# SEE NO EVIL

# SEE NO EVIL

## 19 HARD TRUTHS THE LEFT CAN'T HANDLE

## JOEL B. POLLAK
### SENIOR EDITOR-AT-LARGE, BREITBART.COM

REGNERY PUBLISHING
A Division of Salem Media Group

Regnery® is a registered trademark of Salem Communications Holding Corporation

Cataloging-in-Publication data on file with the Library of Congress
ISBN 978-1-62157-394-4

Published in the United States by
Regnery Publishing
A Division of Salem Media Group
300 New Jersey Ave NW
Washington, DC 20001
www.Regnery.com

Manufactured in the United States of America

10 9 8 7 6 5 4 3 2 1

Books are available in quantity for promotional or premium use. For information on discounts and terms, please visit our website: www.Regnery.com.

Distributed to the trade by
Perseus Distribution
250 West 57th Street
New York, NY 10107

# CONTENTS

## PART I

# SUPPRESSING DISSENT

# CHAPTER 1

# THE LEFT'S WAR ON "TRUTHINESS"— AND TRUTH

## THE LIE:
## The Left speaks truth to power.

Examples:

*"Truthiness is tearing apart our country, and I don't mean the argument over who came up with the word. I don't know whether it's a new thing, but it's certainly a current thing, in that it doesn't seem to matter what facts are. It used to be, everyone was entitled to their own opinion, but not their own facts. But that's not the case anymore. Facts matter not at all. Perception is everything. It's certainty."*
—Stephen Colbert, interview with the *Onion*, January 25, 2006

*"An essential truth of human nature is that frames trump facts. When presented with facts that are inconsistent with the frame through which people view the world, the frame*

3

*will generally win, and inconsistent facts will be discarded
or discounted.”*

*“That's why our top priority has to be the relentless, proud,
self-confident repetition of our frame, our values, and our
vision for the future. We have to activate the progressive
value frame that exists in the minds of swing voters. We
have to set the frame for political debate in America. It's
our job to shape the voters' unconscious understanding of
what constitutes political 'common sense.'”*

—Left-wing organizer and Chicago political veteran
Robert Creamer, 2007[1]

# THE TRUTH:
# The Left suppresses the truth to frame the debate for its own political purposes.

Once, the American Left told itself that it spoke truth to power. Today it cannot even speak the truth to itself.

On November 14, 2015, a day after Paris, France, suffered brutal terror attacks that claimed 129 lives, the three remaining Democratic Party candidates for president stood on a debate stage in Iowa and refused, one after the other, to say that "radical Islam" was responsible.

The perpetrators of the attacks had been identified, leaving no doubt that the so-called "Islamic State," a radical terror group that had arisen in swaths of territory amidst the ruins of Iraq and Syria, had carried out the attacks as part of an effort to project its power worldwide.

And yet these candidates, who wished to lead America against that threat, refused to call it by its name, to state the truth about what had motivated young men to blow themselves up at soccer stadiums, gun down innocent civilians at restaurants, and murder scores more at a rock 'n' roll concert.

Looking back at the year in late December 2015, the economist Thomas Sowell wrote, "Lying, by itself, is obviously not new. What is new is the growing acceptance of lying as 'no big deal' by smug sophisticates, so long as these are lies that advance their political causes." He noted, for example, that when Democratic presidential contender and former Secretary of State Hillary Clinton had been caught by a congressional committee misleading the nation about the cause of the Benghazi terror attacks of September 11, 2012, even as she told the truth to her own family, she won praise instead of condemnation: "Many in the media greeted the exposure of Hillary Clinton's lies by admiring how well she handled herself."[2]

We are witnessing a state of denial in left-wing American politics that is almost terminal. Increasingly, the American Left rejects the truth—not just about the threat of radical Islam, but also about nearly every issue facing our society.

How did it come to this? Especially when the Left prided itself, until recently, on being the "reality-based community"?

The comedian Stephen Colbert mocked conservatives by introducing the term "truthiness" in the opening monologue of the first episode of *The Colbert Report*, his spoof on Fox News and conservatism in general, in 2005.[3]

Colbert said:

> Cause you're looking at a straight-shooter, America. I tell it like it is. I calls 'em like I sees 'em. I will speak to you in plain, simple English.
>
> And that brings us to tonight's word: truthiness.
>
> Now I'm sure some of the Word Police, the "wordanistas" over at Webster's, are gonna say, "Hey, that's not a word." Well, anybody who knows me know [sic] that I'm no fan of dictionaries or reference books. They're elitist. Constantly telling us what is or isn't true, or what did or didn't happen.

Who's *Britannica* to tell me the Panama Canal was finished
in 1914? If I wanna say it happened in 1941, that's my right.
I don't trust books. They're all fact, no heart....
   We are divided between those who *think* with their head,
and those who *know* with their heart. (Laughter)[4]

The term caught on quickly among left-wing critics of President
George W. Bush, who had just led the country to war in Iraq to stop
Saddam Hussein's regime from producing weapons of mass destruction
that were never found.

Colbert explained the term at length the following year in an interview with the satirical newspaper the *Onion*, noting that "truthiness"
was an appeal to authority and emotion, rather than to reason. "Truthiness is 'What I say is right, and [nothing] anyone else says could possibly
be true.' It's not only that I *feel* it to be true, but that *I* feel it to be true.
There's not only an emotional quality, but there's a selfish quality."[5]

"Truth" was a rallying cry on the Left, where critics of the Bush
administration convinced themselves that their opponents cared less for
the concept. And "truthiness" soon joined the term "reality-based community" in the left-wing lexicon. That term was taken from a quotation
from an unnamed Bush adviser who spoke to Ron Suskind for a 2004
*New York Times* article: "The aide said that guys like me were 'in what
we call the reality-based community,' which he defined as people who
'believe that solutions emerge from your judicious study of discernible
reality.' I nodded and murmured something about enlightenment principles and empiricism. He cut me off. 'That's not the way the world really
works anymore,' he continued. 'We're an empire now, and when we act,
we create our own reality. And while you're studying that reality—judi-
ciously, as you will—we'll act again, creating other new realities, which
you can study too, and that's how things will sort out. We're history's
actors...and you, all of you, will be left to just study what we do.'"

Apparently intended as a pejorative, the term "reality-based community" became a badge of honor. The Left saw conservatives as opposed
to science and truth—and motivated instead by power, greed, tradition,

prejudice, and emotion. "Psychologists have found that low-effort thought promotes political conservatism," wrote Katy Waldman at Slate. com, citing science to argue that "right-wing political beliefs arise from a need to manage uncertainty and threat." That did not mean conservatives were stupid, she noted carefully, but it did mean that conservatism appealed to the primitive, "reptilian" part of the human brain. The Left, she implied, aimed far higher.[6]

The Left applies the same conceit to conservative views on specific issues. For example, it is common for liberal politicians to use the term "denialist" to describe conservatives who reject the "consensus" view on climate change, which is ostensibly based in science (though there is nothing scientific in argument by majority rule).

And yet much of the intellectual energy on the American Left today is devoted to suppressing dissent, denying basic facts, and avoiding the truth.

That is not something many on the Left will admit openly, but it is something many know to be the case—especially since the rise of Barack Obama from political obscurity to charismatic leadership.

In his 2009 book *Bloggers on the Bus*, Eric Boehlert, one of the main bloggers at the left-wing Media Matters for America, noted that left-wing bloggers who supported Hillary Clinton in the 2008 election "raised a cautionary flag" about "the rush to crown Obama and demonize Clinton" in online forums.

"Being reality-based was one of the things I thought we prided ourselves on, that we were the rational ones," said blogger Todd Beeton. "We had the facts and therefore we should win."[7]

But Obama brought with him a cohort of community organizers, like Robert Creamer, who were trained and inspried by the radical Saul Alinsky in the 1960s, and who are prepared to violate the truth—to treat it, at best, as a means to an end. And that end is total political power. They believe that if they can "frame" an issue in a way favorable to their candidate or their cause, they can win, regardless of truth. And winning is everything to them—as Clinton was soon to find out.

Once, the term "liberal" suggested open-mindedness, intellectual courage, a willingness to break with dogma in favor of new insight. But today there are, strikingly, two entirely different definitions of "liberal" in our dictionaries.

The Oxford American dictionary, for example, defines "liberal" as "favoring maximum individual liberty in political and social reform."[8]

Merriam-Webster, however, defines "liberal" as "believing that government should be active in supporting social and political change."[9]

These meanings are exact opposites. One favors the individual, the other favors the state. And over time the second definition has become the dominant one among American liberals, who are impatient for "progressive" change.

Some of the increasingly shrill voices on the Left have even given up on liberal democracy itself. The *New York Times* columnist Thomas L. Friedman, for example, wrote that the United States should become "China for a day," using authoritarian powers to impose environmental policies our democratic process is too combative or too corrupt to embrace on its own.[10]

While it is true that dictatorships can achieve great things quickly, it is equally true that they can commit great wrongs irreversibly—as China's damaged environment and smog-filled cities show. Constitutional democracies, with their divided government and checks and balances, may delay action, but they avoid catastrophe. In societies where individuals are free to think and say what they wish, truth—not arbitrary authority—is the standard against which their views are judged.

Today, however, liberals increasingly insist that in the service of greater goals, truth is a secondary value at best. To achieve utopian visions of "social and political change," liberals are willing to punish disagreement, to shut down debate, and, ultimately, to convince themselves of things that are simply untrue.

As the 2016 presidential election unfolded and billionaire Donald Trump mounted an improbable but ultimately successful outsider campaign for the Republican nomination, critics—both left and right—complained that Trump had only a loose respect for truth, at best.

For example, on the day of the Indiana primary, the decisive contest between Trump and Senator Ted Cruz, Trump accused Cruz's father, a

Cuban emigré with a youthful enthusiasm for Fidel Castro, of being involved with the assassination of President John F. Kennedy. He was basing his claim on a story in the *National Enquirer*, which had concluded, rather dubiously, that a man photographed near Kennedy assassin Lee Harvey Oswald was the elder Cruz.[11] Few believed Trump or the *Enquirer*, but the debate seized cable news on a day when Cruz desperately needed to turn out his vote. He fell short, losing every congressional district in Indiana to Trump.

To those who wondered how Trump could run with such a farcical story without losing support, the *Wall Street Journal*'s L. Gordon Crovitz noted that the Obama administration had long since removed the taboo on brazen dishonesty. Obama officials, such as Deputy National Security Advisor Ben Rhodes, for example, openly admitted to the *New York Times* that they had deceived the public about key details of the Iran deal.[12] Crovitz concluded, "As more details such as the role of Mr. Rhodes emerge about how the Obama administration operates, there may be more voters who see Mr. Trump simply as an equal and opposite reaction to Mr. Obama. False narratives and media manipulation worked for Mr. Obama and have empowered Mr. Trump, making him seem to many voters just another flavor of politics as usual."[13] The Iran deal was not the sole example: again and again, from health care to immigration, the Obama administration deceived the public, then congratulated itself for having done so. Those were the new rules of the game—a game Trump was determined to win.

There are still liberals who embrace the essence of the classical liberal political tradition: reason, openness, and individual freedom. But they are a weakened force and a dwindling number.

Few are even willing to engage in rational debate. The abortion issue is the archetypal case. The Left largely refuses even to consider the idea that an unborn baby might actually be a living human being, at any point. The reason is obvious: if a fetus is a live human being, then "disposing of uterine contents" is not a mere medical procedure, but an act of violence—even, perhaps, of premeditated murder. So those on the Left do everything they can to avoid the question of when human life begins.

When they are forced to address it, they find themselves defending an absurd position: that the baby deserves no protection under the law until the moment of birth—or even until the mother takes it home from the hospital—and then suddenly acquires the full complement of human rights. (And, worse, in an attempt to remedy the obvious inconsistency in this leftist position, some philosophers on the Left have even argued for a right to kill babies after they are born.)

In February 2014, journalist Jorge Ramos of the Fusion network asked Cecile Richards, President of Planned Parenthood Action Fund, to say when life begins. She said, "It is not something that I feel like is really part of this conversation.... I think every woman needs to make her own decision. What we do at Planned Parenthood is make sure that women have all their options...." Ramos pressed her. "Why would it be so controversial for you to say when do you think life starts?" he asked. Richards replied, "For me—I'm the mother of three children—for me, life began when I delivered them...but that was my own personal decision."

In another infamous exchange, Republican Rick Santorum of Pennsylvania sparred with California Democrat Barbara Boxer on the floor of the Senate in 1999. At one point Boxer suggested that a child was only a human being once it was completely outside of the mother, and perhaps once it had left the hospital. Santorum allowed her to walk back the claim—perhaps a gaffe—that a newborn only has rights "when you bring your baby home." But he was unsuccessful in urging Boxer to identify when, precisely, a fetus becomes a human being. "I don't want to engage in this," she said.[14]

But others did. In February 2012, philosophers Alberto Giubilini and Francesca Minerva published an article in the *Journal of Medical Ethics* arguing that it should be permissible to perform "after-birth abortion." A newborn baby, they argued, is morally indistinguishable from a fetus: "neither can be considered a 'person' in a morally relevant sense"—because, essentially, neither would notice if it did not exist. And since we allow fetuses to be aborted, the same should hold for newborns:

"Merely being human is not in itself a reason for ascribing someone a right to life."[15]

That may seem outrageous, but it is not easy to distinguish in its underlying principles from Boxer's remark that life begins "when you bring your baby home"—that abortion should be legal up to the point when the mother decides to integrate her newborn into her household.

It is also similar to President Barack Obama's personal position on the issue. During the 2008 presidential campaign, when then-Senator Obama was asked when life begins, he famously said that the answer was "above my pay grade." Yet in the Illinois State Senate, Obama was the most vocal opponent of legislation known as the Born Alive bill, to protect babies that happened to survive abortions. In the course of explaining his opposition to the legislation—as the only member of the state Senate to speak against it on the floor of that chamber—Obama referred to a "fetus, or child, however you want to describe it, is now outside of the mother's womb"—as if a child that had survived an abortion might still not be a human being.

That is an extreme position, but it is no great distance from the position of his party, which is to oppose any restriction on abortion whatsoever. If after-birth abortions were declared legal by the Supreme Court, Democrats would probably support it.

They would, however, prefer not to discuss the issue at all. In September 2015, Vice President Joe Biden—then considering a run for the White House—repeated Obama's "above my pay grade" line. The Left will not engage in rational debate. They will not acknowledge even the possibility of prenatal life. In fact, they will do everything they can to avoid even addressing the arguments on the other side.

The crisis in liberalism is at its most dramatic on college campuses across the nation, which are becoming increasingly intolerant of free speech.

In 2014, the Foundation for Individual Rights in Education (FIRE) reported that "disinvitations" of speakers from college campuses "have been steadily increasing over the past 15 years," and that they had "risen dramatically" in the most recent years studied.

Nine of the ten most-disinvited speakers were conservatives. (The only "liberal" was the unrepentant former Weather Underground terrorist Bill Ayers.)[16]

In addition, universities have begun to provide "trigger warnings" to notify students when they are about to hear or read a controversial idea, or even a word that may have potential associations with race, gender, sexuality, and so forth. Students at the nation's leading "liberal arts" colleges demand "safe spaces" to which they can retreat in the increasingly unlikely event that someone with contrarian views appears on campus to defend them.

That "safety" is often one way. At protests on the University of Missouri campus in 2015, students and faculty—including an assistant professor of media studies—assaulted a photojournalist who attempted to photograph their "safe space" on a public lawn. His rights, and his safety, were unimportant. At Yale, left-wing students tried to shut down a free speech event held on campus by a conservative group, which was able to proceed only with additional police protection—for which the group holding the event had to pay.[17]

If Socrates once said that the "unexamined life is not worth living,"[18] today's universities seem to regard the mildest intellectual challenge as a mortal threat, to be evaded if possible and stamped out if necessary.

The intolerance of the Left is not confined to campus life. It has crept into American political discourse and even our social habits. Ever more boldly, liberals are attempting to suppress opinions and facts that might tend to lead the public to conservative conclusions—or that, at the very least, would lead to open debate on equal footing.

In May 2016, the Gizmodo technology blog reported that Facebook had been suppressing stories from conservative news websites in its "trending news" section, which appeared in a prominent position within users' interfaces when they logged onto their accounts.[19]

Employees responsible for curating the section would "regularly avoid sites like World Star Hip Hop, The Blaze, and Breitbart." Though the orders to do so were never explicit, former employees accused Facebook—which had rapidly become one of the most important news portals in the world—of downplaying conservative-oriented stories, even when they were being widely shared by Facebook users, and promoting stories that management preferred, such as coverage of the Black Lives Matter protest movement. Facebook denied the accusations, but its "trending news" section was exposed as operating less like a computer algorithm and more like a traditional newsroom—with a traditional newsroom's liberal bias.

The result was that Facebook's audience was spoon-fed a skewed perception of what was happening in the world and what was important to others. Reality, as defined by the new elites of Silicon Valley, increasingly reflected their own left-wing political monoculture.

The partisans of the Left know, or suspect, that their ideas would be broadly rejected by the American public. They may believe that ordinary people are simply too stupid to know what is good for them. Regardless, for them, the goal of public debate is not to convince Americans of the truth of left-wing ideas, but to poison the well of public opinion so that the alternatives seem unthinkable, and so that those who openly embrace conservative views are marginalized. They suppress the truth to create a "frame" that excludes dissenting views from public debate. Then the Left can push its own agenda with less resistance.

The Left's rejection of truth goes beyond mere deceit for tactical, political purposes. To lie, as most politicians do (at least occasionally) is one thing. To refuse to distinguish between lies and truth is a very different sin.

In 2004, for example, when CBS News's Dan Rather was caught using forged documents to accuse Bush of dodging military service, the *New York Times* described the documents as "fake but accurate."[20]

After Rather was fired, some liberals continued to defend him, insisting his story could have been true despite the forgery. Robert Redford even made a film, *Truth*, casting Rather in a heroic light.

Often, the Left accepts false stories as long as they tell a "larger truth." For example, in 2010, members of the Congressional Black Congress claimed that they had heard the "N-word" as they walked through a Tea Party demonstration on Capitol Hill.

Andrew Breitbart, my friend and later colleague, offered a $10,000 and then a $100,000 donation to charity if anyone could produce video proof. In fact, video recordings taken from multiple angles showed no racial epithets whatsoever. For the Left, however, the debunking of the "N-word" story still left the "larger truth" of the Tea Party's alleged racism intact.

Similar examples abound, including a false *Rolling Stone* story about rape at the University of Virginia that some on the Left defended because it attempted to expose a broader culture of "male sexual entitlement."[21]

The "larger truth" is always more important than truth itself—even though lies in service of a "larger truth" may have serious, even deadly consequences.

In 2014, for example, a police officer in Ferguson, Missouri, shot and killed a black teenager, Michael Brown, in broad daylight. The teenager's family, and community leaders who rallied to their side, claimed that the policeman had shot Brown in the back as he raised his hands and cried, "Don't shoot!"

None of that turned out to be true. In fact, forensic analysis suggested that Brown had been charging the officer. Moments earlier, he had reached into the officer's patrol car and wrestled for his gun, shooting himself in the thumb in the process. Brown had also just robbed a nearby convenience store, and was found to have marijuana in his system.

But the myth of "Hands up, don't shoot!" triggered nationwide riots and a movement called "Black Lives Matter," which frightened many police away from patrolling black neighborhoods, lest they be accused of racism—or targeted for retribution.

In many cities, crime spiked. Chicago mayor Rahm Emanuel lamented that police "have pulled back from the ability to interdict…they don't want to be a news story themselves…it's having an impact."[22]

The Left's suppression of truth is not just a danger to conservatives, but to the stability of our society itself.

George Orwell recognized truth as the distinguishing virtue of western democracy. He was a socialist, but one who believed—unlike leftists briefly entranced by the Soviet pact with Hitler—that Britain would have to go to war against Nazi Germany to preserve its independence.

Against those who said that imperial Britain was just as bad, or that fighting fascism would require Britain to adopt "fascist" methods, Orwell offered a moral claim that, in his view, decided the matter: "In the last analysis our only claim to victory is that if we win the war we shall tell less lies about it than our adversaries."[23]

What worried Orwell most about totalitarianism—fascist or communist—was not its brutality but its assault on objective truth, especially about history. He warned about "a nightmare world in which the Leader, or the ruling clique, controls not only the future but the past. If the Leader says of such and such an event, 'It never happened'—well, it never happened. If he says that two and two are five—well, two and two are five. This prospect frightens me much more than bombs—and after our experiences of the last few years that is not a frivolous statement."[24]

That passage from Orwell's *Looking Back on the Spanish War* struck a chord with me when I first read it.

At the time I was living in Cape Town, South Africa, working as a freelance journalist. I was born in Johannesburg in 1977, just as my parents were about to leave, having decided they did not want to raise children in an unstable racist society. I returned in 2000 as a Rotary scholar, eager to experience dramatic changes that had come to the country in the intervening years. The new South African Constitution was the world's most liberal, with wide guarantees of socioeconomic rights. From my youthful, left-wing perspective, I hoped to gain political insights I could bring home to America.

But I landed in the midst of the HIV/Aids controversy, when the president of South Africa, Thabo Mbeki, was denying that a virus caused the disease. Then the second Palestinian *intifada* started in the Middle East, and I heard South African leaders making outrageous accusations

about Israel that I knew, from my studies and travels, to be lies. I covered
the Durban racism conference for an American magazine and was
shocked when my left-wing colleagues at the conference denied the obvious antisemitism staring them in the face. That experience sped my
transition from Left to Right.

Later I had the privilege of working for several people steeped in the
finest traditions of liberalism. I worked for Tony Leon, the leader of the
opposition in the South African parliament, who believed that individual
freedom was the best way to fulfill the promise of South Africa's new
democracy, and the best hope for that country's desperately poor millions. Tony spoke out often against what he called "the curse of the
forked tongue," by which he meant the contrast between the country's
professed commitment to constitutional democracy on the one hand and
the corrupt, race-obsessed, illiberal behavior of the post-apartheid government on the other.

At Harvard Law School I worked for Alan Dershowitz , the defense
lawyer, civil libertarian, and loyal Democrat, who made a point throughout his career of supporting the free speech rights of people with whom
he disagreed vehemently. On one occasion, Dershowitz helped anti-Israel
students fight for their right to raise the Palestinian flag on Harvard's
campus—then turned up the day they did so to hand out leaflets
denouncing their cause. Dershowitz taught that in a free society, the
answer to hateful, ignorant, and offensive speech was more speech, not
less.

The best hope for America's future is that classical, muscular liberal
tradition—not the liberalism that places the state before the individual,
substitutes sentiment for reason, and enforces political correctness over
truth.

Ironically, it is American conservatism that is standing up for the
classical liberal values today, even as liberals themselves are abandoning
them. If, as the dictionaries say, the essence of conservatism is the defense
of tradition, then the tradition that conservatives have embraced today
is the American creed of liberal democracy, as expressed in the country's
founding documents and ideals, as well as the timeless virtue of truth.

That is why new conservative movements, such as the Tea Party, have been so effective. The principles for which they fight are shared by most Americans, and the political and social realities to which they are responding are those many in the political class prefer to deny. That is why Andrew Breitbart inspired Tea Party activists by telling them truth was their most effective political weapon. An army of "citizen journalists" with hand-held cameras, he believed, could broadcast the reality the media had no interest in covering.

As Andrew declared in *Righteous Indignation*, his memoir: "Truth isn't mean. It's truth...if there is one thing in religion that speaks to me, it is the idea of absolute truth. In fact, the word truth has meaning only if it's absolute. And absolute truth will set us free...."[25]

No person, or party, has a monopoly on truth—and that is good news. There are liberals who still share the universal principles for which conservatives are fighting today.

One example is Kirsten Powers, a liberal Democrat who has taken a strong stand against the censorship of the academic Left in *The Silencing: How the Left is Killing Free Speech*.[26] Another is Jonathan Turley, the liberal professor at George Washington University School of Law who supports many of Barack Obama's policies, but opposes his use—or abuse—of executive authority to achieve them, undermining Congress and foreclosing the possibility of democratic debate.

In this book, I take a harsh tone with liberals, but I do not believe that liberal Americans and conservative Americans are enemies. I reject the idea that a sizable chunk of the country can simply be ignored or cowed into submission. I believe that there are at least some people on the Left with the intellectual curiosity and the genuine good will to listen to reason.

I know, because I was once a liberal myself. What made me most reluctant to consider conservative ideas was the conviction—partly a self-serving liberal illusion—that being conservative meant being closed-minded.

Now is the time when our fellow Americans need to hear the truth most urgently—delivered patiently, and in a spirit of tolerance and unity.

To restore our nation's unity and promise, we have to return to the civic habits that are essential to self-government—what conservative columnist Charles Krauthammer calls "constitutional decency."

But first, the truths the Left is desperate to suppress must be exposed. Truth is the only basis for real reconciliation.

In the pages that follow, I will explore different examples of truths that the Left refuses to tolerate. Like a child with his fingers in his ears repeating "I can't *hear* you"—or the monkey who holds his hands over his eyes so he will "See No Evil"—progressives do all they can to avoid acknowledging truths that challenge their views. These fall into three broad categories.

**1. Where the Left suppresses dissent**

The first category includes issues where the Left has a plausible argument to make, but progressives still refuse to tolerate dissenting conservative arguments, lest those arguments expose some flaw in liberal ideology.

**2. Where the Left suppresses debate**

The second category includes cases where neither liberals nor conservatives have a clear edge, and where further inquiry might yield better understanding and agreement, yet the Left forecloses that possibility by demonizing its opponents and ending debate.

**3. Where the Left simply suppresses the truth**

The third group of issues includes examples where the Left is unambiguously in the wrong and yet pretends otherwise, using almost any means available to silence critics.

Each case I explore suggests insights into how and why the Left suppresses the truth, as well as the consequences for our democracy and for our society in general.

Our democracy, and our survival, are at stake.

# CHAPTER 2

# GUNS

## THE LIE:
## Gun control is the answer to mass killings.

Examples:

*"We know that other countries, in response to one mass shooting, have been able to craft laws that almost eliminate mass shootings. Friends of ours, allies of ours—Great Britain, Australia, countries like ours. So we know there are ways to prevent it."*

—President Barack Obama, October 2015[1]

*"Repeal the Second Amendment Now. This anachronistic, poorly worded amendment prevents us from passing real gun control measures that will be effective in stopping the ongoing gun slaughter."*

—MoveOn.org petition, November 2015[2]

*"It's controversial, but first thing is all of your—95 percent of your murders, and murderers, and murder victims fit one M.O. You can just take the description, Xerox it, and pass it out to all of the cops. They are male, minorities, 15 to 25. That's true in New York, it's true in virtually every city in America... You've got to get the guns out of the hands of the people getting killed."*

—Former New York City Mayor Michael Bloomberg,
Aspen Institute, February 6, 2015[3]

## THE TRUTH:
## Legal guns deter violent crime, and gun ownership is essential to our concept of liberty.

"By God's Grace, I managed to return fire at the terrorist attackers and they fled the scene."[4]

That is how Pastor Charl van Wyk remembers the St. James Church massacre, a mass shooting during evening services at a congregation in Cape Town, South Africa, on July 25, 1993.

Eleven were killed and 55 were injured. The fact that van Wyk was armed saved many lives.

Today, van Wyk is a missionary, traveling to isolated Christian communities throughout the world and preaching the gospel of gun ownership.

Reflecting on the shooting at the Emanuel African Methodist Episcopal Church in Charleston, South Carolina, June 2015, van Wyk says, "My heart really goes out to the families of those who are feeling the pain of having lost loved ones through this senseless attack." But it would be a mistake, he says, for Americans to enact new gun control laws in response. "Firearms surely make it easier to kill people," he acknowledges, "but firearms also make it easier for people to defend themselves. Removing all firearms from society risks leaving potential victims defenseless."

That is the essential, irreducible truth that stands in the way of sweeping gun restrictions in the United States. People demand the right to defend themselves. And once they have the means to do so, they refuse to part with it. Yet the pressure for gun control is relentless, and has increased in the past few years in the wake of several horrific mass shooting events.

In the hours after the October 2015 shooting at Umpqua Community College in Roseburg, Oregon, where nine innocent people were killed and nine injured, President Barack Obama suggested that the government start confiscating guns, following the example of Australia, where the government forced many civilians to sell their guns back to dealers. The president said, "And, of course, what's also routine is that somebody, somewhere will comment and say, Obama politicized this issue. Well, this is something we should politicize. It is relevant to our common life together, to the body politic."[5]

Critics slammed him: "[T]o make a pronouncement at this time, when, I hate to say it, the bodies are still warm and the wounded are now in surgery, I think is at least premature," said columnist Charles Krauthammer.[6] And yet gun control activists from the president on down, continue using such incidents to advocate for new restrictions, Australia-style confiscations—even for repealing the Second Amendment itself. (Ironically, the president frequently mocks those who think there is "a wild-eyed plot to take everybody's guns away.")[7]

Hillary Clinton, vying for the presidency, even jumped to blame the horrific San Bernardino terror attack of December 2012, in which four-teen innocent people were killed, and twenty-two injured, at a holiday party, on loose gun laws: "I refuse to accept this as normal. We must take action to stop gun violence now,"[8] she tweeted. Not only was the attack an act of radical Islamic extremism, not ordinary "gun violence," but the guns used had been legally bought in California, the state that already has many of the gun restrictions that the left would like to enact nationwide.

When new laws fail to pass, the left blames the National Rifle Association (NRA). In his reaction to the Umpqua shooting, Obama urged the members of the NRA to resist its leadership. Hillary Clinton, on the campaign trail, was more direct: "We have to take on the gun lobby."[9]

In one sense, their reaction is understandable. The horror of mass shootings is unspeakable: the stories of terrified children huddled together and murdered; the people forced to confess their faith and plead for their lives to no avail; the reporter killed on live television as thousands watched in shock; the selfless, fatal acts of heroism by people who block doors with their bodies to save their fellow men and women.

Richard Martinez, the anguished father of Christopher Michaels-Martinez, one of the six students killed in a mass murder at the University of California Santa Barbara in May 2014, became a devoted gun control activist in the wake of the attack. "The kid that killed my son should never have had a gun, and we have to figure out a way so that these things don't happen again," he said.[10]

A sympathetic California legislature passed a law, AB 1014, later signed into law by Governor Jerry Brown, to allow police to obtain a "Gun Violence Restraining Order" (GVRO) to confiscate an individual's weapons upon request by someone who believes that person is a threat to himself or others. The NRA opposed the bill, arguing that restraining orders "can be easily abused and issued in cases where officers lack sufficient evidence for an arrest, but wish to deprive an individual of their right to bear arms."[11]

But the NRA backed a fix to the bill, AB 950, which passed the following year, and allows an individual under a GVRO to surrender his guns to a licensed firearms dealer rather than the police. So reasonable gun regulations are possible. And gun control advocates have a plausible case that more laws are necessary to make sure that deadly weapons do not fall into the wrong hands. The problem is that many of the gun control laws that the Left proposes would have done nothing to prevent past shootings and will do nothing to prevent future ones. And while some people support more gun control as the best response to mass shootings, others seek to arm themselves. It is a natural reaction—one that the left refuses to tolerate.

Ironically, the more that gun control advocates attempt to stamp out the right to bear arms, the more Americans seek to exercise it. Indeed, gun ownership is fundamental to the American concept of liberty.

The American concept of freedom has deep philosophical roots. It was inspired by the English philosophers of the seventeenth century, particularly John Locke. Locke believed that human beings are born equally endowed with liberty. In his *Second Treatise on Government*, Locke wrote that individual liberty exists in the "state of nature," prior to the existence of any government. Yet even then, people must obey natural law, which is that "no one ought to harm another in his life, health, liberty or possessions."[12] And every individual has the right not only of self-defense, but also to enforce natural law.

People unite to create a government—a commonwealth—to improve the enforcement of law and the enjoyment of property, Locke argued. Each individual therefore gives up the right to interpret and execute the law—but the right of self-defense remains. And because the government exists only by the consent of naturally free individuals, the people retain the right to change their government if it abuses its power and violates their freedom.

Locke argued that such revolutions would be rare. Nevertheless, the idea that individuals retain the right to overthrow an oppressive government implies the right to retain the means to do so. And so the right to bear arms stands as a last resort to defend individual liberty from tyranny.

Locke's ideas formed the basis for the American Revolution and the freedoms enshrined in the Constitution that followed soon afterwards. Thus the U.S. Declaration of Independence echoes Locke in its most famous passage: "We hold these truths to be self-evident, that all men are created equal, that they are endowed by their Creator with certain inalienable rights, that among these are Life, Liberty and the pursuit of Happiness."[13]

In contrast, the Canadian equivalent, the Constitution Act of 1867, which retained the Queen as supreme political authority, aimed at "Peace, Order, and good Government."[14] These are fundamentally different aims: one starts with the individual, the other with the Crown or state.

Though the two countries share much in common, that difference in their philosophical orientation is also the reason Americans embrace the right to gun ownership and Canadians do not. Gun deaths are dramatically lower in Canada, but the risk is one Americans have been generally willing to endure to preserve our unique liberty.

In October 2014, a terrorist attacked an unarmed Canadian reservist at the Tomb of the Unknown Soldier in Ottawa, then attempted a mass shooting inside Parliament. He was shot by Royal Canadian Mounted Police Constable Curtis Barrett and Sergeant-at-Arms Kevin Vickers, a ceremonial parliamentary official and former policeman who was—fortuitously—armed with a pistol, which he was licensed to carry.

Perhaps ironically, this Canadian incident tended to reinforce pro-gun arguments in the United States. Indeed, it was a real-life example of the hypothetical situation in which a "good guy with a gun" defends himself and those around him—an individual liberty with a public purpose.

The Left insists that the idea that an armed civilian can prevent a mass shooting is "the myth of the good guy with a gun"—the stuff of movies, perhaps, but not real life.[15] And yet real-life examples abound. In April 2015, for example, an Uber driver stopped a mass shooting in an upscale neighborhood in Chicago by drawing his own gun and shooting a gunman who had been firing into a crowd. (Uber's response was to ban both drivers and passengers from carrying weapons—even lawfully.)[16]

The Second Amendment reads, "A well regulated Militia, being necessary to the security of a free State, the right of the people to keep and bear Arms, shall not be infringed."[17] Advocates for gun control have emphasized the term "Militia" to argue that the right to bear arms applies only in collective, government-run defense organizations.

That argument was rejected—narrowly, but convincingly—in the Supreme Court decision *District of Columbia v. Heller* (2008), which overturned a strict (and rather ineffective) handgun ban in the District of Columbia. The Court held that the Second Amendment had been based on an "inherent right of self-defense" at its adoption and that it "protected an individual right to use arms for self-defense," especially in the home.[18]

That did not mean, the Court said, that the Second Amendment was unlimited, or that no regulations were allowed. As California's AB 950 illustrates, there are regulations that even the most ardent gun rights advocates can support. On guns, the Left has many good arguments— and, in the wake of terrible shootings, perhaps even the better arguments. As the Court acknowledged in *Heller*, it was "perhaps debatable" that "the Second Amendment is outmoded in a society where our standing army is the pride of our Nation, where well-trained police forces provide personal security, and where gun violence is a serious problem."[19]

What the Left does not have is a way to dismiss the arguments for gun ownership. One is the fact that violent crime has fallen as gun ownership has risen in recent decades—and that mass shootings have not risen. Economist John Lott argues that correlation is causation in this case—specifically, that concealed carry laws lower the murder rate:

> Overall, my conclusion is that criminals as a group tend to behave rationally—when crime becomes more difficult, less crime is committed....
>
> Of all the methods studied so far by economists, the carrying of concealed handguns appears to be the most cost-effective method for reducing crime....
>
> Murder rates decline when either more women or more men carry concealed handguns, but the effect is especially pronounced for women.[20]

Lott allows that the data are complex. For example, "concealed handguns might cause small increases in larceny and auto theft," he writes, because criminals turn to inanimate targets when there is a higher chance that victims will carry weapons. But he also notes that the number of cases in which guns deter crime is likely to be underestimated, since guns merely have to be shown, not actually used, to deter many would-be criminals.

For his trouble, Lott has been defamed and attacked by the Left and is frequently the target of such ideologically charged organizations as Media Matters for America. Unable to argue with his facts, they resort simply to a steady string of abuse and slander. As Lott wrote in December 2014, "I have been attacked in over 80 posts on Media Matters over the years. They have even criticized reporters from such places as the *Washington Post* and the *New York Times* just for interviewing me. They have described me as a 'discredited gun researcher.' They have claimed 'Gun Advocate John Lott Lashes out at Trayvon Martin's Mother.'"[21]

Lott went on to describe how Media Matters never allowed him to respond to their accusations, deleting his comments from their website. Only after the intervention of *Washington Post* media critic Erik Wemple did Media Matters allow Lott's comments to appear.

Such treatment, which goes well outside the bounds of a reasoned debate over the social science and the data, is typical of the passion the debate evokes—as well as of the tactics the Left employs to suppress conservative ideas in other areas.

The Left attempts to marginalize Lott—but his data cannot be dismissed.

Another argument the Left cannot answer is that few of the new laws proposed by the Left would have been effective against the mass shootings. Expanding federal background checks for gun purchases, which failed to beat a Senate filibuster in 2013, is favored by a majority of Americans. But as AWR Hawkins of Breitbart News notes, "Of course, the problem with this approach is that the [Umpqua Community College] gunman passed a background check for his guns, as did almost every mass shooter of note in the last eight years."[22] That fact is a powerful argument for Second Amendment advocates, who were able to prevent new federal gun control laws even the wake of such emotional events as the Sandy Hook Elementary School shooting in December 2012.

Another powerful argument is that gun ownership is necessary to prevent tyranny. Gun control advocates deny—and mock—that argument, casting it as a paranoid fantasy. In 2015, the media reacted in horror to Dr. Ben Carson's comment: "I think the likelihood of Hitler being able to accomplish his goals would have been greatly diminished if the people had been armed. I'm telling you there is a reason these dictatorial people take guns first."[23]

The Anti-Defamation League, a left-leaning Jewish civil rights group, said that Dr. Carson "has a right to his views on gun control, but the notion that Hitler's gun-control policy contributed to the Holocaust is historically inaccurate . . . gun control did not cause the Holocaust; Nazism and anti-Semitism did."[24]

But other Jews agree with Carson. An organization called the Children of Jewish Holocaust Survivors actually offers firearms classes to Jews based on the lessons of World War II: "In Europe, the pessimists left. The optimists went to Auschwitz." Supreme Court litigator Stephen P. Halbrook has argued that "German firearm laws and hysteria created against Jewish firearm owners played a major role in laying the groundwork for the eradication of German Jewry in the Holocaust."[25] Even if Jews could not have stopped the Nazis, greater access to firearms could have allowed greater resistance. Crucially, Halbrook notes, Nazi orders to disarm Jews came on the same day as Kristallnacht, the "Night of Broken Glass," November 9, 1938, which many historians designate as the start of the Holocaust.[26]

And when we consider the Civil Rights Movement, it doesn't seem so fanciful that guns could play a role in resisting tyranny. In *This Nonviolent Stuff'll Get You Killed: How Guns Made the Civil Rights Movement Possible*, Charles E. Cobb Jr. observes that "although nonviolence was crucial to the gains made by the freedom struggle of the 1950s and '60s, those gains could not have been achieved without the complementary and still under appreciated practice of armed self-defense."[27]

It was because black activists were prepared to use licensed firearms "to protect themselves and others under terrorist attack for their civil rights activities" that they rarely had to do so. Even Dr. Martin Luther King, Jr. himself owned guns and allowed that the use of violence in self-defense could have profound persuasive value: "When the Negro uses force in self-defense, he does not forfeit support—he may even win it, by the courage and self-respect it reflects."[28]

The history of the Civil Rights Movement, and also the struggle for equal rights after the Civil War, were the basis for another crucial Supreme Court gun rights decision, *McDonald v. City of Chicago* (2010).[29] In *McDonald*, the Court invalidated two Chicago-area hand-gun bans, ruling that the Fourteenth Amendment had "incorporated" the Second, and therefore that the right to bear arms applied against states and cities as well as the federal government.

Along the way the Court considered the struggle against slavery and its aftermath. Even before the Civil War, the Second Amendment had first protected "free soilers" from being disarmed in the struggle over whether Kansas would ban slavery in the 1850s. And then "[a]fter the Civil War, many of the over 180,000 African Americans who served in the Union Army returned to the States of the old Confederacy, where systematic efforts were made to disarm them and other blacks.... Throughout the South, armed parties, often consisting of ex-Confederate soldiers serving in the state militias, forcibly took firearms from newly freed slaves." Ulti-mately the Fourteenth Amendment was passed to ensure the freed slaves' rights. Samuel Alito's majority opinion in *McDonald* notes that even opponents of the Fourteenth Amendment supported gun rights for blacks—arguing that the Amendment was unnecessary because the Second Amendment already protected black Americans' ownership of guns.

That history is frequently, and deliberately, ignored by gun control advocates. Those arguments that the Left cannot defeat it simple ignores or denies.

The gun control movement also attempts to "bracket" discussion of the right to bear arms in general by focusing on a sub-category of guns that it labels "assault weapons." As gun experts note, the term is meaningless.

Assault *rifles*—military-grade automatic weapons—are already restricted. "Assault weapons" are merely guns that look dangerous.

A frequent target is the AR-15, which is so popular—especially among women, for home defense—because it is designed to look like a military weapon. But it is a single-shot semiautomatic gun, meaning that only one bullet is fired with each pull of the trigger, while a new bullet loads. (The term "semiautomatic" is also frequently abused; an ordinary revolver is also "semiautomatic.") The AR-15 became notorious after one was used in the Sandy Hook shooting in December 2012, when twenty children and six adults were murdered. But efforts to ban it have failed, partly because gun owners have rallied around it in the face of misleading arguments against it.

The final tactic of the Left when faced with a truth that cannot be ignored, denied, or bracketed is to ban it—in this case, not only facts about the Second Amendment, but the Second Amendment itself. Democrats have become increasingly bold about suggesting repeal of the Second Amendment and full-scale confiscation of guns. President Obama hinted at confiscation after the October 15 Umpqua shooting, and Hillary Clinton told a town hall meeting the same month that an Australia-style solution—that is, a mandatory gun buy-back—would be worth considering. She also said that "the Supreme Court was wrong" in the *Heller* decision.[30]

A petition at MoveOn.org calls for the U.S. to "Repeal the Second Amendment Now. This anachronistic, poorly worded amendment prevents us from passing real gun control measures that will be effective in stopping the ongoing gun slaughter."[31]

In California, there are laws on the books that ban the *display* of guns—not by liberal Hollywood, which defends its First Amendment rights to use whatever violent imagery it wishes, but in gun stores, where owners are not allowed to use "handgun ads that can be seen from the outside."[32] In the suppression of the Second Amendment, the First Amendment also suffers.

But the Second Amendment is not going to be repealed. There are enough Americans who cherish their right to bear arms as a moral principle and cultural heritage—and they still cross political and demographic lines, even though the two parties are increasingly polarized on the issue. In the wake of Umpqua, the libertarian website Reason.com pointed out that even if gun control advocates could win the support of two-thirds of the U.S. Senate and three-fourths of the states, they would still have to find a way for government to enforce gun control—against a well-armed populace.[33] Though the resistance of one individual or group against the government would be futile, there are enough people willing to die to defend the principle of gun ownership—to force the government to remove their guns "from their cold, dead hands," to borrow a popular NRA slogan—to make confiscation unworkable.

The *Economist* magazine—ruefully—concluded in June 2015, "The America that believes that guns make the country more dangerous—urban, educated, Democratic America—is proposing to disarm the America that is sure (indeed increasingly sure) that safety lies in keeping firearms close by. As a result, nobody is about to disarm anyone."[34] Many gun control activists know that. So passionate pleas for gun control become a political tool—a way to "pander to a core liberal constituency with gun-control rhetoric, all while chasing the votes of the 42% of American households, according to Gallup, that own one."

In their pandering, politicians shamelessly exploit the terror of mass shootings. In January 2011, when a crazed young man killed six and wounded a dozen more—including Democratic Representative Gabby Giffords of Arizona—in a parking lot in Tucson, the Left immediately blamed the conservative Tea Party movement for inspiring the violence, with no evidence for the claim whatsoever. The Left also blamed former Alaska governor Sarah Palin, still a powerful figure on the Right, saying that a 2010 election map "targeting" Giffords's district and others with crosshairs had been a violent message—though Democrats had used similar images. When Palin defended herself, denouncing what she correctly called a "blood libel,"[35] she was accused of politicizing the tragedy! Democrats used Tucson to call for "civility" in politics—a one-sided demand aimed at neutering the new Republican majority in the U.S. House of Representatives, and one that the Left had no intention of honoring itself.

Some also attempted to politicize the movie theater shooting in Aurora, Colorado in July 2012, when a man dressed as Batman opened fire during a screening of *The Dark Knight Rises*, killing twelve and wounding seventy. In the morning after the attack, as details unfolded, ABC News investigative reporter Brian Ross told *Good Morning America* host George Stephanopoulos, "There's a Jim Holmes of Aurora, Colorado, page on the Colorado Tea Party site as well, talking about him joining the Tea Party last year. Now, we don't know if this is the same Jim Holmes. But it's Jim Holmes of Aurora, Colorado."[36]

In fact, there was no Tea Party connection. Once again the perpetrator of a mass shooting turned out to be a psychologically disturbed young man. The same thing was true at Santa Barbara, where the killer wanted personal revenge for being ignored by girls—and began his murder spree by stabbing his roommate and two others to death.

The first mass murderer in recent years with clearly right-wing views was the white supremacist who carried out the Charleston shooting. Democrats tried to blame conservatives in general—"he watches things like Fox News," one claimed[37]—but in his manifesto the killer declared that he had acted precisely because no one else shared his views.

On the other hand, there have been several mass shooters, or would-be mass shooters, with clearly left-wing views. In August 2012, a young man tried to attack the offices of the Family Research Council, a pro–traditional marriage group, in Washington, D.C. He had been a volunteer at the D.C. Center for the LGBT (Lesbian, Gay, Bi-sexual, Transgender) Community at the height of the debate over gay marriage. The shooter found his target on a list of "hate groups" compiled by the left-wing Southern Poverty Law Center (SPLC). He arrived carrying fifteen Chick-fil-A sandwiches, which he intended to leave at the scene as a protest, given the support for traditional marriage by the owner of the restaurant chain. He allegedly began his attack by saying, "I don't like your politics."[38]

In December 2014, two New York Police Department officers were murdered in their patrol car by a man who had posted on the internet his intention of killing police. The deaths occurred in the midst of the nationwide Black Lives Matter protests, after some protesters had called for police to be killed.[39] The media downplayed the shootings' left-wing connections.

The gun debate shows how the Left is willing to use horror and outrage to push an agenda that will not solve the problem at hand, and that in any case has little chance of passing. Worse, Democrats have been willing to risk fomenting violence for the sake of gun control. In Operation Fast and Furious, the Obama administration's Department of Justice smuggled guns across the Mexican border, ostensibly in the hope of tracing them to cartel kingpins, but also, likely to justify new gun regulations at home.[40] The unintended but foreseeable consequence: hundreds of Mexican deaths and the murder of a U.S. Border Patrol agent, Brian Terry.

Precisely because the right to bear arms is fundamental to Americans' traditional notions of liberty, the solution to gun violence may start with liberty—for example, allowing law-abiding citizens to be armed in what are now "gun-free zones" around schools and churches. These restrictions may be well-intentioned, but they advertise soft targets to criminals with no intention of obeying the law. As Charl van Wyk says, "The only person who can stop a bad guy with a gun, is a good guy with a gun." Our liberty, as much as our safety, is at stake in this debate.

# CHAPTER 3

# THE MINIMUM WAGE

## THE LIE:
## Raising the minimum wage helps the poor—and those who oppose it are merely greedy.

Examples:

*"After 14 months since I've called on Congress to reward the hard work of millions of Americans like the ones who we have here today to raise the federal minimum wage, we saw this morning a majority of senators saying 'yes,' but almost every Republican saying 'no' to giving America a raise.... They said no to helping millions work their way out of poverty—and keep in mind, this bill would have done so without any new taxes, or spending, or bureaucracy. They told Americans like the ones who are here today that 'you're on your own'—without even looking them in the eye."*[1]

—President Barack Obama, East Room, White House, April 2014

*"When CEOs and those in charge argue that they do not want to raise the minimum wage so that they can hire more workers, nothing could be further from the truth or more insulting. It appears that we're locked in a battle of minimum wage vs. maximum greed."*[2]

—Al Sharpton, Huffington Post, April 2014

*"Come on. Minimum wage, it's the least we can do."*[3]

—Democratic Senator, Elizabeth Warren
of Massachusetts, January 2014

## THE TRUTH:
## At some point, raising the minimum wage costs jobs, hurting the poor the most.

"Tonight, let's declare that in the wealthiest nation on Earth, no one who works full-time should have to live in poverty, and raise the federal minimum wage to $9.00 an hour."[4]

So said President Barack Obama, delivering the State of the Union address in 2013—his first after being re-elected. The federal minimum wage was—and is, as of this writing—$7.25. But a bidding war was about to begin.

In September 2013, California governor Jerry Brown signed a law raising the state minimum wage from $8 to $10 per hour. And a few months later, President Obama raised his own bid. "I will issue an Executive Order requiring federal contractors to pay their federally-funded employees a fair wage of at least $10.10 an hour," he told Congress in his 2014 State of the Union address, urging legislators to pass a law establishing that level.[5]

Not only the amount but the method had changed—the minimum wage was being raised by executive order, not by legislation.

Others were even more impatient. In April 2014, Seattle became the first major American city to raise its minimum hourly wage to $15. Other cities—San Francisco, Los Angeles—soon followed. Some wanted to go even further. Democratic Senator Elizabeth Warren of Massachusetts suggested in 2013 that the rate should be about $22, based on calculations of labor productivity growth from 1968.[6]

Yet do we even need a minimum wage? Would people really be condemned to low wages if it did not exist? The fact that so few jobs actually pay only the minimum wage suggests not.[7] And if we're going to have a minimum wage, how high should it really be?

Supporters of a minimum wage might give a variety of answers based on what they feel is fair—usually determined not by numerical considerations but by ethical ones. Some would fix on a "living wage"; some would want to raise workers to above the poverty level, and so on. Some economists on the Left argue that the minimum wage would ideally be half the median hourly wage from the year before. That number would be very close to the $10.10 that Obama demanded, which is also close to what the minimum wage would be if it had been indexed to inflation since 1968.[8]

But as conservatives point out, the laws of supply and demand are inescapable. When the price of labor goes up, the demand for labor goes down. Because other wages are pegged to the minimum wage—and so rise when it goes up—the unemployment effects of raising the minimum wage hit workers beyond the relatively small cohort of people who actually earn the minimum wage.

In a monopsony (a labor market with only a single employer), raising the minimum wage could theoretically increase the price of labor without greatly decreasing the demand for it. But we don't have a monopsistic labor market—in most U.S. industries there is a great deal of variety and competition. There are more than 600,000 restaurants in the U.S., for example.[9] In the few sectors (health and education) that are dominated by one large employer (the government), labor unions and political interest groups tend to exercise collective bargaining and lobbying power, and wages already tend to be far higher than the minimum.

Obama's focus on the minimum wage gives the lie to his administration's claim that the economy has recovered from the 2007–8 financial crisis and is healthy again. "Let me start with the economy, and a basic fact: The United States of America, right now, has the strongest, most durable economy in the world," President Obama said in his 2016 State of the Union address. "…Anyone claiming that America's economy is in decline is peddling fiction."[10] But in a true recovery, workers would have seen their incomes rise enough that the minimum wage would not seem an urgent priority. In fact median income has fallen in the United States since Barack Obama took office. Moreover, by September 2015 a record 94.6 million Americans had left the workforce entirely.[11]

The unemployment rate did fall from a double-digit high during Obama's first term to less than 6 percent by late 2015. But employment recovered at the slowest pace of any recovery since World War II. And the boom in the stock market since 2009—often cited by Obama's defenders as proof of economic recovery—has largely been driven by the Federal Reserve's easy money policies, with low and negative interest rates that have kept asset prices rising but left the central bank with few policy tools to intervene to stop any future crises. The recovery was also slowed by a thicket of new laws and regulations. The passage of Obamacare in 2010 created new costs and uncertainties, making hiring more difficult, driving more workers into part-time employment, and raising the cost of health insurance dramatically (instead of decreasing it, as advertised). In addition, the Dodd-Frank financial reforms continue to protect large, "too big to fail" financial institutions while hurting small lenders and community banks, jamming the flow of capital to entrepreneurs. The administration's new efforts to fight "carbon pollution" by executive order (after a Democrat-controlled Congress rejected a cap-and-trade system in 2009) hurt the coal industry—deliberately. And the FCC's new "net neutrality" regulations, which treated the Internet like a telephone company, supposedly in the interest of "fairness," slowed new investment in broadband infrastructure. In a sense, the Obama "recovery" was a transition from an American model to a European model, from growth to redistribution. And as a result, just as in Europe, more people were shut out of the labor market altogether.[12] Left behind were those suffering years out of work—a new "lost generation."

Few Democrats would admit the weakness of the Obama recovery. That is not to say they did not bemoan the state of the economy—but only when the fault could be laid (plausibly or not) at the feet of Wall Street, Republicans, the wealthy, George W. Bush, the Tea Party, or capitalism in general. The one flaw that liberals are prepared to acknowledge has plagued the Obama economy is inequality. The *New York Times* noted in August 2013, "Income inequality in the United States has been growing for decades, but the trend appears to have accelerated during the Obama administration."[13] The irony is rich; Obama has made inequality a target of his policy and his rhetoric during both his presidential campaigns and in office. In 2011, for instance, he endorsed the Occupy Wall Street movement and adopted its "99 percent versus 1 percent" meme in his re-election campaign. In December of that year, Obama gave an address in Osawatomie, Kansas, in which he made it clear that inequality would be the central theme of his re-election campaign:

> The typical CEO who used to earn about 30 times more than his or her worker now earns 110 times more. And yet, over the last decade the incomes of most Americans have actually fallen by about 6 percent.
>
> Now, this kind of inequality—a level that we haven't seen since the Great Depression—hurts us all.[14]

Obama was re-elected on that platform. But he did little to address the problem. He allowed taxes on the wealthy to rise, but crucially, he did little to grow the economy to lift up the bottom part of the economic spectrum. The much-maligned George W. Bush actually grew the economy significantly more than Obama did, though he also inherited a recession (from Bill Clinton).

The Left's explanation for Obama's failure to tackle inequality is that he is beholden to his Wall Street donors and his K Street cronies, the peers with whom he golfs and whose homes he rents on Martha's Vineyard, and the advisers he inherited from the Clinton administration—and in thrall to the conventional wisdom of Washington. Yet the Left's own proposed remedies are simply more of the same policies Obama has already pursued: high taxes, more government intervention; using the bully pulpit of the Oval Office to attack business owners great and small, and a raft of new regulations.

Those on the Left completely ignore the lessons of the past several decades. Like Democratic presidential candidate Senator Bernie Sanders, they still cite Scandinavia, for example, as the model for their brand of democratic socialism—even as the Scandanavian countries themselves have adopted free-market reforms.[15] For many, it is as if the Reagan era and the fall of the Soviet Union never happened.

The news about Obama's economy is not all bad. But the Left's assault on truth has obscured the most important piece of good news. One industry has contributed more to American economic growth than any other in the Obama era—namely, the fossil fuel industry. The U.S. has overtaken Saudi Arabia as the wold's number one producer of oil on President Barack Obama's watch—something that seemed impossible in 2008. The reason is the development of hydraulic fracturing or "fracking," which involves injecting high-pressure liquids into deep rock formations to create cracks that allow oil and gas to be extracted more easily from otherwise unavailable deposits. Coupled with the discovery of vast shale deposits throughout the United States, fracking has revolutionized the oil industry.

Because of fracking—accompanied by a shift to clean-burning natural gas as an energy source—the U.S. economy has been able to grow rapidly in oil-producing regions. The energy boom has kept the U.S. economy afloat despite sluggish growth; a recession and debt crisis in Europe; a stock market collapse in China; and even the persistent obstacles that the Obama administration has placed in the path of oil and gas development. The fracking boom and the shift to natural gas since the

Bush administration have meant that the U.S. has lowered its emissions of carbon dioxide while growing its economy—an achievement no other industrialized country has managed, and without heavy regulations to limit those emissions.

Yet those on the Left have real trouble acknowledging that fact; they oppose fracking even more than it opposes fossil fuel development in general. In New York, environmentalists have succeeded in banning fracking. Jude Clemente notes in *Forbes*, "This controversial decision by Governor Cuomo has even fueled secession talk by the southern part of the state that has sat idly by and watched neighbor Pennsylvania enjoy the huge economic benefits of shale development."[16] Anti-fracking activists deny the benefits of the technology—and believe many false tales about the risks. One is the myth that fracking releases methane into aquifers, so that local residents can set their tap water on fire. In fact, methane leaches naturally into local water and did so long before fracking became possible.[17] The benefit of fracking is one of many economic truths the Left cannot acknowledge. (There are a few exceptions that prove that rule: California Governor Jerry Brown, for example, has resisted calls to ban fracking.) Progressives are simply not going to admit that the fossil fuels industry, not socialist redistribution, is responsible for economic recovery—which will reduce economic inequality. The truth is too difficult to bear.

Economists disagree over whether raising the minimum wage to $9.00, or $10.10, or $22.00, would actually cost jobs or working hours. But it is certain that at some level raising the minimum wage would create unemployment. If the minimum wage were raised to say, $100 per hour, many businesses would close, and those that would not would switch to automated operations. The principle is undeniable. The question is whether politicians have the expertise to set minimum wages at more reasonable levels without hurting employment. Can a one-size-fits-all approach be used without hurting at least some businesses and workers? That question is unfortunately one of many economic problems that is discussed in terms of good intentions rather than practical consequences. Many liberals simply refuse to accept that well-meaning laws like the minimum wage hurt the people they intend to help by making jobs and opportunity more scarce.

Many of the Left's economic proposals rely on the assumption that cost is no obstacle, or that money can always be found somewhere. Their answer to objections about the minimum wage, for example, is that business owners can afford to pay their employees more. When individual business owners claim that they cannot—or that even if they can, their suppliers cannot, so their input costs will rise—advocates for raising the minimum wage tend to ignore their objections.

When critics cite evidence that minimum wage hikes actually have caused job losses—the 2015 loss of restaurant jobs in Seattle, for example, when that city raised its minimum wage—proponents of a higher minimum wage try to minimize the data. The left-wing group Media Matters argued that the job losses in Seattle amounted to "less than 1 percent reduction in the area's restaurant workforce."[18] Later, the group touted a summertime spike in restaurant jobs as proof that critics of the minimum wage hike were wrong,[19] but when jobs went down again in September, Media Matters was silent.

In December 2015 the Federal Reserve Bank of San Francisco published a paper by visiting scholar David Newmark reviewing the existing research on the minimum wage. Newmark concluded that "the overall body of recent evidence suggests that the most credible conclusion is a higher minimum wage results in some job loss for the least-skilled workers—with possibly larger adverse effects than earlier research suggested."[20] Newmark estimated that minimum wage hikes since 2007 have caused "about 100,000 to 200,000" job losses, whose impact must be weighed against the benefit of higher wages for those employees benefiting from the raises. In a subsequent paper, Newmark explained that only about 18 percent of the benefit of raising the minimum wage would actually help the poor, partly because many poor families have no workers at all.[21] Many minimum wage workers—students, for example, who may work part time and still depend on their parents, so that they don't need a "living wage" to support themselves—are from more affluent families. That means the minimum wage is at best an inefficient tool for helping the poor. Newark concluded that "the evidence simply does not provide a strong case for using minimum wages to reduce poverty."

One clue to the folly of minimum wage hikes is the fact that in the most prosperous sectors of the economy employers have to offer more than minimum wages to succeed and grow. In the startup world of Silicon Valley, for example, tech workers are offered compensation in stock options and other benefits in addition to their wages. It is difficult to compare Silicon Valley, with its unique concentration of skills, to other parts of economy. Yet the same principle holds true for unskilled and semi-skilled workers in booming parts of the economy. In North Dakota in the midst of the oil boom in 2014, entry-level jobs at McDonald's, which typically pay wages at or near the federal minimum, paid twice as much—$15—because that was the only way to attract and retain scarce employees.[22] The lesson is that economic growth is a far more reliable way to lift up the poor than the minimum wage.

When finally presented with irrefutable evidence that minimum wages—along with higher taxes, tougher regulations, and other interventions—make life harder for entrepreneurs, liberal policymakers have little empathy. California governor Jerry Brown, for example, said in 2015, "We've got a few problems, we have lots of little burdens and regulations and taxes, but smart people figure out how to make it."[23] Tough luck for entrepreneurs and workers outside the high-tech industry—who are steadily deserting the Golden State.

All things are possible in theory. The trouble begins when we ask: "At what cost?" Or, to put it in politically pointed terms, "Who pays?"

(These are questions the Left prefers to suppress—and not just on the minimum wage. Students at the University of Southern California, for example, struggled to find an answer to that question as they debated a recent resolution to demand the university spend $100 million on "diversity" training. When opponents of the resolution complained that "from [a] fiscal perspective, this will dramatically increase tuition," supporters of the resolution cited Hollywood producer George Lucas's $10 million donation to the university's film school as proof that the money could be found. The task of convincing rich people to donate large sums for "diversity" is, evidently, a job for the grown-ups.)[24]

Again, there is a simple thought experiment that illustrates the problem with arguments for a higher minimum wage. If it should be raised to $15, why not $22? $30? $50? At some level even the most committed advocate for the minimum wage, if he or she is honest, will admit that there is a limit past which jobs would certainly be lost.

The point was illustrated rather comically in Los Angeles, where unions convinced the city council to hike the minimum wage to $15.00 per hour—then demanded that companies with unionized employees should be exempt from the new rule.[25] The demand, widely mocked as hypocritical, demonstrated that even unions understood that the higher minimum wage would cost jobs. They just wanted to make sure those were other people's jobs.

So the principle is clear: at some level, the minimum wage becomes unacceptably high. The question is: Where?

The precise answer could mean the difference between success and failure for a small business, or between employment and unemployment for an entry-level worker. Losing a job—or failing to find one, because the opportunity is never provided—can have a profound effect on young people, for whom early work experiences are a major determinant of future job success.

But for advocates of a higher minimum wage, setting the wage at precisely the right level is less important than the gesture of raising it. Former Obama economic adviser Christina Romer explained in the *New York Times* that "most arguments for instituting or raising a minimum wage are based on fairness and redistribution," not on economic arguments. But, as she pointed out the "fairness" arguments may have severe economic flaws.[26] Romer notes that while relatively few low-wage workers may lose their jobs when the minimum wage is raised, there are other ways that the poor could suffer as a result. Higher wages will be passed on to consumers through higher prices. And higher minimum wages could attract wealthier, more qualified applicants to compete for minimum wage jobs. She concluded that—even from a liberal perspective—there are better ways to help the poor than raising the minimum wage.

Yet to many liberals that is not the point. To them, raising the minimum wage means that workers have a basic level of dignity, represented by their income. Going further, a "living wage" represents the idea that every job should guarantee a certain standard of living. And the idea that minimum wages should rise when corporate profits rise represents the ideal of a more egalitarian society. So you could say these are highly idealistic arguments. (Less charitably, they might also be described as motivated by envy.) In the same way, many liberals argue for tighter regulations on businesses and markets because they believe in the ideal of a centrally managed society, organized scientifically by experts.

The libertarian philosopher Robert Nozick called these ideals "patterned" visions of how wealth should be distributed in society.[27] They are aesthetic visions, painted in the language of morality. Whatever their merit, the inescapable truth that liberals wish to avoid or deny is that they have a cost. And that cost can sometimes be severe.

South Africa—where I was born, and where I studied and worked for several years after college—is a prime example. The country has a massive unemployment problem. The official unemployment rate hovers around 25 percent. The unofficial unemployment rate, which includes those who have given up looking for work, is above 35 percent, representing some 7.7 million people. The World Bank has concluded that the unemployment crisis in South Africa is worse than it was under apartheid.[28] The poor survive by working in the informal economy. Some live an almost cashless existence.

The reasons for unemployment in South Africa are manifold. One is the legacy of apartheid, which not only excluded black South Africans from many occupations and businesses but also deliberately denied them an education that would allow them to develop skills they could use to compete in the labor market. The crisis was compounded by the struggle against apartheid, which saw the imposition of major international sanctions. Some areas of South Africa's economy, such as the energy industry, innovated to deal with new constraints on trade. Still, the damage to the economy as a whole was deep and lasting.

But those pre-1994 problems have been exacerbated by the post-apartheid government. South Africa is the one place in the world where the communists think they won the Cold War, since the fall of the Berlin Wall induced the apartheid government to begin negotiations that would eventually lead to a democratic transition of power. The new government, the African National Congress, gave up its communist policies of nationalizing mines, industry and farmland. But it co-governs with the Communist Party and the trade unions. While its macroeconomic policies have targeted inflation, its labor policies have been far-left.

In 2001, South Africa began applying minimum wages sector by sector. In the years since then, economists have studied the effects. They have concluded that minimum wages did not have an effect on employment or income, though they did tend to reduce the hours worked. The results were "varied and unpredictable."[29] But there was an important caveat: many employers may not have been complying with the new minimum wages: "in four of the five sectors, 40–60% of workers were paid less than the applicable minimum wage." The fact is, the more onerous regulations become, the greater the incentive business owners have to ignore them—and the more they will, if they can get away with it. To survive, they may have no choice.

If the minimum wage did little damage, it certainly did not help. South Africa's unemployment crisis continued to deepen. If anything, the minimum wage laws hurt economic growth, and they are part of a broader set of state interventions that send a clear negative signal to the foreign investors on whom South Africa still depends.

But in South Africa, as in America, an honest discussion of the minimum wage is suppressed by accusations that critics of the policy are greedy, or—especially in South Africa—racist. If you oppose the minimum wage, the implication is that you oppose paying workers an *amount* equal to that particular wage, rather than the attempt to cure poverty by *forcing* all employers to do so. If an economy is booming, workers are paid more, and the minimum wage becomes moot. As Romer notes,

"Robust competition is a powerful force helping to ensure that workers are paid what they contribute to their employers' bottom lines." Employees have less bargaining power when there are few job opportunities. But employees with skills and determination always have a competitive advantage, and can earn far more than the minimum wage as a result. And low-skilled workers are not helped if higher minimum wages price them out of job opportunities.

Another problem with ignoring the real and potential costs of well-intentioned policies like the minimum wage is that our global competitors do not ignore those costs. China, for example, is only interested in raw materials for its factories, markets for its exports, and technology transfers it can adapt and improve. The justice or fairness of what workers are paid is of little concern, ironically, to the communist "People's Republic."

The debate about the minimum wage obscures what is the real challenge for industrialized economies today: growth. Economic growth is what enables people to move out of poverty. It is even what enables statist redistribution policies: without growth, there is less to redistribute among more recipients. For several years now, the U.S. has been growing at a dismal rate, successful only in comparison to Europe's near-zero growth or recession. That has a profoundly negative effect on the country's outlook—though those lucky enough to have investments or retirement accounts, who have seen the stock market rebound, may not be affected—or aware. Today the minimum wage is increasingly a political palliative, often simply a way for a nervous and guilt-ridden elite—aware that it is enjoying massive wealth as the result of inflationary policies while the rest of the country struggles to find opportunities—to feel better about themselves. But tragically the minimum wage debate, which shunts public attention into a clash about fairness and "social justice," precludes a debate about economic growth, the real solution to poverty and inequality.

However much the minimum wage is raised, the basic problem of economics will still be there: people have to toil daily to put bread on the table and build a future. That has been the burden of humanity since

Adam and Eve left Eden—and is also, ironically, part of what makes life worth living. It is because there are costs that we value what we have. By evading the question of costs, or suppressing the answers with accusations of greed, those on the Left make misguided policies like raising the minimum wage more politically feasible. But they also make their ostensible goal—in this case, broader prosperity—harder to achieve.

# CHAPTER 4

# ISRAEL

## THE LIE:
## Israel is the main obstacle to peace in the Middle East.

Examples:

*"Put yourself in their shoes. Look at the world through their eyes. It is not fair that a Palestinian child cannot grow up in a state of their own."*[1]
> —President Barack Obama, Israel, March 2013

*"A two-state solution will be clearly underscored as the only real alternative. Because a unitary state winds up either being an apartheid state with second-class citizens— or it ends up being a state that destroys the capacity of Israel to be a Jewish state."*[2]
> —Secretary of State John Kerry,
> Trilateral Commission, April 2014

*"A lot will have to do with Israel and whether or not Israel wants to make the deal—whether or not Israel's willing to sacrifice certain things. They may not be, and I understand that, and I'm OK with that. But then you're just not going to have a deal."[3]*

—GOP presidential candidate Donald Trump,
Republican Jewish Coalition, December 2015

# THE TRUTH:
# Israel's neighbors do not want peace, and singling out Israel for criticism only encourages its enemies to keep trying to destroy it.

In 2008, I had a public argument with Alan Dershowitz, my law school professor and mentor. The topic was the timeless Yiddish question: "Is it good for the Jews?" Specifically, the dispute was over whether then-Senator Barack Obama would be good for Israel or not. Dershowitz wrote in a blog at the Jerusalem Post, "The election of Barack Obama—a liberal supporter of Israel—will enhance Israel's position among wavering liberals."[4]

Wishful thinking. "We also now know that Obama has associated with the anti-Israel Left for years," I wrote in a response to Dershowitz, noting Obama's close friendships with the racist anti-Israel (and anti-American) pastor Jeremiah Wright, unrepentant domestic terrorist Bill Ayers, and former Palestine Liberation Organization attaché-turned Columbia academic Rashid Khalidi. These were associations the media had done its best to minimize, but they had laid the foundations, I argued, for Obama's future foreign policy.[5]

I was right: Obama turned out to have the worst relationship with Israel of any U.S. president. His supporters pointed to what they called unprecedented security cooperation with Israel, or blamed Israeli Prime Minister Benjamin Netanyahu for the decline in the relationship. But as Israeli Ambassador Michael Oren, a noted historian, concluded, the divide was real, and Obama had created it deliberately to place "daylight" between the U.S. and Israel.[6] Dershowitz, who defended Obama through most of his presidency, finally gave up in September 2015, calling Obama "childish, petty, vengeful" towards the Israeli government.[7]

Over and over, Obama put Israel in a corner on the issue of the Palestinians, who promptly dug in their heels and refused to negotiate. The most significant challenge was Obama's nuclear deal with Iran, which Netanyahu described as an "historic mistake." It lifted economic sanctions in exchange for Iran's agreement to restrain nuclear enrichment—temporarily. Obama hoped the deal would achieve what he called a "new equilibrium" in the region, a balance of power between Shia Iran and the U.S.-aligned Sunni states.[8] But Israel's future in that balance was uncertain.

The problem was not, as some argued, that Obama is an Antisemite. (Ample evidence exists to the contrary.) Rather, the problem was that Obama refused to accept three important truths about the region. The first is that Palestinian terrorism began, has persisted, and will continue with or without Israeli occupation. The second is that Palestinians do not want their own state as much as they want to eliminate Israel. And the third is that Palestinian hostility to Israel is increasingly rooted in fundamentalist Islam, making it impossible to resolve.

These truths have become even more apparent during Obama's administration. Yet he, and the Left, continue to ignore them, blaming Israel. The suppression of truth, in this case, has real-world consequences—not just for Israelis and Palestinians, who remain at war, but for broader U.S. policies in the region and worldwide.

The reality-denial is largely confined to the left side of the American political spectrum.

Recent opinion surveys confirm that roughly two-thirds of the American people side with Israel. That is an historically high level of support, and it has persisted in spite of a cold relationship between Obama and Netanyahu, and despite ongoing conflict in the region.

Even some liberals support Israel. In fact, no issue better illustrates the split between liberals and the hard Left. The Democratic Party still includes a few staunch defenders of Israel, though they have lost political leverage during the Obama era. But in the American academy in particular, and also among the media and policy elite, criticism of Israel is not only common but expected. Indeed, in some social milieus it is considered anathema to declare that you believe Israel has the right to defend itself—all the more so if you stand up for Israel for fighting terror or facing up to the prospect of existential nuclear threat.

Ironically, Alan Dershowitz argues that the best case for Israel is the liberal one—that Israel has a vibrant democracy, treats Jews and Arabs equally, upholds gay rights, fosters high-tech entrepreneurship, and embraces an energetic free press. It is also possible, he notes, to be a critic of Israeli policies—such as Jewish settlement in the West Bank, the chunk of territory that Israel occupied in defensive actions during the Six Day War of 1967 after Jordan, against the pleas of the Israeli government, entered the conflict.

None of that matters to the far Left—which sees Israel through the prism of power—or, to use Obama's preferred term, "fairness." The Jews have a state; the Arabs do not. Israel has a powerful military; its enemies, while cruel, are weak in comparison. That settles most moral questions for the Left. The Left sees Israel as a settler-colonialist state, and judges it according to the moral template of post-colonialism, in which the indigenous links between the Jewish people and the land are disregarded and the Palestinians are not held to the same moral standards that are applied to Israel—or, indeed, to any civilized nation.

That is all nonsense, but the anti-Israel cult is orthodoxy on many university campuses, thanks in part to the profound influence of the late Palestinian postcolonial scholar Edward Said, who gave intellectual heft to what until the 1970s was little more than a terrorist movement. Recent years have seen the emergence of the "Boycott, Divestment, and Sanctions" (BDS) movement, which seeks to isolate Israel the same way apartheid South Africa was once isolated. Israel is cast as a moral pariah, much as the Jew was a social pariah in much of the world for centuries.

The BDS movement often fails to distinguish between protests against Israeli policies such as Israel's presence in the West Bank, on the one hand, and objections to Israel's very existence, on the other.

Indeed, on some university campuses, in some newsrooms, and in some elite circles of opinion it has become impermissible to allow that Israel should exist, or that Israel's founding was a noble historical event worthy of celebration, or that it is a state with any legitimate basis whatsoever.

In 2012 two Israelis who had come to the University of California, Davis to present a pro-Israel perspective were heckled by anti-Israel protestors who disrupted the event. One of the protestors said, "My only purpose today is that this event is shut down. You have turned Palestine into a land of prostitutes, rapists and child molesters." An organizer of the event explained what happened: "They finally allowed the speakers to talk for a few moments here and there. Then they would start screaming again."

In 2015, UC Davis would pass a resolution demanding that the University of California system divest from companies doing business with Israel. As pro-Israel students filed out of the student senate meeting in protest, Muslim students in the auditorium shouted, "Allahu Akbar!" To chant the slogan of Islamist radicals is now more acceptable on a public university campus than to be identified with the Jewish state, the only free country in the Middle East.

This attitude is not confined to college campuses. It has become entrenched in the foreign policy establishment, despite strong support for Israel in Congress.

In the latter half of the twentieth century, "Arabists" at the State Department believed that American interests lay in relations with the oil-rich Arab countries, not the one democratic outpost in the Middle East, which they loathed. Now a generation that regards Israel's power and success as a form of injustice has come of age.

Encouraged by the wrongheaded idea that pro-Israel activists exert too much influence over American foreign policy in general—an idea captured in the 2007 book *The Israel Lobby*—policymakers have sought to marginalize the Jewish state.[9] The perception of American leadership in the region, and the world, has suffered as a result.

The current wave of hostility to Israel kicked off in earnest at the UN World Conference against Racism in Durban, South Africa, in August 2001. The meeting took place at the height of the second, violent Palestinian *intifada*. And it had been clear for months leading up to the conference that Arab regimes and anti-Israel groups intended to use it to draw parallels between Israel and apartheid South Africa. Those parallels were, and remain, false. Israel upholds equal rights for both Jews and Arabs, and Arab Israelis have the vote, something black South Africans never had under apartheid. In the West Bank, Jews and Arabs have been more separated in recent years—but in response to Palestinian terror, not because of racial or religious ideology on the part of the Israelis.

The conference was even worse than expected. At the non-governmental organization (NGO) meetings, anti-Israel activists broke up a meeting on antisemitism. Radical Muslims held protests, chanting Islamist slogans and handing out literature with swastikas alongside Jewish stars. An Egyptian cartoonist distributed caricatures of Jews that could have come directly from the pages of the Nazi-era tabloid *Der Stürmer.* When I personally challenged him to defend what he was doing, he simply shrugged and refused to answer.

The anti-Israel movement had crossed the line into overt antisemitism. And when the conference left South Africa, the hatred remained. The South African government set out on a path of increasing hostility to Israel. Going beyond its Cold War–era loyalty to the Palestine Liberation Organization, the ruling party embraced the global "Boycott, Divestment, Sanctions" (BDS) that had started at the Durban conference,[10] and in 2015 even hosted the leader of the Hamas terrorist group, Khaled Meshaal.[11] Ironically, outside of the media and political elites, a plurality of South Africans sided with Israel over the Palestinians, according to a Pew survey in 2007—a pattern that holds in predominantly Christian countries throughout Africa.

Over the past several decades, Israel has become taboo on the Left. One reason is that left-wing Jews are among Israel's most vociferous opponents. In October 2001, Ronnie Kasrils, a Jewish communist and a minister in the South African government, circulated a petition among "South Africans of Jewish Descent" blaming Israel for the ongoing conflict and calling on Jews to oppose the Israeli government. It gathered few signatures but raised anxiety among South African Jews, who were made to feel that their full citizenship in the new South Africa depended on their denunciation of Israel.

Kasrils set an example for Jewish leftists across the world. In 2003 Tony Judt, late historian of post-war Europe, published an essay in the *New York Review of Books*, "Israel: The Alternative," in which he described Israeli nationalism as an "anachronism" in a post-nationalist world. Judt rejected the two-state solution, instead supporting a "single, integrated, binational state."[12] The most powerful response came from the liberal Leon Wieseltier of the *New Republic*, who pointed out that Judt was essentially calling for Israel's destruction.[13] "A bi-national state is not the alternative *for* Israel. It is the alternative *to* Israel," he argued. Moreover, Wieseltier pointed out, Judt had "given credence to the [right-wing] suspicion that the criticism of Israel's policy is always nothing other than the criticism of Israel's existence." In any case, the idea of a binational state had been floated before, and Arab leaders had rejected it. Wieseltier speculated that Judt was motivated to renounce Israel by social pressure, not the intellectual case against Israel: "I detect the scars of dinners and conferences. He does not wish to be held accountable for things that he has not himself done, or to be regarded as the representative of anyone but himself," he wrote.

But the trickle of liberal defections from support for Israel continued—often at moments of greatest vulnerability for the Jewish state. The liberal commentators Ezra Klein[14] and Jonathan Chait,[15] for example, spoke out against Israel during the Gaza war of 2014—an indisputably defensive conflict for Israel, in which Hamas fired first and attempted to stage mass terror attacks against Israeli civilian targets using a network of tunnels. In 2015, at the height of a Palestinian campaign of knife attacks against Jews, Harvard professor Steven Levitsky and University of Chicago assistant professor Glen Weyl announced they were joining an academic boycott of Israel.[16]

In 2008, those renunciations had taken institutional form with the emergence of a new political group called "J Street" (a play on "K Street," the avenue of lobbyists in Washington, D.C.; there is no "J Street" on the Washington road map). J Street sought to counter the influence of the American Israel Public Affairs Committee (AIPAC), the pro-Israel lobby group. In *The Israel Lobby*, John J. Mearsheimer and Stephen M. Walt had written, "A number of prominent American Jews have also considered founding a new lobbying group explicitly intended to provide a more reasonable alternative to AIPAC." The new group, they wrote, might "bring their influence to bear in more constructive ways."[17] J Street was the result.

While maintaining that it was "pro-Israel" (albeit with no overt identification with the Jewish State or its symbols), J Street encouraged the American government to press Israel for deeper concessions to its enemies. J Street opposed sanctions on Iran, and backed the nuclear deal. It highlighted critics of Israel, such as Richard Goldstone, who accused Israel of war crimes in the 2008–9 war in Gaza (and later retracted). It opposed the Israeli government of Benjamin Netanyahu.

Though officially non-partisan, in practice J Street supported left-wing Democrats almost exclusively. And though it failed to move American public opinion, it helped change the debate within the Democratic Party, where anti-Israel voices that had long been muffled in the interest of appealing to mainstream voters became more outspoken. The influence of J Street was apparent during the 2012 Democratic National Convention in Charlotte, North Carolina, when a floor fight erupted over the abandonment of the party's previous commitments to fighting Palestinian terror and recognition of Jerusalem as Israel's capital. To amend the platform, party elders had to pretend to have won a two-thirds voice vote in favor, as the voices opposed to the anti-Israel amendment clearly prevailed in the hall.

Campuses across the nation continue to be more and more hostile towards Israel—and to Jewish students. After repeated attempts, anti-Israel students at public and private California campuses convinced their student leaders to pass resolutions encouraging divestment from Israeli companies in 2015. Typically, these resolutions required nothing of the Palestinians—or of the students themselves, who never commit to boycotting the Israeli technologies in their cell phones and laptops. And the votes are often marred by procedural oddities, as at Stanford, where a divestment resolution failed—only for a re-vote to be called a week later, when it passed.[18] Increasingly, anti-Israel students express overt anti-semitism. At the University of California, Davis, for example, a Jewish fraternity was defaced with swastikas after the student government's divestment vote.[19]At UCLA, a Jewish student, Rachel Beyda, was turned down by the student government for a judicial position because she was Jewish—until a faculty adviser intervened.

No major university administration actually approved a divestment resolution or supported an anti-Israel boycott. In 2002, in the early years of the BDS effort, Harvard president Lawrence Summers warned during a speech that while there was "much in Israel's foreign and defense policy that can be and should be vigorously challenged...profoundly anti-Israel views are increasingly finding support in progressive intel-lectual communities.... Serious and thoughtful people are advocating and taking actions that are anti-Semitic in their effect if not their intent."[20]

Summers's speech caused an outcry on the Left, which accused him of tarring any criticism of Israel as antisemitic. But Summers was only offering the standard contemporary liberal perspective on Israel: criticiz-ing the state's policies but not its right to exist, which, he said, had been "settled in the affirmative by the world community." For the far Left, though, that didn't go far enough: Israel's existence was itself the prob-lem, and saying so—they claimed—was not antisemitic, but entirely legitimate.

That is an argument that Jewish liberals have struggled to answer. One approach, described above, has been to emphasize the case for Israel as a liberal democracy. "The truth is I support Israel precisely *because* I am a civil libertarian and a liberal," Dershowitz explains in the introduction to his 2003 bestseller, *The Case for Israel*.[21]

Another is to emphasize Israel's positive contributions and achievements. That was the approach taken by the philosopher Hannah Arendt, who was a Zionist but opposed Israeli sovereignty, believing that a Jewish state would never be able to survive a conflict with the surrounding Arab states. In her 1950 essay, "Peace or Armistice in the Near East?," Arendt argued, "The building of a Jewish national home was not a colonial enterprise in which European colonial powers came to exploit foreign riches with the help and at the expense of native labor. Palestine was and is a poor country and whatever riches it possesses are exclusively the product of Jewish labor which are not likely to survive if ever the Jews are expelled from the country."[22] These so-called "artificial" achievements, she said, were a better argument for Zionism than "antisemitism, poverty, national homelessness."

These essentially liberal arguments, however, made little headway against the radical arguments of those on the far Left, who cannot tolerate even the mildest defense of Israel, rejecting the liberal case for Israel as a farrago of excuses for the imbalance of power between Israel and the Palestinians. Judt, for example, acknowledged that Israel is a democratic state, but suggested that its identity as a *Jewish* state negated that argument for its existence: "Israel itself is a multicultural society in all but name; yet it remains distinctive among democratic states in its resort to ethnoreligious criteria with which to denominate and rank its citizens." Judt was wrong: there is no such ranking. Israel's very declaration of independence offers "complete equality of social and political rights to all its inhabitants irrespective of religion, race or sex," and invites "the Arab inhabitants of the State of Israel to preserve peace and participate in the upbuilding of the State on the basis of full and equal citizenship and due representation in all its provisional and permanent institutions."[23] The only unique benefit Jews enjoy, at least formally, is the right to immigrate and claim Israeli citizenship in the first place. That is, after all, the state's raison d'être—to be a refuge where Jews can escape being marginalized and persecuted in the rest of the world and take charge of their own fate in their own country. But to liberals, the right of return is an excuse to claim Israel is violating democratic principles, even though many other Western democracies—Germany, for example—offer the right of return to those that share their heritage. And the fact that Palestinians have rejected a similar state for themselves is immaterial to the Left.

Likewise with Israel's achievements in industry, agriculture, science and technology. To Israel's liberal defenders, it is obvious that Israel's prosperity is the result of the efforts of Israelis, both Jew and Arab. But to Israel's leftist detractors, the "power imbalance" between Israelis and Palestinians—the advantage Israel enjoys in access to international capital and American aid, for example—explains Israeli achievements. That supposed "power imbalance" comes in handy on the question of international law, too—with Israel's most hostile critics asserting that the Jewish state has violated international law—then, when shown that it has not done so, retorting that international law was established by powerful former colonial powers anyway.

But there is one argument for Israel's existence that the Left doesn't have an answer for: the Biblical claim that God gave the land to the Jewish people. It is a theological argument, one Jews have often avoided stating explicitly. It is, however, the core of the argument for Israel—even for secular Israelis. The Zionist movement, after all, rejected an early British offer of settlement in Uganda. Jews also rejected the Soviet alternative to Zionism, which was a Jewish colony in eastern Siberia called Birobidzhan.

The Bible actually anticipates future disputes over the right to the land, as when Abraham insists on paying for a burial cave in Hebron, rather than accepting it as a gift.[24] The Bible also predicts the dispersion of the Jews—and their eventual return. It is precisely because of the religious connection to Israel that Jews have maintained a continuous presence there, even in periods of exile. Ultimately, the religious claim to Israel does what liberal arguments cannot: establish an aboriginal right. But whenever Biblical claims are in conflict with other religious claims, the Left gives those other claims—such as the Islamic religious claim to Jerusalem, which is not even mentioned directly in the Koran—excessive deference.

Unsurprisingly, Palestinians and their leftist allies have tried to suppress the Jewish connection to Israel. It is a staple of Palestinian propaganda to deny that there was ever a Jewish Temple in Jerusalem, for example. Well-meaning American mediators have tried to "bracket" discussion of Jerusalem in peace talks, to no avail: for Palestinians, it is *the* core issue. Even banning Jews from praying at the Temple Mount—a prohibition Israel enforces—is not enough: Palestinians want to bar Jews from visiting it.

The Left suppresses not only the depth of Jewish connection to Israel but also the depth of the Palestinian rejection of the Jewish state. First, whereas the Left contends—and the Obama administration apparently believes—that Israeli settlements are the reason the conflict between Israelis and Palestinians persists, the reality is that Palestinian terrorism is driving the violence. In 2005, Israel withdrew every soldier and settler from Gaza, and the response was more Palestinian terror—rockets, kidnappings, and tunnels. But if the Left acknowledges Palestinian terror at all, it casts it as the desperate response of a people with no other means of defending itself. In reality the Palestinians have chosen terror over a negotiated agreement that would lead to a separate state alongside Israel.

The Palestinians do not want their own state; they simply want to eliminate Israel. Palestinians have no national holidays; they simply observe the date of Israel's founding as the Nakba, or "catastrophe." They have built few of their own institutions and make few economic investments; even if they were, somehow, to replace Israel, they have done little to prepare for their future state.

Palestinian hostility to Israel is essentially religious, not humanitarian or even nationalist. But the increasingly radical Islamist character of the Palestinian cause is muffled in deference to Western left-wing sensibilities. Yet jihad is what many Palestinian leaders are now promising to their people.

Sometimes even genuine friends of Israel prefer not to acknowledge these disturbing truths. At the twentieth anniversary memorial of the assassination of Israeli prime minister Yitzchak Rabin, former President Bill Clinton exhorted Israelis, "...the next step will be determined by whether you decide that Rabin was right, that you have to share your future with your neighbors, that you have to stand for peace, that the risk for peace isn't as severe as the risk of walking away from it. We are praying that you will make the right decision."[25]

That was a frightening leap in moral accounting. As Jonathan S. Tobin of Commentary magazine noted, "Bill Clinton spent the years after he left the White House loudly and bitterly lamenting the fact that Yasir Arafat cost him a Nobel Peace Prize [by rejecting diplomacy].... Each time Israel took the kind of risks for peace that its friends and critics had been urging it to do yet got neither peace nor credit for the sacrifice.... if Clinton were to go to Ramallah and tell the Palestinians that it was up to them to finally make peace, he would not be greeted with thunderous cheers, as was the case in Tel Aviv."[26]

There are real costs to suppressing the truth about the Israeli-Palestinian conflict. Successive American administrations have tried to pressure Israel to make concessions, only to see "the peace process" founder on Palestinian intransigence. Blindness to Palestinian radicalism has often led the U.S. to underestimate radical Islam and its global ambitions. Moreover, the idea that the Israeli-Palestinian conflict is the root of America's problems in the Middle East—a theory embraced by *The Israel Lobby* and the leftists of J Street—has led the U.S. to undermine Israel and other allies, while ignoring the broader threats of Sunni extremism and Iranian Shiite imperialism.

Suppressing the truth about the Israeli-Palestinian conflict has rewarded Palestinians for terror, and raised their expectations about what they can get from negotiations beyond the maximum Israel can offer and still survive, fueling the conflict anew—and proving that there are real life-and-death consequences to the Left's intolerance of truth.

# CHAPTER 5

# CLIMATE CHANGE

## THE LIE:
## Unless we ignore the "denialists" and act now, the planet will be destroyed.

Examples:

*"We, the human species, are confronting a planetary emergency.... Last September 21, as the Northern Hemisphere tilted away from the sun, scientists reported with unprecedented distress that the North Polar ice cap is 'falling off a cliff.' One study estimated that it could be completely gone during summer in less than 22 years. Another new study, to be presented by U.S. Navy researchers later this week, warns it could happen in as little as 7 years. Seven years from now."*[1]

—Former Vice President Al Gore, Nobel Prize Lecture, December 10, 2007

*"We need to limit our carbon pollution.... If it continues year after year, California can literally burn up."*[2]
—California Governor Jerry Brown, August 6, 2015

*"AITC has received funding through the ACT Government Arts Fund for a two week creative development of Kill Climate Deniers.... It is a fictional scenario, and we take as given a common understanding that to depict something does not mean to condone it."*
—Aspen Island Theatre Company, October 2014[3]

## THE TRUTH:
## Warming is less drastic than predicted, and in any case we are already reducing emissions.

Few people in America have more to say about global warming—a.k.a. climate change—than fourth-term California governor Jerry Brown, the liberal icon (and iconoclast) who has made the environmentalist cause the centerpiece of his policy agenda and his political legacy.

The problem: much of what Jerry Brown says about climate change has to be corrected later. In 2014, for example, Brown claimed that climate change could cause sea levels to rise so high that Los Angeles International Airport (LAX) would be underwater. But LAX is over a hundred feet above sea level, and the projected possible rise of the ocean was only four feet over two hundred years. "A 4-foot rise in sea level should have minimal impact on airport operations," airport officials said. Brown's staff admitted tersely, "The governor misspoke about LAX."[4]

The following year, after a series of devastating forest fires, Brown said, "This is a wake-up call. We have to start coming to our senses. This is not a game of politics. We need to limit our carbon pollution.... This is not the way these fires usually behave. If it continues year after year, California can literally burn up."[5] Yet scientists disagreed, saying there was not enough evidence to link forest fires and climate change. Brown was guilty of "noble-cause corruption," one climate change specialist said.[6]

Brown is hardly alone in his exaggerations. Alarmism is a staple of the climate change movement, whose central conceit is that we ought to behave as if the worst outcome possible—or even imaginable—is inevitable. Along the way, activists for the cause suppress contrary information—particularly information about the costs of their proposed remedies.

If the public can be led to believe that California "can literally burn up," that the world's glaciers will melt completely, that winter will never return, that people will starve from drought, and so on, then literally any government intervention can be justified to rescue humanity and the planet.

But occasionally reality seeps in—such as the reality that Brown's ambitious 2015 proposal to cut the state's petroleum use in half by 2030 would result in massive fuel price increases. The result was a backlash from moderate Democrats in the state legislature. Stung by the rare defeat, Brown vowed a "life-and-death struggle" to "change the very basis of our industrial economy"—which may have been the real point all along.[7]

The true agenda of many climate change enthusiasts is to use the power of the federal government—or an international system—to control the economy, down to the everyday choices made by the humblest household. As liberal geographer Joel Kotkin observed in January 2016, "Today climate change has become the killer app for expanding state control."[8] Climate change provides cover for an agenda of total control that the public would never accept were it presented openly—so it must be shrouded in a thicket of lies.

To the Left, climate change is a cultural struggle, a crucial battle in the continuing fight that science must wage against superstition, reason against religion. Yet as Holman Jenkins of the *Wall Street Journal* pointed out rather memorably, "so many who proclaim themselves 'passionate' about global warming cannot string together two sentences indicating any understanding of the subject."[9]

The earth's climate is unfathomably complex, but the basic elements of the climate change theory are not hard to understand; they have not changed much since I studied environmental science at Harvard in the 1990s. The sun heats the earth, the earth radiates heat back to space, and certain gases in the earth's atmosphere trap that heat near the surface. These "greenhouse gases" keep our planet warm enough to sustain life as we know it.

Still, earth's climate is not a static system. Global temperatures change over time, thanks to a variety of factors including sunspots, geothermal activity, volcanic eruptions, and meteor impacts. The composition of the atmosphere has also changed: the creation of oxygen was a major, indeed catastrophic event for life at the time. One of the most important greenhouse gases is carbon dioxide, a colorless, odorless, natural product of breathing and burning that exists in tiny amounts in our atmosphere. It is also the key ingredient in photosynthesis, the process through which plants and plankton make food from sunlight. Without it, we would die.

Since the start of the Industrial Revolution in the mid-nineteenth century, the concentration of carbon dioxide in the atmosphere has been increasing dramatically, from just above 250 parts per million (ppm) to over 400 ppm. Other greenhouse gases have also increased. During the same time, there has been an overall rise in global average surface temperatures. Many scientists think the correlation is no coincidence, and that the more humans burn fossil fuels, the more concentrated greenhouse gases will become, and the more the planet will warm.

There are, however, many complications that this simple story doesn't take into account. One is that there are "negative feedbacks"—natural mechanisms that reduce the effect of carbon dioxide. A warmer surface means more clouds, but clouds reflect solar radiation into space, cooling the planet. Some gases produced by industrial activity are aerosols that cause the atmosphere to cool. And much carbon dioxide is being pulled out of the atmosphere, stored in forests and oceans.

Another complication is that the planet has not warmed as much as our highly sophisticated computer models of climate have predicted. In fact, temperatures have been stagnant for nearly two decades—though at a high level. And our models cannot predict the specific impacts of climate change in any particular place with any precision. The science of climate change—even among true believers—is uncertain.

Faced with these uncertainties, climate change enthusiasts have resorted to invoking majority rule to impose their conclusions—thus the oft-repeated claim that "97 percent of scientists" support the theory that climate change is real and caused by human beings. The 97 percent figure is misleading. In a May 2014 op-ed in the *Wall Street Journal*, Joseph Bast of the Heartland Institute and Dr. Roy Spencer of the University of Alabama argued, "The so-called consensus comes from a handful of surveys and abstract-counting exercises that have been contradicted by more reliable research."[10] One of these "abstract-counting exercises" was from a blogger whose method was so clumsy that authors whose work he had included later complained he misrepresented their views. Dana Nuccitelli, responding to Bast and Spencer, insisted her research showed that of the climate scientists who expressed a view on human-caused climate change, 97–98 agreed with the theory.[11] But it was not clear what exactly they agreed with: the "consensus" is so broad that it takes in views that are skeptical of many claims made by climate change activists. At bottom, the 97 percent argument is not a scientific argument, but a political one. Science is not subject to majority rule; if it were, scientific discovery would be rare, and meaningless. Science is a method of inquiry, not a body of doctrine.

Another element of the overselling of climate change is the term "carbon pollution," which suggests that the problem is not just temperature but toxic substances that pose immediate and concrete threats. The term is designed to create alarm by conflating a potential environmental problem with a real one. There are, in fact, hazardous carbon compounds produced by some industrial activities. But carbon dioxide, the main factor in climate change, is not one of them. The term "carbon pollution" implies that ordinary industrial production and consumption by American households are themselves harmful to the environment. It is a nod to the underlying radical beliefs of the environmental movement, which views human beings as harmful to the planet.

But perhaps the most obvious sleight of hand is the term "climate change" itself. Once it was called "global warming." But when the anticipated warming failed to arrive, activists began to use the more fungible and less predictive "climate change." (In 1975, *Newsweek* published an alarmist article by a scientist warning about global *cooling*.[12])

"Climate change" has the advantage of being "unfalsifiable"—that is, no evidence that could possibly disprove it. Colder as well as warmer temperatures can be evidence of "change," rather than ordinary weather. And because the earth's temperature has always fluctuated, some "change" is virtually guaranteed.

The term "climate change" seems to preclude dissent—and supporters of the theory seem determined to suppress any objections, using methods that are by now familiar. For example, they ignore evidence to the contrary: the temperature plateau; the expansion of ice in the Antarctic; the failure of hurricanes to increase; the failure of polar bears to disappear. One reason meteorologists are more skeptical of climate change than climate scientists is that they are confronted daily with weather phenomena they cannot ignore.

Climate change enthusiasts also attempt to tarnish critics by using a label: "denialist," an all-purpose slur: it applies not only to those who doubt anthropogenic global warming but also to those who doubt warming is happening as fast as the "consensus" claims it is, or who reject the extraordinary policy interventions suggested as a response to a warming planet. The term "denial" is chosen for a reason: it recalls the distasteful ideological project known as "Holocaust denial." Holocaust deniers argue that the Nazis' systematic murder of European Jews either did not happen, or happened on a much smaller scale than six million victims. Holocaust deniers ignore voluminous evidence and even eyewitness testimony. They promote antisemitism under the guise of legitimate historical inquiry.

Climate change activists would like their critics to be as marginalized as Holocaust deniers are. Environmental activist and author George Monbiot wrote in 2006, "Almost everywhere, climate change denial now looks as stupid and as unacceptable as Holocaust denial."[13] Columnist Joel Connolly went further, arguing that "climate change deniers pose a greater danger than the lingering industry that denies the Holocaust."[14]

In some countries, Holocaust denial is a crime. And some on the Left would like to see the same laws applied to climate change. In 2014, Robert F. Kennedy, Jr. wished for a law to "punish" climate change skeptics.[15] In 2015, some twenty scientists wrote to President Barack Obama and Attorney General Loretta Lynch asking them to support "a RICO (Racketeer Influenced and Corrupt Organizations Act) investigation of corporations and other organizations that have knowingly deceived the American people about the risks of climate change."[16]

Some politicians are willing to bring the weight of their office to bear to marginalize "deniers." Republican Representative Raul Grijalva of Arizona sent letters to academic institutions in 2015 demanding information about any outside funding received by skeptical scientists. The letters "convey an unstated but perfectly clear threat," wrote retired Massachusetts Institute of Technology professor Richard Lindzen.[17] "Research disputing alarm over the climate should cease lest universities that employ such individuals incur massive inconvenience and expense—and scientists holding such views should not offer testimony to Congress."

Much of what is labeled as "denial" is not; it is simply the skeptical attitude appropriate to free scientific inquiry. Arguably, a theory that has failed to fulfill the basic scientific task of predicting accurate future results has a long way to go before it can denounce skeptics as crazies or criminals.

A real example of scientific denialism would be the Nazis' denunciation of "Jewish" science. In the 1930s not only were German Jews kicked out of senior academic research posts, but certain scientific ideas were also identified as "Jewish" and suppressed. Nazi ideology regarded the probabilistic, relativistic new field of quantum physics as "Jewish," as opposed to classical physics with its emphasis on firm concepts like mechanics, force, power, and energy. The result was the exodus of some of the world's greatest scientists—a catastrophic strategic loss, since some would go on to produce nuclear weapons for the United States.

Another classic example of denialism was Josef Stalin's embrace of Lysenkoism, a genetic theory that followed the discredited Lamarkian hypothesis of acquired characteristics. Those who subscribed to the (correct) Mendelian view of genetics were marginalized, jailed, and even executed. Stalin preferred Lysenkoism because it was more amenable to communist ideology, which sought to change human beings. Lysenko's ideas also implied that the (deliberately) impoverished Soviet Union could make rapid advances in agricultural productivity with a few clever interventions.

The worst recent example of scientific denialism occurred in South Africa under President Thabo Mbeki, who insisted in 1999 that AIDS was not caused by the human immunodeficiency virus (HIV). AIDS was a "syndrome," he argued; the immune deficiency associated with it was caused by poverty and could only be cured as part of a broader project of economic redistribution. So Mbeki's government refused to allow the prescription of antiretroviral drugs at public hospitals to prevent mother-to-child transmission of the virus. He also attacked those who suggested that heterosexual sex was a prime vector for transmission, accusing them of racist sexual stereotypes. In the place of actual pharmaceutical drugs—which, bizarrely, the government had fought to obtain at discounted prices—Mbeki proposed "African" remedies. The first was Virodene, a drug whose active ingredient turned out to be an industrial solvent. The next was an "indigenous" diet of olive oil, garlic, beetroot, and African potato. The result was hundreds of thousands of needless, preventable deaths. Throughout the crisis, few in Mbeki's own political party challenged his scientific quackery. They feared retaliation, and shared his enthusiasm for redistribution—from rich to poor, from First World to Third—so they remained silent. Mbeki defended his views from criticism in the press by insisting he was simply exercising freedom of speech—while suppressing the voices of those who dared oppose him.

AIDS denialism, like Holocaust denial, hid behind a pretense of genuine scientific skepticism—without a real emphasis on truth or an openness to persuasion. In the climate change debate, ironically, it is the side accusing skeptics of "denialism" that is most hostile to an honest scientific discourse. Activists and politicians misuse the term "denialist" to cover up flaws in their own understanding and recommendations.

Perhaps the most prominent victim of the false charge of denialism is the Danish economist Bjorn Lomborg. In 2001 he published *The Skeptical Environmentalist*: *Measuring the Real State of the World*. The book, which has been updated several times, argues that environmentalists have misused data to exaggerate the scale and urgency of the problems facing the planet in order to create a sense of alarm that would translate into political action. In reality, he argues, the future of the earth is far more hopeful. Lomborg agrees with the environmentalists that climate change is real and that human beings are contributing to it—but he argues that it is not as bad as many are predicting, and that many of the steps prescribed to address it are harmful to us and the environment. He points out that there are far better uses of the world's resources: "…we should not spend vast amounts of money to cut a tiny slice of the global temperature increase when this constitutes a poor use of resources and when we could probably use these funds far more effectively in the developing world."[18]

Lomborg disputes that he is a climate "denialist." Asked by the *New Statesman* in 2010 whether he was a "climate-change denier," he said that he was not: "Because I dared to be skeptical, a lot of people pushed me into the deniers' camp."[19] In fact, Lomborg has given considerable thought to possible solutions to climate change—hardly the approach of someone who is trying to deny that it exists. In another book, *Smart Solutions to Climate Change*: *Comparing Costs and Benefits*, Lomborg subjects various climate change remedies to economic analysis. "Just as with any other problem we face," he writes, "there are many possible remedies, and some of them are much better than others. Not just cheaper, but more effective, more efficient, and—crucially—more likely to actually happen."[20]

For his skepticism, Lomborg has been subjected to more than a decade of abuse. In 2003, the Danish Committees on Scientific Dishonesty investigated Lomborg for "scientific dishonesty." A group of Danish academics actually came to Lomborg's defense with a petition calling for the committees to be abolished.[21] Yet the damage to Lomborg's reputation was deep, and lasting—which was precisely the intent of the scientist-activists who reacted to his arguments by demonizing him.[22]

If anything resembles scientific denialism, it is the way that proponents of the climate change theory defend it in public debate. They frequently resort to alarmist predictions of doom, and they are rarely held accountable when these fail to materialize. In 2007, for example, scientists predicted that the Arctic Ocean would be "ice-free" by the summer of 2013. Former Vice President Al Gore, one of the foremost apostles of climate change and a winner of the Nobel Peace Prize for his efforts, repeated the alarmist prediction. Yet not only did the Arctic ice pack expand, but an icebreaking vessel on a research mission in July 2015 also had to be diverted to help deliver emergency supplies to communities shut in by the ice. And on the other end of the globe, a ship on a mission to study the melting of Antarctic ice in 2014 became stuck in ice, as did another ship sent to rescue it.

Gore's 2006 climate change documentary, *An Inconvenient Truth*, was released to great accolades from scientists and activists and won two Oscars. And yet it contained errors and exaggerations that even some sympathetic experts noted. A judge in the United Kingdom said that while the film was "broadly accurate," it contained nine scientific errors and pushed an "apocalyptic vision."[23]

In 2010, a scandal erupted around the so-called "hockey stick" graph produced by Michael Mann, a climate scientist at East Anglia and (later) Penn State University, showing a rapid increase in temperatures over the last 150 years and suggesting that the rise could continue calamitously. An anonymous leak of a batch of emails seemed to show Mann and other scientists acknowledging that their data were flawed. As James Taylor reported in *Forbes*: "Three themes are emerging from the newly released emails: (1) prominent scientists central to the global warming debate are taking measures to conceal rather than disseminate underlying data and discussions, (2) these scientists view global warming as a political 'cause' rather than a balanced scientific inquiry, and (3) many of these scientists frankly admit to each other that much of the science is weak and dependent on deliberate manipulation of facts and data."[24]

The "Climategate" scandal highlighted just how politicized climate science had become. In 2012, Ivar Giaever, winner of the 1973 Nobel Prize in physics, resigned from the American Physical Society after it declared, "The evidence is incontrovertible: global warming is occurring." Giaever responded: "Incontrovertible is not a scientific word. Nothing is incontrovertible in science."[25]

Many advocates of drastic climate change policies would likely support government intervention in the economy regardless. For some environmentalists, the threat of climate change is a useful pretext to advance their long-held utopian vision of a centrally controlled, scientifically planned society.

That is a radical idea, not a liberal one, and it has come to dominate left-wing political discourse on climate change. A truly liberal approach to climate change would look far different. It would welcome the free exchange of ideas and data, rather than hounding skeptics out of debate and out of jobs. A liberal approach would measure scientific theories, not by how many people signed letters in their favor, but by whether those theories accurately explained and predicted observations in nature. A liberal approach would acknowledge the strong body of evidence in favor of climate change, but also acknowledge the failure of existing computer models, almost all of which have overestimated global warming, as a serious challenge to the hypothesis.

Most of all, a liberal approach to climate change would not presume the need for greater state control of the economy as the solution, but rather would seek to reduce the risks of climate change while preserving the free market, consumer choice, and scientific innovation. There are, in fact, far better alternatives than state intervention. For nearly a decade, the United States has reduced greenhouse gas emissions while growing its economy, largely because of a switch from coal to clean-burning natural gas.

Climate change is a classic "tragedy of the commons," where behavior that is individually rational—fossil fuel use—may be collectively irrational. The answer, as in the case of almost all environmental problems, is to assign property rights over a common resource through either public or private ownership. And given the impossibility of creating a global regime to regulate fossil fuel use—China, for example, which has become the world's leading source of greenhouse gas emissions, has long resisted any real restrictions—the more practical answer is to find technological solutions, which spring from private enterprise more readily than from state control.

The liberal philosopher Karl Popper wrote, "A theory which is not refutable by any conceivable event is non-scientific. Irrefutability is not a virtue of a theory (as people often think) but a vice." He noted that Marxism, like astrology, had become unfalsifiable: when confronted with evidence that contradicted their theory, "the followers of Marx re-interpreted both the theory and the evidence in order to make them agree."[26] The fact that much of the debate on climate change now follows the same pattern is reason for concern not only about the quality of our science but the health of our society. Above all, the degree to which champions of "climate change" are willing to persecute their critics—closing their own minds in the process—ought to give us pause. A free society can afford to tolerate a few people who cling to wrong ideas. It cannot long survive the punishment of legitimate intellectual dissent.

# CHAPTER 6

# THE TWO SEXES

## THE LIE:
## The differences between male and female are arbitrary and artificial.

Examples:

*"For him to say that 'aptitude' is the second most important reason that women don't get to the top when he leads an institution that is 50 percent women students—that's profoundly disturbing to me.... He shouldn't admit women to Harvard if he's going to announce when they come that, hey, we don't feel that you can make it to the top."*[1]
—MIT Biologist Nancy Hopkins, January 2005

*"We've decided not to share Storm's sex for now—a tribute to freedom and choice in place of limitation, a stand up to*

*what the world could become in Storm's lifetime (a more
progressive place?"*[2]

—Kathy Witterick and David Stocker, Toronto,
Canada, January 2011

*"We both know chromosomes don't necessarily mean
you're male or female.... You cut that out now, or you'll
go home in an ambulance."*[3]

—transgender journalist Zoey Tur, *Dr. Drew on Call*, July 2015

# THE TRUTH:
## The differences between the sexes are real and can never be completely negated.

His—or her—name is "Storm." The parents of the new Canadian child born in 2011 chose to raise him (her? it?) without a sex. It was, they explained, "a tribute to freedom and choice," a small step towards gender equality in the world in general, and a way to allow their child to express an authentic self before being made to conform to a gender role. "If you really want to get to know someone, you don't ask what's between their legs," according to David Stocker, the presumed male who identifies as Storm's father.[4]

Two years later, the *Toronto Star* checked in with the family. The parents had still kept Storm's sex a secret, and allowed the child to identify with whatever gender he or she wanted on any particular day. They are not alone: an increasing number of parents are trying the same with their own children, as a visit to a California day care is likely to reveal.

A generation ago, what we now call "transgendered" men and women were fighting for recognition and tolerance. Now, they—or their advocates—are fighting to overturn the dominant culture itself. The University of California decided in 2015 to offer applicants six different options for gender identity: "male; female; trans male/trans man; trans female/trans woman; gender queer/gender non-conforming; and different identity."[5]

At the University of Tennessee Knoxville, the Office for Diversity and Inclusion recommended that instructors use sex-neutral pronouns, including "xe" and "ze," "xim" and "hir."[6] Later, responding to the ensuing controversy, the office helpfully explained: "We no longer use words like, 'crippled,' 'retarded,' or 'crazy' to refer to people with physical and mental disabilities." Somehow words that simply identify what sex a person is—without any connotation of disability—should also be discouraged.[7] The students, or at least their elected representatives, agreed, passing a resolution "endorsing educational efforts and a preferred pronoun policy concerning gender-neutral pronouns" by a thirty-seven to twelve margin in December 2015.[8]

The Left likes to accuse conservatives of a "war on women" around election time. Yet the Left is at war with biological sex difference itself. They are determined to erase any distinction—even nominal ones—between the sexes and to suppress any notion of cultural or even biological difference in an effort to establish its version of equality.

The so-called "war on women," if it ever existed, was lost long before that phrase became a Democratic Party campaign slogan. It ended in 2006 with the surrender of an unlikely enemy: Lawrence H. Summers, president of Harvard University, the Democrat who had served as Secretary of the Treasury under U.S. President Bill Clinton and remained an ally of future candidate Hillary Clinton herself. Summers had already survived several controversies during his tenure at Massachusetts Hall. There was a bitter public dispute with African-American Studies professor Cornel West, whom Summers had asked to do more academic work after West had delved into politics and rap music. There were fights with the faculty over grade inflation. And there were political spats, as when Summers told the Kennedy School of Government that the word "patriotism" was "used too infrequently in communities such as this,"[9] and when he told Memorial Church that some criticisms of Israel were "anti-Semitic in their effect if not their intent."[10]

Then on January 14, 2005, Summers spoke at a National Bureau of Economic Research conference on "Diversifying the Science & Engineering Workforce." The topic was "women's representation in tenured positions in science and engineering at top universities and research institutions." Summers said that he had made "an effort to think in a very serious way about" the topic, and proceeded to summarize current data.[11]

There were "three broad hypotheses" about women's underrepresentation, Summers said: "[T]he first is what I call the high-powered job hypothesis. The second is what I would call different availability of aptitude at the high end, and the third is what I would call different socialization and patterns of discrimination in a search. And in my own view, their importance probably ranks in exactly the order that I just described."

The word "aptitude" triggered a ferocious backlash. As the *Boston Globe* reported at the time, "Nancy Hopkins, a biologist at Massachusetts Institute of Technology, walked out on Summers' talk, saying later that if she hadn't left, 'I would've either blacked out or thrown up.' Five other participants reached by the Globe, including Denice D. Denton, chancellor designate of the University of California, Santa Cruz, also said they were deeply offended, while four other attendees said they were not."

What Summers had tried to explain about "aptitude" was that men showed higher variability in tests: there were more of them at the top and at the bottom. While women's choices between family and career was "the largest phenomenon," and "socialization and continuing discrimination" were "lesser factors," the aptitude factor also explained some of the differences between the numbers of men and women in STEM fields. "I would like nothing better than to be proved wrong, because I would like nothing better than for these problems to be addressable," he said. Note that Summers never said or even implied that women had lower aptitude in the sciences, merely that men and women might have *differences* in aptitude, and that these differences could influence differences in specialization. And Summers was clearly committed to advancing women's career and leadership opportunities, both at Harvard and beyond.

My wife (then girlfriend) happened to be a student in Summers's freshman seminar in the wake of the controversy. He pointed out to the seminar that, among the students admitted to Harvard with perfect scores on the math portion of the SAT standardized test, the women averaged far higher scores on the writing and verbal sections than the men did.

Summers challenged his class to explain how this difference might be related to the underrepresentation of women in the sciences. The answer, as the class of young economists recognized after some Socratic prodding, is the theory of comparative advantage, first developed two centuries ago by David Ricardo. Ricardo had explained that even nations that excel in producing everything can be made better off by specializing in some products and trading them with nations that are worse in everything. Similarly, women might be better than men (have an *absolute* advantage) in both the arts and the sciences, but be better by a larger margin (have a *comparative advantage*) in the arts, and therefore be better off specializing in the arts.

The late Nobel economist Gary Becker agreed with this explanation, writing that it might be true that women are in fact better than men at everything, but that they choose non-scientific careers where they enjoy an even wider advantage. "[W]omen could be better than men at all occupations," Becker wrote, "but would be underrepresented in science if any difference between men and women in scientific aptitudes were smaller than in non-scientific aptitudes." Like Summers, Becker considered difference in aptitude "less important than other forces," but said that more research should be "welcomed."[12]

Such well-intentioned and well-reasoned empirical speculation was not good enough to protect Summers from charges of sexism. As psychology professor Steven Pinker recalled, "An engineering dean called his remarks 'an intellectual tsunami,' and, with equal tastelessness, a Boston Globe columnist compared him to people who utter racial epithets or wear swastikas. Alumnae threatened to withhold donations, and the

National Organization of Women called for his resignation. Summers was raked in a letter signed by more than 100 Harvard faculty members and shamed into issuing serial apologies."[13]

Summers issued a groveling apology in an attempt to make amends: "I deeply regret the impact of my comments and apologize for not having weighed them more carefully.... I was wrong to have spoken in a way that has resulted in an unintended signal of discouragement to talented girls and women," he wrote.[14] That only encouraged his critics. The Faculty of Arts and Sciences passed a vote of no confidence in his leadership, and Summers resigned.

Harvard's left-wing professors had won—and established a new precedent. Merely to acknowledge differences between the sexes was to commit a kind of Orwellian thoughtcrime, a form of impermissible dissent against the new orthodoxy. And those who had supported Summers through previous controversies gave up when he tried to appease his accusers. "Summers's failure to stand up for himself and for the principle of free inquiry when both were under assault—indeed, his collaboration by means of public acts of abasement and contrition before those who would cut off speech and research in order to protect their own tender sensibilities and political agendas—leaves Harvard more enfeebled and more confused about its mission than when he arrived," wrote former Harvard professor Peter Berkowitz.[15]

The Summers controversy showed just how illiberal America's liberal arts establishment had become—especially on differences between the sexes. The intolerance of difference extends to physical, biological difference, which is categorized as a kind of social construct, as arbitrary as any other. As Jonah Goldberg observed, some on the Left "want to turn the word 'woman' into a term of exclusion and oppression."[16]

Meanwhile, others seemed determined to be recognized as women, despite their male chromosomes and anatomy. In 2015, Olympic hero and reality TV star Bruce Jenner came out as transgender. As "Caitlyn," he acquired breast implants, began dressing as a woman, and changed his name. Jenner was instantly fêted as a civil rights hero. (In a society already jaded by sexual pioneers, what was perhaps even more striking was his—now her—admission that she was politically conservative.) Some veteran gay rights activists were skeptical of Jenner, who was curiously late to the struggle—and whose demands for acceptance were relatively conventional.

Today the movement for transgender rights demands not only equal treatment but also a transformation of sex roles themselves. In November 2015, voters in Houston faced a referendum on an equal rights ordinance that, critics said, would have allowed transgender residents to choose male or female restrooms. When voters rejected the ordinance by wide margins, left-wing activists blamed "transphobia." That charge also greeted liberal feminists who dared to doubt the new left-wing orthodoxy. When Germaine Greer said that "a great many women" believed transgender men such as Jenner do not "look like, sound like or behave like women," she was targeted by left-wing activists in Wales who tried to ban her from speaking at the University of Cardiff.[17]

In 2016, when the state of North Carolina passed a law requiring people to use the bathroom that matched their biological sex, the Left pushed back. Hollywood lambasted the state as a haven for hatred. Bruce Springsteen explained that he would cancel a concert in Greensboro because the law was "an attempt by people who cannot stand the progress our country has made in recognizing the human rights of all of our citizens to overturn that progress."[18] Activists likened the North Carolina law to racial segregation under Jim Crow. The Obama administration threatened, then sued the state, declaring that it was in violation of the Civil Rights Act of 1964—as if Dr. Martin Luther King, Jr., a Baptist minister, had any concept of transgender rights.

Calling for a "restroom revolution," CNN columnist John D. Sutter argued that it was "absurd" that anyone "should have to choose a male or female restroom at all." He likened the movement for bathroom equality to the fight against racial segregation. A division that once seemed, to most Americans, simple common sense could only be justified by "bigotry and ignorance," he claimed. "There's little counterargument other that [sic] bias and squeamishness."[19] The objection that many Americans might feel their privacy violated if someone of the opposite sex appeared in their bathroom—or that some might exploit the "restroom revolution" to satisfy their voyeuristic impulses—was ruled out of court.

Novel grievances seemed to proliferate, even though there is hardly a society on earth where women have enjoyed so much equality and achieved so many great things as ours. True, as of this writing Americans have yet to elect a female president—though Hillary Clinton is, or was, clearly the favorite to win in 2016—but there are female governors, female CEOs, female university presidents, and female leaders in almost every other walk of life. One need only look at international sporting competitions to note the dominance of American women. It is no accident that the world's toughest female mixed martial arts fighters are American. American women have staked their claim to the American character, crafting their own version of the American frontiersman—tough, self-reliant, unafraid.

Yet new inequalities continued to be found—or invented. Partly that itself is a function of the American character. Alexis de Tocqueville observed in *Democracy in America*, "When everything is more or less level, the slightest variation is noticed. Hence the more equal men are [and women], the more insatiable will be their longing for equality."[20] Partly, however, oppression is projection—as in the myth of "rape culture," the idea that despite the prevailing culture of political correctness, the country's elite institutions are using rape and fear of sexual assault to subjugate women. The accusation has become a tool with which the left suppresses intellectual dissent on campus.

In 2015, for example, syndicated columnist George F. Will was targeted by feminists because he questioned the inflated statistics being used by the Left and the Obama administration to raise alarm about sexual assault on campus. "One in five women is sexually assaulted while in college, and only 12 percent of assaults are reported."[21] Given that the number of reported assaults is known, Will pointed out, "simple arithmetic demonstrates that if the 12 percent reporting rate is correct the 20 percent assault rate is preposterous."

The real rate must be "approximately 2.9 percent—too high but nowhere near 20 percent." For his trouble, Will was disinvited from giving a talk to female students at Scripps College in California.

Rape does occur on campus, and elsewhere. Fans were stunned when comedian Bill Cosby, a household name, role model, and the recipient of many honorary degrees, was accused by dozens of women of having drugged and raped them. But other accusations fell apart. Perhaps the most spectacular failure was *Rolling Stone*'s 2014 story about a gang rape at the University of Virginia's Phi Kappa Psi fraternity house. Reporter Sabrina Ederly told the chilling tale of a young woman, identified only as "Jackie," who said that she had been assaulted as part of a bizarre initiation ritual.[22] University of Virginia president Teresa Sullivan suspended all campus fraternities, and the Phi Kappa Psi fraternity house was targeted by protests.

But the details did not add up. Subsequent reporting by the *Washington Post* and the *Columbia Journalism Review* uncovered serious errors in the *Rolling Stone* story. Under pressure, the magazine retracted the story. Yet the notion of "rape culture" persisted. Brendan O'Neill of Reason.com noted, "...*Rolling Stone*'s final withdrawal of its story this week, following Columbia's cool dismantling of it, has, perversely, given rise to a chorus of demands that we now focus on the true problem: the epidemic of rape on campus."[23]

Yet other rape stories collapsed, too. A Columbia University student who claimed to have been raped and carried a mattress around campus in protest triggered a lawsuit against the university by the student she had accused, who proclaimed his innocence. Hollywood star Lena Dunham was found to have accused an innocent man of rape in her memoir. Rape happens—but the mythology of "rape culture" has been exposed as a fraud.

Other myths attend the story of women in America today, such as the idea that women are paid less than men for the same work—that, as the liberal moderator of a Republican presidential debate put it, "...working women in this country still earn just 77 percent of what men earn."[24] Many believe that statistic—but it is misleading.

The truth is that the wage gap between men and women is much smaller than that. As Hannah Rosin of Slate wrote in 2013, comparing average weekly wages instead of annual salaries narrows the gap to 81 percent. And when only those men and women working forty hours per week are measured, the gap shrinks again, to 87 percent.[25] Then, Rosin notes, there are other factors. Education and experience play only a small role; today women often have more education than men, and they are gaining on them in experience. Rosin points out, "The big differences are in occupation and industry. Women congregate in different professions than men do, and the largely male professions tend to be higher-paying. If you account for those differences, and then compare a woman and a man doing the same job, the pay gap narrows to 91 percent." As long as men are more likely to choose engineering and women are more likely to choose early childhood education, there will be a wage gap.

Biology plays a role in these career choices. Women bear children. Hence women not only tend to take leave from work to have and to raise children, but also tend to choose occupations with more flexible schedules. The fact that women bear that burden more than men is partly a result of social conventions. But those social conventions reflect an underlying biological reality: men cannot give birth or breastfeed. Some of the differences between the sexes appear to be artificial. But they always emerge again, even after they seem to have been eliminated. George Orwell wrote, "Even in jail, it is said, the female prisoners redden their lips with the dye from the Post Office mail bags." As the classical author Horace famously said: you can drive out nature with a pitchfork, but it always returns.

It is the stubborn persistence of natural differences that triggers the Left's hysteria.

The "social justice warriors" are so hell bent on breaking down gender barriers that they seem to have entirely forgotten the underlying purpose of the institutions that they are using for their radical gender experiments. In August 2015, for the first time, two women graduated from Army Ranger School. "Unlike their male peers, they won't be allowed to try out for the Army's elite 75th Ranger Regiment, a combat-oriented Special Operations Force that continues to bar women," the *Wall Street Journal* noted critically.[26] Whether women would help the military's core mission—killing the enemy—was an afterthought, at best.

Mingling the sexes in elite units is challenging not only because men are stronger but because many of the men do not want women there. Call it sexism, or call it human nature—that male preference, as the conservative Harvard professor Harvey C. Mansfield noted in his 2006 book *Manliness*, has proven impossible to eliminate, even in our by and large gender-neutral society, and especially when life and death are at stake.[27]

Radical feminists understand that; it's the reason they want to be rid of sex differences altogether. Radical feminism began as a reaction to liberal feminism, which sought the integration of women into the workplace and society on equal terms. Borrowing from the Marxist idea that the capitalist mode of production is the foundation of our unequal society, radical feminists argued that the mode of *re*production—sex—was the basis of exploitative relationships throughout our collective life. If sex—and especially pornography, which radical feminists charged with subjugating women—could be transformed, then women would be liberated. That liberation would in turn liberate the rest of humanity.

Some radicals, such as the late Andrea Dworkin, said all sex was rape. But the radicals' extreme notions triggered a backlash—both among liberal feminists, who believed women could and should make their own choices and live with the results, and among conservatives, who argued that the female sex has essential qualities, which have unique value.

In any case, rejecting sex as an instrument of male "oppression" would be self-defeating in the long run. A society failing to reproduce would fail to reproduce girls as well as boys.

And the effort to eliminate sex differences as a way of reducing unfairness also fails because those differences are part of what makes life worth living. Most of the drama and excitement of life, the pleasure of literature and art, the thrill of romance and loss, comes from the complexity of the relationships between men and women.

To some extent, transgenderism is more realistic than radical feminism—at least the transgender movement recognizes that the external trappings of our identity as men or women are fundamental to how we express ourselves as human beings. But lately the transgender movement has joined radical feminism in denying biology any role in shaping identity. Transgender activists are demanding not only space for transgender identity but also a fundamental reorganization of "gender" for everyone else.

They are making their radical demands at a time when the fallout from much more modest changes has made Americans ambivalent about feminism. As women have joined men in the workplace and surpassed men in the academy, men's real wages have stagnated or fallen, while women's real wages have risen (albeit from a lower base).[28] And as men have been dislodged from their traditional breadwinning role, they have not found anything to replace it. As Helen Smith points out, many men are forgoing marriage rather than accept a life defined by domesticity.[29]

And women are not satisfied either. Mansfield notes that women "want a career and they want to be women too. They don't want to be defined, and they do. The challenge to a new feminism is to make sense of those two desires and unite them."[30] They also want to have children, which still requires—until radical improvements in the science of cloning—at least a modicum of male involvement. It also means beating the biological clock. Nature decrees that in reproduction men have the advantage of time—irrationally, unfairly perhaps, but undeniably. In the realm of reproduction, biological differences between the sexes cannot be wished away.

But the denial of sex difference persists—with a profound effect on our political life, not just in new waves of "gender equality" legislation, which somehow never seem to be sufficient, but in the loss of manliness in our society. Manliness is not the unique province of men. Mansfield identifies Margaret Thatcher as "manly," and means that as a compliment. As Clinton acolyte James Carville said of Hillary Clinton in 2008, "If Hillary gave up one of her balls and gave it to Obama, he'd have two."[31]

In political life today, manliness is both increasingly marginalized and sorely missed. That is best seen in foreign policy. The terror attacks of 9/11 reinforced Americans' pride in sheer physical courage, making heroes of policemen, firefighters, and soldiers. Yet the present administration behaves as if the one outcome to be avoided at all costs is a conflict in which Americans would have to fight the enemy face-to-face. In domestic politics, we are afflicted by leaders who lack the essential manliness of leadership; they are good at opposition and criticism, but refuse to govern. That includes the president, who would prefer to mock opponents from afar rather than face them in person—in a classic example of machismo masquerading as masculinity.

It is not clear that our republican form of government can survive the loss of the manly virtue of ambition tempered with restraint. Self-government requires individuals in full possession of themselves, ready both to assert their wills and to bear with the burden of compromise with humility. The politics of constant grievance and protest is not manly—nor is it womanly. It is merely adolescent.

There is no longer any sense in opposing those who wish to challenge traditional sexual roles and invent new ones for themselves as individuals. A liberal society ought to be strong enough to tolerate, even to encourage, such experimentation. But the attempt to deny sex difference altogether can only destroy the freedom to which women, and men, aspire. Nature is ultimately stronger than convention, and when our conventions no longer make room for our nature, other conventions—perhaps illiberal ones—become seductive.

**PART II**

# SUPPRESSING DEBATE

# CHAPTER 7

# MARRIAGE

## THE LIE:
## Support for traditional marriage is bigotry and denies other peoples' rights.

Examples:

*"She gave the worst answer in pageant history. She got booed.... She lost, not because she doesn't believe in gay marriage. Miss California lost because she's a dumb bitch, OK?...She doesn't inspire. She doesn't unite...If that girl would have won Miss USA, California, I would have gone up onstage—I shit you not—I would have gone up onstage, snatched that tiara off her head, and run out the door."*[1]
—Celebrity blogger Perez Hilton, April 2009

*"[T]he opponents of the Supreme Court decision don't want to answer that question because interracial marriage is now*

*so accepted in our society and so recognized as something
that only, you know, really bigoted people oppose. They
don't want to draw the parallel, but the parallel is precise.*"[2]
—CNN legal analyst Jeffrey Toobin, June 2015

*"There really wasn't a good argument on the other side."*[3]
—David Boies, attorney who sued to overturn
California's Proposition 8, July 2014

## THE TRUTH:
## Traditional marriage is legitimate, and its supporters are the ones being bullied.

Answers that beauty pageant contestants give to the questions they are asked onstage are rarely remembered—unless they make mistakes, which live on in infamy.

Yet a question posed to Miss California, Carrie Prejean, at the Miss USA pageant in 2009 caused an instant international news sensation—not because of a mistake by the contestant, but because of one judge's incendiary response.

The question was posed by celebrity blogger—and outspoken homosexual—Perez Hilton. Prejean—whose state had just overturned gay marriage in a controversial referendum in November 2008—drew Hilton's name at random, and he asked her, "Vermont recently became the fourth state to legalize same-sex marriage. Do you think every state should follow suit? Why or why not?"[4]

Prejean answered nervously, but with poise, "Well, I think it's great that Americans are able to choose one or the other. We live in a land where you can choose same-sex marriage or opposite marriage. And you know what, in my country, in my family, I think that I believe that a marriage should be between a man and a woman. No offense to anyone out there, but that's how I was raised, and that's how I think it should be between a man and a woman."

Hilton grimaced and shook his head. He went on to give her a low score, and she went on to lose the pageant. She later said, "When I heard it from him, I knew at that moment after I had answered the question, I knew that I was not going to win because of my answer."[5]

Hilton rushed immediately to the Internet to blast Prejean. He posted a YouTube video in which, still wearing his green suit from the pageant, he described her response as "the worst answer in pageant history," and called her a "dumb bitch."[6]

But Prejean stuck to her guns: "I was raised in a way that you can never compromise your beliefs and your opinions for anything."[7]

With that, Prejean became a heroine to millions of Americans who felt that she was being punished for a widely held belief—a belief that, if he were to be taken at his word, was shared by the President of the United States himself at the time.

The gay marriage issue is a classic example of the second kind of case in which the Left suppresses the truth. A truly liberal approach to gay marriage would allow different rules in different states, perhaps with federal guarantees of non-discrimination for all. But the Left is not satisfied with free choice, lest some make the "wrong" choice. Progressives want to foreclose debate by demonizing and marginalizing traditional marriage supporters.

Proponents of gay marriage have sought to describe it as a "right." Whether that is accurate depends on whether marriage itself is a right. Certainly every individual may choose to get married, but the right to marry is not an *inherent* right in the same way that many other fundamental rights such as freedom of speech and religious liberty are. It is conditional on the consent of another person—and, if conducted in a religious setting, on the approval of community authorities. That makes it a contract. And society limits the terms of the marriage contract, as it does with other kinds of contracts—whether formally through law or informally through culture. We do not allow polygamy, for example, or marriage between close relatives, or marriage with children, and so on.

On the one hand, marriage is about choice (for many of us, the most important choice in our lives). That is a liberal concept. On the other hand, marriage is defined by rules that are determined by tradition—or, if not tradition, another source of authority. That is a conservative idea.

So marriage is not a "right." It is a convention, within which individuals exercise varying degrees of choice. The state's involvement in marriage complicates the issue by conferring benefits on married people that others do not enjoy. But regardless of those benefits, there is a social component of marriage that can never be removed—not even if the state "gets out of the marriage business," as some suggest.

So the question of gay marriage is not really a question of civil rights. Nor is it a question of equality, which is the guise under which it has made its way through the nation's court systems. The question of gay marriage is, and will always be, a question of what society decides marriage should be. Having the courts enforce gay marriage as a matter of equality is merely another way of deciding—allowing a small group of individuals—rather than the people as a whole, or their elected representatives—what marriage is. Calling gay marriage a "right" is a way of concealing that fact by casting the new convention as inherent in human nature.

Making room for gay marriage makes some sense. Different forms of marriage do coexist in other free societies. South Africa, for example, permits polygamy, according to both African customary law and Islamic law, alongside monogamous marriage.

But that is insufficient for the Left, which aims, beyond legalizing gay marriage, to undermine traditional marriage, even in the private sphere. For Perez Hilton, it was not enough that Miss California agreed Americans should be able to "choose same-sex marriage or opposite marriage." Because she stated her own belief in traditional marriage—while allowing for others to choose differently—she had to be destroyed.

That, sadly, is typical of how the gay marriage issue plays out—it's a prime example of the Left suppressing truth to prevent debate.

Opposition to gay marriage is typically portrayed as mere bigotry, like resistance to interracial marriage in the past. (Actually, a good deal of the opposition to interracial marriage came from progressives, on the grounds that such marriages produced genetically inferior children, and that the centrally managed society the Left desired ought to improve the national stock.)

The truth is that interracial marriage has been happening since long before Moses married an Ethiopian in the Book of Exodus. But there is no society in recorded history that has ever practiced homosexual marriage. That alone is not a reason to ban it, but it does tell us something about what humanity has believed the purpose of marriage to be. Marriage has always been a way of organizing reproduction—or, rather, the potential for reproduction. (Abraham and Sarah in Genesis, for example, are the paradigmatic example of marital love—and are childless until a miraculous birth in old age.)

To understand the gay marriage debate—and how the Left is shunting traditional marriage to the margins—it is important to understand how the issue has evolved.

To many people, particularly those who have come of age in the millennial generation, the validity of gay marriage seems almost self-evident. To them, homosexual marriage is something that simply ought to exist, and the socially conscious naturally recoil from discrimination against gay couples.

When I was a passionately left-wing undergraduate at Harvard, I was randomly assigned to live at Dunster House, the one of two predominantly gay residences at the college at the time. The house masters—Harvard's equivalent of resident deans (now to be renamed because the word "master" is a "trigger" mechanism to those with exquisitely sensitive civil rights sensibilities)—hosted Hawaii Governor Benjamin Cayetano at a special reception in December 1996. The courts in Hawaii had just begun to tackle the question of same-sex marriage, and I peppered him with questions about it. To me, a straight but passionately left-wing student, gay marriage was among the more fascinating radical causes of the day.

Exasperated, the governor eventually asked me, "Why, do you want to get married or something?"

To which I replied, to my classmates' amusement, "Thank you, governor, but we've only just met."

Few of my contemporaries—including the gay rights activists on campus, whom I counted as good friends—considered marriage the burning issue of the day. Issues such as discrimination against gays and the military's "Don't Ask, Don't Tell" compromise seemed far more salient.

Gay marriage, as we have seen, is a very new phenomenon, unknown in the history of human civilization. While homosexuality has been present in every society—indeed, whether genetic or chosen, tolerated or persecuted, it has existed almost everywhere—until recently, it has never been sanctified by marriage. The idea that men should be able to form the same unions with each other, or women with each other, that they form with members of the opposite sex was unknown.

For many years, gay marriage was of secondary importance to the gay rights movement. Though gay marriage was first litigated in a U.S. court in 1970,[8] the focus of the gay rights movement at the time was on winning acceptance for homosexuality itself, and equal rights for homosexuals in public life and the workplace. Marriage has become important to the gay rights movement because it symbolizes acceptance and equality, not—primarily, at least—for its own sake, or for the public benefits it sometimes confers.

When the gay rights movement began, homosexuality was illegal almost everywhere in the United States. Anti-sodomy laws began to fall in the 1960s, but as the gay rights movement gained momentum it was struck by the AIDS crisis of the 1980s. The pandemic not only devastated the gay community but also damaged its image. Many Americans saw gays and lesbians as not only deviant, but diseased.

Yet the gay rights movement overcame that obstacle, and others, before marriage even became a subject of debate. Hollywood—tolerant of homosexuality in general, though slow to accept openly gay stars— introduced audiences to sympathetic gay characters in the television shows *Ellen* and *Will & Grace* in the 1990s. Civil rights organizations began to include gay rights among their top priorities. The fight against anti-sodomy laws liberated straight as well as gay couples from government efforts to regulate private morality. Gay culture became a symbol of personal freedom.

Marriage was almost an afterthought until the late 1990s, when the first gay marriage case succeeded briefly in Hawaii. The first gay marriages in the world to be authorized by a state were those legalized by the Dutch parliament in 2000.[9] Gay marriage suddenly became an obsession—both for advocates and opponents. With it came new challenges—gay parenting, gay divorce, and a conflict with what had been a libertine gay counter-culture that resisted marriage as a bourgeois convention. But all along, the symbolic value of homosexual marriage was more important than its practical application.

The movement for gay marriage challenged some traditional norms, but it still abided by others. In Massachusetts, the first state to legalize gay marriage, in 2003, couples wishing to marry must still swear that they are not in violation of "legal impediments to marriage," including:

> No man shall marry his mother, grandmother, daughter, granddaughter, sister, stepmother, grandfather's wife, grandson's wife, wife's mother, wife's grandmother, wife's daughter, wife's granddaughter, brother's daughter, father's sister or mother's sister … No woman shall marry her father, grandfather, son, grandson, brother, grandmother's husband, daughter's husband, granddaughter's husband, husband's grandfather, husband's son, husband's grandson, brother's son, sister's son, father's brother or mother's brother…[10]

Those restrictions still in place—not only against marrying one's in-laws, but also against polygamy and pedophilia—do not just target incestuous unions between blood relatives (which could cause birth defects and thus public health problems), but also unions between those related by marriage alone. In other words, purely moral restraints on who can marry whom, derived from tradition, are still in effect in Massachusetts. It is not clear why these restrictions should stand now that the prohibition against homosexual marriage has fallen.

Advocates of gay marriage typically reject the argument that same-sex marriage will lead to polygamy by way of the same "equal protection" arguments that gay plaintiffs have used to prevail in court. In a 2008 decision legalizing same-sex marriage (an early battle in the long war that was to follow), the California Supreme Court distinguished polygamy from homosexuality on the grounds that polygamy is "inimical to the mutually supportive and healthy family relationships promoted by the constitutional right to marry."[11]

Yet what is "mutually supportive and healthy" is subjective. As Dale Carpenter pointed out at the Volokh Conspiracy legal blog, the court failed to provide "an articulated and non-arbitrary principle distinguishing same-sex marriage from plural marriage."[12] Indeed, a polygamist in Montana has already filed a legal challenge to the law against plural marriage based on same-sex marriage precedents.

It's understandable that advocates for gay marriage resist being placed in the same moral category as polygamists and the proponents of other forbidden unions. The point is not that these unions are morally equivalent to gay relationships—they are not— but rather that the argument for gay marriage is, at bottom, an argument about social conventions, not about rights. It depends on moral conventions that are ultimately at least as arbitrary as those the gay rights movement has toppled.

There are several ways to go about changing social conventions. One is simply to set an example for change—to live according to the new rules that you want instituted. Others may follow, while yet others may protest. But with luck, over time, resistance turns to tolerance, tolerance to acceptance, acceptance to embrace.

Another way is to use the state to impose the change you are seeking. One way to do that is to pass legislation, but that typically involves a campaign for hearts and minds—appealing to fellow citizens and lobbying legislators. Using the court system offers a shortcut: only the judge or a tiny number of judges need be convinced. The latter is the route the gay marriage movement chose, arguing in court that gay couples have an equal right to marry.

Gay marriage advocates hoped to emulate the precedent set by the Civil Rights Movement. It took *Brown v. Board of Education*, the famous 1954 Supreme Court case to end segregation in public schools (then again, it had taken an earlier Supreme Court decision, *Plessy v. Ferguson* in 1867, to enforce it). And more than ten years after *Brown*, in *Loving v. Virginia*, the Supreme Court struck down laws banning interracial marriage, rejecting the argument that such laws were not discriminatory because they applied equally to blacks and whites. The laws, the Court held, infringed on the basic "civil right" to marry, "fundamental to our very existence and survival." But the Court did continue to assume that marriage referred to heterosexual partnerships.[13] There were other precedents, too, by which the Supreme Court mandated sweeping societal change: in 1973 *Roe v. Wade* legalized abortion on the basis of a presumed right to privacy in the Constitution.

But that case divided the nation for decades afterwards, calcifying the debate over abortion in a culture war stalemate. For that reason, the courts were initially reluctant to interfere in marriage laws—at least overtly. And when the Massachusetts Supreme Judicial Court became the first American court to weigh in, in 2003, there was a furious public backlash across the country. Some of the opposition would have arisen anyway, based purely on substance of the policy change mandated by the decision. But the angry reaction was exacerbated by the way the decision had been made—by a small panel of unelected judges. In the years that followed, every time the issue was put to voters, they rejected same sex marriage—even in reliably "blue" states. Every major presidential candidate in 2008 rejected same-sex marriage and made sure the public knew it.

So gay marriage advocates shifted their tactics. They took their case to state legislatures, which began to allow gay couples to unite—some only in "civil unions," to preserve the special status of traditional marriage.

In 2012, when voters in four states faced ballot initiatives on gay marriage, supporters launched advertising campaigns that stressed the idea that gay families were just like everyone else. They emphasized the now generally accepted purpose of marriage—romantic and sexual fulfillment, lifetime companionship—instead of making a blunt argument for equal rights. The result was victory for gay marriage in all four states.

And yet that was not enough for gay marriage advocates, who would not be satisfied with victory in only some states, and who refused to be satisfied with civil unions in those states that had attempted a compromise.

In Illinois, for example, voters returned Democrats to power in 2010 to face a looming budget deficit and pension crisis. Yet among the first business addressed by the legislature was the passage of a law allowing civil unions. And before that legislative term was out, a new bill to allow gay marriage itself was introduced. The bill passed in the next term and was signed into law. The short-lived civil union interregnum was quickly forgotten. (The state's urgent fiscal problems lingered.)

Meanwhile, the court battles continued, and culminated in critical 5–4 Supreme Court decisions. *Hollingsworth v. Perry* (2013), settled the years-long dispute over the California marriage referendum. The trial judge had ruled that favoring traditional marriage had no "rational basis"—that is, no legitimate government purpose. The Supreme Court let the ruling stand.[14]

*U.S. v. Windsor* (2013) invalidated the Defense of Marriage Act of 1996, signed into law by President Bill Clinton, which prevented the federal government from recognizing same-sex marriage. The law was declared unconstitutional on the grounds that it had been motivated by "animus."[15] As Justice Anthony Kennedy wrote, "What has been explained to this point should more than suffice to establish that the principal purpose and the necessary effect of [the Defense of Marriage Act (DOMA)] are to demean those persons who are in a lawful same-sex marriage. This requires the Court to hold, as it now does, that DOMA is unconstitutional as a deprivation of the liberty of the person protected by the Fifth Amendment of the Constitution."[16]

Finally, in 2015, *Obergefell v. Hodges* (2015),[17] the Supreme Court legalized gay marriage throughout the United States, recognizing it as a fundamental right. The majority decision, by Justice Anthony Kennedy, stated that the Court had the power to interpret liberty "as we learn its meaning." That liberty, Kennedy held, included the equal right to marry. (A group of "same-sex attracted men and their wives" had filed an *amicus curie* brief in *Obergefell* rejecting a "one-size-fits-all" approach and defending traditional marriage "because it is endowed with procreative power and complementary capacity." For their trouble they saw their work mocked by liberal critics as "the worst" of a series of "terrible" amicus briefs.)[18]

These three decisions did more than make gay marriage the law of the land. They also enshrined the idea that traditional marriage has no special purpose for which it is worth preserving—whether child-rearing or morality or tradition itself—and that defending it can only be a form of bigotry against same-sex couples. After these decisions, there could be no diversity in forms of marriage, at least in the eyes of the state.

These are fundamentally *illiberal* results—validating Perez Hilton's outburst against Miss California, whose live-and-let-live tolerance has now been rejected as a matter of law. The truth—that gay marriage is a convention like any other, and that traditional marriage might be worth preserving for its own sake—never had its day in court.

Armed with these victories, gay rights proponents pressed their case further. It was not enough that gay couples be allowed to marry: those who held traditional values would be made to endorse the practice.

One strategy used by gay marriage advocates was to compare their struggle to the civil rights struggle of the 1950s and 1960s. They maintained that the fight for equal rights for gay, lesbian, transgendered and "queer" individuals was the logical next step along what President Obama liked to refer to as "the long arc of justice."

There were more than a few problems, however, with the analogy. For one thing, the black community has often been a reliable vote against gay marriage. Indeed Dr. Martin Luther King Jr. took a traditional Christian approach to homosexuality, viewing it as a choice, not a natural or innate feature of those individuals who are drawn to same-sex and other unusual partnerships.

Another problem with the analogy is simply that race and sexuality are different. Race is an ascribed characteristic based on inherent yet largely superficial characteristics; sexuality is expressed through behavior (even if it is also, in many respects, innate). Theoretically, anyone could enter into a traditional marriage to an opposite-sex spouse (as gays and lesbians have done for centuries), but laws against interracial marriage would have unjustly barred anyone from marrying across color lines.

Regardless of the subtleties of argument, the intended effect of the analogy was to cast those who support traditional marriage as bigots, the modern-day equivalent of Bull Connor with his water cannons and flesh-ripping dogs. That argument found resonance in new court cases. In a series of lawsuits, gay plaintiffs sued private business owners—florists, bakers, photographers—who served gay clients without fuss but declined to participate in gay weddings because of their Christian faith. In one case, *Elane Photography v. Willock*, New Mexico's Supreme Court ruled that a business owner had to participate in a gay wedding as the "price of citizenship," despite her personal beliefs.[19] The Supreme Court declined to hear her appeal.

A similar controversy arose in Washington State, where a florist declined to provide floral arrangements for a gay marriage and was sued by the state. The florist protested that the issue had nothing to do with her feelings about homosexuals, towards whom she said she was tolerant. The issue was the institution of gay marriage itself, which she did not wish to endorse—and participating in a wedding would a very public form of endorsement.[20]

What was striking about these cases was their pettiness. It is not as if gay couples looking for photographers, wedding cakes, or floral arrangements could not have found them elsewhere. The impulse to sue was driven by the desire to eliminate any religiously based opposition to gay marriage—to single out and humiliate and defeat anyone who would dare stand up for his or her traditional beliefs, and to defeat a few signal defendants as a warning to any others.

The bullying was relentless, and everywhere. In "liberal" Silicon Valley, the newly-appointed CEO of Firefox, Brendan Eich, was forced to step down after it was revealed that he had contributed $1,000 to the Proposition 8 campaign for traditional marriage. There was no room for political diversity in progressive Silicon Valley.

Ironically, some of the repression was carried out under the "anti-bullying" banner. Sex columnist and gay rights icon Dan Savage, ran campaigns titled "No H8" and "It Gets Better," and they were endorsed by a White House eager to demonstrate its gay rights credentials to impatient activists.

In April 2012, speaking to a conference of high school journalism students, Savage tore into the Bible and Christian beliefs, literally bullying religious students in front of their peers, mocking their beliefs as "bullshit" and trashing some of the Biblical texts that sustained the core of their personal faith.[21]

If it were possible for an entire electorate to be bullied, then California's would qualify. The voters chose traditional marriage in 2008 by passing Proposition 8, then saw state officials refuse to defend the law and the courts strike it down. When in 2015 Indiana attempted to pass a law that would have guaranteed the religious freedom of private business owners, the state was hounded by the media into amending the law within a week—even though it was little different from federal law and laws in other states.

And so the gay rights movement became an Inquisition instead of a force for liberation, attacking the diversity and tolerance at the heart of our national culture—as well as a cherished institution that has long been the basis for virtue in our democratic society.

# CHAPTER 8

# THE CONSTITUTION

## THE LIE:
## We have a "living Constitution" whose meaning changes with the times.

Examples:

*"...I do not believe that the meaning of the Constitution was forever "fixed" at the Philadelphia Convention. Nor do I find the wisdom, foresight, and sense of justice exhibited by the Framers particularly profound.... For a sense of the evolving nature of the Constitution we need look no further than the first three words of the document's preamble: 'We the People.' When the Founding Fathers used this phrase in 1787, they did not have in mind the majority of America's citizens."*[1]

—Justice Thurgood Marshall,
Hawaii, May 1987

*"And so, when we get in a tussle about abortion or flag burning, we appeal to a higher authority—the Founding Fathers and the Constitution's ratifiers—to give us more direction. Some, like Justice Scalia, conclude that the original understanding must be followed and that if we strictly obey this rule, then democracy is respected.*

*Others, like Justice Breyer, don't dispute that the original meaning of constitutional provisions matters. But they insist that sometimes the original understanding can take you only so far—that on the truly hard cases, the truly big arguments, we have to take context, history, and the practical outcomes of a decision into account.*

*. . . I have to side with Justice Breyer's view of the Constitution—that it is not a static but rather a living document, and must be read in the context of an ever-changing world.*

*How could it be otherwise?"*

—Senator Barack Obama,
*The Audacity of Hope*, 2006

*"The originalist perspective in theory is designed to counter what many offer as activist judges legislating from the bench. This is a focus-group-tested canard designed to obfuscate reality by relying on the mythical deity of the framers of the Constitution. . . .*

*Though I would not consider myself on an intellectual par with James Madison, I would say that I have a better understanding of what 'We the people of the United States in order to form a more perfect union' looks like in the 21st century than he does."*[2]

—Byron Williams, Huffington Post,
June 2012

## THE TRUTH:
## The Constitution means what it says, and it was always meant to be a bulwark against the "transformation" of our republic.

"Now, Mizzou, I just have two words for you tonight: five days. Five days. After decades of broken politics in Washington, and eight years of failed policies from George W. Bush, and 21 months of a campaign that's taken us from the rocky coast of Maine to the sunshine of California, we are five days away from fundamentally transforming the United States of America."[3]

The pledge to "fundamentally transform" America would haunt critics of the Obama presidency. To conservatives, it was a hint of Obama's true ideological agenda, which he had carefully hidden until the last days of the campaign, when the stock market had crashed and his victory was almost inevitable. Apparently Obama cared less about fixing America and more about changing it.

The suspicion that Obama was committed to transforming America radically was deepened by the infamous remarks of Obama's incoming chief of staff, Rahm Emanuel, who told the *Wall Street Journal* in November 2008, shortly after Obama's historic victory: "You never want a serious crisis to go to waste.... This crisis presents the opportunity for us to do things that you could not do before."[4]

Several years later, Obama tried to back away from his pledge to "fundamentally transform" the county, telling Bill O'Reilly of Fox News in 2014 that he had meant it merely as a generic promise to restore an America where "if you work hard, you get ahead." But that wasn't the truth—and his supporters knew it.

Obama's definition of transformation was never spelled out, but one of his campaign advisers, radical Chicago activist Robert Creamer, had written a manual that Obama strategist David Axelrod called the "blue-print."[5] Creamer's manifesto, *Listen to Your Mother*: *Stand up Straight*! *How Progressives Can Win*, partially written while Creamer was serving a federal prison sentence for fraud, laid out an ambitious agenda for the "democratization of wealth."[6]

Another illustrative definition of "fundamental transformation" comes from South Africa, one of Obama's original political inspirations. (He first became politically active when he joined anti-apartheid protests in New York while finishing his undergraduate years at Columbia.) The post-apartheid government used the term "transformation" to describe a program of radical affirmative action that was in theory meant to redistribute wealth and opportunity to the poor (though, in practice, it largely enriched the ruling party).

Whether it amounts to genuine redistribution or the enrichment of the regime, that kind of "transformation" is at odds with the written constitution of a liberal democracy—even a constitution like South Africa's, which is more statist than our own. In either case, "transformation" means giving the central government immense powers to redress perceived injustices.

And it was clear from the start that Obama's own ideas about the Constitution went even further than standard Democratic Party post–New Deal redistributionist fare. His thinking had more troubling roots, in a school of thought called Critical Race Theory (CRT), which holds that the United States, its Constitution, and its laws are all corrupted by white supremacy—so much so that not even equal rights are enough to make ours a truly just system.

CRT has its roots in Critical Legal Studies (CLS), which paints laws and institutions as a reflection of underlying power relations. Rather than take common legal concepts for granted—"truth," for example—CLS claims that traditional legal doctrines are only tools by which the powerful ensure that our legal institutions favor their own interests. CRT applies the same kind of analysis, but with an emphasis on race.

One of the pioneers of CRT was Derrick Bell, a Harvard Law School professor who was well known at the time the Obamas studied there.

Bell argued that white supremacy was deeply enshrined in the American legal system, since the Constitution itself was drafted, in part, by white slave-holders. Because the institution of property that our Constitution protects implies the subjugation of black people, black Americans would never find real redemption within the economic system established by that Constitution. They will always be "faces at the bottom of the well"—the people against whom the rest of America defines itself.[7] The only remedy for systemic racism, he argued, is a new set of socioeconomic rights that will redistribute property.

Bell had a deep influence on Obama's thinking. Just how deep is suggested by a video unearthed by the late Andrew Breitbart shortly before his death in 2012—a rarely seen film of Obama introducing Bell at a Harvard student rally for faculty diversity in 1991. Left-wing critics mocked the embrace of the two men as "hug-gate"—but in fact the connection was strong. A few years later, Obama taught Bell's ideas to his students at the University of Chicago[8] and asked Bell to review and blurb his memoir, *Dreams from my Father.*[9]

Obama has shown an affinity for Bell's ideas throughout his presidency—in his Supreme Court appointments in particular. His first appointee, Sonia Sotomayor, once said that "a wise Latina woman with the richness of her experiences would more often than not reach a better conclusion than a white male"[10] in judging cases. His second, Elena Kagan, once lectured on CRT—a fact she was not asked about during Senate confirmation hearings. In 2015, Obama said that America is "not cured" of racism—that it is "part of our DNA that's passed on"[11]—pure Critical Race Theory.

Even more telling is a 2001 interview that then–state senator Obama gave to WBEZ-FM, Chicago's National Public Radio affiliate, in which he criticized the Warren Court of the 1950s and 1960s. Despite the many gains the Civil Rights Movement achieved during that era, he said, the Court had not gone far enough: "If you look at the victories and failures of the civil rights movement and its litigation strategy in the court. I think where it succeeded was to invest formal rights in previously dispossessed people, so that now I would have the right to vote. I would now be able to sit at the lunch counter and order as long as I could pay for it I'd be OK. But, the Supreme Court never ventured into the issues of redistribution of wealth, and of more basic issues such as political and economic justice in society."[12] The idea that courts would or should have redistributed wealth is straight from Critical Race Theory, which prescribes socioeconomic rights as the only way to save the American legal system. Obama went on to tell WBEZ that one of the "tragedies" of the Civil Rights Movement was that it had been so focused on the courts, and not on building "the actual coalition of powers through which you bring about redistributive change."[13]

Yet the Supreme Court had in fact moved in the direction of giving the federal government greater power to intervene in the economy and to redistribute wealth—backing away from the laissez-faire principles of the now-infamous 1905 case of *Lochner v. New York*. In *Lochner*, the Court had struck down a state law regulating bakers' hours on the grounds that it interfered with the individual freedom of contract, which the Court said was a substantive right protected by the Fourteenth Amendment's Due Process clause.[14] In other words, to the *Lochner* court it was more important to protect the individual worker's right to make contracts than to guarantee socially useful or acceptable contracts, however well intentioned. The *Lochner* precedent—which would be demonized by generations of law professors—held into the New Deal era, during which the Court struck down President Franklin D. Roosevelt's ambitious programs. But the *Lochner* era ended, after unprecedented pressure on the judiciary, with *West Coast Hotel Co. v. Parrish* (1937), in which the Court upheld a state minimum wage law, opening the floodgates to further government regulation of the economy.[15] In *Wickard v. Filburn* (1942), the Court ruled that the federal government had the power to regulate a farmer's wheat under the Interstate Commerce Clause, even if he intended it only for his own consumption.[16]

From there, the federal government's power to regulate the economy was virtually unimpeded. Liberal legal scholars even told Congress during the debate over Obamacare that the federal government could, theoretically, compel citizens to eat broccoli.[17] That argument was rejected by the Court in the Obamacare case—but the Court still upheld Obamacare under the taxation power, showing just how statist the Court had become.

Conservatives struggled to push back. The *Lochner* precedent was of little use—not just because it had been overruled, but because it implied that there was a set of natural or substantive rights protected by the Constitution that were not explicitly identified in it,[18] and liberal justices had used similar reasoning in finding a right to privacy that protected abortion in *Roe v. Wade*—complicating any effort to revive *Lochner*.

Instead, in the 1970s and 1980s, conservatives turned to originalism—which, put simply, is the idea that the Constitution means what it says, and nothing more. It can be interpreted, of course, but only in light of the text itself, and the terms it uses should be understood as they would have been at the time when they were written.

By far the most influential originalist was the late Justice Antonin Scalia, a powerful dissenting voice on the Court when it ruled along liberal lines. Though he was rarely the decisive vote, Scalia's originalism made him the most influential if not the most powerful justice on the Court.

Originalism has a powerful internal logic. All of us, to some extent, are originalists: in private contracts, and real estate deals, and employment disputes, people focus on the precise meaning of individual words. Modifications can be made, but by mutual—usually written—agreement, not according to a vague evolving understanding about what the terms of the deal ought to be.

Originalism simply applies the same reasoning to the Constitution. Critics regard it as too strict and simplistic. In reality, originalism is liberating and creative: it merely shifts the task of changing the Constitution back to the legislatures and to the people, where—according to the amendment process laid out in the Constitution itself—that responsibility rightfully belongs.

Originalism is so compelling that legal scholars on the Left have started using it to make their own arguments. As law professor Eric A.

Posner noted in 2011, "The left wing of the Supreme Court long resisted originalism but has allowed itself to be sucked into it. Most notably, the 2008 gun control case, *District of Columbia v. Heller*, featured warring constitutional histories about gun rights from the majority and the dissent. Meanwhile, many liberal law professors have thrown in the towel, endorsing originalism or a version of it but arguing that the original sources indicate liberal rather than conservative constitutional norms."[19]

Originalism does not always lead to conservative policy conclusions—just as the "living constitution" approach need not necessarily produce liberal outcomes. One case in which originalism aligned with what left-wing arguments was *Hamdi v. Rumsfeld* (2004), in which an American who had been detained without charge as an enemy combatant challenged his imprisonment. The Supreme Court majority found that Hamdi could be detained, though he had to "be given a meaningful opportunity to contest the factual basis for that detention before a neutral decisionmaker."[20]

Justice Scalia, who, ironically, was later derided as "a cheerleader for the administration's terrorism policies," wrote a strident dissent in which his liberal colleague John Paul Stevens joined. Citing the English common law on the writ of *habeas corpus* at the time it was incorporated into the Constitution, Scalia found that Hamdi was "entitled to a habeas decree requiring his release unless (1) criminal proceedings are promptly brought, or (2) Congress has suspended the writ of habeas corpus."[21]

While originalist analysis yields some results welcome to the Left, and some left-wing judges have adopted originalist arguments, the Left in general would prefer that the judiciary simply defer—not to the executive or to the legislature branches of the government, but rather to "social justice." Typically, social justice, as defined by the Left, means economic leveling, mediated by the power of the state. Courts are expected to rule not on the basis of rights, laws, or precedent, but based on that goal.

Because the American legal system does not (yet) work this way, the Obama administration has adopted a hostile posture towards the judiciary—something not seen since FDR threatened to restructure the Supreme Court to stop it from striking down his New Deal legislation.

One way Obama has undermined the courts is by simply defying rulings that he does not like. In 2010, for example, there was a major oil spill in the Gulf of Mexico when the *Deepwater Horizon*, an offshore rig owned by BP, suffered a catastrophic blowout at a wellhead on the ocean floor. The accident had less environmental impact than was initially feared, but it did initially seem to confirm the Left's suspicions of the oil industry. The Obama administration reacted with a sweeping moratorium on all offshore drilling activity in the Gulf. That triggered a lawsuit to challenge the moratorium, and U.S. District Judge Martin Feldman overturned the ban as being overly broad. The administration then issued another moratorium. The judge found the Obama administration had acted in contempt of court: "Each step the government took following the court's imposition of a preliminary injunction showcases its defiance," he said.[22]

There was a similar fiasco in 2014 and 2015, when several states challenged President Obama's unilateral executive actions on immigration, particularly the Deferred Action for Childhood Arrivals, or (DACA). That policy delayed the deportation of millions of foreign nationals and directed that they be given driver's licenses, work permits, and the like—all in defiance of Congressional will and most state policies. Several states joined together in a lawsuit to challenge the president's new ruling, as well as the new benefits it conferred at state taxpayers' expense. After the judge ruled against the administration's attempt to have the case dismissed, the Obama administration continued to process applications from illegal aliens for "deferred" status, defying the federal judge and misleading him. In response, the furious judge threatened to hold the Department of Justice itself in contempt of court.[23] (Attorney General Eric Holder had already been held in contempt of Congress for failing to provide documents relating to Operation Fast and Furious.)

Throughout, the attitude of the Obama administration towards the judiciary was to try to get away with whatever it could. Obama apparently felt no obligation to lead by example and show respect to the courts.

The administration also committed sins of omission—as when it declined to defend the Defense of Marriage Act (DOMA) from constitutional challenge, thought it was required to defend the law even if it disagreed with it.

Not content with defying court rulings and abandoning its constitutional responsibilities, Obama also bullied the courts over matters pending adjudication. The most notorious case was *NFIB v. Sebelius* (2012),[24] the Obamacare case, which tested the constitutionality of Obama's singular domestic policy initiative. The challenge concerned the policy's "individual mandate," which requires every individual to purchase insurance; the issue was whether Congress has power to force such a purchase, on penalty of a fine, under the Commerce Clause.

Initially, Democrats mocked the idea that Obamacare might be unconstitutional. But the case against the individual mandate appeared more compelling as the case developed, and the oral arguments before the Supreme Court went badly for the administration. Liberals began to fear—and conservatives to hope—that the law might be overturned.

It was then that Obama took to the podium: "I'd just remind conservative commentators that for years what we've heard is the biggest problem on the bench was judicial activism or a lack of judicial restraint— that an unelected judge would overturn a duly constituted and passed law."[25]

Obama had misstated not only the conservative critique, but the very definition of "judicial activism." Conservatives do not object to the principle of judicial review, which has been a core part of our judicial system since *Marbury v. Madison* (1803). If a law defies the Constitution, conservatives are happy for the courts to strike it down—however "duly constituted and passed" it may be. What conservatives object to is judges legislating from the bench, imposing their personal beliefs on the nation—declaring laws unconstitutional because they offend against modern sensibilities about social justice rather than the actual words of the Constitution. *That's* what conservatives mean by "judicial activism."

While Obama's spokespeople scrambled to explain that, yes, the former *Harvard Law Review* editor did understand judicial review, Chief Justice John Roberts appeared to take the president's attack to heart, and was rumored to have switched his vote. Instead of overturning the law,

Roberts wrote a majority opinion in which he redefined the individual mandate as a "tax" rather than a penalty. The individual mandate failed under the Commerce Clause, he said—but survived under the taxation power.

Later, when a second challenge to Obamacare arose in *King v. Burwell* (2015),[26] the president again spoke out—this time saying the Court should not have taken the case in the first place. Though the 6–3 decision was more firmly in the administration's favor than the 5–4 *NFIB v. Sebelius*—Anthony Kennedy having switched back to the liberals' side— once again the Chief Justice handed down a flawed ruling that gave the impression that he had labored hard to avoid overturning Obama's prized domestic achievement.

It is unusual for the executive branch to weigh in on pending cases. In the controversial Kim Davis case of 2015, when a Democratic Party county clerk was jailed for contempt of court for failing to provide same-sex couples with marriage licenses, appeals to the Kentucky governor, also a Democrat, to intervene went nowhere because he declined to interfere with a matter that was already before the courts. Obama, the supposed constitutional law scholar, was never so deferential.

Perhaps the most shocking of Obama's efforts to undermine the judiciary was his first. During the 2010 State of the Union address, Obama took on the contentious *Citizens United* case, with six of the nine Justices seated in the House chamber in front of him—silent and respectful, as decorum required.

*Citizens United* case was a 5–4 decision that found that corporations (and unions) could spend unlimited amounts of money to advocate for candidates in elections—on the grounds that free speech extends to associations of individuals as well as to individuals themselves, and that campaign contributions are a form of speech.

In his address, Obama said, "With all due deference to separation of powers, last week the Supreme Court reversed a century of law that I believe will open the floodgates for special interests—including foreign corporations—to spend without limit in our elections."[27] Supreme Court Justice Samuel Alito, seated silently in the well of the chamber with several of his colleagues, shook his head and mouthed the words, "Not true."

Alito's response set the media and the Democrats alight. But what was more striking was the way the Democrats in the chamber, led by New York Senator Charles Schumer, had leapt to their feet in applause for the president. The Court had been humiliated in front of the whole nation. It seemed a calculated attempt to bully the judiciary and undermine its political independence.

Obama's attack on the Court was perhaps a form of payback for the *Bush v. Gore* (2000) decision, which effectively resolved the deadlocked 2000 presidential election in Bush's favor.[28] With Republican appointees siding with Bush and Democrat appointees backing Gore, Democrats tended to regard the decision as a political one. But actually, the Gore team had sealed its own fate when it failed to call for a statewide recount of votes in Florida, the decisive state, choosing only to count votes in four Democrat-heavy counties. Democrats had also hurt themselves by approving a "butterfly ballot" in Palm Beach county that caused thousands of Democrats to cast erroneous votes for arch-conservative Pat Buchanan. A later independent recount showed that Bush had, in fact, earned more votes. And if the courts had not intervened, the Republican-led House of Representatives would have put Bush in office, following the Constitution's deadlock procedures. Regardless, Democrats used *Bush v. Gore* to portray the Court as a partisan institution.

Obama's attitude towards the courts might have been expected to be different, given his past service on a law school faculty, his work as a civil rights attorney, and his editorship at the *Harvard Law Review*. Instead of leading with an example of respect for the judiciary, however, he stepped up the attack on the Court.

Ironically, despite Obama's bluster about *Citizens United*, the Democrats subsequently proposed a constitutional amendment to regulate corporate political speech—falling back on the process for constitutional change that is mandated by the actual words of the Constitution, and thus affirming the originalist logic of the Court's decision. Obama may have hurt the Court's image, but he could not dent its logic.

Still, Republicans failed to mount an effective defense of judicial independence. In 2013, the Senate faced a fight over the D.C. Circuit Court of Appeals, an appellate court that plays a very important role in reviewing federal regulation, since many of the challenges to federal agencies are filed in the jurisdiction where those agencies are based. As Obama expanded the scope and power of federal regulations, control of the D.C. Circuit became even more important. When Obama took office, there had been an informal "balance" of four Republican appointees and four Democrat appointees, with three vacancies on the eleven-seat court. Suspecting that Obama planned to upset that balance, Republican senator Chuck Grassley of Iowa sought to shrink the D.C. Circuit to eight judges—a move entirely within the jurisdiction of Congress, and justified in part by the court's slow workload.

In response, Democrats threatened to invoke the "nuclear option"— an end to the filibuster rule, according to which the Senate must reach a sixty-vote supermajority in order to end debate and proceed to a vote on laws and appointees. The filibuster is not part of the Constitution or the law; it is merely a rule of the Senate, adopted by a majority vote. But over the course of several decades it has become a cherished protection for the minority party in the Senate, and a way to of ensuring a more deliberative, consultative process that has made the Senate a more moderate place to conduct the government's business than the highly partisan House.

During the Bush administration, moderate Republican John McCain had rebelled against his own party leadership by organizing a "Gang of 14" to protect the filibuster rule, at a time when it benefited the minority Democrats who wanted to block the president's judicial nominees. Now, however, no one on the Left was willing to reprise McCain's principled stand.

In 2013, Senate Majority Leader Mitch McConnell reportedly reached a compromise in which Republicans would agree to allow President Obama to appoint nominees to the Consumer Financial Protection Bureau—a new agency with sweeping, arguably extra-constitutional powers—and in return, Democrats would agree not to invoke the "nuclear option."[29]

Yet in 2014 the Democrats did just that, with Majority Leader Harry Reid changing the Senate rules to end the filibuster for judicial and high-level executive nominees. The White House began stacking the D.C. Circuit and other courts with administration-friendly leftist judges.

Republicans were left with nothing but outrage. They failed to defend judicial independence—by, for example, standing up against Obama's Supreme Court nominees or censuring Obama for his attempts to bully the Supreme Court. And their failure to take effective action made their commitment to originalism seem half-hearted at best.

And that is a shame, because the debate over originalism shows that there are certain truths that, if conservatives have the courage to fight, the Left cannot easily suppress.

# CHAPTER 9

# RACE

## THE LIE:
## Racism is in our nation's "DNA," and it is irresolvable without radical political change.

Examples:

*"Though this nation has proudly thought of itself as an ethnic melting pot, in things racial we have always been and continue to be, in too many ways, essentially a nation of cowards."*[1]

—Attorney General Eric Holder,
Department of Justice, February 2009

*"I love the fact that people are talking and dealing with the institutional racism that has existed in this country and been ignored. I feel like it's another '60s moment, where*

*the people themselves had to expose how ugly they were before things could change. I'm hopeful that that's happening now."[2]*

—Director Quentin Tarantino,
summer 2015

*"It is incontrovertible that race relations have improved significantly during my lifetime and yours, and that opportunities have opened up, and that attitudes have changed. That is a fact.*

*What is also true is that the legacy of slavery, Jim Crow, discrimination in almost every institution of our lives—you know, that casts a long shadow. And that's still part of our DNA that's passed on. We're not cured of it."[3]*

—President Barack Obama, Podcast with Marc Maron,
June 2015

## THE TRUTH:
## Racism has faded significantly and is all but eliminated as a real problem.

Few expected the election of Barack Obama to the presidency in 2008 to resolve all of America's lingering racial problems. But the country had arguably taken a giant step toward realizing Dr. Martin Luther King Jr.'s dream of a nation where people "will not be judged by the color of their skin, but by the content of their character."[4] Obama's opponent, John McCain, acknowledged in his concession speech the historic achievement of "the election of an African-American to the presidency of the United States." McCain declared, "Let there be no reason now for any American to fail to cherish their citizenship in this, the greatest nation on Earth."[5]

Black Americans seemed to agree. A CNN poll on the eve of Obama's inauguration found that more than two-thirds—a higher percentage, in fact, than of white Americans—agreed that King's dream for America had been fulfilled.[6]

But some on the left feared that Obama's presidency would let Americans off the hook. So they worked tirelessly—beginning even before the election—to deny that America had changed in any significant way. One Hollywood writer called Obama "the 'Magic Negro'.... there to assuage white 'guilt' (i.e., the minimal discomfort they feel) over the role of slavery and racial segregation in American history."[7] Immediately after the election, another leftist publicly criticized Obama for an insufficiently radical "weak ass stand on race."[8]

Initially Obama seemed to represent what most Americans—black or white—hoped the country would achieve. Scholar Shelby Steele observed during the election that Obama "embodies something that no other presidential candidate possibly can: the idealism that race is but a negligible human difference."[9] Obama's success seemed genuine, and earned: "He was *special* because he was clearly more than an 'affirmative action baby,' someone who could succeed without the ministrations of white guilt."[10] Still, at the same time, Steele wrote, Obama seemed "driven by a determination to be black,"[11] which sprang from "a personal angst, not from an oppression in society."[12] He resolved the complexity of his own identity by "exaggerat[ing] black victimization in America."[13]

Steele thought the contradictions between Obama's two personas—the "bargainer" and the "challenger"—would prevent him from winning the election. But a sudden economic crisis, favorable treatment from the media, and the skilled use of social media by his campaign secured his victory.

It was only once he reached office that the contradictions emerged. In his own mind, perhaps, the president was reprising the role of Harold Washington, the first black mayor of Chicago, who had been an inspiration to the young Obama when he was a community organizer. Even in office, Mayor Washington faced racist opposition from the ethnic white Democrats whose machine he had broken. Obama seemed to see his Republican opponents in Congress the same way. And soon a presidency that had great potential to unite suddenly became the most divisive in recent history.

Eight years after left-wing activists went door to door canvassing for Obama, they were back in the streets chanting "Black lives matter!" and daring the police to react. University campuses were seized by a paroxysm of protest as students occupied administration buildings demanding greater racial sensitivity from their sympathetic but bewildered professors. It was as if the Obama presidency had never happened.

The angry rhetoric not only contradicted the hopeful sentiments of 2008: it also misrepresented the reality of life in America—a society that was in fact less racist than ever before. In the late 1950s, according to Gallup, only a slim plurality of Americans said they would vote for a black candidate for president. By the late 1990s, 95 percent said they would.[14] And the change in attitudes about race went further than politics: in 1958, only 4 percent of Americans approved of black-white marriage, yet by 2013, 87 percent approved (96 percent of blacks and 84 percent of whites).[15]

Blacks and whites disagree about how much progress has been made. According to a 2015 Gallup poll, 43 percent of whites believe that civil rights for blacks have improved "greatly," while only 21 percent of blacks felt the same. Yet overwhelming majorities of both blacks and whites believe there has been *some* improvement.[16] The lingering differences are between blacks' and whites' perceptions of the criminal justice system: a majority of whites have confidence in it, compared to 37 percent of blacks. Yet overall, blacks and whites agree that there has been progress.[17]

Today most American institutions, public and private, are eager to help black Americans close the gaps with their white compatriots. Affirmative action is the norm in tertiary education. Where it has been rolled back, as in California, it has been replaced by remedial programs aimed at bringing promising yet struggling black students closer to par with their white and Asian classmates. And educational outcomes for black students have actually improved under this new regime, even if fewer attended the institutions at the apex of the state's public university system.[18]

The enduring blight of inner cities is where America's racial inequities are still most glaring. Yet those cities are largely governed by minorities and by Democrats committed (in theory) to policies of economic redistribution. Ironically, the isolation of these communities has deepened as successful black families have moved elsewhere.

While undoubtedly there are still many obstacles facing black Americans, racial discrimination is arguably not the primary one, or even a major one. If it were, the rapid success of black immigrant communities from Africa and the Caribbean would not have been possible.

Though it is politically risky to say so, there are factors within the black community that hold it back. Roughly 30 percent of white children are born out of wedlock today; about 70 percent of black children are. That is a significant factor driving racial inequality. So too is a popular culture in minority communities that emphasizes victimization and rebellion, often to the exclusion of virtues held dear by earlier generations.

Meanwhile, at the nation's elite universities, Princeton students demanded a special "safe space" for black students in 2015,[19] and Occidental College students demanded "physicians of color...to treat physical and emotional trauma associated with issues of identity."[20] These are demands not for *equal* treatment, but for *special* treatment, on the grounds that the university campuses themselves—the most left-wing institutions in America—maintain a "systemic racism" that cannot be corrected without special interventions.

The present spate of student activism was actually foreshadowed—if not inspired—by the "Rhodes Must Fall" protests in South Africa at the University of Cape Town. In March of 2015, Cape Town students who had walked past an old statue of Cecil John Rhodes every day for years without complaint suddenly decided that it was an unwelcome relic of colonialism. (The fact that the university grounds themselves, set against the spectacular slopes of Table Mountain, were donated by Rhodes seemed not to matter.)

After weeks of demonstrations, with protesters flinging feces at the statue (in a "poo protest"), the university agreed to remove it. That victory galvanized a national student movement for free university education, dubbed "Fees Must Fall." South African President Jacob Zuma canceled a planned tuition increase for 2016, handing the students another victory—and another reason to escalate the protests, which turned violent on some campuses. By February 2016, protesters at the University of Cape Town were ransacking university buildings and burning portraits of white people[21]—even those painted by anti-apartheid artists.[22]

The story of the South African protests reached—and helped inspire—protests in the United Kingdom, where Rhodes scholars demanded the "Rhodes" name be removed,[23] and it also found American activists through social media.[24]

There are some interesting parallels between South Africa and the United States, at least in terms of the Left's approach to redressing past injustice. South Africa achieved a dramatic racial reconciliation in the mid-1990s with its first democratic elections and its new liberal constitution. But then, as we have seen, the new ruling party, the African National Congress (ANC), began to implement a new agenda called "transformation." In theory, transformation means reversing the discrimination of the past, so that every institution reflects the demographics of the country as a whole. In practice, the ANC uses transformation to enrich its leaders, including billionaires who still qualify as "historically disadvantaged individuals."

The results have been a return to race-consciousness, and white flight—first from the public to the private sector, then from the private sector abroad. The country's economy and civil service have lost valuable skills. Those who suffer most are those whom "transformation" is theoretically intended to help—the poor black majority most in need of job opportunities and most dependent on public services. With nothing to offer an increasingly restless population, the ruling party focuses on symbolic struggles—renaming streets and removing statues. The inequalities are less striking in the U.S., and the problems far less urgent, but the pattern is the same.

Despite the utopian fantasies of racial reparations and redistribution, the actual, lived experience of policies like "transformation" is not just that they fail to help black people, but that black people do far better in their absence. The elimination of racial discrimination creates new opportunities, but the effort to intervene on behalf of disadvantaged minorities often creates new obstacles. When these are swept aside by more conservative governments, outcomes for black people improve.

In the city of Cape Town, for example, the opposition Democratic Alliance (DA) narrowly won an election in 2006 against the ruling ANC, which had applied ambitious racial quotas in municipal contracts. Contracts were frequently awarded to ruling party insiders rather than to the most qualified bidder at the most competitive price. When the DA government took over, it rolled back affirmative action and racial quotas to the legal minimum. The effect was to remove the entrenched advantage of ANC cronies and to open up city contracts to a much wider array of entrepreneurs. And in the first year alone, Cape Town increased the number of contracts awarded to black-owned businesses by 10 percent. Meanwhile, city services improved dramatically, as the emphasis shifted from the skin color of the person cashing the city check to the quality of the service he or she provided. Elsewhere in South Africa, where race remained the most important priority of government—as it had been during apartheid, albeit with the roles of black and white reversed—services continued to decline, and hope to fade.

Though affirmative action has been less extreme in the United States, it has followed an essentially similar pattern, benefiting a relative few while leaving the many behind—and sowing new seeds of resentment. It is a rejection of Dr. King's vision, as well as that of the black abolitionist hero Frederick Douglass, who famously said, "Everybody has asked the question, and they learned to ask it early of the abolitionists, 'What shall we do with the Negro?' I have had but one answer from the beginning. Do nothing with us! Your doing with us has already played the mischief with us."[25] His was a vision of black self-reliance, not perpetual victimization and grievance.

From his global study of affirmative action, economist Thomas Sowell concluded, "Despite sweeping claims made for affirmative action programs, an examination of their actual consequences makes it hard to support those claims, or even to say that these programs have been beneficial on net balance—unless one is prepared to say that any amount of social redress, however small, is worth any amount of costs and dangers, however large."

That leaves some room for debate. But it is a debate the Left would rather not have, because—as in the Proposition 209 case, when Californians passed a referendum to ban affirmative action—it stands to lose if the actual evidence is presented. In one of the last cases he heard, *Fisher v. University of Texas*, Justice Antonin Scalia raised an argument that had been presented in the briefs to the court suggesting that black students who attend a "less-advanced" or "slower-track school" than the University of Texas enjoy better career outcomes because they are not being "pushed ahead in classes that are too fast for them."[26] The social science data backs Scalia[27]—who may have been raising the point hypothetically, as judges often do during oral arguments. For his trouble, he was excoriated by the Left (and by Donald Trump) as a racist.[28] Instead, those on the left short-circuit debate by insisting that the one option that may *not* be considered is the non-racial ideal for which Douglass fought and King marched. Non-racialism, in which each individual is judged based on his or her own merit, has been redefined as a form of racism.

The 2012 Obama re-election campaign abandoned the 2008 rhetoric of racial reconciliation, portraying Republican policies as deliberately hostile to black Americans. Republican Mitt Romney is "going to put y'all back in chains," Vice President Joe Biden told a largely black audience in Virginia.[29] Obama's campaign refused to apologize, saying the metaphor was apt given Romney's pledge to reduce regulation on Wall Street. Such race-baiting rhetoric was more than a campaign strategy; it was a return to the president's religious roots in Jeremiah Wright's Trinity United Church of Christ, where Obama and his family worshipped for two decades. The precepts that Wright preached over those years demonstrate the depths to which the Left will sink to retain race as a dividing factor in American life. Wright's church embraced what it called the "Black Value System," which included "Disavowal of the Pursuit of 'Middleclassness,' as well as tithing to black institutions and pledging 'allegiance' to black leaders.[30] Obama wrote in his first memoir, *Dreams from My Father*, that he was drawn to Wright's church precisely because of its mix of faith and politics. Later, then-senator Obama would take the name of his second memoir, *The Audacity of Hope*, from one of Wright's sermons. Wright offered Obama a kind of authenticity within the black community. The future president married his wife in the church, had his daughters baptized in the church, and gave the church significant sums of money. It was far from a fleeting association.

The mainstream media belatedly caught up to the story in 2008, publishing videos of Wright shouting "God damn America" and calling the 9/11 terror attacks "America's chickens come home to roost."[31] Association with that kind of racism and anti-American vitriol should have been enough to sink any campaign for president.

But the Left, and the media, rallied around Obama and the idea that it was natural for a black American—even one aspiring to *lead* America—to feel a sense of resentment towards America. And Obama defended his association with Wright in a March 2008 speech in Philadelphia with the grandiose title, "A More Perfect Union."[32] The future president criticized Wright's views but declared: "I can no more disown him than I can disown the black community."

The speech was hailed by the progressive commentariat. Noted Obama admirer Chris Matthews of MSNBC called it "a speech worthy of Abraham Lincoln.... One that went beyond 'I have a dream,' to 'I have lived the dream but have also lived in this country.'"[33] The *New York Times*' Maureen Dowd called it "momentous and edifying."[34] The glowing reception rescued Obama's campaign.

But the speech was, in fact, a "brilliant fraud," as conservative commentator Charles Krauthammer pointed out at the time.[35] Obama had failed to denounce some of Wright's worst beliefs. But he soon severed ties with Wright after all, when a substitute preacher at Wright's church mocked Hillary Clinton from the pulpit. Obama was able to weather the controversy, cushioned by the Left's willingness to reject, or doubt, King's color-blind vision.

In much the same way, the progressive media establishment would go on to heap praise, money, and awards on Ta-Nehisi Coates, the left-wing blogger who published a popular memoir on race in America, *Between the World and Me*, in 2015. Written as a letter to his fifteen-year-old son, the book offered a bleak, almost hopeless portrait of race relations in the United States, a country that denies "you and me the right to secure and govern our own bodies."[36]

Coates warns his son that he, like other black people, can be killed by police with impunity, merely for the crime of existing. "There is nothing uniquely evil in these destroyers or even in this moment," he writes. "The destroyers are merely men enforcing the whims of our country, correctly interpreting its heritage and legacy.... You must never look away from this."[37]

The book dwells on a recent series of sensational cases in which black people have been killed by police. But the facts matter little to Coates. He refers, for example, to "the killers of Michael Brown"—the teenager who attacked a police officer in Ferguson, Missouri, and was shot while charging him.[38] The Left claimed Brown held his hands up in surrender, saying, "Don't shoot." But an investigation by the sympathetic Department of Justice failed to corroborate that story. Several witnesses, in fact, said that "they would have felt threatened by Brown and would have responded in the same way" as the police officer.[39] Coates allows that "Michael Brown did not die as so many of his defenders supposed"[40]— yet still calls the police his "killers."

Coates writes that his disillusionment with America was sealed the day he learned that his friend and classmate Prince Jones had been killed by a police officer in Maryland in controversial circumstances. Only several pages later does Coates reveal that the police officer was black. Coates describes watching the World Trade Center burn on September 11, 2001—and feeling no sympathy: "I could see no difference between the officer who killed Prince Jones and the police who died, or the fire-fighters who died. They were not human to me."[41]

This is pure Reverend Wright stuff—or Derrick Bell, the Harvard professor who described black people as "faces at the bottom of the well," against whom the rest of society defines itself. (Commentators have misidentified Coates as the source of the "faces at the bottom of the well" metaphor.[42]) "[P]erhaps being named 'black' was just someone's name for being at the bottom," Coates meditates.[43] But while Bell offered at least some hope of redemption, Coates offers none—save in Paris, or the seclusion of Howard University, which he calls "The Mecca." The America he condemned retaliated...by awarding Coates the MacArthur "genius" grant and the National Book Award.

There is no gainsaying the fact that there is an enduring mistrust between black communities and law enforcement authorities. But it is telling that so many of the episodes that form the basis for that mistrust have been fudged, exaggerated, or fabricated outright.

One of the more infamous examples is the case of Tawana Brawley, who was allegedly "attacked, scrawled with racial slurs, smeared with feces and left beside a road wrapped in a plastic bag" in New York State. Brawley and the Reverend Al Sharpton accused the Duchess County prosecutor, Steven Pagones, of having joined in the attack. Pagones sued for defamation and won, as the allegations were proven false.[44]

Then there are cases where the facts are clear, and yet large numbers of people in the black community believe an alternate version of events that is little more than fantasy.

In 1995, when O.J. Simpson was acquitted of murdering his ex-wife and her lover, many black Americans rejoiced, seeing him as a symbol of the mistreatment of black men by the criminal justice system. Yet in 2013, when George Zimmerman was acquitted of murdering a teenager named Trayvon Martin, the black community reacted with outrage and dismay.

In other circumstances, the half-Hispanic Zimmerman might have been seen as a sympathetic figure, another minority being railroaded through the courts by a prosecutor with a political agenda. But

Zimmerman had the misfortune of being labeled as "white" by an erroneous Associated Press report. That was all Al Sharpton needed to portray Martin's killing as a racist act, prejudicing large portions of the public against Zimmerman and casting Martin as an icon of black suffering. President Obama weighed in: "If I had a son, he'd look like Trayvon," he said.[45]

The media played along, reporting one false story after another about Zimmerman: that he had highlighted Martin's race on a 911 call, when in fact he had only mentioned it at the prompting of the dispatcher; that Martin had not hurt him, when in fact bloody photographs of his injuries showed that he had been telling the truth. The civil rights establishment, which has long prided itself on standing up for defendants against the state, abandoned Zimmerman completely.

There certainly are cases when police use deadly force against civilians—black and white—without justification. In April 2015, a police officer in Charleston, South Carolina, shot and killed an unarmed black man, Walter Scott, whom he had been chasing on foot. The officer was quickly charged with murder. The case immediately faded from the headlines: it was an example of the criminal justice system working well, and therefore of little interest to professional political activists.

Two months later, a new horror hit Charleston. A twenty-one-year-old white supremacist, Dylann Roof, walked into an historic black church, Emanuel A.M.E., on a Wednesday evening, prayed with the pastor and the congregants, and then shot nine to death, including the Reverend Clementa C. Pinckney. The country recoiled in horror. South Carolina's Republican governor, Nikki Haley, called for the removal of the Confederate flag from the grounds of the state Capitol, and state legislators gave their assent soon afterwards, in a gesture of reconciliation that shone in the midst of an unspeakable loss.

In his eulogy for the dead, President Barack Obama cast the Charleston shooting as an indictment of the broader society: "For too long, we've been blind to the way past injustices continue to shape the present. Perhaps we see that now. Perhaps this tragedy causes us to ask some tough questions about how we can permit so many of our children to languish in poverty, or attend dilapidated schools, or grow up without prospects for a job or for a career. Perhaps it causes us to examine what we're doing to cause some of our children to hate."[46] For good measure, he added a strident appeal for gun control.

And yet what was so striking about the Charleston shooting was how atypical it was. Roof even explained in a manifesto that he had acted precisely because no one else would: "We have no skinheads, no real KKK, no one doing anything but talking on the internet [sic]. Well someone has to have the bravery to take it to the real world, and I guess that has to be me."[47] The killer's isolation was evidence of America's decency, in spite of our troubled past.

I look at my own son, who has pale skin and blue eyes and yet is a direct descendant of Clements Kadalie, the first black trade unionist in Africa—a man whose opposition to racial segregation was so vehement that even the ANC considered him too radical. Shall I tell my son that the color of his skin condemns him to guilt, and shame? Shall I tell him that his ancestry entitles him to preferential treatment and restitution? Or shall I teach him to embrace the principles that are his country's heritage, and its hope?

It is true that racism, and racial violence, persists in America. But it is also true that racism is in retreat. The Obama years were a wasted opportunity for reconciliation; indeed, opinion polls suggest Americans consider race relations worse now than when Obama took office.[48] But our progress as a nation is undeniable—if we only allow ourselves to embrace it.

# CHAPTER 10

# IMMIGRATION

## THE LIE:
## It is un-American to restrict entry to refugees and other immigrants.

Examples:

> *"Family Guy creator Seth MacFarlane has spoken out against the Arizona immigration law that allows police officers to request proof that people are in the United States legally if they have 'reasonable suspicion' that those people aren't. 'Nobody but the Nazis ever asked anybody for their papers,' MacFarlane told Reuters Television. 'Walking down the street, a cop can come up to you and say "May I see your papers?"—I think they should be required to ask that question in German if the law sticks around.'"*[1]
>
> —Mandi Bierly, *Entertainment Weekly*, May 2010

*"We can have a legitimate debate about how to set up an immigration system that is fair and orderly and lawful.... But when I hear folks talking as if somehow these kids are different from my kids, or less worthy in the eyes of God, that somehow they are less worthy of our respect and consideration and care—I think that's un-American."*[2]
—President Barack Obama, Des Moines, September 2015

*"I don't want anybody to be down right now about what's going on in the Republican Party.... Appealing to the baser side of human nature. Working on this notion of xenophobia in a way that hasn't occurred in a long time. Since the Know-Nothing party back at the end of the nineteenth century."*[3]
—Vice President Joe Biden, Washington, D.C., September 2015

## THE TRUTH:
## Americans are open to immigration—as long as the border is secure.

"Give me your tired, your poor, Your huddled masses yearning to breathe free." The famous line from Emma Lazarus's poem, "The New Colossus," which is engraved on a plaque at the Statue of Liberty, has become almost as much a cliché as the immigration debate itself.

Over the past decade, the question of immigration reform has become an intractable political problem. Proposals emerge in Congress, only to be shot down by both the Left and Right. Republicans attack each other over the issue in primary races, and Democrats use it as a cudgel in general elections. Voters do not consider immigration a top priority, yet it dominates and divides our nation.

And yet there is a broad consensus on what to do. A Gallup poll in August 2015 showed that nearly two-thirds of Americans "favor a plan to allow immigrants who are living illegally in the U.S. to remain in the country and become citizens if they meet certain requirements over time." That figure includes 50 percent of Republicans.[4]

But there is another two-thirds majority on the immigration question: those Americans who want the country's borders to be secured before any changes to the nation's immigration laws. A 2013 Fox News poll that found 78 percent support for a "path to citizenship" also found that 68% of Americans wanted border security first. That included nearly two-thirds of Democrats.[5] These are not bigots; they are people legitimately concerned about national security, the economy, and the rule of law.

And they have reason to worry. In 1986, President Ronald Reagan signed into law the Immigration Reform and Control Act, popularly known as Simpson-Mazzoli for its bipartisan sponsors. It granted amnesty to three million illegal aliens, allowing them to become citizens. At the same time, it provided for improved border security measures, so that the 1986 amnesty would be the last.

As Fred Barnes observed at the *Weekly Standard*: "The amnesty went into effect immediately.... But strengthened enforcement never happened—that was the flaw—and the bill produced a perverse result. Rather than halt the flow of illegal immigrants, the 1986 law actually spurred millions more to come. Crossing the border was easy, jobs were plentiful, and the chance of being deported was slim, including for those who overstayed their temporary visas. There are now at least 11 million illegals in the country—and perhaps, some argue, millions more."[6]

Yet the Left rejects legitimate concerns about immigration, dismissing opposition to immigration reform as mere bigotry and xenophobia. That poisons the public debate, making it impossible to solve the problem despite broad public agreement on how immigration reform should be carried out.

The Left conflates different kinds of opposition to immigration. In fact, very few critics of immigration reform oppose it due to xenophobia or nativism. Certainly there are those who oppose most forms of immigration, including legal immigration. But that does not automatically make them bigots. There are two legitimate arguments against further legal immigration.

One is the cultural objection. Many immigrants from Latin America and elsewhere in the Third World come from societies where the political ethos is oriented towards socialism and statism. There is a danger of reinforcing a culture of entitlement and undermining the traditional American emphasis on individual achievement. With immigrants from Islamic countries, there is also the risk that new arrivals may hold values at odds with our own—including radical Islam. And we may be attracting such immigrants faster than we can assimilate them. One of the terrorists who carried out the San Bernardino massacre in December 2015 came to the U.S. legally, on a K-1 fiancé(e) visa. Background checks failed to discover her radical beliefs or deadly ambitions.

The other legitimate argument against legal immigration is economic. Legal immigrants represent new competition for American workers—not just at the low-skilled end of the labor market, but at the top end as well, where tech companies exploit the H1-B visa program to import workers, leaving many skilled Americans out in the cold. In addition, while some immigrants pay into our nation's entitlement system, many others have become a burden on our public services and welfare programs.

And of course more Americans object to illegal immigration than to legal. Estimates vary as to how many illegal aliens are actually in the country, from 11 million to 30 million. Many of those here illegally take advantage of government services that that are already stretched thin, barely providing for the needs of U.S. citizens. A minority of these illegal aliens are criminals, including violent criminals. Thanks to inadequate border security, Mexico's drug cartel wars have started to bleed over into the U.S. There is also the risk that more terrorists will cross that border, or enter the country legally and then stay illegally. In the summer of 2014, thousands of unaccompanied children crossed into the country, overwhelming the border patrol. Chinese couples have taken advantage of our laws of birthright citizenship to deliver "anchor babies" in the U.S. before returning home.[7] Few Americans believe the government is managing the problem well.

Yet the Left treats such concerns as a form of racism. That is how progressives described Arizona's 2010 immigration law, SB 1070, which directed state and local police to enforce federal immigration laws that federal authorities were neglecting. The Left called the law racist, even comparing Arizona to Nazi Germany because it allowed police to ask people to prove they were in the country legally. (Ironically, that "racist" provision was the one part of the law that survived Supreme Court review.)[8]

One of the Left's favorite tactics is to argue that because we are a "nation of immigrants," we have no basis, moral or otherwise, to object to allowing more immigrants into the country or legalizing those already here illegally. President Barack Obama has made that argument repeatedly. In January 2013, he said, "Unless you're one of the first Americans, Native Americans, you came from somewhere else; somebody brought you."[9] In November 2014, he said, "There have been periods where the folks who were already here suddenly say, 'Well, I don't want those folks,' even though the only people who have the right to say that are some Native Americans."[10] And in September 2015, he repeated that "unless you are a Native American, your family came from someplace else."[11] Vice President Joe Biden followed suit, telling an audience that same month that Republicans were like "the Know-Nothing party back at the end of the nineteenth century."[12]

This line of argumentation implies, absurdly, that the only morally consistent immigration policy America can possibly have is an open-border policy, allowing anyone to immigrate at will. The argument that America is a "nation of immigrants" also relies on a flawed premise, as controversial conservative author Ann Coulter pointed out in an interview with Jorge Ramos of the Fusion network. "The first people here back in the 1600s were not immigrants," she told him. "They were settlers. They came to a society continent [sic] that had no country. They created this country. The Dutch, mostly the British, created America."[13]

They shared a common cultural heritage and embraced a unique set of values that were influenced heavily by the Protestant faith. Those who arrived later, regardless of faith or background, were expected to embrace those original values—not to reshape the country's founding creed to their liking.

Where the Left sees the U.S. as a wealthy society that has the means to support millions more new arrivals, Coulter hones in on the source of that prosperity, which is not natural abundance or colonial exploitation, but rather the principles of liberty. Those are principles that even native-born Americans struggle to understand, and that have largely been abandoned in public schools and popular culture. It is not bigotry to worry that the rapid pace of immigration is challenging our ability to transmit those values to new immigrants—especially when the most radical immigrant advocacy groups, like La Raza ("The Race"), reject them.

Ironically, the Left has disrupted recent efforts at immigration reform more often than the Right. Mark Salter, a former chief of staff and speechwriter to Republican Senator John McCain of Arizona, recalled in 2011 that it was then-senator Barack Obama himself who often disrupted bipartisan efforts at immigration reform when Republicans controlled Congress and the White House. For example, Salter wrote, Obama was nominally part of a bipartisan effort to draft a comprehensive immigration reform bill, but he repeatedly insisted on changes to the legislation that were "invariably the same demands made by the AFL-CIO, which was intent on watering down or killing the guest-worker provisions." Instead of working out disagreements, Salter wrote, Obama "remained adamant in his positions and unwilling to compromise." Obama "not only refused to oppose the amendments that would hurt [a 2007 immigration reform] bill's chances of passage, but actually sponsored some of them."[14]

Obama and the Left were determined not to allow immigration reform to undermine the narrow interests of Big Labor—and they were even more determined not to allow a Republican president to take credit for an issue they hoped to use to rally Latino voters in the future. It is more useful for Democrats to cast Republicans as bigots than to fix the broken system.

Indeed, Democrats never cease casting Republicans as xenophobic, even when ostensibly trying to rally their support for immigration reform. In 2013, Democratic Representative Luis Gutierrez of Illinois appeared alongside Republican Representative Paul Ryan of Wisconsin at the City Club of Chicago to discuss their joint efforts at promoting a new immigration reform bill. Gutierrez could not resist the opportunity to play on racial and class guilt in his description of illegal aliens: "Who are they? You know who they are. They pour the water in your glass when you go to dinner. And they wash the dishes before and after they pour that water in your glass.... You drink the water, you drink the Chardonnay, right? You eat the fruit, and the salad, and you let them take care of your kids and mow your lawn. And now it is time, at the end of the day, after they sweat and they toil that they can receive the same satisfaction in being a citizen of the United States of America just like you."[15] In fact, as Mark Levin has pointed out, many "jobs that are stereotypically thought to comprise mainly immigrants actually comprise mostly American citizens," including maids and housekeepers.[16] Gutierrez's demagoguery not only hides the truth but undermines the legitimate policy arguments for immigration reform and exacerbates social and political divisions that make reform more difficult.

The Left denies a series of basic truths about immigration and border security. For example, it is routine on the Left to deny that border security is, in fact, a serious problem. The progressives have several standard arguments on this point. One is the contention that the government has done as much as it possibly can to secure the border. President Obama made that assertion in an infamous 2011 speech in El Paso, Texas. From the White House transcript:

> [THE PRESIDENT]: We have gone above and beyond what was requested by the very Republicans who said they supported broader reform as long as we got serious about enforcement. All the stuff they asked for, we've done. But even though we've answered these concerns, I've got to

say I suspect there are still going to be some who are trying
to move the goal posts on us one more time.

AUDIENCE MEMBER: They're racist!

THE PRESIDENT: You know, they said we needed to triple
the Border Patrol. Or now they're going to say we need to
quadruple the Border Patrol. Or they'll want a higher
fence. Maybe they'll need a moat. (Laughter.) Maybe they
want alligators in the moat. (Laughter.) They'll never be
satisfied. And I understand that. That's politics.[17]

(Note that the White House left the interjection in the transcript.)

Yet the president's claim was untrue, as even the left-leaning Politi-
Fact acknowledged.[18] The federal government had failed to implement
the Secure Fence Act of 2006, which required double fencing along the
border.

A second argument against better border security is the claim that
net migration is zero, or even negative, on account of a weak U.S. economy. In November 2015, for example, a Pew study was released showing
net negative migration to Mexico from 2009 to 2014.[19] But as conservative writer Daniel Horowitz pointed out, there had been a huge spike in
crossings from 2014 to 2015, after the Obama administration announced
radical changes to immigration policy.[20]

Other arguments include the idea that it is impossible to secure a
frontier that is nearly two thousand miles long, given limited personnel
and the variety of terrain that the fence would need to cross. Yet new
high-tech border fences in Israel have reduced illegal crossings almost to
zero. Though Israel is a small country, its technology could be scaled up,
given the political will.

Another tactic is to change the subject. That explains Operation Fast
and Furious—ostensibly meant to track smuggled guns, but likely a
pretext to create momentum for firearms restrictions—which ended with
the death of Border Patrol agent Brian Terry.

One of the supreme ironies of the immigration debate is that when President Obama had the opportunity to pass legislation in 2009–10, with a Democratic majority in the House and a filibuster-proof supermajority in the Senate, he failed to do so—disappointing Latino voters to whom he had promised to make immigration reform a priority. Congress resisted left-wing proposals for a "Dream Act" to allow children brought to the country illegally—so-called "Dreamers"—to achieve legal status.

But in 2012 Republican Senator Marco Rubio of Florida, a Tea Party favorite with Cuban immigrant roots and a large immigrant constituency, proposed his own legislation. Obama realized quickly that he had been outflanked. But instead of offering his own version of legislation to Congress, Obama announced a series of unilateral executive actions to allow "Dreamers" to stay in the country—what critics called a "Dream Act by fiat." Rubio, disgusted, noted that Obama had poisoned the debate, making it harder to move any legislation through Congress.

In 2013, Rubio tried again, this time with a bipartisan "Gang of Eight" whose bill passed the Senate. Obama kept his distance, partly at the urging of immigration reform advocates. But the Left undercut Rubio by refusing to sequence reforms so that border security came first, dooming the legislation in the House.

So Obama decided to act unilaterally again, announcing a new policy—cynically, after his party's crushing defeat in the 2014 midterm elections—that effectively legalized millions of illegal aliens. The problem with the new Deferred Action for Parents of Americans (DAPA) was that Obama had argued, repeatedly, that he had no power to create such a policy.[21] He was not the "emperor," but the president, he had reminded impatient Latino activists. Predictably, DAPA ran into legal challenges, as Republican governors sued to prevent their states from being forced to grant legal documents to illegal aliens.

The biggest victims, however, were legal immigrants. Obama's unilateral policies flooded the U.S. Citizenship and Immigration Services (USCIS) with applicants for deferred action, causing massive delays in processing the applications of those trying to immigrate legally. As even the *New York Times* reported, would-be legal immigrants were stranded abroad, with relatives and spouses of U.S. citizens stuck overseas.[22]

Meanwhile, Obama and other politicians—including Republicans—continued to pander to illegal aliens, invariably portraying them as altruistic, eager future patriots. The effect was to denigrate the honesty and commitment of legal immigrants who had taken the care to follow the country's laws. And in the end it was all for naught, as the courts struck down DAPA on administrative grounds, leaving immigrants—both legal and illegal—in the lurch.

The Left refused to learn the lessons of that experience. Hillary Clinton promised in May 2015 that she would go "even further" than Obama. "I will fight to stop the partisan attacks on the president's executive actions," she said.[23]

The fact that the president can declare for years—correctly—that he has no power under the Constitution to legalize millions of illegal aliens, only to attempt exactly that later, with his party's support, is a sign of the decline of the rule of law and the rise of the rule of men. "Executive amnesty" risks undermining the reason many immigrants come to the United States in the first place.

The rule of law is critical—as I can attest from personal experience, twice over. My parents immigrated to the U.S. from South Africa in the 1970s, just as they were about to start professional careers—my father as a doctor, my mother as a physical therapist. Though both came from relatively humble backgrounds, they could have expected a life of comfort and privilege in the bubble-world of white South Africa. Instead they chose to leave for frigid Chicago, leaving family and friends behind. The reason they did so is that they did not want to raise children in a society with immoral racial codes, which virtually guaranteed future civil unrest, or worse.

A generation later, my wife Julia, born into a multi-racial family, stood to claim every new privilege that post-apartheid South Africa offered. An Ivy League-educated, "historically disadvantaged" woman, she could have risen rapidly through the ranks of the corporate hierarchy and political leadership. She chose instead to settle in the U.S., serving in the U.S. Navy Reserve and going through the legal immigration process. Rather than a life where opportunities for rent-seeking would have come easily, she preferred to live in a society where success was earned and the fruits of success were less vulnerable to theft or seizure.

The fact that people give up lives of relative wealth elsewhere to become Americans is a reminder of what makes America truly special. We are a destination for "tired…poor…huddled masses" not hungry to eat, but "yearning to breathe free." America attracts a self-selecting group of bold entrepreneurs—precisely because devotion to the rule of law and our written Constitution provides a foundation for astonishing success. We tamper with that model at great peril.

The present-day status quo on immigration is itself corrosive of the rule of law. But that is a reason to craft immigration reform properly— through Congress, with an emphasis on border security. Executive action by a president who has failed to enforce existing law risks destroying more than political civility.

Instead of embracing America's laws, constitution, and values, many of the left-wing activists who advocate amnesty for illegal immigrants are actively hostile to the very country the beneficiaries wish to join. In 2014, for example, amnesty activists in Murrieta, California, burned an American flag during a protest on the Fourth of July.[24] The year before, immigration activists gathered at the Los Angeles City Hall to demand that Republicans who lead the U.S. House of Representatives pass immigration reform or else face political "extinction."[25] Spanish is spoken from the podium at immigration rallies, with nary an American flag in sight. That is hardly a way to convince Americans to support the cause.

Elected Democrats, who ought to know better, often encourage such behavior. In 2010, when then–Mexican president Felipe Calderón addressed Congress, Democrats leapt to their feet after he slammed Arizona's controversial immigration law, which merely enforced Congress's own statutes. The fact that Mexico's own immigration laws are far harsher towards illegal aliens was simply ignored. The Obama administration actually reported Arizona's law to the United Nations as part of a review by the Human Rights Council, whose members include some of the world's worst human rights abusers.

Much of the left's political rhetoric on immigration is aimed at corralling Latino voters. But ironically, many Hispanic or Latino Americans also oppose illegal immigration. When the city of Huntington Park, California, appointed two illegal aliens to civic commissions, locals—including legal immigrants—rose up in protest. One, Francisco Rivera, told the city council at a public hearing, "I don't have anything against immigrants. But there's a difference between 'immigrant' and 'illegal immigrant.'"[26]

Later, in an interview with Breitbart News, he expanded on those sentiments: "I literally remember this one guy, he must have been about 19 years old, bald, holding a Mexican flag. He looked at the sheriff and he literally told the guy, 'F- the USA.'...People need to understand that not every immigrant supports immigration reform and I do not approve of it. You don't cut in front of people in line and expect not to pay the consequences...."[27]

That is a perspective the Left would prefer to ignore or suppress.

Being an American is a privilege that deserves to be approached with a sense of awe, not a sense of entitlement. There are many possible solutions to the immigration problem, but the Left short-circuits debate by ignoring the border, dismissing the Constitution, and accusing opponents of bigotry. Better to keep the issue alive for the next election, apparently, than to solve it.

# CHAPTER 11

# GOVERNMENT

## THE LIE:
## Only government can help the truly needy.

Examples:

*"There is nobody in this country who got rich on his own. Nobody. You built a factory out there—good for you! But I want to be clear. You moved your goods to market on the roads the rest of us paid for. You hired workers the rest of us paid to educate. You were safe in your factory because of police forces and fire forces that the rest of us paid for. You didn't have to worry that marauding bands would come and seize everything at your factory, and hire someone to protect against this, because of the work the rest of us did. Now look, you built a factory and it turned into something terrific, or a great idea—God bless. Keep a*

*big hunk of it. But part of the underlying social contract is you take a hunk of that and pay forward for the next kid who comes along."*[1]

—Senator Elizabeth Warren, September 2011

*"If you get sick, America, the Republican health care plan is this: 'Die quickly.' That's right. The Republicans want you to die quickly."*[2]

—Representative Alan Grayson, speaking in the House of Representatives, September 29, 2009

*"In the richest nation on Earth, far too many children are still born into poverty, far too few have a fair shot to escape it, and Americans of all races and backgrounds experience wages and incomes that aren't rising, making it harder to share in the opportunities a growing economy provides. That does not mean, as some suggest, abandoning the War on Poverty. In fact, if we hadn't declared 'unconditional war on poverty in America,' millions more Americans would be living in poverty today."*[3]

—President Barack Obama on the Fiftieth Anniversary of the War on Poverty, January 2014

## THE TRUTH:
## The free market—not government welfare—has liberated the truly needy all over the world.

The moral core of the leftist creed is the claim that government intervention and economic redistribution are necessary to sustain and uplift the poor. That utopian belief faltered in the 1970s and retreated in the 1980s and 1990s, but it returned with a vengeance after the financial crisis of 2007–8.

On January 8, 2009, less than two weeks before being inaugurated as the forty-fourth President of the United States, president-elect Barack Obama spoke at George Mason University. He laid out an agenda for the first months of his presidency and a governing philosophy—an unmistakably left-wing set of principles that placed government at the center of society: "It is true that we cannot depend on government alone to create jobs or long-term growth, but at this particular moment, only government can provide the short-term boost necessary to lift us from a recession this deep and severe.

"Only government can break the cycle that is crippling our economy—where a lack of spending leads to lost jobs which leads to even less spending; where an inability to lend and borrow stops growth and leads to even less credit."[4]

Obama would go on to sign a massive $862 billion stimulus, which the White House promised was necessary to keep the unemployment rate below eight percent.[5] But unemployment kept soaring anyway, reaching double digits before finally falling—largely because of dropouts from the labor force—while growth remained below 3 percent for the duration of his presidency.[6]

Undaunted, Obama went on to push through a de facto nationalization of health insurance, massive new regulations in the financial services industry, and the effective conversion of the Internet to a public utility.

The old liberal creed of the Bill Clinton era was that government assistance was meant to be a helping hand, or a safety net, not the permanent source of support for large swathes of society. In his 1996 State of the Union address, President Clinton said, "We know big Government does not have all the answers. We know there's not a program for every problem. We know, and we have worked to give the American people a smaller, less bureaucratic Government in Washington. And we have to give the American people one that lives within its means. The era of big Government is over...."

"But we cannot go back to the time when our citizens were left to fend for themselves."[7]

That was a straw man argument, but one that defined the limits of the liberal vision of government: not big enough to dominate, but strong enough to help the truly needy. The rest was up to individuals, albeit in cooperation with each other: "Our individual dreams must be realized by our common efforts," President Clinton said.

Whether Clinton's party has shifted left, or its members are simply less shy about their real beliefs, today's Democrats seem to believe that because there are some things government *must* do, there is *nothing* government should not do. They ignore the basic truth that some of what government does for the people not only fails, but is also dangerous to our freedom.

The American Recovery and Reinvestment Act of 2009 is a case in point. President Obama touted it boldly, even brashly, making personal visits to the recipients of federal grants. Much of the money went to state and local government to shore up failing budgets and prevent public sector job cuts (and to keep dues flowing to public-sector unions). But some went to private companies—including, most infamously, Solyndra, a maker of solar panels in Silicon Valley, which received half a billion dollars in loan guarantees before failing calamitously.

For more than a year, the Obama administration treated Solyndra as a prime example of the success of the stimulus. Both President Obama and Vice President Joe Biden made high-profile visits to the company. But the reality was that the company could not compete with Chinese manufacturers, and it soon collapsed.

In the public sector, state and local governments struggled to spend the stimulus money on projects that would create jobs right away. The "shovel-ready jobs" that Obama had promised turned out not to be so "shovel-ready," as Obama himself later joked.[8] But the waste of nearly a trillion dollars was no laughing matter. Voters knew that the bill for all the new spending—which ballooned the fiscal deficit and the national debt—would eventually have to be paid.

The Tea Party was born in the wake of the stimulus; it swept the country by tapping into the widespread conviction that there are some things government ought not do. Many in the media were caught by surprise at the rise of the new conservative wave. Some were simply incredulous that Americans would want tax cuts or less government spending. Others mocked conservatives for wanting to maintain military spending—was the military, too, not part of government?

The idea that there might be priorities among different uses of public money and that defense might be the first among those priorities—since it is truly something that only government can do—was apparently unthinkable to the Left. The Left was determined to reduce defense spending—even though many military jobs were truly "shovel-ready."

Another thing that many on the Left found impossible to understand was that increasing the government's power could prove dangerous to individual freedom. Many feared the George W. Bush administration, complaining about the government's expanded surveillance powers after the terrorist attacks of September 11, 2001. But those on the Left found it impossible to believe that a government whose powers were ostensibly devoted to socially desirable outcomes such as economic redistribution and environmental regulation could abuse those powers.

In fact, as we shall see, the Obama administration would prove the most abusive since the Nixon years, targeting its political opposition and the media for harassment and worse. Even when evidence of those abuses emerged, the Left continued to deny that harm had been done.

Before those abuses had emerged, Obama had passed Obamacare, the biggest expansion of government power since the New Deal. The new law meant that the federal government controlled one-sixth of the economy, as well as life-and-death decisions for hundreds of millions of patients.

For a century, progressive reformers of both parties had tried, and failed, to create a national health care system. A 1993 effort led by then–first lady Hillary Clinton failed, and triggered a massive Republican backlash in the midterm elections of 1994. What had changed by 2009 was that Democrats now had a supermajority in the Senate, a historic figure in the White House, and a sense of opportunity.

Despite some flaws, however, the American health care system was doing rather well. Some 85 percent of patients were happy with their health insurance.[9] Of the thirty million uninsured, many were between jobs or had chosen not to buy insurance. The major complaint was rising costs—which Republicans had tried to address by passing a new benefit, Medicare Part D, covering prescription drugs (the new program, though expensive, came in under budget).[10]

The main driver of high costs in health care was the fact that most health care was paid for by a third party—an insurance company or the government, not the patient or the provider.

And Obamacare did nothing to resolve that problem. Instead it overhauled the entire health insurance market—including for the vast majority of formerly happy customers—to subsidize the newly insured. It would have been simpler to transfer money to the uninsured to buy insurance, but it would have been less politically palatable, and it would not have allowed government to set the terms of the policies.

Obamacare was sold as a market-friendly reform—and one that would not affect people who already had insurance: "If you like your plan, you can keep your plan. If you like your doctor, you can keep your doctor," President Obama said, literally dozens of times.[11] In the end, millions would lose both their plans and their doctors.

It turns out that managing the health insurance market for a few million people is difficult enough—and for three hundred million, it is nearly impossible. Worse, the supposedly tech-savvy Obama administration could not manage the task of setting up online insurance markets. The federal healthcare.gov website did not work on launch day, or for weeks afterward; some state exchanges, such as Oregon's, never worked at all.

Soon, costs skyrocketed as the young, healthy patients who were expected to subsidize older, sickly patients simply avoided the exchanges and paid the (cheaper) fine instead. Aside from the expansion of Medicaid in some states, Obamacare could boast few accomplishments and looked to have a bleak future.

There are some government programs that work very well. A few regularly make their way into political talking points: Social Security, which virtually ended extreme poverty among the elderly; the G.I. Bill, which opened career opportunities for millions of veterans; and the food stamp program, which has ballooned in recent years, but has reached millions of children in desperate need. The failures and unintended consequences of many other government programs, however, are typically ignored—because they tend to reinforce the value of limited government.

In his 2014 book, *Why Government Fails So Often and How It Can Do Better*, Peter H. Schuck offers a glimpse of some successful government policies.[12] One is the interstate highway system. Once championed by the Left, and still featuring occasionally in defenses of taxation—à la Elizabeth Warren—the system is now detested by the Left for cultivating Americans' love of the automobile. They prefer that we be forced onto public transportation. (Few of the foremost champions of public transportation, with the exception of Vice President "Amtrak Joe" Biden, bother to use it.)

The Earned Income Tax Credit is another successful program. "A principal reason for its popularity," Schuck reports, is that it encourages work."[13] There are problems with the EITC, including fraud, and the fact that "the effective marginal tax rate at the benefit phase-out level is high,"[14] discouraging work beyond a certain point. But overall, it is successful, and has proved popular among both parties, though it may eventually be eliminated as part of broader tax reform.

As Schuck points out, successful government programs share one trait: "*To succeed, then, the programs largely needed to engage the actors' self-interest; they did not need to create new values or transform deeply rooted behaviors*" [emphasis in the original]."[15] That is where Obamacare failed—it expected individuals, especially the young and healthy, to buy more expensive insurance out of a sense of social responsibility.

Ending or reforming failed government programs can be very successful, as Schuck points out in the case of airline deregulation and welfare reform under two liberal Democrats, Jimmy Carter and Bill Clinton. With deregulation, the prices of flights fell, routes expanded, and service improved. While the airlines have been through their ups and downs, including consolidations and security scares, deregulation of the skies has been a boom to the economy as a whole. And the Welfare Reform Act of 1996—much of which the Obama administration has now undone by removing work requirements—worked: "Almost every index of child well-being except obesity improved.... more are employed, and they are less poor than they were before the 1996 law."[16] But today's Left lobbies to add bureaucracy and remove accountability.

There is room for debate about government programs—but the Left suppresses that debate, ignoring the lessons of the past and casting opponents of government as hard-hearted or self-interested. Demonizing their opponents also makes it easier for those on the Left to abuse government powers to harass conservatives, journalists, and other critics.

In May 2013 it emerged that the Internal Revenue Service had been singling out applications for non-profit status by conservative groups and subjecting them to additional scrutiny and delay. Organizations that had the words "9/12," "Tea Party," and even "Patriot" were targeted. Though a few liberal groups were screened, they generally received the coveted non-profit status that makes the difference between fundraising success and failure. Conservative groups, however, were left hanging, and their activities ground to a halt—at the very time when they could have made a difference in the 2012 election.

When Congress first asked the IRS about reports of political targeting in 2012, IRS Commissioner Douglas Shulman denied them.[17] Yet Tea Party groups, pro-life groups, and other conservative organizations reported facing a battery of questions—such as what books the group discussed, what speakers attended meetings, and—most ominously—who their donors were. (In one case, the IRS passed confidential donor information about the National Organization for Marriage to the group's left-wing opponents.[18])

In May 2013, IRS official Lois Lerner revealed, through an answer to a planted question at a law conference, that the Department of the Treasury had investigated the targeting of conservative groups. In fact, the Obama administration was already aware of the abuse in mid-2012 but said nothing.[19] Presumably, doing so would have caused a public outcry, and perhaps affected the result of the 2012 elections.

Meanwhile, the Obama re-election campaign had mobilized every liberal non-profit organization it could—including Organizing for Action, Obama's own 501(c)4, which the IRS had approved easily for non-profit status when it applied. And the grassroots army of the Tea Party movement had effectively been frozen, or demobilized. The *Wall Street Journal*'s James Taranto concluded, "The history books should record Obama's re-election with an asterisk to indicate that it was achieved with the help of illicit means."[20]

At first, the Obama administration purported to be shocked by the IRS scandal. President Obama described it as an "outrage" in May 2013.[21] That was enough to dissuade the media from asking questions about White House involvement. Yet by December, Obama felt bold enough to mock the scandal: "suddenly everybody's outraged."[22] Worse yet, Lerner escaped any punishment, even when she failed—blaming a hard drive failure—to produce emails that Congress had demanded. And the IRS continued to stonewall Congress. There were calls for the impeachment of new IRS Commissioner John Koskinen.

The IRS scandal highlighted the potential for abuse of power by the executive. And there are many other agencies with vastly expanded powers that can be abused—at times in open defiance of Congress.

The Environmental Protection Agency (EPA) is the most notorious. It has attempted to not only to regulate greenhouse gases, but also to redesign the nation's electricity grid—all without a mandate in legislation passed by the people's representatives in Congress. Legal challenges to the EPA's Clean Power Plan are still winding their way through the courts, but the Supreme Court granted a stay in February 2016 against the regulations, which face serious constitutional challenges.[23] As

Harvard's Laurence Tribe—a progressive and early teacher of environmental law—opined in the *Wall Street Journal*:

> The Clean Power Plan would set a carbon dioxide emission target for every state, and the EPA would command each state, within roughly a year, to come up with a package of laws to meet that target. If the agency approves the package, the state would then have to impose those laws on electric utilities and the public.
>
> ...But such federal commandeering of state governments defeats political accountability and violates principles of federalism that are basic to our constitutional order.
>
> Even more fundamentally, the EPA, like every administrative agency, is constitutionally forbidden to exercise powers Congress never delegated to it in the first place. The brute fact is that the Obama administration failed to get climate legislation through Congress. Yet the EPA is acting as though it has the legislative authority anyway to re-engineer the nation's electric generating system and power grid. It does not.[24]

The Left defends such power grabs by citing good intentions. Such is the case with "Net Neutrality," the new policy through which the Federal Communications Commission (FCC) supposedly will equalize Internet access between the rich and poor.

Net Neutrality became the pet cause of Silicon Valley billionaires, many of whom remain fashionably left-wing despite their enormous success in a capitalist—and largely unregulated—industry. Ostensibly, Net Neutrality is needed to prevent Internet service providers (ISPs) from slowing or blocking data for those paying less for bandwidth. But without differential pricing, there is no way for private companies to recoup investment in the physical infrastructure that makes the Internet work.

What the Silicon Valley lobbyists promised was "smart" regulation. What the FCC delivered, instead, was a decision to regulate the Internet as a public utility—like an old, stodgy telephone monopoly—under Title

II of the Communications Act of 1934. Predictably, as a result, "major ISPs reduced capital expenditure by an average of 12%, while the overall industry average dropped 8%" in the policy's wake, the *Wall Street Journal* reported.[25]

The Silicon Valley leftists advocating Net Neutrality had trouble understanding that the kind of government intrusion they resented in some areas—surveillance, for example—could be so destructive of their own industry. It seems that the Left is very effective at hiding the truth about government excess—from even itself.

To many on the Left—especially Millennials raised after the Cold War, who were taught little about what we fought for, and why—the idea that "only government" can provide may seem quite natural. Yet it contradicts the very founding principles of America.

Some on the Left actually understand that, and insist that the election of 2008 was indeed a mandate to "fundamentally transform" America. On the other hand, many Americans who supported Obama—including many liberals—naively did so in the belief that he intended to restore stability to a struggling system, not to introduce new shocks and radical changes.

Some conservatives saw the Obama's "only government" speech before his inauguration, which we looked at at the beginning of this chapter, as a confirmation of their suspicions about his true left-wing agenda. To more sympathetic observers, though, the "only government" argument did not appear to be so radical—it seemed to fit in with Americans' common understanding of economic history, shaped by the ideas of John Maynard Keynes.

Keynes believed that prolonged economic depressions were caused by self-reinforcing drops in aggregate demand. Thus only government had the ability to borrow and to spend enough to boost aggregate demand and shock the economy out of its slump. But in his "government only" argument, Obama was not referring solely to the extreme circumstances of economic depression: he applied the "only government" principle to job creation and "long-term growth," not just to rescuing the economy from the brink. Keynes would never have accepted the idea that government ought to be the prime factor in the economy, with the private sector secondary.

In any case, if "only government" can save us in emergency situations, what is to prevent government from demanding control in other circumstances? Will government recognize the economic liberty of citizens if it believes they owe it their very survival?

In security matters, the government certainly is the only source of salvation. But that is why the Constitution includes provisions to prevent the extraordinary powers of the government in wartime from hanging over into peacetime. The much-neglected Third Amendment prevents the forcible quartering of soldiers in citizens' homes except in times of war, for example. And the Second Amendment is the ultimate bulwark against tyranny.

Fundamentally, what Obama's argument misses is that the Founders believed that even in extreme circumstances—such as John Locke's "state of nature"—individuals would be able to provide for themselves, and each other. The reason for creating government in the first place was not to provide for basic economic needs, but to secure economic gains within an impartial system of justice.

The left-wing worldview is not only socialist but also highly paternalistic. It presumes that human beings are in fact unable to provide for themselves, or even to act in common, without the power of the state to guide them. It is an authoritarian mentality masked in the guise of liberation.

If we want to find examples of the problems that Obama's "only government" philosophy creates, we need not revisit communist Europe or the stagnant statist economies in the post-colonial world. We need only look at areas of the U.S. where Democrats have been given free rein to promote the "only government" ideal.

These include, first of all, our nation's cities, most of which have been run exclusively by Democrats for generations. The federal, state, and local governments have pumped untold billions of dollars into the cities with little to show for it. Urban Americans are more dependent on government than ever, the prospect of reducing government assistance evokes horror, but the cities remain mired in poverty, crime, and every other kind of dysfunction.

Native American communities are another example. In many places, the paternalistic role of the federal government—established by treaty and reinforced by liberalism—has made distant Washington, D.C., the main driver of community life on Indian reservations. The result, for many tribes, is continued dependence, generation after generation— despite the public perception of casino wealth.

In the inner city and on the reservation, the problem is that increasing the government's powers, even with the best of intentions, tends to institutionalize its control and to erode the self-governing habits necessary for the cultivation of liberty, or for the creation of the prosperity that the rest of America increasingly take for granted. As Alexis de Tocqueville noted nearly two centuries ago, centralized power cannot coexist with freedom or private wealth.

That is not to say that traditional liberal (or libertarian) philosophy would exclude the possibility that government might play an important role in times of crisis. As even F. A. Hayek admitted, "It may well be true that the most effective method of providing against certain risks common to all citizens of a state is to give every citizen protection against those risks."[26]

Hayek was perhaps referring to large, calamitous events, such as natural disasters, and not to general economic malaise. Regardless, what Hayek rejected is that *only* government can perform that role. The notion that "only government" can provide *in extremis* has been twisted by the Left into the idea that only government ought to provide in general.

The debate over the size and role of government in our society is the essential controversy at the heart of our politics. When allowed to develop freely and openly, that debate creates a useful and productive tension—one that encourages healthy competition as well as compromise. But in the service of asserting vastly expanded government powers, the Obama administration has suppressed its critics, inadvertently proving true one of the main arguments against expanding the centralized power of the state.

Giving the government—even, and especially, a government that proclaims its good intentions—too much power creates temptations for abuse, whether that power is provided to fight a terrorist threat or to revive a struggling economy. There must be safeguards against government power, or else that power will live on well past emergencies—which is exactly what some, especially on the Left, intend. They hide the dangers of government power from the public, and from themselves, under the shroud of good intentions.

Those who claim to use the immense powers of government for good are capable of using those powers to repress those who doubt their motives and draw attention to their failures. Thus the abuses of the Obama administration will come fully to light only belatedly, when the present abusers of government power no longer hold its reins in their hands.

# CHAPTER 12

# WAR

## THE LIE:
## War doesn't achieve anything; we should never resort to force.

Examples:

*"We don't need a surge of troops in Iraq—we need a surge of diplomacy and politics. Every knowledgeable person who has examined the Iraq situation for the past several years—Baker and Hamilton, senior military officials, junior officers—has drawn the same conclusion—there is no military solution in Iraq. To insist upon a surge is wrong."[1]*
—Senator Christopher Dodd, Des Moines, Iowa, April 2007

*"Obama has as President created a new climate in international politics. Multilateral diplomacy has regained a central position, with emphasis on the role that the United*

*Nations and other international institutions can play. Dia-*
*logue and negotiations are preferred as instruments for*
*resolving even the most difficult international conflicts.*"[2]

—Nobel Prize Committee, October 2009

*"It is really a stunning willful choice by President Putin*
*to invade another country. Russia is in violation of the*
*sovereignty of Ukraine. Russia is in violation of its inter-*
*national obligations. Russia is in violation of its obligations*
*under the U.N. Charter, under the Helsinki Final Act. It's a*
*violation of its obligations under the 1994 Budapest Agree-*
*ment. You just don't in the twenty-first century behave in*
*nineteenth-century fashion by invading another country on*
*completely trumped up pretext.*"[3]

—Secretary of State John Kerry, CBS News's *Face the Nation*,
March 2, 2014

# THE TRUTH:
## Only if we are willing to go to war can we have peace.

Among the many debates truncated by the Left's suppression of the
truth, the debate over American foreign policy has suffered the most—
with the most serious consequences.

We have, as the Left is wont to remind us, the world's largest and
most powerful military—and yet the idea of using it to protect American
interests or allies is now almost politically impossible. Because war is
never an option, at least to many of our current leaders, the only real
choices available are surrender or compromise—on increasingly worse
terms over time.

In December 2015, for example, as the Western world attempted to respond to terror attacks by the so-called Islamic State (ISIS, ISIL, or "Daesh"), Shepard Smith of Fox News voiced a widely shared skepticism about using America's military power: "I remember hearing, you know, not that very long ago that, you know, we'd be greeted as liberators, and that this was going to work out just great, and weapons of mass destruction and yellowcake from Niger. And every time we take another step it seems like we're doing something—the moderate rebels in Syria, who were going to fight and win this, and there turned out to be a grand total of zero of them. You just wonder when all of this rhetoric that turns out to mean nothing—zero boots on the ground, no troops, not going to go do what ISIS wants, you wonder when that will all come together and America will go, 'You keep not telling us the truth and you keep sending our men home dead by the thousands.' When at some point do we go we need a real strategy here that doesn't involve what ISIS demands?"[4]

For fear of doing "what ISIS demands"—going to war with them—the nation's media and political elite seemed prepared to allow ISIS to continue beheading Americans. For fear of war, the country's leaders are prepared to live with increasing terror.

It should be stipulated at the outset that American governments, whether Democratic or Republican, have rarely excelled at strategic thinking in national security and foreign policy. Separated from the tumult of the world by two oceans, and focused on "Manifest Destiny" rather than imperial conquest, Americans are traditionally insular. We are willing to fight and die for distant people in faraway lands, but it is telling that many of our best strategic thinkers—Henry Kissinger, for instance—have their origins abroad.

Since the end of the Cold War, the pattern of each new administration has been to reverse the policies of the old. The result has been incoherent policy and unstable leadership. After nearly eight years of war under George W. Bush, for instance, Barack Obama has been determined to avoid a war—or, at least, avoid winning one.

The specter of the Iraq War still hangs over American politics. While the experience of the Vietnam War created skepticism about war in general, the legacy of Iraq has been skepticism about American leadership. Ironically, the U.S.-led coalition not only won the Iraq War but stabilized the country after a difficult occupation.

But the story the Left tells about the Iraq war is that Bush lied to the world about the Iraq's weapons of mass destruction (WMD), then exploited Americans' fears of terrorism to prod the country into an ill-advised war that was at least partly aimed at benefiting business interests close to the administration, and pushed by a coterie of "neo-conservatives" obsessed with helping Israel.

It was certainly a "war of choice," and yet war was inevitable unless we wanted to allow Saddam Hussein to defy the United Nations. It was Bill Clinton who had first embraced regime change in Iraq. Bush, ironically, came into office looking for a different option. On September 11, 2001, everything changed: politically, as well as strategically, the president could not afford the risk of a nuclear-armed dictator in Iraq.

Former Pentagon official Douglas Feith recalled that the Bush administration considered an attack on Iraq immediately after 9/11. "One of the reasons for including Iraq...was to call attention to the danger of weapons of mass destruction and the fact that key states that support terrorism were also interested in WMD.... Important as the Iraq problem had been beforehand, it looked graver and more urgent after 9/11."[5] Though the president decided not to confront Iraq at that time, the potential threat Iraq posed to the U.S. remained.

Even Secretary of Defense Donald Rumsfeld regarded war with Iraq "as a last resort," Feith writes, yet "it was not clear that we had an effective alternative."[6] Bush's moment of decision came after Saddam defied the United Nations in December 2002, refusing to comply with international inspections and resolutions: "War would be risky.... But leaving Saddam in power would be risky, too. Reasonable people differed then, and differ now, on whether war was the right choice."[7]

What was missing was a grasp of the tactical difficulty of rebuilding Iraq, and of the strategic consequences of a power vacuum in the heart of the Middle East, which would tempt Iran's regional ambitions. Amazingly, despite those mistakes, and against objections from Democrats and some military leaders, Bush launched a "surge" in Iraq that defeated a terrorist insurgency and restored American deterrent power and even some diplomatic credibility.

The Iraq surge ranks among the most astonishing successes in recent American military history. Behind it was a simple tactical idea: the U.S. had invaded with too few troops to maintain order. By committing resources to the fight, the U.S could not only defeat terrorists in battle, but also win the trust of the Sunni Arabs, once they understood that America was in Iraq to stay.

Al Qaeda had advanced in Iraq after Saddam Hussein fell partly because of a sense among the Sunni population that the new Shiite-dominated Iraq threatened their security, which had been protected to at least some extent by the Baathist regime. Iran's support for Shiite militias heightened those fears and brought the country to the precipice of a bloody religious civil war. Terrorists swarmed to the country, convinced that it was the ultimate battlefield against the infidel West, while Iran backed even some Sunni terrorists in an effort to make life difficult for the U.S.

Though many Democrats had supported the initial invasion, the party's solution to the challenges of rebuilding was complete withdrawal from Iraq. Then-senator Joe Biden of Delaware proposed partitioning the country into ethnic zones. The glaring flaw of both these plans is that they would have condemned Iraq to civil war and genocide. They also would have signified a major American defeat in the War on Terror.

So Bush committed more troops, instead of withdrawing. And in a striking—and rare—display of political acumen, he convinced Democrats, who had just retaken Congress in the fall of 2006, not to stop the Surge, even as the party's leaders continued to insist that the war had been a failure.

The result was a dramatic drop in casualties, both military and civilian, in Iraq. The surge also prompted the "Sunni Awakening," a decision by local Sunni Arab leaders to side with the U.S. and reject Al-Qaeda. Democrats refused to give the surge credit even for that victory. Obama actually argued that Sunnis had decided "after the Democrats were elected in 2006, you know what, the Americans may be leaving soon, and we are going to be left very vulnerable to the Shi'as." In fact the U.S. military presence was the key to shifting Sunni opinion. It was only in September 2008 that Obama was willing to acknowledge that the surge had "succeeded beyond our wildest dreams."[8] By then Iraq was no longer the defining issue of the presidential campaign.

The Left refused to admit the surge had worked, for political reasons: Obama's opponent, John McCain, had backed it. And in any case, many Democrats had a dogged commitment to the idea that war is never, or rarely, the solution. That belief would define the military policies of the Obama administration.

What was curious about Obama's condemnation of the war was how hollow it was. In the race for the nomination he challenged then-senator Hillary Clinton on the basis of her vote to authorize the invasion of Iraq. He had opposed the war, he said—though he never had the opportunity to vote on it, and his speech at a Chicago anti-war rally in 2002 had to be re-staged for a campaign advertisement, since no full recording of it seemed to exist.[9]

And after his election, caught between the idealism of progressive anti-war sentiment, and the duties of Commander-in-Chief, Obama led half-hearted war efforts that achieved little, and eroded the philosophical basis of his own opposition to military action.

In Libya, for example, Obama went to war without the required authorization from Congress, under the banner of a new theory called "Responsibility to Protect"—the idea that war is justified in order to save civilian populations from atrocities. Given Republican deference to the military, Obama probably could have obtained the necessary authorization. Instead, he relied on resolutions of the UN Security Council and the Arab League to provide legitimacy for military action, while ignoring Congress entirely. This was a flip-flop for Obama, and also for State Department legal adviser Harold Koh, who as dean of the Yale Law School had protested George W. Bush's use of executive powers in the war on terror. Now, Koh advised Obama that he did not have to obtain congressional authorization under the 1973 War Powers Resolution because the U.S. was not engaged in "hostilities"—even as it was bombing Muammar Gaddafi's regime.

Koh's former colleagues were aghast. "Where is the Harold Koh I worked with to ensure that international law, human rights and the Constitution were honored during the Bush years?" one protested.[10] But President Obama followed along, writing to Congress that he did not have to end U.S. involvement in the war after sixty days, as required by law when Congress has not authorized military action, because the U.S. had already handed control over to NATO and was merely playing "a supporting role in the coalition's efforts."[11]

Obama's inattention to Congress was matched only by his inattention to Libya itself, where the chaotic fall of Gaddafi's regime unleashed terrorist bands across North Africa. When terrorists attacked the U.S. consulate compound in Benghazi on September 11, 2012, Obama showed little interest in exercising the executive power he had so jealously defended the year before. After a briefing by defense officials early in the evening, Obama took little notice of the events in Benghazi. He went to bed and flew to Las Vegas for a campaign fundraiser the next day.

Obama shredded what was left of his philosophical consistency on the question of U.S. military interventions a year later, in making the case for limited air strikes against Syria. Initially the Obama administration, and Democrats in general, considered Syrian dictator Bashar al-Assad a "reformer," as Secretary of State Hillary Clinton put it.[12] In the waning months of the Bush administration, several leading Democrats made pilgrimages to Damascus to meet with Assad and to show a contrast with Bush's more aggressive posture toward the Syrian regime.

But Assad proved himself a mass murderer. So in 2012 Obama warned of military action against the dictator if he crossed the "red line" and used chemical weapons—but when Assad did, Obama did nothing.

Stung by criticism of his inaction, Obama began to prepare the way for war. Ironically, the justification his administration used was *exactly* the justification the Bush administration had used for going to war in Iraq without UN Security Council approval. UN Ambassador Samantha

Power tried to explain the administration's posture to National Public Radio:

> INSKEEP: So let me just make sure that I'm clear on this. You're saying that something needs to be done and it is time to go outside the legal system, outside the legal framework. You believe it is right to do something that is just simply not legal.
>
> POWER: In the cases of—we've seen in the past, there are times when there is a patron like Syria backed by Russia. We saw this in Kosovo as well, where it was just structurally impossible to get meaningful international action through the Security Council. And yet, in this case, you have the grave breach of such a critical international norm in terms of the ban on chemical weapons use, it is very important that the international community act so as to prevent further use.[13]

The only difference between Bush's plan for Iraq and Obama's plan for Syria was that Bush won Congress's approval—and that Bush was intent on succeeding.

Two years later, Obama would send special forces to Syria after all, to fight the so-called Islamic State, while telling the nation there were no "boots on the ground." This was not a lie so much as a semantic dodge: "boots on the ground"[14] typically refers to combat divisions, though the public could be forgiven for thinking the presence of *any* ground troops qualified. It was an example of Obama's preference for special operations forces, which had been heroically successful in the raid on Osama bin Laden's compound in May 2011. But special operations could only achieve limited tactical objectives, not broader strategic aims—and that is where Obama's deep leftist philosophical resistance to war remained solid. The results were often catastrophic.

In Iraq, for example, Obama famously withdrew all U.S. forces by 2011, far earlier than military leaders had wanted, and despite warnings, later fulfilled, that Iraq was not read to handle its own security.

In 2009, he had ordered a "surge" of his own into Afghanistan—after months of dithering, and sending far fewer troops than the military said it needed. Crucially, he set a timeline for withdrawal—satisfying anti-war Democrats, but undermining confidence in the mission. As American casualties mounted in Afghanistan, Obama began to look for an exit, going so far as to release five senior Taliban commanders from Guantánamo Bay in exchange for an American deserter, hoping to speed negotiations—without telling Congress in advance, as required by law.

That was just one example of Obama's flouting existing laws and constitutional restraints on the president's powers in war—and in diplomacy. On Libya, as we have seen, Obama flouted the War Powers Resolution. On Iran, he did far worse, flouting the Treaty Clause of the Constitution itself.

Article II, Section 2, Clause 2 of the Constitution provides, "The President ... shall have Power, by and with the Advice and Consent of the Senate, to make Treaties, provided two thirds of the Senators present concur...." President Obama was fully capable of passing treaties—even controversial ones—with Republican votes. In late 2010, for example, the Senate ratified the New START treaty with Russia, despite concerns that its nuclear cuts were one-sided in Russia's favor, and despite worries that Russia would interpret the treaty as a ban on future U.S. deployment of missile defense systems—which it did, almost immediately.

But when the president pursued a nuclear deal with Iran, he avoided the Senate entirely. Obama had been set on negotiations with Iran long before he became president, when he vowed to meet its leaders "without preconditions."[15] In 2009, when pro-democracy protesters rose up against the Iranian regime, Obama did nothing to help them, believing that the goodwill that the lack of American intervention built with the regime would help bring it to the negotiating table. And throughout his presidency, he resisted sanctions on Iran—sanctions for which he would take credit.

Obama began secret talks with the regime as early as 2011, then began public negotiations with the announcement of an interim deal in November 2013. Not only did the deal flout existing UN Security

Resolutions—supposedly Obama's standard of legality—by allowing Iran some nuclear enrichment, but it contained a cascade of concessions to the Iranian regime. The promise of "anywhere, anytime" inspections; the promise of full disclosure of the possible military dimensions of Iran's nuclear program; the promise to stop Iran's ballistic missile development—all were broken.

That was likely why Obama sought to avoid the Senate: he knew the Iran deal could not possibly be ratified. So instead he sought to classify it not as a treaty but as an "executive agreement"—the sort of government-to-government understanding typically used for minor matters.

Democrats offered no resistance to Obama's blatant usurpation of the Senate's constitutional powers. And instead of resisting, Republicans offered a half-measure: the Iran Nuclear Agreement Review Act, a.k.a. the "Corker bill." The legislation provided that the Iran deal had to be reviewed by both houses of Congress, effectively lowering the threshold for passage to a simple majority—and to one-third, if Obama's vetoed Congress's rejection of the deal. Obama first threatened to veto the Corker bill, then let it become law, and finally never had to abide by even its flimsy limits on his power: Senate Democrats filibustered the Iran deal, allowing Obama to implement an "executive agreement" unilaterally that—by his own admission—allowed Iran to begin openly developing nuclear weapons in as little as a decade.

What was so striking about the debate over the Iran deal was that Obama accused its *critics* of colluding with the enemy. "It's those hard-liners chanting 'Death to America' who have been most opposed to the deal. They're making common cause with the Republican caucus," he said in a speech at American University, to laughter and applause from the audience of students.[16]

Rarely had a President of the United States made such an incendiary accusation about the political opposition. Aside from the inaccuracy of the attack—the chants of "Death to America" were led by high officials of the Iranian regime itself, with which Obama had just forged the deal—what was striking was Obama's callous disregard for civility.

Obama declined opportunities to climb down from his accusation, telling friendly CNN interviewer Fareed Zakaria, "What I said is absolutely true, factually."[17] It would not be the last time Obama made such a claim. In November 2015, amidst concerns that terrorists might infiltrate refugee populations, as several had done in Europe, Obama excoriated Republicans—from abroad—for resisting the resettlement of Syrian refugees in the U.S., calling their rhetoric a "potent recruitment tool" for the so-called Islamic State.[18]

Obama has repeatedly accused critics of his foreign policy of wanting war. As he said in his blistering speech at American University on Iran: "Now, when I ran for President eight years ago as a candidate who had opposed the decision to go to war in Iraq, I said that America didn't just have to end that war—we had to end the mindset that got us there in the first place." That "mindset" included "a preference for military action over diplomacy," he said, among other faults, and had led the world to disastrous stalemate in Iraq.

The problem with Obama's argument is that the result of his diplomacy were consistently poor. His "reset" with Russia led to America's unilateral abandonment of missile defense systems in Europe that had been painstakingly negotiated with Poland and the Czech Republic—and to Russia's invasion of Ukraine and annexation of Crimea. Obama's push for Israeli-Palestinian peace, including continual calls for new Israeli concessions, merely emboldened Palestinians to make more extreme demands and alienated Israelis. His efforts to achieve global agreements on climate change led to deals that were cosmetic at best. The Iran deal was the nadir—negotiated even as Iran imprisoned innocent Americans and led chants of "Death to America."

The sad irony about the Left's preference for diplomacy is that unless America's enemies believe it is willing and capable to go to war American diplomacy is essentially worthless. By signaling to America's rivals that he would rather accept any agreement—or any retreat—rather than go to war, Obama ensured constant diplomatic humiliation.

And, in fact, that appeared to be the goal. Obama seemed to accept America's role in the world grudgingly. In 2010 he said that America needed to be involved in conflict resolution, because "whether we like it or not, we remain a dominant military superpower, and when conflicts break out, one way or another we get pulled into them."[19]

McCain, his opponent from 2008, retorted: "We are the dominant superpower, and we're the greatest force for good in the history of this country, and I thank God every day that we are a dominant super-power."[20]

The Left's hostility to war is not simply a reaction to the horrors of war; it reflects an ambivalence about American leadership—and America itself. In 2008 McCain pointed out that Obama never used the word "victory" when describing America's wars abroad.[21] "Victory" grates on the Left—because many progressives do not believe that America has the moral standing to lead and win.

Ironically, one of the most coherent defenses of the use of force was provided by the president himself, in his speech accepting the Nobel Peace Prize in 2009, an award that was almost laughably premature given that Obama had not yet spent a year in office. Obama noted that "the most profound issue surrounding my receipt of this prize is the fact that I am the Commander-in-Chief of the military of a nation in the midst of two wars." Though he had opposed one of those wars—the word "Iraq" did not appear once in his speech—he defended military strength in principle: "There will be times when nations—acting individually or in concert—will find the use of force not only necessary but morally justified…. I face the world as it is, and cannot stand idle in the face of threats to the American people."[22]

And yet in the face of *actual* threats and attacks—such as the beheadings of Americans by the so-called Islamic State—Obama was reluctant to send more than a token force to defend the American people. In facing the danger of a nuclear-armed Iran, which vowed "Death to America" and tested ballistic missiles even *after* the Iran deal in defiance of the UN Security Council, Obama refused to use sanctions, let alone military force. His defense of "just war" was a purely rhetorical one, not backed by any real commitment. It suggested that he knew what was right but chose to do the opposite—meanwhile avoiding honest debate and accusing his critics of wanting war and colluding with the enemy.

War is not the only or even the primary tool of foreign policy. Yet unless America can wage war effectively, much of what we take for granted about our world—the rapid advance in prosperity, the relative freedom of movement and communication—would not exist. Liberty has constant enemies, and power has constant rivals.

As Leon Trotsky is reported to have said, "You may not be interested in war, but war is interested in you." That remains the truth of our world, and in the end we will not be able to avoid the obvious conclusion: that we must be prepared to fight for what we value.

# PART III

# SUPPRESSING TRUTH

# CHAPTER 13

# ISLAM

## THE LIE:
## Islam has nothing to do with terror.

Examples:

*"What's the famous saying about local newscasts, right? If it bleeds, it leads, right? You show crime stories and you show fires, because that's what folks watch, and it's all about ratings. And, you know, the problems of terrorism and dysfunction and chaos, along with plane crashes and a few other things, that's the equivalent when it comes to covering international affairs."*[1]

—President Barack Obama, interview with Vox, February 2015

*"They kill anybody who isn't them and doesn't pledge to be that. And they carry with them the greatest public display of misogyny that I've ever seen, not to mention a false claim regarding Islam. It has nothing to do with Islam; it has*

*everything to do with criminality, with terror, with abuse,
with psychopathism—I mean, you name it."[2]*

—Secretary of State John Kerry, U.S. Embassy in Paris,
November 2015

*"If it's county employees having some type of a banquet
there, that takes on more of a domestic militia group, an
anti-government domestic militia group wanting to attack
the government than it does international terrorism where
they're usually on suicide mission."[3]*

—CNN analyst Tom Fuentes, December 2, 2015

# THE TRUTH:
## Unless we can name and fight the enemy, we are condemned to lose.

On December 2, 2015, a county employee in San Bernardino, California left an office holiday party, quietly. He returned with his wife—both of them armed to the teeth—and opened fire.

Before fleeing, Syed Farook and Tashfeen Malik had killed fourteen of the colleagues who had thrown Malik a baby shower just months before, and wounded twenty-one more.

During their terror spree, Malik posted a message to Facebook under an alias, pledging allegiance to the so-called caliph of the Islamic State, the terrorist fiefdom occupying parts of Iraq, Syria, and Libya.

In early reporting, however, the media described the shooting as a likely attack on the town's Planned Parenthood abortion clinic—even though that facility was over a mile away. Later, analysts speculated that the perpetrators were part of an anti-government "domestic militia."[4] Democratic presidential candidates tweeted about gun control. President

Barack Obama mused about yet another mass shooting; he would talk about possible "workplace violence" for days.

And yet by the first day's end, it was clear to anyone who wasn't committed to the administration's spin that the attack had been an act of radical Islamic terrorism. Forty-eight hours after the first shots were fired, the Federal Bureau of Investigation (FBI) finally classified it as such.

It was not the first time the Left had minimized the threat of radical Islam. Earlier in 2015, Muslim terrorists attacked the offices of *Charlie Hebdo*, a satirical French weekly, in Paris, killing ten people and a police officer. Two days later, radical Islamists attacked a kosher market, taking hostages and killing four people.

Much of the Western world recoiled in horror. But the Europe editor of the *Financial Times* felt that *Charlie Hebdo* had it coming. In an article that was later retracted and deleted, he said the newspaper's cartoons had been "stupid."[5] President Barack Obama declined to join other world leaders at a rally in Paris. He described the killings at the kosher market as "random," as if radical Islamists had not singled out a Jewish target.[6] He refused—as he had throughout his presidency—even to utter the phrase "radical Islam."

The Left's effort to deny the reality and danger of radical Islam goes far beyond the trite observation that not every Muslim is a terrorist, and not every terrorist is a Muslim—ignoring the plain connections among countless terror attacks worldwide.

Some try to defend the denial on strategic grounds. Hillary Clinton, for example, has said that she declines to use the phrase "radical Islam" because it could offend Muslims, who might then become more outraged. In an extraordinary exchange with former Clinton White House aide George Stephanopoulos on ABC News' *This Week*, she elaborated:

> STEPHANOPOULOS: ... You've also been reluctant to say we're fighting radical Islam. And I wonder why not. Isn't it a mistake not to say it plain, that the violence is being pushed by radical elements in that faith?

CLINTON: Well, that's a different thing. Radical elements who use a dangerous and distorted view of Islam to promote their jihadist ambitions, I'm fine with that. I say it all the time and I go after Islamic, too.

STEPHANOPOULOS: So what's the problem with "radical Islam"?

CLINTON: Well, the problem is that that sounds like we are declaring war against a religion....[7]

The many Muslims who are the primary victims of radical Islam would beg to differ.

The problem with the Left's denial is more than semantic. It means that the United States and much of the West simply refuse to understand the origins of the threat and are failing to fight against it in the realm of ideas. Instead our government is willfully, needlessly blind to the extremism being preached in some of our mosques and spirited across our borders.

The denial about radical Islam is an example of the third and most egregious category of cases in which the left suppresses the truth: those issues on which the left is completely wrong and simply wishes to hide the truth. The most the Left is willing to allow is that radical Islam is a response to the West's colonialism, imperialism, and oppression.

This denial is built on a deep foundation—a belief that there is no absolute right or wrong, that the West's values are not inherently superior; that freedom is not worth defending. Ironically, by avoiding the challenge of radical Islam, so-called "liberals" are accepting a kind of intolerance that is fatal to liberalism itself.

Clinton's assumption that radical Islam is indistinguishable from the religion itself is not what many Muslims believe—but it is what radical Muslims proclaim.

There are essentially three defining features of radical Islam. The most obvious feature is its method: violence, directed against innocent people. Another is its utopian vision, hearkening back to the Islamic caliphates of the medieval era, which radical Muslims wish to recreate and to expand. The third feature is a sense of urgency—one common to many millenarian cults, but which, when combined with its violent tactics and fantasies of conquest, gives radical Islam a particularly deadly potency.

Some Western critics agree that radical Islam is inseparable from the faith itself. Their argument goes beyond quoting inflammatory passages in the Qur'an—for which there are often parallels in the Bible—to the nature of Islamic law and civilization. Against these arguments stand the examples of societies in which Muslims have been able to live relatively peacefully, and to coexist with people of other faiths, for centuries.

Regardless, the danger of radical Islam *exists*, and it is a global challenge. Opinion surveys repeatedly demonstrate that while only a minority of Muslims are radicals, it is a significant minority—and one whose beliefs are often supported by the majority. Oppression of women is nearly universal in the Muslim world—not just dress codes, but female genital mutilation, honor killings, and kidnappings are widespread. These practices even continue quietly within insular immigrant communities in the West. And despite the hostility to women— and gays, and other non-Muslims—the Left still refuses even to name the problem.

Rather than acknowledge radical Islam, the Left tries to deny that it exists—and to silence and shame those who recognize it. One of the most egregious cases is that of Ayaan Hirsi Ali. Born in Somalia and raised in Kenya, she fled from an arranged marriage and sought refugee status in the Netherlands. There, Hirsi Ali quickly assimilated to European culture and eventually became one of that country's most prominent politicians, playing a leading role in criticizing the insular Islamic culture imported by many recent immigrants, which is ill at ease with liberal Dutch mores.

Eventually, Hirsi Ali's criticism of Islam attracted the attention of Muslim extremists, who targeted her and a filmmaker with whom she had worked, Theo van Gogh, who was eventually murdered. The weak response of the Dutch government prompted Ali to emigrate to the United States, where she has continued her activism, writing several books about Islam and feminism.

In the spring of 2014, Brandeis University, originally founded as a haven for Jews who suffered discrimination in the Ivy League, invited her to deliver its commencement address and accept an honorary degree. It was a timely honor, given the recent advance of the Islamic State terror group and its subjugation, enslavement, and rape of non-Muslim women.

And then, suddenly, Hirsi Ali was disinvited and her honorary degree was rescinded. The reason: her large oeuvre of writings critical of Islam had triggered a protest from within the university. The administration announced, "[W]e cannot overlook certain of her past statements that are inconsistent with Brandeis University's core values."[8]

It was a total shock to Hirsi Ali. "What was initially intended as an honor has now devolved into a moment of shaming," she said.[9] Instead of delivering her remarks at Brandeis, Hirsi Ali published them in the *Wall Street Journal*, urging the West to take the challenge of Islamic fundamentalism more seriously: "We need to make our universities temples not of dogmatic orthodoxy, but of truly critical thinking, where all ideas are welcome and where civil debate is encouraged...."[10]

The Left did not see it that way: Hirsi Ali was only one of many critics of Islam to suffer "disinvitation."

And while President Obama offered occasional rebukes to political correctness on campus, his official policy was not just to deny radical Islam but also to punish its critics.

In 2009, the Obama administration joined the Egyptian government of Hosni Mubarak in sponsoring a supposed "free speech" resolution that preserved the ability of Islamic states to criminalize criticism of their faith. In 2012, while radical Islamists were attacking the U.S. embassy in Cairo on the anniversary of 9/11, the Obama administration tweeted criticism of an obscure anti-Islamic video on YouTube, appearing to blame American blasphemy for the attack. The administration would go on to blame the same video, falsely, for the terror attack on the U.S. consulate in Benghazi, Libya later that night—even though Secretary of State Hillary Clinton's own emails, revealed by a congressional investigation, demonstrate clearly that she knew better.

Nevertheless, in the days that followed the Benghazi attack, President Obama continued to talk about the video, telling the UN General Assembly, "The future must not belong to those who slander the prophet of Islam."[11] Mollie Hemingway of The Federalist, a conservative website, responded: "The problem of such cowardly rhetoric in the face of Islamist violence certainly didn't begin with President Obama and Hillary Clinton but they should be called to account for their tepid defense of free speech and freedom of the press."[12]

They were not called to account. And in 2015, after the San Bernardino attacks, Attorney General Loretta Lynch went even further, reassuring American Muslims that she would prosecute criticism of Islam that "edges towards violence,"[13] in blatant contradiction of Americans' First Amendment right to free speech.

Obama's adherence to the leftist line on radical Islam in spite of so many attacks is a novelty for the U.S. government. President Jimmy Carter tried to reconcile with the Iranian regime after the Islamic Revolution, but stopped that initiative when Americans were taken hostage. George W. Bush reassured Americans that Islam is a "religion of peace," but he insisted that Muslims choose sides: "Either you are with us, or you are with the terrorists."[14] In contrast, Obama pretended that radical Islamic terror did not exist. While he continued and expanded Bush's policy of using drones to target terrorists, Obama's overall theory was that Muslim extremists could best be managed by integrating them into the normal political life of their countries—perhaps on the Turkish model, where an Islamist party took power and adopted pro-market policies (alongside politically repressive ones).

To that end, Obama was determined to strip his rhetoric of anything that might possibly be construed as offensive to fundamentalist Islam— and to show that he understood the Islamic world's perspective. In an historic speech to the Muslim world in Cairo in June 2009, Obama recited a list of Muslim complaints about the West, saying that he had "come to seek a new beginning between the United States and the Muslim world."[15] He cut funding to pro-democracy groups and relaxed restrictions on banned Islamist organizations—such as Egypt's Muslim Brotherhood, specially invited to his speech.

Two years later, the Arab Spring had spread through the region. At first, Obama's instinct was to stand by the regimes he had appeased. He then flip-flopped and sided with the Muslim Brotherhood, which went on to win Egypt's 2012 elections. When the Brotherhood's illiberal rule provoked the biggest mass protests in human history, the Obama administration urged Egyptians not to rise up against their government; they ignored him. His Sunni outreach in tatters, Obama turned to the Shia regime of Iran. Meanwhile, the rise of the Islamic State underlined the complete failure of the the president's Middle East policy.

On the home front, Obama's attempts to appease the Muslim world coincided with an increase in radical Islamic terror attacks. Far from decreasing the radicals' appetite for violence, Obama's strategy arguably lowered America's defenses.

On his first day in office, for example, Obama signed an executive order directing that the prison at Guantánamo Bay, Cuba, be closed down within a year. Congress refused to appropriate funds for the transfer, since few Americans wanted the world's most dangerous terrorists on our home soil.

So the Obama administration sped up releases from the facility. Freed prisoners often returned to field of battle. And instead of bringing new terrorists to the prison, the administration either brought them to trial in the civilian court system, in which the government could not interrogate them for very long after their initial arrest, or simply killed them in the field.

When interrogations did take place, they did not involve the "enhanced interrogation techniques"—such as waterboarding—that the Bush administration had used, and that Obama called "torture." Obama had been eager to prosecute Bush-era interrogators, but an inquiry by the Department of Justice did little but damage morale.

The result of Obama's attempt to dismantle the legal and intelligence apparatus of the War on Terror was that the government failed to monitor suspected terrorists, and to extract information from terrorists once they were caught.

On Christmas Day 2009, for example, a young Islamic radical named Umar Farouk Abdulmutallab attempted to detonate explosives hidden in his underwear while on a Northwest Airlines flight from Amsterdam to Detroit. Initially, the administration claimed that he had acted alone; later, ties to international terrorism were found. But the administration's new interrogation team failed to question Abdulmutallab before he was read *Miranda* rights, allowing him to refuse to respond.

In 2010, another disaster was narrowly avoided when a bomb inside a car in Times Square failed to detonate. Again the Obama administration insisted that the bomber acted alone; again, he turned out to have been part of a larger conspiracy.

There seemed to be little interest in intelligence on terrorism. Four years after the successful raid on Osama bin Laden's compound in Abottabad, Pakistan, Fox News reported that the administration had analyzed only ten percent of the intelligence trove that the U.S. Navy Seals had found. After the Boston Marathon bombing in April 2013, it emerged that Russia had warned U.S. authorities about the Tsarnaev brothers, but the Obama administration had not acted on the intelligence.

While the government did stop several terror plots—including some that may remain unknown to the public—the sense of public vulnerability only continued to grow, reinforced by the president's lackadaisical attitude.

In November 2009, an Army psychiatrist named Nidal Hasan opened fire on fellow soldiers while shouting "Allahu Akbar!," killing thirteen and injuring thirty. It was the worst terrorist attack on U.S. soil since 9/11. But in his first opportunity to respond, President Obama, speaking at a meeting with Native American leaders, opened with jovial "shout-outs" to some of the gathered dignitaries before finally turning to the grave news.[16] In 2012, after learning of the Benghazi attacks, Obama did not maintain contact with his national security team. He let events unfold and headed to Las Vegas for a fundraiser the next morning.

The people who suffered most from Obama's refusal to recognize the threat of radical Islam were those whom he had left behind in his withdrawal from American leadership in the Middle East. In Iraq, Obama did almost nothing to save Christian communities—many of them centuries old—that had been overrun by the marauders of the Islamic State. U.S. forces intervened to help relieve the Yazidis—members of an ancient pre-Christian civilization—only after intense media coverage created public pressure on Obama to help. And the administration did woefully little to arm the pro-American Kurdish *peshmerga*—the only local force capable of taking the fight to the Islamic State. In Israel, the Obama administration was quick to condemn violence by Israelis against Palestinians, but slow to condemn far more frequent Islamist terror against Jews.

The most chilling example of Obama's attempt to suppress the reality of radical Islam came in February 2015, when the president addressed the National Prayer Breakfast. The Islamic State had just released a gruesome video of the execution of a Jordanian pilot who had been brought down over Syria. The desperate pilot was trapped in a cage and burned alive.

In his remarks, Obama said, "So how do we, as people of faith, reconcile these realities—the profound good, the strength, the tenacity, the compassion and love that can flow from all of our faiths, operating alongside those who seek to hijack religious for their own murderous ends?

"Humanity has been grappling with these questions throughout human history. And lest we get on our high horse and think this is unique to some other place, remember that during the Crusades and the Inquisition, people committed terrible deeds in the name of Christ."[17]

So the atrocities of the Crusades, centuries ago, were used to excuse the atrocities of radical Islam in the present day. Obama added, "In our home country, slavery and Jim Crow all too often was justified in the name of Christ"—as if Christianity had not been crucial to undoing both.

Obama's refusal to admit the danger of radical Islam was reflected by fellow Democrats—such as Secretary of State John Kerry, who produced troubadour James Taylor to comfort Parisians while declaring Islam had "nothing to do" with terror. Obama's denial created an impatience among the public that was exploited by businessman Donald Trump, who swiftly rose to the top of a crowded Republican presidential field by promising tough action on illegal immigration and, after the San Bernardino attack, caused a sensation by demanding an end to all Muslim immigration.

It was an audacious, offensive proposal (though it was not, as many of its left-wing detractors claimed, unconstitutional). Because Trump's proposed ban covered even tourists and visitors, it would have caused great damage to American trade, diplomacy, and even national security—given that the U.S. depends on foreign informants for intelligence about radical Islamists abroad. Yet it framed the threat of radical Islam in clear, if overly broad, terms. It was no answer to the problem—but it was more of a response than Democrats' opportunistic proposals for new gun control laws, or the repeated exhortations by the president and his cabinet not to indulge "Islamophobia" or anti-Muslim discrimination.

The truth about Muslim communities in the contemporary world is a mess of contradictions. For several years (2000–6), I lived in the heart of the Muslim community of Cape Town, South Africa—first in the working-class industrial enclave of Salt River, then in the picturesque Malay Quarter, or Bo Kaap, on the slopes of historic Signal Hill. I joined my neighbors in fasting for Ramadan; I took Arabic lessons with a local imam; I went to weddings and memorials. I immersed myself in the serene beauty of the faith.

I also saw the dark side—the political fulminations in local media about distant wars and grievances; the exaggerated sense of betrayal; the perpetual suspicion of Jews. I saw how radical Islam held a utopian appeal even for thoroughly assimilated Muslims, who took comfort in the idea that an ideal Islamic life was still possible, somewhere.

I learned two lessons. One was that military defeats for radical Islam, anywhere in the world, resonated throughout the world. Losses generated outrage—but also shattered illusions. When Saddam Hussein was found hiding in a "spider hole," rather than on the battlefield where he had sent countless young men to die, it did much to deflate the romance of jihad.

The second lesson was that moderate Muslims do exist—though not in the way the West seems to expect.

There are three types of "moderate" Muslims. There are lapsed Muslims, who are largely irrelevant and uninterested. There are dissenting Muslims, few in number. And then there are many Muslims—perhaps the silent majority—who simply wish to get on with their lives, and will do so, given the opportunity.

The question is how to reach these moderate Muslims, the better to push back against radicals who dominate the political and religious conversation. Though outsiders, we do have a moral obligation to our fellow human beings to intervene if necessary. It's also in our self-interest to prevent the Islamic world from self-destructive turbulence that has already begun to hurt us as well.

War is not the only tool at our disposal—and as recent experiences has shown, it may often be a counterproductive one. One possible avenue for reform is, perhaps counterintuitively, to improve literacy in the Islamic world. There are many Muslims who cannot read the Qur'an for themselves in the original Arabic and thus are perpetually dependent on authorities to tell them what it says and how to think about it. If we want, as some suggest, an Islamic "Reformation," then just as the printing press helped spread the Protestant Reformation, greater literacy may help to spread an enlightened Islam, one prepared to interact peacefully with the rest of the world.

There are some new leaders in the Muslim world who are confronting radical Islam. One is Egyptian President Abdel Fattah el-Sisi, who overthrew the Muslim Brotherhood government and won subsequent elections. In a speech at Al-Azhar University in Cairo, a center of Sunni Islamic scholarship, he said, "Is it possible that 1.6 billion people [Muslims] should want to kill the rest of the world's inhabitants—that is 7 billion—so that they themselves may live? Impossible!...I say and repeat again that we are in need of a religious revolution."[18] While he is no democrat, el-Sisi deserves support.

But more than helping moderate Muslims, who will be effective—at best—at the margins or over a long time, what the West can do here and now to counter radical Islam is to revive its own values—the moral values of our Judeo-Christian tradition, and the classical virtues of our Greek and Roman philosophical heritage.

Radical Islam flourishes in a vacuum. That vacuum is especially pronounced in Europe, where socialism has bound the individual more closely to the state than to faith or even self. We may find the courage to name radical Islam as the enemy, but neither a military nor an ideological struggle can be won if we do not know the alternative for which we are fighting.

# CHAPTER 14

# ENTITLEMENTS

## THE LIE:
## Social Security and Medicare will always be there for us.

Examples:

*"So here's the thing. Social Security is not in crisis."*[1]
—President Barack Obama, Columbus, Ohio, August 2010

*"The truth is, these programs aren't in crisis."*[2]
—President Barack Obama, 50th anniversary of Medicare,
August 2015

*"Not even the most pessimistic prognosticators thought
Social Security would be bankrupt anytime soon...."*[3]
—Democratic Party activist Robert Creamer, *Listen to Your
Mother: Stand up Straight! How Progressives Can Win*, 2007

# THE TRUTH:
## Unless we reform entitlements, they will collapse—and our economy with them.

Greece is not typically a place that generates much news interest for most Americans. But in recent years, Americans have watched events in Greece in fascination and horror.

In 2009, it became clear that the Greek government could no longer pay its debts. Unable to borrow, Greece needed the European Union to bail it out—or it would default and exit the euro currency system, throwing the world economy into turmoil.

The simple, or perhaps simplistic, answer to Greece's problems was for it to spend less on its generous welfare state. The *New York Times*, a cheerleader for Obamacare, noted that the Greek reforms aimed at "removing the state from the marketplace in crucial sectors like health care."[4]

Many Americans see Greece's budget deficits, lavish spending, and inadequate workforce as a sign of things to come in this country. When Barack Obama came into office, America was still reeling from a financial crisis. He spent massive amounts on "stimulus," and deficits and debt skyrocketed.

Worse, Obama added the massive new entitlement of Obamacare. Through creative accounting—taxing for ten years, spending for six—the Democrats managed to have the so-called "Affordable Care Act" scored as a deficit reducer. In reality, it depended on future bailouts by the taxpayer. Some critics speculated that it had been set up to fail and be replaced by fully socialized medicine.

The Greece analogy was sufficiently compelling that the Left worked diligently to dislodge it from the public imagination. Leading that effort was the *Times*'s resident left-wing economist, Paul Krugman, who believed that the Obama administration should have spent even *more* money in economic stimulus in early 2009 to shock the economy into growth. Krugman insisted that the U.S., unlike Greece, had "a clear path back to economic recovery."[5] He pointed to projections of rising tax revenues, faster economic growth, and falling budget deficits. Still, even Krugman had to admit, "That said, we do have a long-term budget problem"—one that he had once berated the previous administration for ignoring.[6]

That problem is driven not just by excessive spending but by "mandatory spending"—Social Security, Medicare, and the other entitlements that account for over 60 percent of the federal budget before a penny is spent on non-entitlement government programs.

Krugman wrote that "we should ignore those who pretend to be concerned with fiscal responsibility, but whose real goal is to dismantle the welfare state—and are trying to use crises elsewhere to frighten us into giving them what they want."[7] But Krugman's political enemies could disappear from the face of the planet, and the welfare state would still be on a path to self-destruction. There are too many beneficiaries, drawing too much from too few contributors.

The details are grim. We have two problems. The first concerns our non-entitlement or "discretionary" spending—everything else the federal government does, from national defense to education to food stamps. We almost always spend more on these functions than we take in through taxes. That would not necessarily be a bad thing, if the difference weren't so large. Some amount of deficit spending helps stimulate the economy. The difficulty is that we have been spending so much that we have an enormous national debt—and it has doubled since Obama took office. When Obama was sworn in in 2009, the debt was about $10 trillion; when he leaves in 2017, it will have reached $20 trillion.

Even more important than the amount of debt is its relation to gross domestic product (GDP), the sum total of all goods and services we produce in a year. According to the Federal Reserve, our debt-to-GDP ratio hovered around 60 percent for the twenty years leading up to 2008 and the financial crisis.[8] Then President Bush bailed out the banks, the lenders, and the large insurers through the Troubled Asset Relief Program

(TARP). And then there was the near-trillion-dollar "stimulus," which boosted debt-to-GDP to 100 percent by 2012, which is roughly where it remains. That means we would have to devote all of our economic efforts—everything we produce or earn—to paying off the debt for one year to erase it completely. There are three ways to dispose of that kind of debt: economic growth, inflation, and default. And right now, economic growth looks stagnant by historical standards.

The other problem with our public finances is our entitlements. Social Security was created during the New Deal as a kind of pension system. People regard it as a savings plan, but it is actually a direct transfer from young workers to a growing number of retirees. And thus it is an increasingly shaky plan. "The 2015 Trustees' Report estimates that the current Social Security system is not generating enough revenue to stay in balance past 2033," *Forbes* notes.[9]

Medicare was established during the 1960s as part of President Lyndon B. Johnson's ambitious Great Society reforms. It covers health care for the elderly—but has also made that care more expensive, since there are no incentives to keep costs down. It has also made health care more scarce; many doctors refuse to accept Medicare patients. The government says that Medicare is set to become insolvent by 2030—unless the government starts rationing care.

These are the challenges we face. We are setting ourselves up for national bankruptcy and all that comes with it. Already we are struggling to pay for our defense. And our political debates have become zero-sum games, fights over dwindling resources.

Yet the Left pretends none of this is happening—that the government faces no serious financial crisis whatsoever. And it maligns anyone who says otherwise or offers solutions. Occasionally, when it is politically convenient—usually when a Republican is in power— left-wing politicians will acknowledge fiscal reality. On the campaign trail in 2008, for example, then-senator Barack Obama called President George W. Bush "unpatriotic" for adding to the debt: "The problem is, is that the way Bush has done it over the last eight years is to take out a credit card from the Bank of China in the name of our children, driving up our national debt from $5 trillion for the first 42 presidents—#43 added $4 trillion by his lonesome, so that we now have over $9 trillion of debt that we are going to have to pay back—$30,000 for every man, woman and child. That's irresponsible. It's unpatriotic."[10]

Of course, Obama's own contribution to the debt would more than double Bush's.

Obama also talked up entitlement reform before taking office. In the second presidential debate, Obama promised: "...we're going to have to take on entitlements and I think we've got to do it quickly. We're going to have a lot of work to do, so I can't guarantee that we're going to do it in the next two years, but I'd like to do it in my first term as president."[11]

As president-elect, Obama confirmed his promise to the *Washington Post*. "What we have done is kicked this can down the road. We are now at the end of the road and are not in a position to kick it any further," he said. "We have to signal seriousness in this by making sure some of the hard decisions are made under my watch, not someone else's."[12]

Yet once he took office, Obama's enthusiasm for reforming entitlements mysteriously disappeared. Instead, he reverted to the default position of his party, which was not only to block any attempt to fix Social Security and Medicare, but to deny that there are any problems with these ailing entitlements. On the first of August 2015, for example, President Obama devoted his weekly address to the fiftieth anniversary of Medicare. He declared, "Today, we're often told that Medicare and Medicaid are in crisis. But that's usually a political excuse to cut their funding, privatize them, or phase them out entirely—all of which would undermine their core guarantee. The truth is, these programs aren't in crisis."[13]

He added, "Nor have they kept us from cutting our deficits by two-thirds since I took office." That claim, a frequent Democratic talking point, counts Obama's performance on the debt only from the 2009–10 fiscal year—leaving out the first nine months of Obama's presidency, including the massive $862 billion stimulus.

One official disagreed with Obama's assessment of Medicare: "…if you look at the numbers, then Medicare in particular will run out of money and we will not be able to sustain that program no matter how much taxes go up. I mean, it's not an option for us to just sit by and do nothing."

That official was President Obama himself, speaking at a press conference in 2011, in a rare moment of candor, perhaps prompted by re-election concerns.[14]

Not every Democrat was as cynical in covering up the truth. In 2009, House Majority Whip Representative Steny H. Hoyer, Maryland Democrat, called for immediate action on debt and entitlements in a speech to the Bipartisan Policy Center:

> The recklessness we have seen from so many consumers, and from Wall Street, found an echo in the recklessness of the federal government. For years, our government has lived far beyond its means—and we see now that when we over-rely on debt, things can turn very ugly, very quickly. If a fiscal meltdown comes, there will be no one to bail out America.
>
> What we face is not just an accounting issue, but a moral issue. And turning a blind eye to our long-term challenges would not only be irresponsible—it would be dangerous to our nation's continued success.…
>
> Today, I want to talk about the hard decisions it will take to get our fiscal house in order and control the spiraling costs of our entitlement programs, especially Social Security, Medicare, and Medicaid. But I come here today with a good deal of optimism, because never in recent memory has the American public been so focused on the danger of debt and so ready to turn responsibility into a powerful political issue. As a result, we have a very short window of time in which to act—and the sooner we act, the easier we will find solutions, both politically and substantively.[15]

Perhaps it was easier for Hoyer to speak boldly because he could still blame the damage on Obama's predecessor. In any case, the entitlement reform he demanded never happened.

In 2007, left-wing activist and Democratic strategist Robert Creamer (who in 2005 had been convicted of check kiting to bankroll his political activities) crowed about Democrats' defeat of Social Security reform under Bush. He denied the reality of the problem. "Not even the most pessimistic prognosticators thought Social Security would be bankrupt anytime soon," he said.[16] And he revealed the real reason Social Security is important to the Left, regardless of the numbers: "Social Security, as much as any other program of our government, embodies progressive principles...and that the most efficient way to promote these things is through the only truly democratic institution we have—our government."[17] Reality had to be denied to preserve that statist vision.

To suppress the truth about entitlements and to discourage reform, the Left uses tactics that have become known as "Mediscare"—frightening the public, and seniors in particular, into believing that any change in the entitlement programs, even to improve them, threatens benefits.

The classic case of "Mediscare" was in 1989, when left-wing activists bullied Illinois Democrat Dan Rostenkowski, the powerful chair of the House Ways and Means Committee, over the Medicare Catastrophic Coverage Act of 1988. The act, which had been passed by bipartisan majorities in Congress and signed by President Ronald Reagan, was an attempt to help seniors avoid major out-of-pocket expenses by adding a small premium to the program. But it was an expense few wanted for a benefit they did not feel they needed.

As the *New York Times* explained in 2013, "The dramatic climax came on Sept. 17, 1989, when Representative Dan Rostenkowski, the gruff and burly chairman of the Ways and Means Committee, was hectored in his Chicago district by a band of angry older voters. They surrounded and blocked his car and forced him to escape on foot before he could make his automotive getaway. A news crew caught the episode on camera." The Catastrophic Coverage Act was soon repealed.[18]

The ambush of Rostenkowski was partly orchestrated by Jan Scha-kowsky, a left-wing "advocate" for seniors who ten years later would be elected to Congress from Illinois's 9th District. Schakowsky, married to Creamer, is a steadfast opponent of entitlement reform. I witnessed her "Mediscare" tactics firsthand when I ran for Congress against her in 2010 and her campaign sent mailings to the district claiming that I planned to destroy Social Security and Medicare. (She won by a large margin.)

"Mediscare" tactics have been very effective at defeating entitlement reform and those who embrace it. In 2005, newly re-elected President George W. Bush made Social Security reform his top priority. He hoped to allow individuals to invest some amount of their payroll tax contribu-tions in private accounts. But the Left's scare tactics quickly turned public opinion against any such reforms, and the plan never even came up for a vote in Congress.

In 2008, Representative Paul Ryan, now Speaker of the House, but then merely a member of the congressional minority, created a plan called the Path to Prosperity, aimed at saving both Medicare and Social Security by moving them towards a model of individual insurance and savings, respectively. At first the plan attracted few co-sponsors, but when Repub-licans took the House in 2010 on a wave of conservative Tea Party sup-port, Ryan became the House Budget Committee chair and his plan was embraced by the new majority.

In response, a left-wing group produced an ad depicting Ryan push-ing an elderly woman in a wheelchair to the edge of a cliff and then tipping her over to her death. Erica Payne, the activist responsible for the ad, defended it without apology to Neil Cavuto of Fox News:

> CAVUTO: ... you are telling anyone who wants to tackle this, this is how we're going to treat you?
>
> PAYNE: I think that I'm actually doing something different. What I would like to do—I think we are in a really impor-tant moment in our country.
>
> CAVUTO: You're fear-mongering, Erica.

PAYNE: And we have important choices to make. And I want to just make sure that people understand the choices. Look at what is happening. Learn about the issues, and really focus.

CAVUTO: Do you think you elevated the debate with that?

PAYNE: I think what I did was I highlighted that we have got a lot senior citizens who are going to be in a really bad spot if we don't make the right moral choices in this budget debate.

CAVUTO: But what if we do nothing, Erica? . . . [19]

She never answered.

The Left has never provided an answer for our entitlement crisis, short of calling for more taxes on the rich. And that's no solution. The rich are such a small percentage of Americans that they simply don't have enough money to pay for the ballooning entitlements, even if they were taxed at 100 percent. And the much larger middle class, where the bulk of the money is, will reject having to pay for them. So the Left persists in a fantasy that the programs can continue as they are, hiding from the fact that eventually they will collapse—and drag the rest of the economy with them.

In 2012, Representative Ryan confronted then–Secretary of the Treasury Timothy Geithner at a House Budget Committee hearing: "Leaders are supposed to fix problems. We have a $99.4 trillion unfunded liability. Our government is making promises to Americans that it has no way of accounting for them. And so you're saying yeah, we're stabilizing it but we're not fixing it in the long run. That means we're just going to keep lying to people. We're going to keep all these empty promises going."[20]

Geithner's response: "We're not coming before you to say we have a definitive solution to our long-term problem. What we do know is that we don't like yours."[21]

Instead of dealing with the challenge of existing entitlements, Democrats promised to add new ones the country could not afford. In addition to Obamacare, in 2015 President Obama proposed two free years of community college. Socialist senator Bernie Sanders of Vermont went even further in his 2016 presidential campaign, promising "free college" to young Americans.[22]

In most countries, governments eventually reach the limit of their ability to borrow from credit markets. But cutting spending means facing steep political opposition from interest groups that have become dependent on government largesse. So to continue massive spending, indebted governments eventually have to print money, increasing inflation, which impoverishes the country (Zimbabwe); ask for additional loans, increasing their indebtedness even more (Greece); or default on their loans, which makes it much harder for them to recover in future (Argentina).

The U.S. has escaped those options only because the dollar remains the world's primary reserve currency. But many U.S. states—typically, those governed by left-wing Democrats—provide examples of what happens when governments live beyond their means and cannot print money.

In Illinois, President Barack Obama's home state, the levels of debts and unfunded liabilities are staggering. By 2014, the state owed roughly $30 billion in debts, had about $100 billion in unfunded pension liabilities,[23] and carried annual budget deficits of roughly $6 billion.[24] A budget showdown in the fall of 2015 saw the state suspend payments to lottery winners. Illinois cannot print money, so it must either raise taxes dramatically and cut spending drastically or find a way to declare bankruptcy—each of which has major costs.

The U.S. government still enjoys relative financial confidence in the global markets, even though ratings agencies downgraded its debt rating in 2011. The federal government can still borrow at low rates, which means that the temptation to spend liberally is still strong. The only brake on federal spending came in 2010, with the rise of the Tea Party—one of the few populist movements in the world to demand less government spending, not more.

The Tea Party success in the midterm elections of 2010 ended left-wing fantasies about the federal government bailing out highly indebted states like Illinois. But it did not succeed in stopping the continued rise of federal government spending. In one showdown after another, Republican leaders in Congress have caved to pressure from the White House when the debt ceiling—the legal limit of the federal government's ability to borrow money—loomed.

In the first and most important showdown in 2011, Congress and the White House agreed to the Budget Control Act, which raised the debt ceiling provided that both parties could agree on a new plan to cut the deficit. If they failed to agree (which they did) automatic cuts to new spending—half defense, half social programs—kicked in. The "sequester" marked the first time since the Korean War that federal spending had fallen for two straight years. But by 2014, even that deal had begun to unravel, as Republican leaders, eager to avoid new showdowns, agreed to budget deals that "busted" the spending caps.

House Speaker Paul Ryan has continued to propose ways to rescue the nation's entitlements. Social Security would be the easiest to reform. Ryan's past proposals call for a gradual raising of the retirement age, while allowing younger workers to contribute to individual savings accounts. On Medicare, Ryan joined liberal Democratic senator Ron Wyden of Oregon in 2011 to introduce a plan that would allow Medicare patients to choose between government health insurance and private insurance; the government would provide "premium support"—which critics called a "voucher"—rather than direct health insurance benefits. In both cases, the changes would be phased in for those under fifty-five, allowing those in or near retirement to use the current system.

The response from the Obama administration has been downright hostile. In 2011, Obama invited Ryan to a special speech on the budget at George Washington University. But instead of offering an olive branch, Obama used the occasion to attack Ryan directly. Ryan's plan "would lead to a fundamentally different America than the one we've known certainly in my lifetime," Obama said, adding: "I believe it paints a vision of our future that is deeply pessimistic." He listed people he said Ryan's plan would hurt—students, seniors, poor children.[25]

That ended any hope for bipartisan reform of America's entitlements.

By the early 2016 presidential primaries deficits, debts and entitlements had faded from the forefront of political debates. That was partly because of a general sense of despair about either party having the leadership, or the will, to face the problem. The resurgence of radical Islamic terror as a political preoccupation was also a factor.

But the two issues are not unrelated. The nation's ability to counter growing threats was hampered by the erosion of the nation's military, the one area of federal spending that the Obama administration had little interest in increasing. It was unclear where the funds for a military buildup could be found in the future, in the increasingly likely event that one would be needed.

As Admiral Mike Mullen, then–chairman of the Joint Chiefs of Staff, warned in 2011, "The biggest threat we have to our national security is our debt.... The interest on our debt is $571 billion in 2012, and that's notionally about the size of the Defense Department."[26]

President Obama, and the Left in general, are content to deny the truth about America's financial vulnerabilities, leaving the challenge to future generations—when it may already be far too late.

# CHAPTER 15

# POVERTY

## THE LIE:
## The only reasons for opposing the government's redistributive policies are racism and greed.

Examples:

> *"It's almost as if Republicans are actively striving to get a reputation for being mean to poor, hungry people."*[1]
> —Andrew Leonard, Salon, January 2012

> *"Their philosophy is simple: You are on your own."*[2]
> —President Barack Obama, Burlington, Vermont, March 2012

> *"It's no shocker when [Paul] Ryan—or other libertarians—denounce government assistance programs for breeding dependency and preventing recipients from developing a robust work ethic. But Ryan contends all this assistance*

*leads to a cultural problem.... And by tying this depraved culture to inner-city Americans, Ryan presents an analysis that can be read to include a racial component."*[3]

—David Corn, *Mother Jones*, March 2014

# THE TRUTH:
# Unless we change our policies, the poor are doomed to remain in poverty.

On May 13, 2011, former Speaker of the House Newt Gingrich launched his presidential campaign with a speech to the state convention of the Georgia Republican Party. Among the reasons cited by the architect of the 1994 Republican Revolution and the landmark 1996 welfare reform for his candidacy was the need to reduce poverty and dependence among the American people.

"Would you rather have food stamps, or a paycheck?...President Obama is the most successful food stamp president in American history. More people are on food stamps today than at any point in American history—and he's proud of it!" Gingrich said. "I would like to be the most successful paycheck president in American history."[4]

The media and the Left pounced on Gingrich's comments as if they were evidence of racism. Gingrich denied that claim outright and repeated the line about a "food stamp president" often on the campaign trail. On one occasion he offered to explain to the National Association for the Advancement of Colored People (NAACP), the country's leading black advocacy organization, why his policies were the opposite of racist—"why the African American community should demand paychecks and not be satisfied with food stamps."[5] That merely triggered a new round of controversy.

The facts actually support Gingrich's claim about Obama's performance. The number of Americans making use of the food stamp program would grow to 47.8 million by December 2012, an all-time record.[6] The growth under President Obama was a staggering 15.8 million recipients, the highest under any president.

At the time Gingrich made the claim, the media's fact-checkers were eager to point out that George W. Bush had overseen slightly more growth in the food stamp rolls in his eight years than Obama had in his three.[7] (Few cared to examine the data once Obama had overtaken Bush.) While the administration suggested, somewhat plausibly, that the increase was largely due to the depth of the recession, Gingrich and others charged that Obama cared more about creating beneficiaries than breadwinners.

Already so much of our political debate is geared towards the poor and issues of inequality that one could be forgiven for forgetting that the United States is the richest and most prosperous society civilization has ever produced—and not just at the top of the heap.

From the New Deal, which addressed the sudden poverty of millions thrown out of work and off the land during the Great Depression; to the Great Society, which declared "War on Poverty" at the crest of the post-World War II boom; to the Reagan era's Earned Income Tax Credit; to George W. Bush's vision of an "ownership society"; to Obamacare, American politics has aimed at solving the problem of poverty.

The notion that the state should care for the poor and the vulnerable is a relatively new one, not only in the history of the United States but also the history of civilization itself. It emerged with the rise of socialism in the late nineteenth century and the efforts of "Progressive" reformers early in the twentieth. Ultimately, it was Franklin Delano Roosevelt's New Deal that helped cement the idea of government as a provider for the poor in the American consciousness—even though some of the New Deal policies arguably made the Depression worse.

In Roosevelt's 1941 State of the Union address—what became known as his celebrated "Four Freedoms" speech—FDR described "freedom from want" as one of the four basic freedoms (the others being freedom of speech and expression; freedom of religion; and "freedom from fear"). Freedom from want, "translated into world terms, means economic understandings which will secure to every nation a healthy peacetime life for its inhabitants everywhere in the world,"[8] said FDR. And it was governments that were ultimately responsible to provide that material sustenance to their citizens, as of right.

But the evidence is that free markets, not government, are the best way to fight poverty. Government's most ambitious efforts—most recently, President Lyndon B Johnson's "War on Poverty"—have failed dismally.

In 2014, in observance of the fiftieth anniversary of the War on Poverty, the House Budget Committee—then led by Representative Paul Ryan—noted,

> Despite trillions of dollars in spending, poverty is widespread:
> In 1965, the poverty rate was 17.3 percent. In 2012, it was 15 percent.
> Over the past three years, "deep poverty" has reached its highest level on record.
> About 21.8 percent of children live below the poverty line.[9]

In contrast, there is increasing evidence from around the world that free enterprise and economic growth are the keys to fighting poverty, while government intervention is a virtual guarantee of poverty and poor societies. Hundreds of millions of people, in fact, have been pulled out of extreme poverty in the past few decades since communism began to fall. The most remarkable example is China, which began to abandon its Maoist economic policies and adopt elements of a free-market economy under Deng Xiaoping in the early 1980s.

A World Bank report in late 2014 affirmed that the global poverty rate had all but collapsed since the late 1970s—perhaps the most extraordinary achievement in the history of human civilization.[10] The reason was the expansion of the free economy—free trade, the free movement of capital, the free flow of ideas. This is an achievement that the Left has carefully suppressed, clinging to outdated myths of capitalism's failure.[11] The World Bank report received virtually no attention in the media and was barely noticed by politicians.

One of the chief ways in which the Left tries to hide the truth about free markets is by using fear. Progressives portray capitalism as a desperate free-for-all in which a few will dominate and millions will struggle in vain. Their rhetoric was anticipated decades ago by Ayn Rand in her novel *Atlas Shrugged*, where the rail industry is pressured to embrace an "anti-dog-eat-dog rule" that prevents "destructive competition." Another piece of anti-capitalist legislation in the novel, the Equalization of Opportunity bill, prevents any one individual from owning more than one business. It's all supposed to be in the service of fair play, but shuts down the competition that enables the free market to create wealth and lift people out of poverty.[12]

President Barack Obama unwittingly echoed Rand's anti-capitalist villains when he attacked the Republican Party's supposed "you're-on-your-own" economics in his re-election campaign. In Burlington, Vermont, in March 2012, he declared, "Their philosophy is simple: You are on your own. You're on your own. If you are out of work, can't find a job, tough luck, you're on your own. You don't have health care—that's your problem—you're on your own. If you're born into poverty, lift yourself up with your own bootstraps even if you don't have boots. You're on your own. They believe that's their—that's how American has advanced. That's the cramped, narrow conception they have of liberty. And they are wrong. [Applause.] They are wrong.

"In the United States of America, we are greater together than we are on our own."[13]

These were not new arguments. They were almost word-for-word the same things Obama had said in his speech accepting the Democratic Party's nomination for president in 2008.[14] The argument never changes—partly because scaring people about the alternative to left-wing policies works to obscure their failure, and partly because the Left simply has no other ideas.

Obama does not merely argue that economic liberty fails; he labels it un-American. In so doing, he denies reality and the principles of the American Revolution and the Constitution.

The concepts of self-ownership and self-reliance were central to the thinking of John Locke, and they were the moral ideals to which America's forefathers aspired, however imperfectly. They understood—and Obama does not—what Tocqueville would observe in the mid-nineteenth century: that while Americans were almost obsessive about improving their material lot, they also joined in countless associations to help each other and to advance common interests. Tocqueville called this "self-interest properly understood." When Obama contrasts the free market with doing things "together," he is setting up a false choice. Americans have always cooperated in the marketplace and in civil society—with no need for government programs to bring them together.

And perhaps the worst kind of isolation is that felt by those who depend on government but whom government fails to help—the millions who lost their health insurance to Obamacare, the veterans dying on Veterans Affairs waitlists on Obama's watch, the children trapped in failing public schools because the Obama administration refuses to allow them vouchers to attend private or parochial schools. But they are invisible.

Given the American people's broad experience of government failure, it is increasingly those at the top of the socioeconomic pyramid—who rely least on public services—that retain faith in utopian policies. Skepticism of the free market has become deeply embedded in our nation's political and intellectual elite, which has tilted sharply left in recent years. One shared mistaken belief is the idea that the relatively unfettered capitalism of the late nineteenth and early twentieth centuries was a kind of Dark Age of grinding poverty and inequality—when really it was a time of rising prosperity and flourishing philanthropy.

The nation's lawyers have a name for this supposedly benighted time: it is "the *Lochner* era," named for the 1905 case *Lochner v. New York*, in which, as we saw in chapter 8, the Supreme Court overturned a state law restricting the working hours of bakers.[15] *Lochner* was only one of many cases in which the Court struck down laws and regulations that amounted to government interventions in the economy.

In his famous dissent to the *Lochner* decision, Justice Oliver Wendell Holmes Jr. maintained that the Constitution does not mandate a "laissez faire" economic system. That dissent is quoted in legal textbooks and even in international judicial opinions. Yet few bother to quote the relevant sentence, which is also skeptical of statism, in full: "But a Constitution is not intended to embody a particular economic theory, *whether of paternalism and the organic relation of the citizen to the state* or of laissez faire [emphasis added]."[16]

Contrary to the Left's view—which is the orthodoxy in America's law schools—the Court in *Lochner* was not merely an appendage of the "robber barons" of the railways and the industrial trusts. The *Lochner* Court was deeply concerned with freedom of contract—an idea that was particularly salient in the years after the Civil War and Emancipation, when millions were finally at liberty to hire out their labor as they wished.

The end of the *Lochner* era in the mid-1930s meant that the government's power to intervene in the economy was unleashed—and the Great Depression took a turn for the worse. The American economy would not recover until World War II—partly because of massive government spending, but also because government regulations on vital industries were eased to accelerate production.

The true story of the *Lochner* court deflates the idea that American justice "evolved" from a benighted era of industrial servitude to the sunny uplands of the welfare state. That fiction obscures the profound concept of individual economic emancipation behind *Lochner*—which is the seed of the prosperity we still enjoy.

As Newt Gingrich learned when he was running for president, one of the most frequent—and, sadly, most effective—tactics the Left uses to suppress free market alternatives and silence those who point out the failure of statist "solutions" for poverty is to accuse critics of racism. That puts critics of the failed welfare state on the defensive, forcing them to defend themselves from a sensational charge—while the programs themselves escape scrutiny.

The argument is that since many black people are poor cutting back on government spending for the poor is racist in effect, if not intent. Cutting government jobs is also racist—because a disproportionate number of public employees are black. The theory is that a bloated government payroll has historically been viewed as illegitimate because black people fill are overrepresented in government jobs. "The assault on public sector employees seems to build on [a] history of racism, causing African-American workers to suffer disproportionately during this recovery," one left-wing economic analyst has written.[17]

It does not matter whether the criticism of government programs and their pernicious effects on the black community comes from someone who has tried to help that community, or even from that community itself. In March 2014, Representative Ryan told an interviewer that one reason for chronic poverty was "this tailspin of culture, in our inner cities in particular, of men not working and just generations of men not even thinking about working or learning the value and the culture of work." For that accurate observation, he was accused of racism.[18]

One black leader who agrees with Ryan is Bob Woodson of the Center for Neighborhood Enterprise. He told the *Wall Street Journal* that the poor would benefit most from less government intervention—particularly from the easing of the occupational licensing requirements that have raised the barrier to entry for many would-be entrepreneurs.[19] But voices like Woodson's are regularly ignored by professional civil rights activists, for whom government services are a way to access public funding.

Public aid is often a boon for private contractors. In April 2013, the Government Accountability Institute (GAI) exposed how large companies and financial institutions made big profits off contracts with the government (including state governments) to process food stamps through electronic benefits transfer (EBT) transactions. As the number of recipients expanded, so did profits. "What companies have realized is there's good money to be made in the poverty industry," said the GAI's Peter Schweizer. "Shrinking the size of government will only occur when we reduce the incentives corporations and individuals have to see government swell."[20]

But that is unlikely to happen as long as honest debate about poverty is quashed. The distortion of the debate is deliberate. Writing in 2007, two years before Obamacare, Democratic strategist Robert Creamer crafted a strategy for pushing health reform: "To win we must not just generate understanding, but emotion—fear, revulsion, anger, disgust."[21]

And so they did, accusing opponents of Obamacare of racism, among other outrages. Then-Speaker of the House Nancy Pelosi marched through a large crowd of Tea Party protesters at the U.S. Capitol with her gavel in her hands and members from the Congressional Black Caucus (CBC) at her side, in an attempts to liken the fight for expanded government health insurance to the fight for voting rights and desegregation. As we have seen, the CBC members made the false accusation that the Tea Party demonstrators had shouted "the N-word" at them as they walked by.

Not content with portraying opponents as racists, the Left also paints critics of statism as paid agents of rich billionaires and powerful corporations. Democratic senator Barbara Boxer of California told Chris Matthews of MSNBC that the constituents showing up at town hall meetings around the country to protest Obamacare were not to be taken seriously because they were "well-dressed middle-class people in pinks and limes... [the] Brooks Brothers Brigade." She added, "This is all planned. It's to hurt our president and it's to change the Congress."

Matthews agreed, speculating that "the health insurance companies" were bankrolling the protests. "Do you think they're behind these so-called AstroTurf demonstrations? That they're not really grassroots?"[22] The left eventually settled on the Koch brothers—leading industrialists, philanthropists, and libertarians—as the imagined culprits.

In fact the "AstroTurf" was on the other side. Pro-Obamacare activists bused paid members of the Service Employees International Union to town halls. An Obama administration-aligned group, Health Care for America now, was caught on camera planning to sneak placards into a public meeting and block constituents from asking questions.[23]

Nevertheless, the demonization of the foes of big-government redistribution continues. In 2014, Ryan introduced a new policy to fight poverty, including a plan to replace unwieldy federal programs with block grants to the states so that they could launch new, innovative efforts to help the poor find work and move ahead. Even some more thoughtful liberals were impressed. Former Secretary of Labor Robert Reich, who had resigned from the Clinton administration to protest welfare reform, said of Ryan's plan, "This is something that is very new and different from the Republican Party."[24]

But the plan never gained traction—partly because conservatives were preoccupied with budget battles and Ryan's proposal would not have reduced overall spending, but largely because the Left had tarnished Ryan as a racist.

That is how existing poverty policies—which doom successive generations of Americans, predominantly black and Latino, to poverty—are maintained: those who wish to change those policies, giving the poor more responsibility and opportunity, are silenced or ignored. The voices calling for reform are a little harder to silence when they come from the poor themselves. Indeed, if there is hope in the poverty debate, it is to be found in the pushback by black and Latino communities on education reform.

One of the first acts of the Obama administration when it took office in 2009 was to cut spending on the D.C. Opportunity Scholarship Program, a voucher system that had allowed a small number of mostly African-American children in the nation's capital to attend private schools using the money that otherwise would have been spent on their behalf in the failing public system.

Obama's cuts to the D.C. voucher program came at a time of extreme profligacy, when the federal government was spending (and wasting) hundreds of billions of dollars on stimulus projects, including in education. The reason Obama and his party hastened to cut the Opportunity Scholarships was that the Democrats' allies in the teachers unions could not tolerate an example of vouchers' success.

Then–Secretary of Education Arne Duncan, who poses as a reformer, defended the administration's decision: "At the end of the day, we can't be satisfied with saving 1 or 2 percent of children and letting 98 or 99 percent down."[25] In other words, because the program could not help everyone, it should help no one.

There are at least two successful major education reform efforts under way at this time. One is vouchers. The other is the charter school movement, in which community groups seek permission from state governments to start their own schools, funded by the public but managed independently, and largely beyond the reach of the teachers unions, which oppose charters bitterly.

Other reform efforts have aimed at improving the accountability of schools and teachers by punishing failure and rewarding merit. These reforms have slightly more support on the Left—partly because the Obama administration has been able to use them to exercise more federal control over education, as it did in its "Race to the Top" policy, which offered states federal money in exchange for desired reforms. The Common Core is another case of a reform idea that was originally embraced by conservatives but has now been rejected, as federal authorities use it to implement their own desired curriculum.

The challenges to reform remain formidable: the Department of Justice sued Louisiana over its school voucher system on the spurious grounds that black students benefiting from vouchers left behind public schools whiter than they had been before. The Fifth Circuit Court of Appeals ruled in favor of Louisiana in November 2015, restoring hope for reform—and showing that it is possible to win the argument on poverty with the Left.[26]

The Left's claim that only government can help the poor, like its denial of radical Islam, is simply wrong. To suppress the truth, the progressives have to paint their conservative critics as bigots. For good measure, they throw in the sentimental defense that even if the results are poor, their motivations are pure—beyond reproach.

Because the Left's argument is framed in moral terms, albeit faulty ones, the answer to it must also be a moral argument. Pursuing policies that condemn the poor to poverty and dependence is not only wasteful, but also immoral. We can't claim we don't know the results.

Arthur Brooks, the president of the American Enterprise Institute, points out that "we rarely hear a moral defense for free enterprise from our politicians."[27] The only moral case is made by the Left: that it is cruel to cut government poverty programs, and inequality itself is a moral evil requiring intervention (in the interests of "social justice").

That is why, Brooks, says, "despite the fact that surveys find a large majority of Americans think the government is too big and trying to do too much—we acquiesce to larger and larger government from both parties." The need to make the moral case for free enterprise, not least as a path out of poverty, is urgent, he says.

The moral case for capitalism has three parts, according to Brooks. The first is the argument from the right to "earned success." This is similar to John Locke's argument that everyone has the right to the fruits of his or her own labor. But Brooks adds the empirical observation "that people who say they have earned their success are our happiest citizens," rich or poor.

The second argument is from "fairness"—not in the sense of material equality, but in the sense of everyone having the same chance to advance by playing by the same set of rules. "For most Americans," Brooks points out, "a fair society is one in which hard work, creativity, and honest competition result in financial reward."

The third argument for the free market, Brooks says, is about "the rights of the poor." Far from impoverishing them, as the Left claims, capitalism has lifted hundreds of millions of people out of extreme poverty in the space of a few decades—and can do even more.

Making those arguments—especially the last—is very difficult, given that the Left's efforts to suppress the good news about capitalism have been so thorough and so successful. That is why exposing government failures and aligning with the poor themselves on issues such as education reform are important.

When cracks in the dam of lies start forming, we can know that the truth will—eventually—burst through.

# CHAPTER 16

# PROCESS

## THE LIE:
## The political process is not important. Results are the only thing that really matters.

Examples:

*"So Washington gets very concerned about these procedural issues in Congress.... What the American people care about is the fact that their premiums are going up 25, 40, 60 percent, and I'm going to do something about it."*[1]
— President Barack Obama, interview with Fox News, March 2010

*"This is what democracy looks like!"*[2]
— hundreds of demonstrators inside the Wisconsin State Capitol, February 2011

*"To solve the serious problems facing our country, we need to minimize the harm from legislative inertia by relying more on automatic policies and depoliticized commissions for certain policy decisions. In other words, radical as it sounds, we need to counter the gridlock of our political institutions by making them a bit less democratic."*[3]

—Peter Orszag, former Obama White House
budget director, September 2011

# THE TRUTH:
## The process required by the Constitution prevents mistakes and protects liberty.

Late at night on Sunday March 30, 2003, bulldozers rumbled onto the tarmac at Meigs Field, an airport on a Lake Michigan peninsula in front of the majestic Chicago skyline, well known to pilots and aviation enthusiasts from flight simulator programs.

Working secretly and under cover of darkness, the construction crews carved six giant Xs into the airport's runways, rendering them inoperable, leaving sixteen airplanes virtually stranded.

It was not an act of terror or a daring feat of vandalism. It was a deliberate and effective move by Mayor Richard M. Daley, who had decided to resolve a long-running dispute over the fate of the airport by simply destroying it—ripping up not only the runways, but an agreement he had reached with the state's former Republican governor.

A city official left a message on an answering machine at the Federal Aviation Administration at 2:00 a.m. on March 31 politely informing the federal government that the airport had been closed.

An air traffic controller driving to Meigs for the start of his 6:00 a.m. shift learned about the closure from the radio news. The rest of the city read about it in April 1 headlines: "Daley rips up Meigs runways in surprise raid," the *Chicago Tribune* announced.[4]

But it was no April Fool's Day prank.

In a press conference, Daley cited terror concerns, noting that the runway was close to the city's many skyscrapers. "We have done this to protect the millions of people who live, work and visit our downtown Chicago in these very uncertain times," he said. "And not just our tallest buildings, but the hundreds of thousands of people who attend not only the Taste of Chicago and the Grant Park concerts, our museum park, Navy Pier, our water filtration plant, who will be using our beaches and visiting our museums."[5]

*Tribune* columnist Eric Zorn called Daley's midnight raid "an exercise in autocracy so brazen that it was downright amusing." He added: "Pro-Meigs forces argue no, that the little airport handled important medical and rescue flights and helped control and secure the airspace over the city, and that the [terror] threat posed by Meigs is so speculative that the demolition is an act of paranoia. You think maybe this was worth a discussion?"[6]

But after the city paid a small fine to the FAA, there was nothing more to discuss. "Hizzoner" the mayor had his way, and the rest of his party fell into line. This was politics "the Chicago way."

Some of Daley's close allies, such as political consultant David Axelrod and former staffer Valerie Jarrett, were soon to become household names. And watching the airport incident closely was an obscure state senator, Barack Obama, who had just decided to run for federal office.

Six years later, President Barack Obama sat in the Oval Office and spoke with Fox News' Bret Baier, defending his new health care reform bill, the Patient Protection and Affordable Care Act, or "Obamacare." Baier noted that Democrats were discussing procedural tricks to avoid a final vote in the House of Representatives, and that special deals for Nebraska and Louisiana, derided by critics as "the Cornhusker Kickback" and "the Louisiana Purchase," had already been used to secure votes.

Obama brushed aside such questions about process. "I don't spend a lot of time worrying about what the procedural rules are in the House or the Senate," Obama said. "What I can tell you is that the vote that's taken in the House will be a vote for health care reform."[7]

Baier continued to press the point. "I know you don't like to talk about process, but…there are a lot of people around America that have a problem with this process," he said.

"I've got to say to you, there are a lot more people who are concerned about the fact that they may be losing their house or going bankrupt because of health care," Obama said. "Washington gets very concerned about these procedural issues in Congress," but the rest of the country did not care. According to the president, they simply wanted affordable health care, by any means necessary.

Obama's argument was straight out of the Daley playbook. Axelrod, now ensconced in the White House as Obama's political adviser, had made a similar argument in 2005, defending Daley from accusations of corruption. Though as a younger man he had opposed political patronage, Axelrod explained in the *Tribune*, he had come to see that corruption was not just an inevitable part of government, but a desirable one: "When a congressman responds to the president's request for support for a judicial nominee or a trade deal by replying that he'd like the president's backing for a new bridge in his district, he's fighting for his constituents. If the money for that bridge is approved over a worthier project elsewhere, should the deal between the two officials become a crime?"[8] Few would dare to praise corruption so openly, but those on the Left tend to share the same belief—that the policy ends justify the procedural means.

But that is emphatically not what the Framers of the Constitution believed. They designed an elegant system of checks and balances—complex, but not complicated—because they understood that a fair process offered the best protection against abuses of power and costly mistakes.

Democrats are perfectly capable of following correct constitutional procedures, when it's convenient to them. But when it's not, the Left suppresses the truth about how our system of government is supposed to work.

President Woodrow Wilson, in many ways Obama's ideological forebear, shared many of the same views about the political process. The

Constitution's separation of powers, he argued, made government less scientific, less efficient, and even less democratic.

In a campaign speech in 1912, published in 1913 as an essay entitled "What is Progress?," Wilson made an explicit argument against the Constitution's procedural safeguards.[9] "The laws of this country have not kept up with the change of economic circumstances in this country," he said. "The system set up by our law and our usage doesn't work,—or at least it can't be depended on; it is made to work only by a most unreasonable expenditure of labor and pains."

Wilson argued that the Constitution had been written according to the "Newtonian" science of its day. Its checks and balances had been "a sort of imitation of the solar system," Wilson said. "Politics in their thought was a variety of mechanics." But times had changed: "The trouble with the theory is that government is not a machine, but a living thing. It falls, not under the theory of the universe, but under the theory of organic life. It is accountable to Darwin, not to Newton." And the kind of government America needed in the twentieth century depended on unity, not opposition. "No living thing can have its organs offset against each other, as checks, and live. On the contrary, its life is dependent upon their quick co-operation, their ready response to the commands of instinct or intelligence, their amicable community of purpose."

Thus, Wilson said, he was "forced to be a progressive"—to "adjust" American laws and institutions to the needs of the present day. "All that progressives ask or desire is permission—in an era when 'development,' 'evolution,' is the scientific word—to interpret the Constitution according to the Darwinian principle; all they ask is recognition of the fact that a nation is a living thing and not a machine."

He favored a gradual change over a sudden, revolutionary one: "You must knit the new into the old." Still, he had contempt for the old. "The Declaration of Independence did not mention the questions of our day," he argued. Instead of checks and balances, which Wilson believed were vulnerable to manipulation by special interests, the American system should be "co-operative as in a perfected, co-ordinated beehive." Eventually, "a generation or two from now," a new, utopian age would be reached "where the whole talk of mere politicians is stilled, where men can look in each other's faces and see that there is nothing to conceal."

In fact, human beings are not bees, but unique individuals with different dreams, desires, and destinies. What Wilsons' proposed "Darwinian" reforms ignored was that the primary purpose of the Constitution's checks and balances is to protect the individual liberties of American citizens, not just to produce better policy outcomes.

With the benefit of a century of hindsight, it is also clear that governments organized as "perfected, co-ordinated beehives" produce inferior outcomes—military defeat, social stagnation, and economic collapse. That's true of socialism, and also true even in far milder, democratic forms of "progressive" government. Obama's Chicago has been a virtual one-party state for generations—one that cannot seem to overcome urban blight, rising crime, and looming fiscal disaster.

Ironically, Chicago may have contributed to Obama's suspicion of checks and balances in government, and of political opposition in particular. The city of Chicago held a fascination for Obama, as for many other left-wing activists. It was where the New Left had confronted the Democratic Party and the Chicago Police Department over the Vietnam War, where community organizer Saul Alinsky had developed his *Rules for Radicals*.[10] In the early 1980s, when Obama first became involved in politics, Chicago was where Harold Washington was making history as the first African-American to be elected mayor, breaking the back of the Democratic Party's white ethnic political machine, as we have seen in chapter 9.

When Washington took office in 1983 he faced stiff opposition from the Democratic Party bosses, who were determined to hold onto power. They formed a twenty-nine-vote majority in the fifty-member city council to block Washington's agenda. Locals called the standoff "the Council Wars."

Obama was watching the drama unfold from his new perch on the South Side of Chicago. "More than anything, I wanted Harold to succeed," he would later write in *Dreams from My Father*, his first memoir.

"[L]ike my real father, the mayor and his achievements seemed to mark out what was possible; his gifts, his power, measured my own hopes."[11]

Unable to move the city council, Washington began using his executive powers to circumvent it. He never gave in on the issues, and he used speeches to appeal over the heads of the elected legislators to the public—a model Obama would later follow. Finally, after special elections brought more Washington allies into the council, the aldermen were divided 25–25, and Washington held the tie-breaking vote. He went on to win re-election easily, but died tragically from a heart attack early in his second term, before he could enact his ambitious second-term agenda.[12]

In his memoir, Obama considered Washington's legacy. "At the margins, Harold could make city services more equitable," Obama wrote. But "nothing seemed to change" for the city's poorest.[13] The lesson Obama drew was that executive action was appropriate to overcome political opposition—but that it had to be big, bold, and brazen.

That has been the rule in the Obama presidency. Whereas Ronald Reagan put economic stability first and waited until his second term to enact his bolder policy reforms, Obama made health care reform—covering one-sixth of the American economy—his most urgent priority. And when Obama encountered obstacles, whether political, procedural, or even constitutional, he simply pressed ahead, using whatever executive powers he had, and some that he did not, to advance his highly ideological agenda.

One of the more well-known cases in which Obama flouted the procedures mandated by the Constitution involved Obama's appointments to the National Labor Relations Board (NLRB), a theoretically nonpartisan body dating back to the New Deal, whose decisions shape the fate of the American economy. Appointments to the NLRB are made by the president, subject to the approval of the Senate. But in January 2012 Obama made three appointments to the NLRB without Senate approval. "The move was a big score for labor and Obama's allies on the left, who congratulated the president for muscling past Republicans bent on blocking his agenda," Politico reported.

To put his nominees on the NLRB, Obama used a measure known as a "recess appointment." Recess appointments when the Senate is not in session are allowed by the Constitution because of the sheer difficulty of gathering (and keeping) a quorum of Senators in Washington, D.C., during an era before even steamboats and railways, let alone cars and airplanes.

But in January 2012 the Senate was not actually in recess. It had merely adjourned in the middle of a congressional session; it was holding short *pro forma* sessions each day precisely to prevent a recess. As Ken Klukowski of Breitbart News reported, "Obama took the unprecedented step of declaring that, for purposes of the Constitution, the Senate is in recess whenever there are not enough senators present to conduct business, even if the Senate claims it is still in session."[14] That would have given Obama the power to make appointments to principal offices whenever the Senate went to lunch.

More than two years later, in *Noel Canning v. NLRB*, the Supreme Court found the president's actions unconstitutional in a unanimous 9–0 decision, an unusually powerful rebuke. "[W]hen the appointments before us took place," wrote Justice Stephen Breyer, "the Senate was in the midst of a 3-day recess. Three days is too short a time to bring a recess within the scope of the Clause. Thus we conclude that the President lacked the power to make the recess appointments here at issue."[15]

In a concurring opinion, Justice Scalia said the Court's ruling had been too narrow—that *any* appointment not made during "the intermission between two formal legislative sessions" was not a valid recess appointment.[16]

That did not discourage the Obama administration from continuing to circumvent Congress in every way possible—and it also was defying the courts, as we saw in chapter 8. In negotiating the nuclear deal with Iran, for example, the White House rejected the notion that it would have to submit the agreement to the Senate for a ratification vote of two-thirds of those present, as the Constitution requires for treaties with foreign governments. Instead the administration insisted that the Iran deal was simply an "executive agreement."

Secretary of State John Kerry, testifying before the Senate Foreign Relations Committee, argued that the agreement was not even binding:

"With respect to the talks, we've been clear from the beginning. We're not negotiating a 'legally binding' plan. We're negotiating a plan that will have in it a capacity for enforcement. We don't even have diplomatic relations with Iran right now."[17] But if the agreement was not "legally binding," there was no way for the White House to make good on its guarantees that Iran would be blocked from building nuclear weapons.

Later, when the House Foreign Relations Committee asked Kerry why the Iran deal was not a treaty, Kerry replied, "I spent quite a few years ago trying to get a lot of treaties through the United States Senate. And frankly, it's become physically impossible. That's why. Because you can't pass a treaty anymore."[18] In fact, the Senate had ratified several treaties on Kerry's watch.[19] And in any case, the difficulty of persuading the people's elected representatives to rubber stamp the administration's initiatives was no excuse for that administration to act unilaterally, in defiance of the Constitution's requirements. The President of the United States simply has no right to enter into treaties with other nations without the consent of the Senate—it's a shared power. If the Senate refuses to give that consent, the Constitution mandates that the treaty fail.

And yet the Obama administration resorted to the very same tactic when negotiating a climate change treaty with nearly two hundred other nations in Paris, France, in December 2015. There was no way to deny that that agreement was a treaty. Thus the Obama administration made sure that the most important parts of the agreement, including emissions limits and $100 billion in annual grants to developing nations, were non-binding. As the UK *Guardian* noted, "Negotiators sealed the deal after changing provisions that would have triggered a requirement that the agreement be approved by the U.S. Congress."[20] The Obama administration would simply ignore the Senate and proceed as if the treaty had the force of law.

What is most damning is that the Obama administration has shown it is capable of consulting Congress or showing deference to the people's elected representatives. Long before he announced his support for gay marriage, President Obama pushed for the repeal of "Don't Ask, Don't Tell"—the Bill Clinton policy that prevented open homosexuals from serving in the armed forces. In that case, Obama did not circumvent Congress—though, as commander-in-chief, he could have done so, constitutionally. Instead he waited until the military had studied the issue and Congress had deliberated about it. In 2010, the Don't Ask, Don't Tell Repeal Act passed with bipartisan support. The change was accepted widely and immediately, and it remains the least controversial of Obama's gay rights policies.

But Obama only adheres to process when he wants to evade responsibility. In general, he shares the Left's general contempt for legal boundaries, constitutional principles and parliamentary procedure.

The Left's understanding of democracy was on full display in 2011, when Governor Scott Walker of Wisconsin and the newly elected Republican state legislature proposed public sector labor reforms that would have allowed unions to continue bargaining for wages but not for benefits. Fourteen Democratic members of the legislature fled to Illinois to prevent a quorum that would have allowed the Republican proposals to come to a vote. At the state capitol itself, thousands of demonstrators gathered for weeks of protests. Some occupied the capitol building itself. Excited by the scale of their protests, which drew national media coverage, and the seeming helplessness of state authorities to stop them, demonstrators adopted the refrain: "This is what democracy looks like!"

The fact that Wisconsin voters had actually put Republicans in power in a free and fair election was not, evidently, "democracy."

The "This is what democracy looks like!" chant was also popular with the Occupy Wall Street movement, which began in lower Manhattan in September 2011 and spread throughout the country and the world. In city after city, demonstrators built tent cities in public and private spaces, illegally squatting in protest against economic inequality and capitalism in general.

Occupy, which purported to have no official leaders, developed a concept of "democracy" that was participatory in the extreme, featuring a curious technique for holding discussions and making decisions. The Occupy activists would gather at "General Assembly" meetings where, in lieu of a microphone or bullhorn, the crowd would repeat, phrase by phrase, every single word spoken by whoever was addressing the meeting. All decisions were to be made by consensus: there were no votes, but participants showed approval or disapproval by waving their fingers—"up twinkles" for yes, "down twinkles" for no.

In 2014, the Black Lives Matter movement became the latest to adopt "This is what democracy looks like!" as a protest refrain. After the shooting death of black teenager Michael Brown by a Ferguson, Missouri, police officer, demonstrations sprang up around the country, sometimes turning violent. In Berkeley, California, demonstrators celebrated their "democracy" as they claimed ownership of the streets and illegal protests segued into vandalism and violence.

At one protest in Minnesota, the phrase took on a grim irony. Demonstrators had chanted "Pigs in a blanket, fry 'em like bacon" at police, and yet members of the police force had done their best to be accommodating. As the *Minneapolis Star-Tribune* reported, "One St. Paul officer told a reporter that Black Lives Matter St. Paul had been cooperative in working with police. 'This is what democracy looks like,' he said."[21]

There are two kinds of process—or, rather, the lack of it—that appeal to the Left. One is the authoritarian approach preferred by Woodrow Wilson and Obama, in which checks and balances are ignored and all opposition is presumed to be in bad faith. The other is the mass action of the Wisconsin protests, the Occupy protests, and the Black Lives Matter movement, in which "democracy" sweeps aside all order and institutions—including even, in Wisconsin, elections.

But these are really two sides of the same coin. By disrupting existing institutions, mass protests create an opening for sympathetic executives to assert, and exert, sweeping powers. Again and again, the Obama administration has endorsed the most radical protests on the president's watch, including Occupy, offering caveats about law and order but congratulating the protesters for their public-mindedness.

In 2015, for example, when mass student protests led to the unexpected resignation of University of Missouri president Tim Wolfe, White House spokesperson Josh Earnest said proudly, "I think this also illustrates something that the president talked a lot about in the context of—in his campaign, that a few people speaking up and speaking out can have a profound impact on the communities where we live and work."[22] As Wolfe resigned, the noble "Mizzou" demonstrators were busy roughing up journalists, including a sympathetic photographer who wanted to document their tent city on campus.

The Left wants to repress what democracy *really* looks like—at least the constitutional democracy enshrined in the republican institutions of our Constitution and restrained by the protection of our individual liberties and a system of checks and balances. The Left's version of democracy represents the excessive form of democracy about which Alexis de Tocqueville warned in the nineteenth century—mass rule that he warned could lead to the "tyranny of the majority" and a despotism more powerful and pervasive than any that existed under the divine right of kings in Europe.

One way for conservatives to push back is to lead by example. Republican senator Mitch McConnell of Kentucky, for example, restored some of the powers of the opposition when Republicans took power in the Senate after 2014. While the Democrats under Senator Harry Reid had blocked Republicans from offering amendments, McConnell restored the amendment process.

Yet as the Obama administration continued to defy the Senate, conservatives began to argue that McConnell should repay the Democrats by abolishing the filibuster, which helps the minority party block legislation, and which Reid had weakened. The danger is a tit-for-tat competition in which Democrats and Republicans vie with one another to dismantle the procedural safeguards to our republican liberties.

More than retribution, what America needs is illumination—constant reminders of why we have a constitutional process and what democracy in America is truly meant to be.

# CHAPTER 17

# CHRISTIANITY

## THE LIE:
## America is not a Christian nation.

Examples:

*"Whatever we once were, we are no longer a Christian nation—at least, not just. We are also a Jewish nation, a Muslim nation, a Buddhist nation, and a Hindu nation, and a nation of nonbelievers."*[1]

—Senator Barack Obama,
Call to Renewal Conference, June 2006

*"Among developed nations, America stands alone in these [Biblical] convictions. Our country now appears, as at no other time in her history, like a lumbering, bellicose, dimwitted giant."*[2]

—Sam Harris, *Letter to a Christian Nation*, 2006

*"No matter how many Christians live here, we are not a Christian nation. For the sake of people of all faiths and of no faith, we should hope we never become one."*[3]
—Author Peter Manseau, Fox News, March 2015

# THE TRUTH:
## Christianity is the key to our freedom.

When President Barack Obama addressed the National Prayer Breakfast in February 2015, as we have seen in chapter 13, he posited a moral equivalence between the excesses of medieval Christianity and those of radical Islam today, reminding his audience that "people committed terrible deeds in the name of Christ."[4]

Despite the ensuing controversy, Obama repeated a similar criticism of Christianity two months later, in the midst of a controversy over religious freedom laws designed to protect private businesses from being forced to accept same-sex marriage. "On Easter, I do reflect on the fact that as a Christian, I am supposed to love. And I have to say that sometimes when I listen to less-than-loving expressions by Christians, I get concerned," he said.[5]

Critics noted that Obama's remarks came days after a terror attack in Kenya in which 147 Christian students had been slaughtered by Muslim gunmen.

For Obama, as for much of the Left, Christianity is a perpetual punching bag, held in particular contempt as the dominant faith of the most powerful country in the world. The history of Christianity in the New World is taught to students today as a story of oppression by colonialists and conquerors. In 2015, when Pope Francis canonized Junipero Serra—one of the pioneers of southern California, in both a religious and a practical sense—statues of the eighteenth-century Franciscan were vandalized across the Golden State.[6]

Whatever the misdeeds of the past, Christians are the most persecuted religious group in the world today—more so even than Jews, who at least have a state willing to rescue Jews in peril, by force if necessary.[7] In China, Christianity—other than the Communist Party–sanctioned variety—is persecuted. In Libya, the terrorists of ISIS beheaded Coptic Christians on the beach and videotaped the event for global consumption. In Iraq, the so-called Islamic State has emptied the country of much of its Christian population.

And yet there are few speaking up for the persecuted Christians of the world.

Ironically, Christians today are the people most willing to sacrifice for others. That is true not only of charities and of faith-based organizations that proselytize among the beneficiaries of their generosity. It is also true of Christians who advocate peace in far-flung regions such as Sudan, where American Evangelicals helped broker a respite in a long civil war.

It is also true of ordinary Christian Americans, who put their lives at risk to join the armed forces in great numbers, often sacrificing to protect vulnerable Muslims—whether Kosovar Albanians at risk of persecution by Serbian Christians, Iraqi Muslims at risk from each other, or Jews imprisoned in concentration camps by Nazi Germany.

Christians embody the very values American liberals purport to champion.

Indeed, Christianity is the source from which America's freedom springs. The first settlers include pilgrims fleeing religious persecution, and concepts unique to Christianity shaped the intellectual and ideological foundations of American democracy.

But the left suppresses these undeniable historical facts. The left-wing writer Ta-Nehisi Coates, for example, defending President Obama in the Atlantic, claimed that the president's prayer breakfast speech had been misinterpreted—partly, he contended, because of racism.

In truth, Coates said, the president's remarks had been accurate; he had wanted to convey "faith leavened by 'some doubt.'" The terror of the Islamic State, Coates said, required "understanding the lure of brutality, and recalling how easily your own society can be, and how often it has been, pulled over the brink."[8]

His defense reflected the common view on the Left: Christianity is a malevolent force in our democracy—the weapon of an intolerant majority against religious minorities, and people of no religion. Leftist activists are doing their best to drive Christianity out of all our institutions. Atheists object to the traditional town nativity scene, and left-wing agitators urge the Pentagon to curb religious expressions by Christians in uniform.

At best Christians are seen as naïve dupes, clinging to superstitions they barely understand and values that they routinely violate in their own behavior. At worst they are seen as would-be Inquisitors eager to oppress others, especially blacks, women, and gays.

In his remarks at the National Prayer Breakfast, Obama claimed, "In our home country, slavery and Jim Crow all too often was justified in the name of Christ." That is true—but it is also true that the abolitionist movement and the civil rights movement drew on Christian teachings on the inherent dignity of the individual and the equality of human beings before God.

For Obama to entirely neglect the redemptive side of Christianity was a particularly glaring oversight, particularly given that he began his career as a community organizer in a Catholic church. As he notes in his memoir *Dreams from My Father*, Obama was drawn to the Reverend Jeremiah Wright's church precisely because of the way Wright connected Christian worship with anti-apartheid activism. Though Wright's radicalism left little room for true Christian compassion—the September 11 terror attacks were "America's chickens come home to roost," he said—Obama could not have been oblivious to the fact that Wright's politics at least purported to be drawn from the Christian faith.

The fact is that Christian civilization has done more than any other to advance freedom, in no small part because Christianity recognizes the moral life of the individual outside the state.

And that is precisely why the Left hates it.

Arthur Koestler—a Jew and Zionist—best expressed the difference between the Christian idea and its rivals in his anti-communist novel, *Darkness at Noon*: "There are only two conceptions of human ethics, and they are at opposite poles. One of them is Christian and humane, declares the individual to be sacrosanct, and asserts that the rules of arithmetic are not to be applied to human units. The other starts from the basic principle that a collective aim justifies all means, and not only allows, but demands, that the individual should in every way be subordinated and sacrificed to the community.... Humbugs and dilettantes have always tried to mix the two conceptions; in practice, it is impossible."[9]

Moreover, within Christendom, the dissenting Protestant sects stood apart for their belief that an individual may connect to God on his own. That high value on the individual has driven America's political and economic success.

The attraction of the Christian faith and lifestyle is more powerful than anything that the Left has been able to offer. At best, socialism can create ephemeral communities—like the tent cities of Occupy Wall Street—that only last a short time and often self-destruct.

The appeal of Christianity is that it offers more than mere materialism. The Left offers a critique of material wealth, but it remains locked in a materialistic worldview, offering redistribution of material goods as the remedy. In contrast, Christianity acknowledges the material world but seeks to transcend it—not only with promises of life in the hereafter, but with the insistence that individuals have an inner spiritual dignity.

In his seminal text *Conscience of a Conservative*, the late Barry Goldwater observed that while conservatives were often accused of materialism because of their association (fair or not) with the interests of the wealthy, in reality it was conservatism's opponents who were obsessed with material questions. He noted that "...it is Socialism that subordinates all other concerns to a man's material well-being. It is Conservatism that puts material things in their proper place...."

What is missing from political culture on the American Left is a sense of how important Christianity is to the liberties we enjoy—how "under God," inserted into the Pledge of Allegiance to distinguish the American creed from communism, actually reflected the underlying assumption that had already guaranteed "liberty and justice for all," at least in theory, throughout American history.

Instead, Christianity is often discussed as if it were a system of intolerance and repression—with an attitude little changed from the disdain expressed a century ago by H. L. Mencken, who saw the Christian faith as a creed of the easily duped and the socially pathetic. Attacks on Christianity are widely resorted to as a cheap means of expressing intellectual sophistication and identifying as cosmopolitan. Christian principles may occasionally be invoked by the Left—but only to justify government redistribution of income, which hijacks the Christian concept of charity.

Meanwhile, the Christian nations of the world struggle to muster a response to the advance of radical Islam, both far away and within their own borders. Facing the self-doubting Christian societies of the West, radical Islamists are undoubtedly reassured by the relative strength and resilience of their own faith.

When it comes to religion, the United States has always been different from the European countries. One of the characteristic features of American life, observed nearly two hundred years ago by Alexis de Tocqueville, has been widespread religious observance. Tocqueville noted that religious faith persisted in America, ironically in spite of—or perhaps because of—the lack of an official state church. He concluded that the independence of church and state from one another in the U.S. meant that, unlike in his native France, political upheavals were not accompanied by religious ones and faith remained a stable foundation for society.

Today, however, there are cracks in that foundation. A decline in the traditional family lifestyle that was once sustained by religious faith and practice has coincided—some would say, has been caused by—the advance of the welfare state over the past several decades. A healthy liberal secularism, in which people of different faiths and no faith at all can mix and mingle peacefully—is giving way to an aggressive anti-religious left-wing political agenda.

The American Left has defined religious freedom as the freedom *from* religion. And yet the Founders who defined our civil liberties saw religious faith as central to the mores and habits that would guide government and governed alike to respect those liberties.

As Thomas Jefferson famously wrote, "Can the liberties of a nation be secure when we have removed a conviction that these liberties are the gift of God?"[10] Or, as William Penn put it, "Men must be governed by God or they will be ruled by tyrants." The Quaker founder of Pennsylvania did not mean that Americans ought to live in a religious state. But he understood that unless the social mores and ideas of the general populace reflected virtues of the sort promoted by faith, then anarchy and immorality would reign and self-government would be insufficient to maintain social order. Then only monarchy would do, and democracy would have failed.

Even the late Christopher Hitchens, one of the best known critics of Christianity and religion in general, had to admit that the alternative had sometimes been worse. In his 2007 polemic *God is Not Great: How Religion Poisons Everything*, Hitchens claimed that it was "impossible to argue that religion causes people to behave in a more kindly or civilized manner."[11] Yet he also acknowledged that "secular totalitarianism has actually provided us with the *summa* of human evil."[12]

Some left-wing resentment of Christianity derives from the fact that Christianity has come to play a greater role in American politics in recent years. The political mobilization of Christians, especially Evangelical Protestants, in various organizations and under different names—the religious right, the Christian right, the "Moral Majority," and so on—has had a profound effect on American politics from the 1970s onward, shaping Congress, the Supreme Court, and popular culture.

The foundation for the new era of Christian politics was laid by the rapid spread of a telegenic new national form of Evangelical Christianity, largely through the successful ministries of the Reverend Billy Graham and others, who were able to use the media of television and radio to reach millions of Americans. They shaped a religious revival that reprised the Great Awakening of early American history.

Originally, the Evangelical movement was not necessarily Republican, or even politically conservative. It is telling that America's first Evangelical president, one who claimed to have been "born again" for Christ, was not a Republican but a Democrat, Jimmy Carter.

It was the courts that provoked the Evangelical movement to embrace conservatism. A series of increasingly left-wing decisions by the Supreme Court from the 1950s through the 1970s triggered growing outrage as a group of unelected lawyers essentially rolled back the moral framework of American society.

The changes began with the Supreme Court's 1962 decision in *Engel v. Vitale*, striking down prayers in schools.[13] The most notorious case, of course, was *Roe v. Wade*, the 1973 decision that legalized abortion by reading a right to privacy into the 14th Amendment.[14] Abortion was already on the way to being legalized democratically in many states, but the Supreme Court decision halted that movement in its tracks, triggering a backlash that continues to this day.

Politically active Evangelical Christians began linking themselves more tightly to the conservative movement in the 1970s, and that alliance reached its apogee in the presidency of Ronald Reagan, who built a successful coalition that united social conservatives with fiscal conservatives—a coalition that continues to define the Republican Party today.

Democrats have long viewed the alliance of these two factions with a mixture of contempt and dismay—contempt for what they see as the odd union between those arguing for smaller government power and those arguing for greater government intrusion into private life on moral grounds; and dismay because the combination has proved so potent and enduring.

But what balances the two sides of the Republican equation is more than mere political convenience or the cynical exploitation of the poorer Americans who also tend to be socially conservative—as alleged by left-liberals like Thomas Frank.

The two sides of conservatism—traditional morality and capitalist prosperity—are intimately connected, and they have been for centuries. The sociologist Max Weber traced the energies of capitalism to the dissident sects of Protestantism, who saw success in this world as evidence of God's grace.[15]

More fundamentally, Christianity's emphasis on individual moral choices and personal salvation strengthened the idea of individual rights given by God—rights that exist prior to government. Thus even libertarians like Kentucky Republican senator Rand Paul, who says "I want a government really, really small—so small you can barely see it,"[16] also argues that the government should outlaw abortion—and he's not just making a play for the votes of social conservatives. In the view of the pro-life libertarian, the first (and perhaps only) legitimate purpose of the state is to protect the lives and liberties of its members. Since the right to life is the most fundamental right, the state has the duty to protect it.

The political power of social conservatives has waned somewhat over time, thanks to the dominance of popular culture. Though opposition to abortion has held steady, for example, opposition to gay marriage has collapsed with amazing speed—partly under the weight of cultural pressure from Hollywood and judicial pressure from the courts, but also because of the fundamentally tolerant nature of American society.

Still, religion remains a potent political force in American life, and the link between liberty and faith is the core of what is called American exceptionalism.

Barack Obama views American exceptionalism, erroneously, as merely a kind of natural patriotic attachment of the sort common to all nations. "I believe in American exceptionalism, just as I suspect that the Brits believe in British exceptionalism and the Greeks believe in Greek exceptionalism," he infamously said during his first year in office.[17] The truth is that American exceptionalism derives from the Protestant tradition that took root in American soil. That tradition prized literacy, rejected hierarchy, and valued human industry because, properly applied, it would express God's presence in the world. Thus the Protestants who were the first American settlers believed that Augustine's ideal "City of God" could in fact be found in the City of Man—in America.

Fundamentally, the American Christian tradition is not only a religious creed but also a humanistic one. And while it certainly has had its share of superstitions, oddities, fraudulent preachers and self-seeking prophets, American Christianity provided our country with a moral foundation that worked in tandem with what Tocqueville described as "self-interest." By "self interest properly understood," he meant the impulse of ordinary Americans to pursue their own—perhaps greedy and self-indulgent—desires, but to do so in a way that was socially useful, or at least not socially harmful. This delicate balance, according to Tocqueville, was nurtured by the religion of most Americans, which was situated within the broader secular structure of American life, in which individuals were simultaneously members of a variety of overlapping associations through which they pursued their own goals with a sense of public purpose.

Thus while capitalism and freedom encouraged an atomistic, ambitious, fractured, and ever-changing society, the ritual and structure of religion, congregation, township, and association wove the social fabric tightly. That is the essence of American exceptionalism, and Christianity is fundamental to it.

American Christianity manages to be fervent and ecumenical at the same time—another exceptional feature. In February 2015, Peter Manseau, writing for the liberal website Salon, praised Obama's first inaugural address for its explicit mention of a wide variety of faiths, including atheism. It was, he said, "the first time a newly elected president used the occasion to give voice to the diversity of religious life among its people"—and he contrasted Obama's inclusivenesss favorably with the homage paid by previous American presidents to the Christian tradition.[18] "[Obama's] simple declaration of a catalogue of beliefs surprised many because there persists, among believers and nonbelievers alike, an assumption that the United States is, for better or worse, a Christian nation," Manseau wrote. But "we should hope that the new president [inaugurated in 2017] will be aware enough of history to reaffirm a truth that should be self-evident: A country as complex as ours cannot be captured by a single religious idea."

In fact, religious diversity is essential to America's religious foundation. The Christian tradition from which America benefits is actually a *Judeo*-Christian tradition. The idea of law—both human and God-given—as the bedrock of society dates to the Hebrews of the Old Testament. The notion of writing laws and handing their interpretation to judges was not unique to ancient Jewish civilization, but was perfected by it. Later, that high valuation for law found expression in the British common law tradition that is the basis for American jurisprudence.

Even the Muslim world has contributed, indirectly, to the American democratic experiment (though not in the grand way often claimed by President Obama, who favors a revisionist history that virtually writes Muslims into the Founding and omits mention of Islamic pirates as early enemies of the United States). It was the Islamic world that preserved the writings of the ancient Greek philosophers and historians, when the Europe of the Middle Ages was barely literate. The works of Aristotle, Plato, and other classical Greek thinkers went on to inspire the Renaissance, and then the Enlightenment, and they were studied closely by the Framers of the U.S. Constitution, when there were not many contemporary examples of democracy to study.

What is lost when faith recedes from public life is that sense that there is something prior to government, and to business: namely, the inner life and inherent dignity of the individual. Many of the interlocking rights and guarantees, checks and balances, freedoms and liberties that secular life depends on are ultimately only guarded by the idea of individual dignity, which comes only from the Judeo-Christian tradition.

The great pagan philosophers valued the individual life—but only for a few: for the Platonic philosopher-king, who was free to recommend the execution of everyone over a certain age, the better to achieve the most perfect Republic; or for the class of men designed by nature to be masters and not slaves (the life of the mind was supposed to be their exclusive preserve).

Other faiths provide models that do not preclude democracy and individual liberties, but they would be unlikely to promote them if left to their own devices. Islam literally means "submission," and its ideal political model is not the democratic republic achieving worldly prosperity, but the Islamic caliphate conquering vast swathes of territory, forcibly bending all knees to the one true God. Its people are subjects, not citizens.

Even Judaism, which provided the ethical foundations on which subsequent Christian ideas were built, does not lend itself to democracy. The ideal Jewish political system is rule by scholarly judges and—if necessary—by a king. The fact that Israel is a democracy today, when so many Israeli Jews immigrate from countries with no real democratic tradition themselves, owes more to British parliamentary tradition than Jewish law.

Christianity upholds individual dignity while balancing the prerogatives of the individual with precepts of faith and a framework of ritual. That notion of the free but bounded self is the essence of republican democracy and an open society. The Christian faith not only undergirds our system of individual rights and civil liberties, but is responsible for the concept of the individual—whose liberation from religion the Left now demands. Our society accommodates a wide spectrum of religious diversity, and it can tolerate atheism. But nothing can replace the essentially Christian concept of the individual—except for the utilitarian prerogatives of the state.

Yes, as Obama notes, and the Left reminds us constantly, Christianity has been guilty of terrible atrocities—against Jews, against Muslims, against the colonized peoples of the world, against fellow Christians. And yet compared to its rivals, there is no other faith that has done more to spread freedom. We would mourn its absence were it ever to disappear from our public life, as some desire.

# CHAPTER 18

# THE MEDIA

## THE LIE:
## There is no liberal bias in the American media.

Examples:

> *"It's silly that there's a liberal bias in media. Obviously, there are liberal voices and there are conservative voices. But overwhelmingly, media in the United States, television, newspapers and that sort of thing, the bias shifts towards the right. It's a center-right media in this country."*[1]
>
> —Bob Herbert, former *New York Times* columnist, MSNBC, April 2013

> *"I'm part of the mainstream media, but my viewpoint is pretty clear. I think what people don't like is when they*

*feel that there are biases at work that are unannounced.
And I think the mainstream media is biased but not in any
partisan way."*[2]

—MSNBC host Christopher Hayes,
*The Daily Show with Trevor Noah*, November 2015

*"[The New York Times'] liberal reputation makes it all that
much more valuable as a counterintuitive megaphone for
conservative propaganda."*[3]

—David Brock, *Killing the Messenger*, 2015

# THE TRUTH:
## The media have a left-wing bias, and it affects what many Americans believe.

My friend, colleague, and mentor Andrew Breitbart passed away suddenly on March 1, 2012. He died just four days before we were due to launch the new version of Breitbart.com. Andrew's vision for the website—which had formerly been a passive domain linking to news wire stories—was to create a conservative news source that would break news rather than simply linking to or commenting on stories from the mainstream media. He intended to take on the liberal media—and defeat it. Though our hearts were broken, the management and staff worked around the clock over the next four days to launch Breitbart.com—on time, on schedule, on target, to fulfill his dream.

Andrew had grown up in the affluent liberal clime of West Los Angeles, one of two adopted children in a loving Jewish family. He was Boy Scout and class clown rolled into one. He made it to Tulane University in New Orleans, a top-tier school—but passed through it in a par-tied-out haze. And he was lucky he did, he later reflected: by slacking off, he missed out on the politically correct dogma being drilled into his classmates' brains.

As he recalled in his memoir,[4] Andrew returned to L.A. with no clear direction—waiting tables, delivering pizzas, and schlepping movie scripts from one Hollywood office to another. If he had any political ideas at all, they were liberal at best, nihilist at worst.

But under the influence of his girlfriend's father, the conservative actor Orson Bean, he began to think about politics more seriously. He turned Rush Limbaugh on in the car. He met a young salesman named Matt Drudge, who would go on to create the Internet's most important news portal. And he had an epiphany while watching the confirmation hearings for Supreme Court Justice Clarence Thomas. The way a conservative black jurist was being smeared as a sexual predator set Andrew off—and down the warpath against what he came to call the "Democrat-media Complex."

The "Complex" was Andrew's shorthand for the journalistic establishment, over 90 percent of whom vote Democrat,[5] as well as the liberal culture brokers of Hollywood. "Culture is upstream from politics," he would often say. Through popular culture and media, Hollywood influences Americans who otherwise have no interest in politics to view society through a political prism that suits the Left's purpose, which is to create doubt and dissatisfaction within American society and so make people more receptive to revolutionary, socialist change.

The Complex's most powerful weapon, Andrew believed, was the façade of objectivity. The media's liberal bias was the truth it could not afford to report, because once people understood the filter through which their information was delivered, they would be less manipulable and might start to push back.

The media denies that they have any such bias—or argue that, if they do, their bias has no real effect on how Americans see the world, much less on how they vote. A Facebook editor argued against the claim that the website's "trending news" section had suppressed conservative stories by claiming that the site used "rigorous guidelines" for curating news topics.[6] Those guidelines included comparing news stories from conservative sites to ten large mainstream outlets, only two of which were conservative. A story from one of those two outlets—Fox News and the *Wall Street Journal*—*might* be considered legitimate if the BBC, the *New York Times*, CNN, and NBC also covered the same topic.[7] The idea that most mainstream outlets might have a left-wing bias never, apparently, entered the editorial equation.[8] Some on the Left have even argued that the media are too conservative, owing to the profit-making motives of most media corporations. And if they are criticized from both the Left and the Right, that must be proof that the media are in the middle—exactly where they ought to be, objectively.

So the argument went—until Tim Groseclose, a political scientist and economist at UCLA, became involved. Groseclose, now at George Mason University, was a rare conservative on a California campus, and one of the many L.A. conservatives Andrew emboldened. He decided to use empirical methods to test whether the media did, in fact, have a liberal bias—and, if so, what the effect of that bias was on public opinion.

Groseclose explains his research at length in his 2011 book, *Left Turn: How Liberal Media Bias Distorts the American Mind*.[9] He borrows the political quotient (PQ), a common measurement in political science that assigns numerical values to political views on a scale from 0 (most conservative) to 100 (most liberal). Using data on how often different media outlets cite liberal and conservative think tanks, he assigns each source a slant quotient (SQ). And, finally, he asks whether, and how much, the media's SQ affects the average voter's PQ—in other words, how media bias affects political perceptions.

The results are astonishing: "every mainstream national news outlet in the United States has a liberal bias," he shows.[10] Only a few, including the *Washington Times* and Fox News's Special Report, lean to the right. "But even these supposedly conservative news outlets are not far right [emphasis in the original]," Groseclose says. "For instance the conservative bias of Special Report is significantly less than the liberal bias of CBS Evening News."[11]

Furthermore, Groseclose finds: "The effects of media bias are real and significant. My results suggest that media bias aids Democratic candidates by about 8 to 10 percentage points in a typical election [emphasis in the original]."[12] While the average voter has political views corresponding to a score of 50 on the PQ scale, that is only because of media bias. Without media bias, the average voter's views would be 20 points more conservative—"approximately 25 or 30," Groseclose writes.[13] That means they would share the views of Fox News host Bill O'Reilly, or of the population of Orange County, one of the few Republican-leaning areas in the blue state of California.

For his trouble, Groseclose has been attacked viciously by the Left and the academic establishment. But no one can dispute his numbers or methods.

Groseclose also disputes the "corporate media" theory, which has been a favorite of the Left since at least the 1960s. "This theory says that despite the liberal views of journalists, their reporting will be centrist— and maybe even conservative—because of pressure from their corporate bosses," he says.[14] The basic problem with this theory is that the supply of journalists is so overwhelmingly liberal that in the unlikely event a conservative owner finds a conservative journalist or two, they will still be overwhelmingly outnumbered by their liberal colleagues, on whose views and output they are unlikely to have much of an effect.

But the "corporate media" theory still has some fans. Its most prominent exponent is David Brock, a conservative-turned-liberal who founded Media Matters for America, a George Soros–funded non-profit that exists to defend Democratic Party politicians and to trash conservative media outlets.

Brock is close to Hillary Clinton—whom he once smeared, before switching sides—and runs a political action committee, American Bridge 21st Century PAC, that supports Clinton's 2016 campaign for president. To that end, he has published defenses of Hillary Clinton's conduct surrounding the Benghazi terror attack in Libya in 2012, as well as attacks on journalists who have dared to explore Clinton's long history of cronyism and cover-ups.

In September 2015, Brock accused the reliably liberal *New York Times* of being a shill for conservatives. "As it concerns Clinton coverage, the *Times* will have a special place in journalism hell," he wrote in a book defending Clinton.[15] He also accused the *Times*'s former Washington bureau chief, Carolyn Ryan, of turning the newspaper into a "megaphone for conservative propaganda."[16]

The *Times* pushed back, telling Politico, "David Brock is an opportunist and a partisan who specializes in personal attacks. We've seen him lash out at some of our aggressive coverage of important political figures and it's unsurprising that he has now turned personal. He's wrong on all counts."

There is a small kernel of truth in Brock's critique. Groseclose writes that "to some extent, I also agree with the 'corporate media' theorists in one regard. That is, many corporate bosses pressure their journalists not to report in the far-left manner the journalists desire."[17] The reason may be simpler than political bias: corporate media executives realize that the American public is far less liberal than the journalists in the newsroom, and they do not want to lose profits by alienating readers.

Hillary Clinton probably does receive an unusual amount of scrutiny—for a Democrat—but for reasons that have nothing to do with conservative bias. One reason is that she and her husband have a long history of acrimonious relations with the press. That makes some journalists—Ron Fournier, for example, who has covered the Clintons since their days in the Arkansas governor's mansion—more inclined to criticize Clinton. Another reason is that Clinton is the Democratic Party frontrunner. Leaders in both parties receive more attention than candidates who have less chance of winning.

But the most important reason Hillary Clinton may attract more criticism is that both times she has run for president, she has faced an opponent further to the left—Barack Obama in 2008 and Bernie Sanders in 2016. The left-wing bias of many journalists could very well make them more inclined to give more positive coverage to Sanders and more negative coverage to Clinton. In doing so, journalists may also make the presidential race more competitive than it would otherwise have been, given Clinton's large early lead in national polls and fundraising. A closer race generates more public interest—more clicks, more subscriptions, and more job security.

Whatever the reason, conservative bias at the *New York Times* is the least likely explanation. And certainly Clinton's own dubious conduct—such as her decision to install a private e-mail server in the bathroom of her New York home for her official communications as Secretary of State—have helped to provoke the media's interest.

Brock's improbable accusations of conservative bias against one of the most left-wing media outlets in the country, repeated and weaponized by leading members of the political establishment, are disturbingly reminiscent of tactics that have undermined press freedom in other countries.

In South Africa, where I was born and where I first cut my journalistic and political teeth after college, the post-apartheid ruling party, the African National Congress (ANC), repeatedly accuses the country's media of bias against the government. That bias, the ANC alleges, is motivated by racism—on the part of reporters, editors, and owners. The fact that many journalists were among the fiercest critics of the apartheid regime doesn't stop the ANC, whose leaders still cling to Cold War-era secrecy and resent any media criticism. They see the free press—and political opposition—as "counter-revolutionary" obstacles to their political agenda.

In 2000, under pressure from the ruling ANC, the South African Human Rights Commission conducted a probe into racism in the media. The atmosphere surrounding the investigation was McCarthyist. Journalists were ordered to testify under threat of imprisonment and had to respond to an absurd preliminary roster of claims. An editorial criticizing the government's performance in garbage collection, for example, was said to be a sign of "deep-seated racialised anxiety about dirt."[18]

In the years since, the ownership of South African media has become more racially diverse, but the ruling party's suspicion of a free press has not abated. The ANC has attempted to pass a "secrecy" bill—ostensibly to protect information vital to national security but actually aimed at discouraging the sort of investigative reporting that embarrasses the ruling party.

Abuses of press freedom like those in South Africa may seem unlikely in the U.S., where that freedom is protected by the First Amendment. Yet in 2012 investigative journalist Matthew Boyle, then of the Daily Caller (now Breitbart), revealed that the Department of Justice had colluded with Brock's Media Matters to monitor conservative journalists, including me.[19] Moreover, the American media voluntarily submits itself to intense, almost coercive, political pressure.

Obama would never have been elected in 2008 had it not been for the media's efforts to hype his candidacy despite his sparse résumé, to cover up his many mistakes, and to pursue his critics. The press behaved, at times, almost as if they were acting on his instructions. Yet journalists have not been treated worse by a president since Richard Nixon. The first signs of trouble appeared on the campaign trail, when Obama was frequently unwilling to talk to journalists. In one case, the Obama team irritated journalists by flying them from Washington to Chicago on the campaign airplane, only belatedly revealing that Obama was not actually on the flight—and then leaving them to find their own way home.

Journalists who were critical of the Illinois senator—such as Stanley Kurtz, who wrote about Obama's ties to domestic terrorist Bill Ayers— were targeted; the campaign labeled Kurtz a "kook," though his charges were completely accurate. Kurtz's appearance on a Chicago-area radio show prompted Obama supporters to jam the phone lines, making an honest debate all but impossible.

In office, Obama touted his administration as the "most transparent ever." That claim rested largely on the unprecedented release of White House visitor logs. But staff simply worked around the supposed transparency by taking important meetings with lobbyists offsite. Moreover, as Andrew Breitbart pointed out, the administration would not confirm the identities of people who appeared on the list, making it useless. "The visitor logs that have been released are problematic, because they are simply lists of names, with no way to verify whether a specific name belongs to a particular person," he wrote, adding that the White House had "created a haystack that can hide a needle."[20]

The administration also became notorious for evading, delaying, and redacting responses to Freedom of Information Act requests for documents. Hillary Clinton's notorious "homebrew" e-mail server was in part a way of evading such requests. The Obama press shop also began to circumvent the White House press corps by using non-traditional, pop culture–oriented media sources—such as Inside Edition, YouTube channels, and podcasts—to get their message out. And the administration used White House photographer Pete Souza to show flattering, admiring pictures of the president rather than allowing pool photographers to take their own.

Even more ominous was the White House's war on conservative media, including Rush Limbaugh and especially Fox News, which the Obama White House specifically attempted to freeze out of interviews and press briefings. In Obama's second term, it emerged that the administration had gone even further with one specific Fox News reporter, James Rosen, tapping his phone and even his parents' telephones to determine who had leaked him information about North Korea's nuclear program. The investigation, Attorney General Eric Holder told Congress, was not an attempt to prosecute a journalist—though the court that authorized the warrants for the searches and surveillance had been told the opposite, meaning that Holder had likely perjured himself. Later it was revealed that the Department of Justice had tapped more than twenty phone lines at the Associated Press. The scandal could have— and, as some said, should have—been a turning point for Obama's relations with the media.

But Obama refused to apologize, and the press continued to defend him. Obama's response when each scandal broke was to express outrage, to claim that he had only learned of the scandalous conduct from the news, and to promise to stop whatever abuse had taken place. The media dutifully followed his script—and then moved on, leaving Obama to reverse himself at leisure.

The media would never have given any other president—certainly not a Republican president—anything like the leeway it gave Obama. The fact that they would not defend their own freedoms is a sign of how poorly they understood the value of press freedom, and of the extent of their own bias.

Even when admitting bias, journalists ascribe that bias to anything other than left-wing partisanship. MSNBC host Chris Hayes, appearing on The Daily Show on Comedy Central—a reliable font of left-wing views—told new host Trevor Noah that "the mainstream media is biased but not in any partisan way. I think there are certain biases we have. We have bias towards spectacle."[21] One of the media's favorite spectacles just happens to be attacking conservatives. As a conservative journalist, one soon learns the rules of the game. Conservatives are rarely invited onto a network to offer a straightforward opinion. But conservatives who are willing to attack other conservatives find numerous platforms for their views. And if, as a conservative journalist, you do or say something controversial, providing the mainstream media a potential opening to criticize you, you may find a few unexpected and polite mainstream media requests in your email inbox, inviting you to participate in your own potential public demise. In other words, they typically invite conservatives on only when their appearance can be used against conservatism.

That is what nearly happened to me in March 2012, a week after Andrew Breitbart's passing, when I was invited onto CNN's morning show, hosted by Soledad O'Brien. The request referred to the recent release of video footage of a young Barack Obama embracing Critical Race Theory proponent Derrick Bell at Harvard Law School (see chapter 9), which Andrew had teased in the weeks before his death, and which we had just released. I came prepared to talk about Obama's relationship with Bell, but as I sat in CNN's L.A. studio, preparing to join the show via satellite, it became clear that O'Brien intended to bury Andrew, not to praise him.

In that moment, I asked myself what Andrew would have done in the same situation. The answer came to me: question the premise.

Andrew understood that the key to mainstream media bias is the way the media frames issues. Resist the frame, and you can force the debate onto a level playing field.

I was explaining the Critical Race Theory to which Bell subscribed, when O'Brien interrupted me:[22]

> O'BRIEN: OK. So then let's go back to the clips that I just showed. What part of that was the bombshell? Because I missed it. I don't get it. What was a bombshell?

> POLLAK: Well, the bombshell is the revelation of the relationship between Obama and Derrick Bell. Obama didn't just lead a protest—

> O'BRIEN: OK. So he's a Harvard law student and Harvard law professor, yes?

> POLLAK: That's correct. And Derrick Bell is the Jeremiah Wright of academia. He passed away but during his lifetime he developed a theory called critical race theory which holds that the civil rights movement was a sham and that white supremacy is the order and it must be overthrown. Barack Obama—

> O'BRIEN: So, that is a complete misreading. I'll stop you there for a second. Then I'll let you continue. That is a complete misreading of critical race theory, as you know. That's an actual theory. You could Google it and someone would give you a good definition of it. So, that's not correct.

> POLLAK: Well, in what way—in what way is it a critical misreading? Can you explain to me? Do you know what critical—explain to your readers what critical theory race is.

> O'BRIEN: I'm going to ask you to continue on. I'm just going to point out that that is inaccurate. Keep going. Tell me what the bombshell is. I haven't seen it—

POLLAK: Well, wait a minute. You've made a claim — you've made a claim that my characterization of critical race theory is the opposite of Martin Luther King, is inaccurate. You're telling your viewers that. But you're not telling why it is.

Eventually, one of O'Brien's co-panelists, Jay Thomas, interjected,

THOMAS: Are you frightened that some black people are going to do something to you? You have a group of individuals—if you and I were black we would be madder than hell, but we're not. And so, we are white people. There are more white people than black people. And so there's a struggle that's been going on and so in a struggle you talk about a lot of things. There's anger. There's resentment. And so, what are you frightened of? What do you think Barack Obama's going to do? Is there a secret black movement that's going to start killing white people? What are you talking about? As a white guy.

POLLAK: I'm glad you played the racism card. You've accused me of being a racist.

THOMAS: White. I've accused you of being white. It's all I've accused you of.

POLLAK: No, you've accused me of being afraid of black people. And it doesn't deserve a response. But let me respond anyway.

THOMAS: Sure.

POLLAK: No, I'm not afraid black people are going to be violent and take over the country. What I'm pointing out is that there's a pattern in Barack Obama's associations with Derrick Bell, with Reverend Wright, and it carries over into his governance because his Justice Department won't treat black civil rights violators the same way it treats white civil rights violators. That there's a racial pattern in which justice is enforced and it gives us a sense of how Barack Obama thinks about these issues.

At every point when he could have followed the path of Martin Luther King, he threw in his lot with the Jeremiah Wrights and Derrick Bells of the world.

I must admit that I was tempted to tell Thomas that the only black person I was legitimately afraid of was my mother-in-law. But I decided to leave my family out of the argument—which I won.

O'Brien revisited the issue the following Monday. But this time she did not invite me to defend my views. She merely discussed me with another guest in my absence—prompting *Washington Post* media critic Erik Wemple to quip, "As a CNN viewer, I'll gladly take the initial, contentious segment over O'Brien's chorus-of-consensus do-over."[23]

The episode drove home for me the lesson that the most important way that media bias works is by framing the discussion. For the media's gatekeepers, determining which political views are legitimate and which are not is more important than determining which are true and which are false. Even purported "fact-checking," now a cottage industry, is affected by the bias of the journalists who run the fact-check websites. PolitiFact, for example, run by the *Tampa Bay Times*, has been shown to punish Republicans more harshly than Democrats for factually questionable statements.[24] The *Washington Post*'s fact-checker, Glenn Kessler, questions Republicans more often than Democrats, and has admitted that his ratings are "subjective."[25]

The only way to force the Left to acknowledge the reality of media bias is to confront them with it. For that reason, the emergence of the conservative new media—from talk radio to Fox News to the Drudge Report and beyond—has been both a blessing and a curse. The proliferation of new outlets has brought new strength and coherence to the conservative movement and provides space for the airing of ideas that the Left has long and effectively sought to repress. But there is a downside: the emergence of conservative media accelerated the conservative withdrawal from American public life—from academia, cultural institutions, public radio, cinema, and pop culture. True, these spheres had all been colonized by the Left—but it was a crucial tactical error that rather than fighting back many conservatives chose the splendid isolation of their own media bubble.

There is no need to hide. Andrew Breitbart led by example. With truth on our side, all we need is courage.

# CHAPTER 19

# SEE THE GOOD IN AMERICA

## THE LIE:
## American democracy is broken and doomed to fail without radical political change.

Examples:

*"Once again, the democracies are having grave difficulty pulling their economies out of a prolonged economic slump. Once again, they are suffering from parliamentary deadlock and loss of faith in democratic institutions. The American version reflects a radically obstructionist Republican Party taking advantage of constitutional provisions that Madison (and Obama) imagined as promoting compromise; instead, the result is deadlock."*[1]

—Robert Kuttner, *The American Prospect*, March 2015

*"America's constitutional democracy is going to collapse.*

*"Some day—not tomorrow, not next year, but probably
sometime before runaway climate change forces us to seek
a new life in outer-space colonies—there is going to be a
collapse of the legal and political order and its replace-
ment by something else. If we're lucky, it won't be violent.
If we're very lucky, it will lead us to tackle the underlying
problems and result in a better, more robust, political system. If we're less lucky, well, then, something worse will
happen."[2]*

—Matthew Yglesias, Vox, October 2015

*"I am pledged, if elected president of the United States, to
bring about a political revolution where millions of people
begin to stand up and finally say enough is enough, this
great country and our government belong to all of us, not
just a handful of billionaires."*

—Senator Bernie Sanders, Democratic presidential debate,
December 2015

## THE TRUTH:
## American democracy remains robust—if we have
## the courage to use its tools.

This book has reviewed the many ways in which the Left suppresses the
truth in political debates. Even where they have a plausible case to make,
those on the Left work to suppress any truths that might form the basis for
dissent. Where there are closely argued policy differences, progressives
shortcut debate by obscuring facts and marginalizing conservative

viewpoints. And when they are completely in the wrong, the partisans of the Left simply deny reality.

But there is one chink in their armor: namely, the prospect of political change. Despite the Left's domination of the mainstream media, Hollywood, and government agencies, conservatives have been able to mobilize political opposition.

In 2009, shortly after President Barack Obama took office and began pursuing an aggressive left-wing agenda, veteran Democratic political strategist James Carville published a book entitled *40 More Years: How the Democrats Will Rule the Next Generation*.[3] But less than two years later, Republicans won the most dramatic midterm election victory in nearly a century, taking over sixty seats in the House, six seats in the Senate, six gubernatorial elections, and hundreds of seats in state legislatures in the 2010 midterm elections. The shift in party representation at the state level meant that the drawing of new congressional districts would largely be in Republican hands, allowing them to shut Democrats out of power in the House for a decade. It was an astonishing affirmation of the health of American democracy, which was resisting one-party dominance and radical political change.

So the Left has increasingly resorted to the argument that American democracy is "broken"—and only greater centralization of power can save it. As Joel Kotkin noted at the Daily Beast, "Increasingly the call is not so much for a benevolent and charismatic dictator, but for an impaneled committee of experts to rule over our lives." Those arguments, he added, gained momentum after "the 2010 Republican congressional sweep."[4]

Meanwhile, Obama pressed ahead with his progressive agenda as if the 2010 elections had never happened. And he did the same after 2014, launching executive-driven policies on immigration, foreign policy, and climate change that evaded Congress and in some cases violated what he himself had said were the constitutional rules.

The Left defended these power grabs, proclaiming that Obama had previously been *too* bipartisan and that now he was forced to act unilaterally. Robert Kuttner, co-editor of the liberal *American Prospect*, for example, argued that "it is hard to recall a Democratic president more genuinely eager to accommodate the opposition than Barack Obama," though he provided no evidence for the claim.[5]

The idea that America has become "ungovernable" is not new. As Christopher Chantrill pointed out at the *American Thinker*, "Liberals were saying exactly the same thing in 1980, thirty years ago, in the darkest days of the Carter administration. The mess of inflation, recession, Iran hostages, and gas lines, they decided, was not a direct result of stupid Carter administration policy. It was a sign that America's best days were behind us, and that there was nothing to do but decline gracefully."[6] But, Chantrill added, "You'll remember that U.S. voters in the fall of 1980 had a different idea. They decided to elect a B-movie actor to the presidency." Ronald Reagan was considered unelectable, but he led the nation back to prosperity, global supremacy, and self-respect.

The most astonishing political story of 2015 was the rise—and rise—of Donald J. Trump, the real estate billionaire and reality television star who decided to run for president and defied expectations by surging to the lead in the Republican primary. Here was a man who had only recently "come out" as a Republican, and who had caused party leaders to squirm uncomfortably in 2011 when he challenged President Barack Obama to prove that he had been born in Hawaii and not, in fact, in Kenya. Trump flirted briefly with the idea of running in 2012, but decided not to.

When Trump finally announced his bid for the presidency in June 2015, *Vanity Fair* called it a "shocking twist."[7] Many observers mocked his ambitions, wondering if it was all just a show. Most presumed Trump would fail. Democrats used Trump's announcement as an opportunity to mock Republicans: Trump "adds some much-needed seriousness" to the Republican field, the Democratic National Committee announced.

And then Trump began to soar—first in New Hampshire, then everywhere.

The Republican establishment was mortified. Asked what he would do if Trump won the nomination, Republican former Los Angeles mayor Richard Riordan said, "I would probably go find a deserted island."[8]

The political commentariat struggled to understand what was going on. Some on the Left ascribed Trump's success to the bigotry of the conservative political base, which was responding to Trump's strong stance against illegal immigration. Pulitzer Prize–winning *Wall Street Journal* columnist Bret Stephens called Trump's supporters "vulgarians": "The leader isn't the problem. The people are. It takes the demos to make the demagogue."[9]

Stephens's fellow *Journal* columnist, former Reagan speechwriter Peggy Noonan was more sympathetic, pointing out that that Trump's rise "rests on two issues: opposition to illegal immigration to the U.S. and an obvious and visceral rejection of political correctness and the shaming and silencing it entails."[10] To fathom the depth of Trump's appeal, it is necessary to understand just how extreme the Left's political correctness has become—on immigration, as on other issues—and to grasp the frustration that many Americans feel with the Republican opposition, which seems to lack the will or the courage to fight back.

In October 2015, for example, America's college campuses exploded in protest as left-wing student activists challenged university administrators to address perceived racism—not just on campus, but in society at large. Students at the University of Missouri demanded that the university president write and read publicly a letter in which he "must acknowledge his white male privilege."[11] At Yale, left-wing students protested against a residential college administrator who had defended students' rights to wear offensive Halloween costumes because "free speech and the ability to tolerate offense are the hallmarks of a free and open society."[12] At Occidental College in Los Angeles, where President Barack Obama spent his early college years, students demanded that campus safety officers, who were already unarmed, stop wearing bulletproof vests. They also demanded that Occidental hire "physicians of color," who, they believed, could best "treat physical and emotional trauma associated with issues of identity."[13] Publisher Roger Kimball called these students "crybullies," radicals who used claims of their own hurt feelings to force others to accept their will.[14] And unlike previous outbreaks of political correctness over the past several decades, this was no mere academic issue, confined to ivy gates and ivory towers.

There is not one area of American life that has not been targeted by the Left, from the classroom to the bedroom. Today, for example, in supposedly libertine California, radical AIDs activists are passing ordinances requiring actors in pornographic films to wear condoms and protective goggles—not just to protect the performers, but to send a message about safe sex to the audience. And if the radical Left has its way, the "ladies' room" and the "men's room" will be phased out. The urinal—enviro-friendly waterless or otherwise—will be a relic of a past era.

The Left is even trying to force the game of football out of existence. The campaign goes far beyond concern for concussions that might affect athletes' long-term neurological health. It is a war against the masculine values of the game itself. Progressive columnist Peter Beinart has complained, "In big-time football, morality is measured in wins and losses,"[15] and worried about teaching his son to love the game lest he grow up with "heartwarming memories of sitting alongside his old man watching other men pulverize their bodies and minds."[16]

In September 2015 even President Obama felt compelled to speak out against the cult of political correctness: "I think you should be able to—anybody who comes to speak to you and you disagree with, you should have an argument with 'em. But you shouldn't silence them by saying, 'You can't come because I'm too sensitive to hear what you have to say.' That's not the way we learn either."[17] It was a statement he would feel compelled to repeat in the months that followed, telling the graduating class at Howard University, "[D]on't try to shut folks out, don't try to shut them down, no matter how much you might disagree with them."[18]

And yet this was the same president who insisted that the Washington Redskins football team change their name;[19] who claimed that Republicans who objected to his deal with Iran were making "common cause" with America's enemies; and who in 2008 had referred to *Democrats* in small-town America as people who "get bitter, they cling to guns or religion or antipathy to people who aren't like them or anti-immigrant sentiment or anti-trade sentiment as a way to explain their frustrations."[20]

President Obama did not really oppose political correctness; on the contrary, he depended on it. Suppressing conservative ideas and objections was necessary if he were to continue bending—and breaking—the constitutional rules that had bound every one of his predecessors. He humiliated Congress, behaving in a manner that conservative commentator Charles Krauthammer called "constitutionally indecent."[21] The president directly violated the letter of the Constitution, but more often he violated its spirit and vision.

The problem is not, as liberal pundits would have it, that the federal government is being prevented from working properly by a political opposition fueled by conservative billionaires. The problem is that the federal government already does too much of what the American people do not want it to do, and they do not trust it to do more. Obama's insistence on doing what he likes, in defiance of the will of the people's elected representatives, has only deepened the partisan divide. He, and the Left, are the cause of the very dysfunction they claim to cure.

Faced with the constitutional challenge Obama presents, the Republican opposition in Congress has actually been reluctant to use the tools at its disposal—such as blocking appointees, refusing to fund the federal government, or passing articles of impeachment. One of the few such efforts, the attempt by Republican Senator Ted Cruz of Texas to defund Obamacare before it was implemented in October 2013, led to a government shutdown in which Republican opposition to Obama cracked easily.

One tactic Republican leaders in Congress did try was suing the president in federal court, hoping that the judiciary—though it has become more liberal since Obama took office—would protect legislative prerogative and the public interest. While Congress occasionally prevailed, as we saw in chapter 16, the result was simply to increase the power of another branch of government, one even less accountable than the executive. As Mark Levin—not just a radio host, but also a litigator—observed: "I really do cringe at this idea that the elected branch of government turns to the unelected branch of government, and in essence empowers the other branch to make these decisions."[22] When Congress lost in court, Obama was only emboldened further.

Levin laid out his own proposed remedy in a 2013 book, *The Liberty Amendments*. He noted that the Framers had provided two ways to amend the Constitution under Article V. The first, which is most familiar, is a two-thirds vote in Congress for an amendment followed by ratification in three-fourths of the states. The second option, which has never been used, is a process that may be initiated by two-thirds of the states on their own—a "convention for proposing amendments."[23] It was precisely because the Framers feared the unchecked expansion of federal and executive power that they provided that backup method for amending the Constitution. To that end, Levin has not only proposed holding a convention of the states but also provided eleven amendments that he believes would restore and reinforce the original purpose of the Constitution, fortifying it against slow erosion by an over-powerful federal government.

Levin's proposal remains a long shot. Meanwhile, from the perspective of the average right-of-center voter as of 2016, the Republicans have been worse than disappointing. In 2010, riding the Tea Party wave, the GOP promised to repeal Obamacare and balance the budget. When they failed, Republican leaders said they could do little unless they controlled both houses of Congress. So voters gave Republicans power in the Senate in 2014. But that made no difference, either. Republicans passed massive spending bills of the sort that had provoked the Tea Party and failed to repeal Obamacare or to stop the Iran deal. GOP leaders protested that they could do little until they won back the White House. But after Mitt Romney's crushing loss in 2012, conservatives were loath to leave the choice of candidate to the Republican establishment.

So conservatives began to look elsewhere for leadership, and for people who would stand up for the truths that the Left had driven out of debates in Washington. One of these was Kim Davis, a county clerk in Kentucky who refused to provide marriage licenses to same-sex couples and was eventually jailed for contempt of court. Some conservatives argued that her conduct was no more unconstitutional than the Supreme Court's decision creating a fundamental right to same-sex marriage in the first place. If the Left could violate the rule of law with impunity, so could the Right.

This was the environment in which Donald Trump thrived. Americans were looking for strong leadership, and for a candidate who would stand up against the fictions of the Obama administration, the Left, and the media.

But there were reasons to worry about what a Trump presidency might mean. He was brash, often ill-informed, and—by his own admission—divisive. He mocked and threatened to sue journalists who dared criticize him. His promises sometimes exceeded the bounds of what was practical, constitutional, or lawful. He vowed, for example, to build a "big, beautiful wall" on the border with Mexico—and to make the Mexican government pay for it, somehow.

Trump also said he would keep Muslim immigrants and tourists out of the country until the federal government "can figure out what is going on" (which, given the depth of government dysfunction, might be never). As we have seen in chapter 13, though the idea is not unconstitutional, it would cause immense damage to trade and diplomacy. Trump even proposed killing the families of terrorists—which, as his rival for the Republican nomination Rand Paul pointed out, would violate the Geneva Conventions. America was still reeling from the damage and division caused by one chief executive who feels free to disregard the boundaries of the Constitution. It is unclear whether or how the country can survive another.

Another concern was Trump's penchant for exaggeration and fabulist tales. For example, in November 2015, Trump told an audience at a campaign rally that "thousands and thousands" of Muslims had celebrated the destruction of the World Trade Center from rooftops in New Jersey. It was an absurd claim on its face: if thousands of Muslims had celebrated in public, it would have been widely remembered. Trump insisted that he had seen a television report about it—and soon enough, a report from CBS New York surfaced, documenting that eight people in a building "swarming with suspects" had indeed been seen celebrating on the roof.[24] But eight is not "thousands"—and "thousands" lends itself to sweeping conclusions about American Muslims in general, rather than a small group of radicals. The truth matters.

Whatever happens in the 2016 presidential election and beyond, America will need more than a strong president to prevail over the many challenges the country faces. Indeed, the U.S. Constitution was written with the goal of restraining what strong leaders can do.

What is more important is to restore the health of our democracy by restoring truth to its rightful place in American political discourse. Reviving the truths the Left wishes to deny will begin to make a truly open political debate possible, one in which our country can finally find the right solutions to its dilemmas—and in which citizens can hold the people in power accountable for their actions.

Restoring truth begins with resisting the petty totalitarianism of the campus Left.

Author Wendy Kaminer, writing in February 2015 in the *Washington Post*, recalled an encounter with political correctness on the campus of Smith College, an all-female—and almost uniformly progressive—institution.[25] Kaminer had participated in a panel discussion on free speech, and bizarrely the transcript of the event was accompanied by a content warning, lest student readers encounter a particularly offensive word or idea. The dangerous word in question turned out to be "crazy," which the transcript described as an "[ablist slur]." Other "slurs" were also bracketed, so that the entire discussion carried a kind of stigma—even though the purpose of the discussion itself had been to open minds to challenging such stigmas. Kaminer warned that "the soft authoritarianism that now governs many American campuses" is "teaching future generations of leaders the 'virtues' of autocracy" rather than democracy. And this form of thought control is almost entirely self-imposed.

The unthinkable must be made thinkable again on our university campuses. That means resisting attempts to disinvite people—even those whose views are objectively offensive—or to exclude "dangerous" ideas. Academic institutions that play by totalitarian rules should be shamed. And we must be vigilant lest the totalitarian habits of the ivory tower continue to creep into the rest of our discourse.

One arena where conservatives have pushed back successfully is online. Against efforts like Facebook's attempt to filter out conservative news and the bizarre editorial policies at Buzzfeed that effectively preclude views supporting Donald Trump,[26] conservatives like Milo Yiannopoulos have pushed back on Twitter and in other forums, creating a new fan base and new conversations. The tech world may be overwhelmingly left-wing, but the tools it creates can be used for conservative purposes just as well, given creativity and courage.

Another way to assert the many truths the Left wishes to deny or suppress is to promote examples of conservative success—not least in the many states that are now governed by Republican governors, which are providing the perfect laboratories for policy experimentation, but elsewhere as well.

Public sector labor reform, formerly unthinkable, has worked in Wisconsin and has spread elsewhere. Reform of race-based affirmative action in California led to lower enrollment of black students at the state's most competitive universities—but also to better career outcomes for those black students who went to universities better geared to their abilities. Abroad, a new border fence in Israel—the kind of boundary American lawmakers pretend is impossible or impractical—has reduced illegal crossings from the West Bank and Egypt to nearly zero. These are all real-world, practical examples of success that according to the dogma of the Left should be impossible.

In addition to promoting conservative policy success, we must do more to bring the Left's core agenda out of the shadows. We cannot let the other side hide behind criticism of our ideas, defining themselves merely in silhouette, against everything conservative. We must force the Left's obscured dogmas into the harsh light and show what they actually represent and would achieve if their ideas were taken to their logical conclusions.

Perhaps most important, in the age of Trump, we should remind Americans that it is all right to offend the powerful—and even all right to be wrong. As Karl Popper pointed out, the mark of a truly scientific theory is that it be falsifiable: there must be conditions which, if observed in reality, would negate the theory. Otherwise, a theory is not a scientific hypothesis but a religious belief. Today much of our political debate revolves around propositions—on climate change, minimum wage hikes, appeasing the Muslim world, and so on—that are never measured against reality. Under the influence of the repressive Left, we have developed the habit of judging political ideas not by whether they work in reality but by whether they exhibit the correct motivations.

In the 2012 presidential elections, for example, many conservative commentators simply would not believe polls showing Barack Obama with a sizable lead against Mitt Romney. The polls sampled too many Democratic voters, we argued. But the polls were right, of course. In fact, the most liberal firm, Public Policy Polling—the one with the greatest incentive to inflate Democratic polls—was the most accurate of all.

My colleague John Nolte did some soul-searching and wrote an apology to readers:

> We were dead wrong about the polls. . . .
>
> That doesn't mean our ideas are wrong or that the GOP must change its core convictions. But it does mean that tactically we have to wrap our heads around the fact that Democrats have the ability to summon enough voters required to eke out victory. . . .
>
> The good news is that we won't be caught off guard again.[27]

It was the Democrats who were caught off guard in 2014; they repeated conservatives' wishful thinking from two years earlier. As pollster Nate Silver observed: "For much of this election cycle, Democrats complained the polls were biased against them. . . . The Democrats' complaints may have been more sophisticated-seeming than the 'skewed polls' arguments made by Republicans in 2012. But in the end, they were just as wrong. The polls did have a strong bias this year—but it was toward Democrats and not against them."[28] That failure to learn from conservatives' mistakes shows the hazards of tuning out the opposition.

One of the hazards of the Internet age is that mistakes live forever. In heated political debates, there is always the temptation to discredit a current adversary by bringing up a past error. But if, instead of bludgeoning people with their past errors, we allow them to admit they are wrong—and survive!—they are more likely to be honest, rather than suppressing the truth. That lesson in tolerance would benefit liberals and conservatives alike. Showing honor and respect for those who at least strive, albeit imperfectly, for the truth—rather than celebrating those who are most brazen in defying it—will restore truth as a universal standard, and bring decency back to our political discourse.

Above all, we must reject the lie that American democracy has failed. The Left repeats that lie in order to justify its increasing centralization of power—and it is a lie the Left does not actually believe.

Even as Trump surged in the Republican presidential primary, on the Democratic side Senator Bernie Sanders of Vermont, a self-described socialist who spent his honeymoon in the Soviet Union, built a surprisingly strong campaign on a promise to wage a "political revolution" against a political system that, he alleged, had been corrupted by "billionaires."

Waging what had been considered a hopeless fight for the nomination, Sanders began drawing huge audiences, picking up celebrity endorsements, and filling stadiums on the campaign trail. By the fall of 2015, he even led Hillary Clinton, the Democratic Party's presumptive nominee, in polls in New Hampshire and Iowa. Asked by CNN's Wolf Blitzer whether he had expected to do so well, Sanders replied: "So, you want me to tell you the truth.... Yes, I'm stunned." His own success seemed to contradict his insistence that the system was rigged.

The only people who persist in their belief that American democracy is irreparably doomed are the marginal right-wing extremists who invade abandoned federal wilderness outposts in the dead of winter, and the elite members of the left-wing establishment who are indifferent to the principles that undergird their own success.

The truth about American democracy is liberating for the Left as well as the Right; it can restore faith in the principles that we do, at the core, share in common. The key is to seek truth—and, when it is found, to defend it. The assault on constitutional democracy can be defeated, Andrew Breitbart said, "by presenting unvarnished truth after unvarnished truth."

Fundamentally, what American democracy needs is not stronger leaders but stronger citizens—citizens armed with the truth.

# Notes

## CHAPTER 1

1. Robert Creamer, Listen to Your Mother: Stand Up Straight! How Progressives Can Win (Santa Ana: Seven Locks Press, 2007) 578.
2. *Thomas Sowell, "Remembering 2015," RealClearPolitics, December 29,* 2015, http://www.realclearpolitics.com/articles/2015/12/29/ remembering_2015_129149.html.
3. Stephen Colbert, The Colbert Report, Comedy Central, October 17, 2005.
4. Stephen Colbert, "The Word–Truthiness," The Colbert Report, broadcast on Comedy Central, October 17, 2005, http://www.cc.com/video-clips/63ite2/the-colbert-report-the-word—-truthiness.
5. Stephen Colbert, interview by Nathan Rabin, A.V. Club, January 26, 2006, http://www.avclub.com/article/stephen-colbert-13970.
6. Katy Waldman, "The Science of Truthiness," Slate, September 3, 2014, http://www.slate.com/articles/health_and_science/science/2014/09/ truthiness_research_cognitive_biases_for_simple_clear_conservative_ messages.2.html.
7. Todd Beeton, quoted in Eric Boehlert, Bloggers on the Bus: How the Internet Changed Politics and the Press (New York: Free Press, 2009) 127.
8. The New Oxford American Dictionary, 2nd ed., s.v. "liberal."
9. *Merriam-Webster Online*, s.v. "liberal," accessed November 16, 2014, http://www.merriam-webster.com/dictionary/liberal.

10. Thomas L. Friedman, *Hot, Flat, and Crowded: Why We Need a Green Revolution—and How It Can Renew America* (New York: Farrar, Straus and Giroux, 2008), 371.

11. J. R. Taylor, "Ted Cruz's Father — Caught With Jfk Assassin," National Enquirer, April 20, 2016, http://www.nationalenquirer.com/celebrity/ted-cruz-scandal-father-jfk-assassination/.

12. David Samuels, "The Aspiring Novelist Who Became Obama's Foreign-Policy Guru," *New York Times*, May 5, 2016, http://www.nytimes.com/2016/05/08/magazine/the-aspiring-novelist-who-became-obamas-foreign-policy-guru.html?_r=0.

13. L. Gordon Crovitz, "Trump and the Obama Effect," *Wall Street Journal*, May 9, 2016, http://www.wsj.com/articles/trump-and-the-obama-effect-1462738574.

14. Barbara Boxer, "Partial-Birth Abortion Ban Act of 1999—Motion to Proceed." 145:18 (October 20, 1999), 26034.

15. Alberto Giubilini and Francesca Minerva, "After-Birth Abortion: Why Should the Baby Live?" *Journal of Medical Ethics*, February 23, 2012, http://jme.bmj.com/content/early/2012/03/01/medethics-2011-100411.full.

16. Foundation for Individual Rights in Education, "Disinvitation Report 2014: A Disturbing 15-Year Trend," May 28, 2014, https://www.thefire.org/disinvitation-season-report-2014/.

17. Zach Young, "Free Speech, Not Disruption," *Yale Daily News*, November 9, 2015, http://yaledailynews.com/blog/2015/11/09/young-free-speech-not-disruption/.

18. Plato, *Plato in Twelve Volumes*, vol. 1, trans. Harold North Fowler, (Cambridge: Harvard University Press, 1966), f. 38a.

19. Michael Nunez, "Want to Know What Facebook Really Thinks of Journalists? Here's What Happened When It Hired Some," *Gizmodo*, May 3, 2016, http://gizmodo.com/want-to-know-what-facebook-really-thinks-of-journalists-1773916117.

20. Maureen Balleza and Kate Zernike, "The 2004 Campaign: National Guard; Memos on Bush Are Fake but Accurate, Typist Says," *New York Times*, September 15, 2004, http://www.nytimes.com/2004/09/15/us/the-2004-campaign-national-guard-memos-on-bush-are-fake-but-accurate-typist-says.html.

21. Katie McDonough, "'It Makes Me Really Depressed': From UVA to Cosby, the Rape Denial Playbook That Won't Go Away," *Salon*, December 4, 2014, http://www.salon.com/2014/12/04/it_makes_me_really_depressed_from_uva_to_cosby_the_rape_denial_playbook_that_wont_go_away/.

22. John Byrne, "Emanuel Blames Chicago Crime Uptick on Officers Second-Guessing Themselves," *Chicago Tribune*, October 13, 2015, http://www.chicagotribune.com/news/local/politics/ct-emanuel-fetal-police-met-20151012-story.html.

23. George Orwell, *As I Please 1943–1945: The Collected Essays, Journalism and Letters*, vol. 3, ed. Sonia Orwell and Ian Angus (Boston: Nonpareil), 88.

24. George Orwell, "Looking Back on the Spanish War," *My Country Right or Left 1940–1943: The Collected Essays, Journalism, & Letters of George Orwell*, vol. 2 (Boston, Nonpareil, 2000), 259.

25. Andrew Breitbart, *Righteous Indignation: Excuse Me While I Save the World!* (New York: Grand Central, 2011), 159.

26. Kirsten Powers, *The Silencing: How the Left is Killing Free Speech* (New York: Regnery, 2015).

## CHAPTER 2

1. Barack Obama, "Statement by the President on the Shootings at Umpqua Community College, Roseburg, Oregon," White House, October 1, 2015, https://www.whitehouse.gov/the-press-office/2015/10/01/statement-president-shootings-umpqua-community-college-roseburg-oregon.

2. "Repeal the Second Amendment Now." Petition. MoveOn.org, accessed November 18, 2015, http://petitions.moveon.org/sign/repeal-the-second-amendment-6.

3. Michael Bloomberg, Remarks at Aspen Institute, February 6, 2015, audio via Chuck Ross, "Here's Audio From The Event Michael Bloomberg Is Trying To Block From Being Broadcast [AUDIO]," Daily Caller, February 16, 2015, http://dailycaller.com/2015/02/16/heres-audio-from-the-event-michael-bloomberg-is-trying-to-block-from-being-broadcast-audio/.

4. Charl van Wyk, quoted in AWR Hawkins, "Survivor of 1993 Church Massacre: 'By God's Grace I Managed to Return Fire,'" Breitbart News, June 19, 2015, http://www.breitbart.com/california/2015/06/19/survivor-of-1993-church-massacre-by-gods-grace-i-managed-to-return-fire/.

5. Barack Obama, Roseburg Statement, ibid.

6. Charles Krauthammer, "Did President Obama Prematurely Politicize Oregon Shooting?" *Fox News Special Report*, October 2, 2015, http://nation.foxnews.com/2015/10/02/did-president-obama-prematurely-politicize-oregon-shooting.

7.   Barack Obama, "Remarks by the President to U.S. Conference of Mayors,"
     White House, June 19, 2015, http://www.whitehouse.gov/the-press-
     office/2015/06/19/remarks-president-us-conference-mayors.

8.   Hillary Clinton, Twitter post, December 2, 2015, 12:26pm, https://twitter.
     com/HillaryClinton/status/672149874046083072?ref_src=twsrc%5Etfw.

9.   Hillary Clinton, quoted in Philip Rucker, "Hillary Clinton's Push on Gun
     Control Marks a Shift in Presidential Politics," *Washington Post*, July 9,
     2015, https://www.washingtonpost.com/politics/clinton-makes-big-gun-
     control-pitch-marking-shift-in-presidential-politics/2015/07/09/4309232c-
     2580-11e5-b72c-2b7d516e1e0e_story.html.

10.  Richard Martinez, quoted in John Rogers, "Father of UCSB Shooting
     Victim Continues Fight for Gun Reforms," *Associated Press*, May 23,
     2015, http://www.dailynews.com/government-and-politics/20150523/
     father-of-ucsb-shooting-victim-continues-fight-for-gun-reforms.

11.  National Rifle Association-Institute for Legislative Action, "Anti-Gun Bills
     Must be Stopped in Sacramento," July 31, 2014, https://www.nraila.org/
     articles/20140731/california-anti-gun-bills-must-be-stopped-in-
     sacramento.

12.  John Locke, *Second Treatise of Government*, Book II. § 6.

13.  U.S. Declaration of Independence.

14.  Constitution Act, 1867, pt. VI, s. 91 (Can.).

15.  Matt Valentine, "The Myth of the Good Guy With the Gun," *Politico*,
     October 5, 2015, http://www.politico.com/magazine/story/2015/10/
     oregon-shooting-gun-laws-213222.

16.  AWR Hawkins, "Uber Bans Guns After Driver Uses One to Stop
     Attempted Mass Shooting," Breitbart News, June 21, 2005, http://www.
     breitbart.com/big-government/2015/06/21/uber-bans-guns-after-driver-
     uses-one-to-stop-attempted-mass-shooting/.

17.  Bill of Rights, U.S. Constitution.

18.  *District of Columbia v. Heller*, 554 U.S. 570, 44 (2008).

19.  Ibid., 64.

20.  John R. Lott, Jr., *More Guns, Less Crime*: *Understanding Crime and Gun
     Control Laws*, 3rd ed. (University of Chicago Press: Chicago, 2010),
     20–21.

21.  John R. Lott, Jr., "Media Matters, the Facts and Me," *Fox News,*
     December 9, 2014, http://www.foxnews.com/opinion/2014/12/09/media-
     matters-facts-and-me/.

22.  AWR Hawkins, "Hillary Clinton Pushes Change Allowing Victims to Sue
     Gun Makers in Wake of Oregon Attack," Breitbart News, October 5,

2015, http://www.breitbart.com/big-government/2015/10/05/hillary-clinton-pushes-change-allowing-shooting-victims-sue-gun-makers-wake-oregon-attack/.

23. Ben Carson, quoted in AWR Hawkins, "Ben Carson: Armed Jews Could Have Curtailed Holocaust," October 25, 2015, http://www.breitbart.com/big-government/2015/10/09/ben-carson-armed-jews-curtailed-holocaust/.

24. Jonathan A. Greenblatt, quoted in Vanessa Williams, "Carson: ADL's Statement That Gun Control Did Not Cause the Holocaust Is 'Foolishness,'" *Washington Post*, October 9, 2015, https://www.washingtonpost.com/news/post-politics/wp/2015/10/09/ben-carson-jewish-group-talking-foolishness-on-holocaust/.

25. Stephen P. Halbrook, "Nazi Firearms Law and the Disarming of the German Jews," *Arizona Journal of International and Comparative Law* 17:3 (2000): 484.

26. Ibid., 516.

27. Charles E. Cobb Jr., *This Non-Violent Stuff'll Get You Killed: How Guns Made the Civil Rights Movement Possible* (New York: Basic Books, 2014), 1.

28. Martin Luther King, Jr., quoted in Cobb, 112.

29. *McDonald v. City of Chicago*, 561 U.S. 742 (2010).

30. Hillary Clinton, quoted in Alana Goodman and Stephen Gutowski, "Leaked Audio: Clinton Says Supreme Court Is 'Wrong' on Second Amendment," *Washington Free Beacon*, October 1, 2015, http://freebeacon.com/politics/leaked-audio-clinton-says-supreme-court-is-wrong-on-second-amendment/.

31. "Repeal the Second Amendment Now," Petition. MoveOn.org, accessed November 18, 2015, http://petitions.moveon.org/sign/repeal-the-second-amendment-6.

32. Richard Sharp, "Gun Store Owners Challenge California Law in Federal Court," KCRA News, November 11, 2014, http://www.kcra.com/news/local-news/news-sacramento/gun-store-owners-challenge-california-law-in-federal-court/29652348.

33. Austin Bragg, "How to Create a Gun-Free America in 5 Easy Steps," *Reason*, October 7, 2015, https://reason.com/reasontv/2015/10/07/how-to-create-a-gun-free-america-in-5-ea.

34. Lexington, "Why Gun Control Is Doomed," *Economist*, June 19, 2015, http://www.economist.com/blogs/democracyinamerica/2015/06/charleston-and-public-policy.

35. Sarah Palin, "Sarah Palin Responds to Tucson Shooting," YouTube video, 7:42, CBS News, January 12, 2011, https://www.youtube.com/watch?v=KhcDh0-_5m4.

36. Brian Ross, quoted in "Good Morning America: Aurora Shooter Could Be A Tea Party Member," *Townhall*, July 20, 2012, http://townhall.com/tipsheet/townhallcomstaff/2012/07/20/good_morning_america_aurora_shooter_could_be_a_tea_party_member.

37. Todd Rutherford, interviewed by Jake Tapper, *The Lead with Jake Tapper*, CNN, June 18, 2015, http://www.realclearpolitics.com/video/2015/06/18/sc_state_rep_todd_rutherford_charleston_shooter_did_this_because_he_watches_things_like_fox_news.html.

38. Tony Lee, "FBI: FRC Shooter Had 15 Chick-fil-A Sandwiches; Said 'I Don't Like Your Politics,'" Breitbart News, August 16, 2012, http://www.breitbart.com/big-government/2012/08/16/fbi-frc-shooter-had-15-chick-fil-a-sandwiches-box-of-ammo-said-i-don-t-like-your-politics/.

39. NBC News, "Video Shows NYC Protesters Chanting for 'Dead Cops,'" NBC New York, December 15, 2014, http://www.nbcnewyork.com/news/local/Eric-Garner-Manhattan-Dead-Cops-Video-Millions-March-Protest-285805731.html.

40. Sharyl Attkisson, "Documents: ATF used 'Fast and Furious' to make the case for gun regulations," CBS News, December 7, 2011, http://www.cbsnews.com/news/documents-atf-used-fast-and-furious-to-make-the-case-for-gun-regulations/.

## CHAPTER 3

1. Barack Obama, "Remarks by the President on Raising the Minimum Wage," White House, April 30, 2014, https://www.whitehouse.gov/the-press-office/2014/04/30/remarks-president-raising-minimum-wage.

2. Al Sharpton, "Minimum Wage vs. Maximum Greed," Huffington Post, February, 4, 2014, http://www.huffingtonpost.com/rev-al-sharpton/minimum-wage-vs-maximum-g_b_4725368.html.

3. Elizabeth Warren, "Elizabeth Warren: Raising The Minimum Wage Is 'The Least We Can Do,'" HuffPost Live January 28, 2014, http://www.huffingtonpost.com/2014/01/28/elizabeth-warren-minimum-wage_n_4681412.html.

4. Barack Obama, "Remarks by the President in the State of the Union Address," White House, February 12, 2013, https://www.whitehouse.gov/the-press-office/2013/02/12/remarks-president-state-union-address.

5.   Barack Obama, "President Barack Obama's State of the Union Address,"
     White House, January 28, 2014, https://www.whitehouse.gov/the-press-
     office/2014/01/28/president-barack-obamas-state-union-address.

6.   Peter Weber, "The Case for $22-an-Hour Minimum Wage," *The Week*,
     March 19, 2013, http://theweek.com/articles/466521/case-22anhour-
     minimum-wage.

7.   Drew Desilver, "Who Makes Minimum Wage?," Pew Research Center,
     September 8, 2014, http://www.pewresearch.org/fact-tank/2014/09/08/
     who-makes-minimum-wage/.

8.   Drew Desilver, "5 Facts about the Minimum Wage," Pew Research Center,
     July 23, 2015, http://www.pewresearch.org/fact-tank/2015/07/23/5-facts-
     about-the-minimum-wage/.

9.   Statista, "Number of Restaurants in the United States from 2011 to 2015,"
     accessed January 4, 2016, http://www.statista.com/statistics/244616/
     number-of-qsr-fsr-chain-independent-restaurants-in-the-us/.

10.  Barack Obama, "Remarks of President Barack Obama—State of the Union
     Address As Delivered," White House, January 13, 2016, https://www.
     whitehouse.gov/the-press-office/2016/01/12/remarks-president-barack-
     obama---prepared-delivery-state-union-address.

11.  Caroline May, "Record 94,610,000 Americans Not in Labor Force,"
     Breitbart News, October 2, 2015, http://www.breitbart.com/big-
     government/2015/10/02/record-94610000-americans-not-labor-force/.

12.  Jeffry Bartash, "Share of Americans in Labor Force Shrinks to 38-Year
     Low," MarketWatch, October 2, 2015, http://www.marketwatch.com/
     story/share-of-americans-in-labor-force-shrinks-to-38-year-
     low-2015-10-02.

13.  Anna Bernasek, "Income Gap Grows Wider (and Faster)," *New York
     Times*, August 31, 2013, http://www.nytimes.com/2013/09/01/business/
     income-gap-grows-wider-and-faster.html.

14.  Barack Obama, "Remarks by the President on the Economy in
     Osawatomie, Kansas," Osawatomie High School, Osawatomie, Kansas,
     December 6, 2011, https://www.whitehouse.gov/the-press-
     office/2011/12/06/remarks-president-economy-osawatomie-kansas.

15.  Jeff Jacoby, "No, Bernie Sanders, Scandinavia Is Not a Socialist Utopia,"
     *Boston Globe*, October 15, 2015, https://www.bostonglobe.com/
     opinion/2015/10/15/bernie-sanders-scandinavia-not-socialist-utopia/
     lUk9N7dZotJRbvn8PosoIN/story.html.

16.  Jude Clemene, "Why New York's Fracking Ban For Natural Gas Is
     Unsustainable," *Forbes*, June 7, 2015, http://www.forbes.com/sites/

judeclemente/2015/06/07/why-new-yorks-fracking-ban-for-natural-gas-is-unsustainable/.

17.   Eric Hand, "Methane in Drinking Water Unrelated to Fracking, Study Suggests," *Science*, March 30, 2015, http://www.sciencemag.org/news/2015/03/methane-drinking-water-unrelated-fracking-study-suggests.

18.   Craig Harrington, "Fox Hypes Cherry-Picked Data to Attack Seattle Minimum Wage," Media Matters for America, August 11, 2015, http://mediamatters.org/research/2015/08/11/fox-hypes-cherry-picked-data-to-attack-seattle/204889.

19.   Craig Harrington and Alex Morash, "Latest Seattle Jobs Numbers Disprove Fox's Minimum Wage Misinformation," Media Matters for America, August 25, 2015, http://mediamatters.org/blog/2015/08/25/latest-seattle-jobs-numbers-disprove-foxs-minim/205155.

20.   David Newmark, "The Effects of Minimum Wages on Employment," *FRBSF Economic Letter,* December 21, 2015, http://www.frbsf.org/economic-research/publications/economic-letter/2015/december/effects-of-minimum-wage-on-employment/.

21.   David Newmark, "Reducing Poverty via Minimum Wages, Alternatives," *FRBSF Economic Letter,* December 28, 2015, http://www.frbsf.org/economic-research/publications/economic-letter/2015/december/reducing-poverty-via-minimum-wages-tax-credit/.

22.   Brian A. Shactman, "Unemployed? Go to North Dakota," *USA Today*, August 28, 2014, http://usatoday30.usatoday.com/money/economy/story/2011-08-27/Unemployed-Go-to-North-Dakota/50136572/1.

23.   Jerry Brown, quoted in Dale Buss, "Texas v. California: This Ain't Over When Toyota Leaves," *Forbes*, April 30, 2014, http://www.forbes.com/sites/dalebuss/2014/04/30/texas-v-california-this-aint-over-when-toyota-leaves/.

24.   Adelle Nazarian, "USC Students Debate, Delay Vote on Mandatory 'Diversity' Classes," Breitbart News, October 28, 2015, http://www.breitbart.com/california/2015/10/28/usc-diversity-delay-vote/.

25.   Heesun Wee, "LA Union Wants to Be Exempt from $15 Minimum Wage," CNBC, July 30, 2015, http://www.cnbc.com/2015/07/30/la-union-wants-to-be-exempt-from-15-minimum-wage.html.

26.   Christina D. Romer, "The Business of the Minimum Wage," *New York Times*, March 2, 2013, http://www.nytimes.com/2013/03/03/business/the-minimum-wage-employment-and-income-distribution.html.

27.   Robert Nozick, *Anarchy, State, and Utopia* (New York: Basic Books, 1974) 156.

28. "South Africa Unemployment Is Worse Now Than at the End of Apartheid," BusinessTech, August 17, 2015, http://businesstech.co.za/news/government/95983/south-africa-unemployment-is-worse-now-than-at-the-end-of-apartheid/.

29. Haroon Bhorat and Natasha Mayet, "The Impact of Sectoral Minimum Wage Laws in South Africa," Econ 3x3, June 10, 2013, http://www.econ3x3.org/article/impact-sectoral-minimum-wage-laws-south-africa.

## CHAPTER 4

1. Barack Obama, "Remarks of President Barack Obama to the People of Israel," White House, March 21, 2013, https://www.whitehouse.gov/the-press-office/2013/03/21/remarks-president-barack-obama-people-israel.

2. John Kerry, quoted in Josh Rogin, "Exclusive: Kerry Warns Israel Could Become 'An Apartheid State,'" *Daily Beast*, April 27, 2014, http://www.thedailybeast.com/articles/2014/04/27/exclusive-kerry-warns-israel-could-become-an-apartheid-state.html.

3. Donald J. Trump, quoted in Adam Chandler, "Donald Trump Breaks with the GOP on Israel," *Atlantic*, December 3, 2015, http://www.theatlantic.com/politics/archive/2015/12/donald-trump-gop-israel/418737/.

4. Alan Dershowitz, "Why I Support Israel and Obama," *Jerusalem Post*, October 15, 2008, http://cgis.jpost.com/Blogs/dershowitz/entry/why_i_support_israel_and, also available at, http://www.huffingtonpost.com/alan-dershowitz/why-i-support-israel-and_b_135660.html.

5. Joel B. Pollak, "Right of Reply: Compare Records, not Rhetoric," *Jerusalem Post*, October 22, 2008, http://www.jpost.com/Opinion/Op-Ed-Contributors/Right-of-Reply-Compare-records-not-rhetoric.

6. Michael Oren, *Ally: My Journey Across the American-Israeli Divide* (New York: Random House, 2015).

7. Alan Dershowitz, interview by Steven Malzberg, "The Steve Salzburg Show," *Newsmax*, September 3, 2015, http://www.newsmax.com/Newsfront/alan-dershowitz-barack-obama-chidish-petty/2015/09/03/id/673526/.

8. David Remnick, "Going the Distance: On and Off the Road with Barack Obama," *New Yorker*, January 27, 2014, http://www.newyorker.com/magazine/2014/01/27/going-the-distance-david-remnick.

9. John J. Mearsheimer and Stephen M. Walt, *The Israel Lobby and U.S. Foreign Policy* (New York: Farmer, Straus and Giroux, 2007).

10. Jeremy Gordin, "South Africa's Ruling Party Endorses BDS Campaign Against Israel," *Ha'aretz*, December 21, 2012, http://www.haaretz.com/

israel-news/south-africa-s-ruling-party-endorses-bds-campaign-against-israel.premium-1.486195.

11. Herb Keinon, "South Africa Hosts Hamas Leader Mashaal, Prompting Angry Protest by Israel," *Jerusalem Post*, October 19, 2015, http://www.jpost.com/Israel-News/Politics-And-Diplomacy/South-Africa-hosts-Hamas-leader-Mashaal-prompting-angry-protest-by-Israel-427405.

12. Tony Judt, "Israel: The Alternative," *New York Review of Books*, October 23, 2003, http://www.nybooks.com/articles/archives/2003/oct/23/israel-the-alternative/.

13. Leon Wieseltier, "What Is Not to Be Done," *New Republic*, October 28, 2003, https://newrepublic.com/article/62173/what-not-be-done.

14. Ezra Klein, "Why I Have Become More Pessimistic about Israel," *Vox*, July 30, 2014, http://www.vox.com/2014/7/30/5948839/why-i-have-become-more-pessimistic-about-israel.

15. Jonathan Chait, "Israel Is Making It Hard to Be Pro-Israel," *New York*, July 29, 2014, http://nymag.com/daily/intelligencer/2014/07/why-i-have-become-less-pro-israel.html.

16. Steven Levitsky and Glen Weyl, "We Are Lifelong Zionists. Here's Why We've Chosen to Boycott Israel," *Washington Post*, October 23, 2015, https://www.washingtonpost.com/opinions/a-zionist-case-for-boycotting-israel/2015/10/23/ac4dab80-735c-11e5-9cbb-790369643cf9_story.html.

17. Mearsheimer and Walt, 333.

18. Alexis Garduno, "Senate Reverses Divestment Vote, Passes Resolution," *Stanford Daily*, February 27, 2015, http://www.stanforddaily.com/2015/02/17/senate-reverses-divestment-vote-passes-resolution/.

19. Emily Alpert Reyes, "Jewish Fraternity at UC Davis Defaced with Swastikas," *Los Angeles Times*, February 1, 2015, http://www.latimes.com/local/lanow/la-me-ln-jewish-fraternity-davis-swastikas-20150201-story.html.

20. Larry Summers, "Address at Morning Prayers," Memorial Church, Cambridge, Massachusetts, September 17, 2002, http://www.harvard.edu/president/speeches/summers_2002/morningprayers.php.

21. Alan Dershowitz, *The Case for Israel* (Hoboken: John Wiley & Sons, 2003), 12.

22. Hannah Arendt, "Peace or Armistice in the Near East?," *Review of Politics* 12:1 (January 1950), 56–82.

23. "Declaration of the Establishment of the State of Israel," Isreal Ministry of Foreign Affairs, May 14, 1948, http://www.mfa.gov.il/mfa/foreignpolicy/

peace/guide/pages/declaration%20of%20establishment%20of%20 state%20of%20israel.aspx.

24. Genesis 23.

25. Bill Clinton, quoted in Jonathan S. Tobin, "Sorry Bill, It's Not Up to Israel," *Commentary*, November 1, 2015, https://www. commentarymagazine.com/foreign-policy/middle-east/israel/bill-clinton- israel-peace-process/.

26. Ibid.

## CHAPTER 5

1. Albert J. Gore, "Nobel Lecture," (lecture, Olso City Hall, Oslo, Norway, December 10, 2007).

2. Jerry Brown, quoted in Joel B. Pollak, "Scientists: Jerry Brown Wrong to Link Fires, Climate Change," Breitbart News, October 19, 2015, http:// www.breitbart.com/big-journalism/2015/10/19/scientists-jerry-brown- wrong-to-link-fires-climate-change/.

3. Aspen Island Theatre Company, "Statement on Kill Climate Deniers," Facebook note, October 1, 2014, https://www.facebook.com/permalink. php?story_fbid=381964428626289&id=332059103616822.

4. Jerry Brown, quoted in William Bigelow, "Jerry Brown Warns LAX Will Have to Be Moved Due to Global Warming; Update: Aide Corrects," Breitbart News, May 15, 2014, http://www.breitbart.com/ california/2014/05/15/jerry-brown-warns-lax-will-have-to-be-moved-due- to-global-warming/.

5. Brown, quoted in Pollak, "Scientists: Jerry Brown Wrong to Link Fires."

6. Roger Pielke, quoted in Pollak, ibid.

7. Jerry Brown, quoted in Joel B. Pollak, "Jerry Brown Vows 'Life-and-Death' Struggle to 'Change …Our Industrial Economy,'" Breitbart News, September 10, 2015, http://www.breitbart.com/california/2015/09/10/ jerry-brown-vows-to-change-our-industrial-economy/.

8. Joel Kotkin, "How Liberals Are the New Autocrats," *Daily Beast*, January 3, 2016, http://www.thedailybeast.com/articles/2016/01/03/how-liberals- are-the-new-autocrats.html.

9. Holman Jenkins, "The Next Climate Scandal?," *Wall Street Journal*, November 4, 2015, http://www.wsj.com/articles/the-next-climate-scandal- 1446594461?alg=y.

10. Joseph Bast and Roy Spencer, "The Myth of the Climate Change '97%,'" *Wall Street Journal*, May 27, 2014, http://www.wsj.com/news/articles/SB10 001424052702303480304579578462813553136.

11. Dana Nuccitelli, "The Wall Street Journal Denies the 97% Scientific Consensus on Human-Caused Global Warming," *Guardian* (UK), May 28, 2014, http://www.theguardian.com/environment/climate-consensus-97-per-cent/2014/may/28/wall-street-journal-denies-global-warming-consensus.

12. Peter Gwynne, "The Cooling World," *Newsweek*, April 28, 1975, 64.

13. George Monbiot, "The Threat Is from Those Who Accept Climate Change, Not Those Who Deny It," *Guardian* (UK), September 20, 2006, http://www.theguardian.com/commentisfree/2006/sep/21/comment.georgemonbiot.

14. Joel Connelly, "Deniers of Global Warming Harm Us," *Seattle Post-Intelligencer*, July 10, 2007, http://www.seattlepi.com/local/connelly/article/Deniers-of-global-warming-harm-us-1243264.php.

15. Robert F. Kennedy Jr., quoted in Cheryl K. Chumley, "RFK Jr. Wants Law to 'Punish Global Warming Skeptics,'" *Washington Times*, September 23, 2014, http://www.washingtontimes.com/news/2014/sep/23/robert-kennedy-jr-we-need-laws-punish-global-warmi/.

16. Jagadish Shukla, quoted in James Delingpole, "Climate Alarmists to Obama: Use RICO Laws to Jail Skeptics!" Breitbart News, September 19, 2015, http://www.breitbart.com/big-government/2015/09/19/climate-alarmists-obama-use-rico-laws-jail-skeptics/.

17. Richard Lindzen, "The Political Assault on Climate Skeptics," *Wall Street Journal*, March 5, 2015, http://www.wsj.com/articles/richard-s-lindzen-the-political-assault-on-climate-skeptics-1425513033.

18. Bjørn Lomborg, *The Skeptical Environmentalist: Measuring the Real State of the World*, 23rd ed. (Cambridge: Cambridge University Press, 2014), 322.

19. Sophie Elmhirst, "The NS Interview: Bjørn Lomborg," *New Statesman*, September 24, 2010, http://www.newstatesman.com/environment/2010/09/interview-gay-climate.

20. Bjørn Lomborg, *Smart Solutions to Climate Change: Comparing Costs and Benefits* (Cambridge: Cambridge University Press, 2010).

21. Alison Abbott, "Social Scientists Call for Abolition of Dishonesty Committee," *Nature* 421 (2003): 681, http://www.nature.com/nature/journal/v421/n6924/full/421681b.html.

22. Andrew C. Revkin, "Environment and Science: Danes Rebuke a 'Skeptic,'" *New York Times*, January 8, 2003, http://www.nytimes.com/2003/01/08/international/europe/08SKEP.html.

23. Judge Michael Burton, quoted in Sally Peck, "Al Gore's 'Nine Inconvenient Untruths,'" *Telegraph* (UK), October 11, 2007, http://www.telegraph.co.uk/news/earth/earthnews/3310137/Al-Gores-nine-Inconvenient-Untruths.html.

24. James Taylor, "Climategate 2.0: New E-Mails Rock The Global Warming Debate," *Forbes*, November 23, 2001, http://www.forbes.com/sites/jamestaylor/2011/11/23/climategate-2-0-new-e-mails-rock-the-global-warming-debate/.

25. Ivar Giaever, quoted in Philip Sherwell, "War of Words over Global Warming as Nobel Laureate Resigns in Protest," *Telegraph* (UK), September 25, 2011, http://www.telegraph.co.uk/news/earth/environment/climatechange/8786565/War-of-words-over-global-warming-as-Nobel-laureate-resigns-in-protest.html.

26. Karl Popper, "Science as Falsification," *Conjectures and Refutations* (London: Routledge and Keagan Paul, 1963), 33–39.

## CHAPTER 6

1. Nancy Hopkins, quoted in Daniel J. Hemel, "Summers' Comments on Women and Science Draw Ire," *Harvard Crimson*, January 14, 2005, http://www.thecrimson.com/article/2005/1/14/summers-comments-on-women-and-science/.

2. Kathy Witterick and David Stocker, quoted in Jayme Poisson, "Parents Keep Child's Gender Secret," *Toronto Star*, May 21, 2011, http://www.thestar.com/life/parent/2011/05/21/parents_keep_childs_gender_secret.html.

3. Zoey Tur, quoted in Ian Hanchett, "Watch: Tur Threatens To Send Breitbart's Ben Shapiro Home in an Ambulance During Jenner Discussion," Breitbart News, July 16, 2015, http://www.breitbart.com/video/2015/07/16/watch-tur-threatens-to-send-shapiro-home-in-an-ambulance-during-jenner-discussion/.

4. David Stocker, quoted in Jayme Poisson, "Remember Storm? We Check In on the Baby Being Raised Gender-Neutral," *Toronto Star*, November 15, 2003, http://www.thestar.com/life/parent/2013/11/15/remember_storm_we_check_in_on_the_baby_being_raised_genderneutral.html.

5. University of California, quoted in Jacob Kohlepp, "Calif. Students Now Given Six 'Gender Identity' Choices on College Admissions Applications," College Fix, July 27, 2015, http://www.thecollegefix.com/post/23519/.

6. Jess Staufenberg, "University of Tennessee Switches Gender-Specific Pronouns 'He' and 'She' for 'Xe' and 'Ze' to Promote Inclusivity,"

*Independent* (UK), August 29, 2015, http://www.independent.co.uk/news/ world/americas/university-of-tennessee-switches-gender-specific-pronouns-he-and-she-for-xe-and-ze-to-promote-10478034.html.

7. Rickey Hall, Office for Diversity and Inclusion, "Clarification on Gender-Neutral Pronouns Article," University of Tennessee Knoxville, September 1, 2015, http://diversity.utk.edu/2015/09/no-policy/.

8. MJ Slaby, "UT Students Endorse Gender-Neutral Pronouns," *Knoxville News Sentinel*, December 3, 2015, http://www.knoxnews.com/news/local/ ut-students-endorse-gender-neutral-pronouns-ep-1398513880-361266381. html.

9. Lawrence H. Summers, "Remarks at Public Service Awards Dinner" (speech, Kennedy School of Government, Cambridge, MA, October 26, 2001).

10. Lawrence H. Summers, "Address at Morning Prayers" (speech, Memorial Church, Cambridge, MA, September 17, 2002).

11. Lawrence H. Summers, "Remarks at NBER Conference on Diversifying the Science & Engineering Workforce" (speech, Harvard University, Cambridge, MA, January 14, 2005).

12. Gary Becker, "Comment on Gender Differences in Scientific Achievement," *Becker-Posner Blog*, January 30, 2005, http://www.becker-posner-blog. com/2005/01/comment-on-gender-differences-in-scientific-achievement-becker.html.

13. Steven Pinker, "Sex Ed," *The New Republic*, February 13, 2005, https:// newrepublic.com/article/68044/sex-ed.

14. Lawrence H. Summers, "Letter from President Summers on Women and Science" (letter, Harvard University, Cambridge, MA, January 19, 2005).

15. Peter Berkowitz, "Summers's End," *Weekly Standard*, March 6, 2006, http://www.weeklystandard.com/Content/Public/ Articles/000/000/011/913ykmyh.asp.

16. Jonah Goldberg, "Liberals Now Find Gender Identity Itself Oppressive," National Review Online, June 5, 2015, http://www.nationalreview.com/ article/419347/lefts-war-women-jonah-goldberg.

17. Germaine Greer, interview by Kirsty Wark, "Germaine Greer: Transgender Women Are 'Not Women,'" BBC, October 24, 2015, http://www.bbc.com/ news/uk-34625512.

18. Bruce Springsteen, "A Statement from Bruce Springsteen on North Carolina," April 8, 2016, http://brucespringsteen.net.

19.  John D. Sutter, "'We need a restroom revolution,'" CNN, May 9, 2016, http://www.cnn.com/2016/05/09/opinions/sutter-gender-neutral-restrooms/index.html.

20.  Alexis de Tocqueville, *Democracy in America* (New York: HarperCollins, 1969), 538.

21.  George F. Will, "Colleges Become the Victims of Progressivism," *Washington Post*, June 6, 2014, https://www.washingtonpost.com/opinions/george-will-college-become-the-victims-of-progressivism/2014/06/06/e90e73b4-eb50-11e3-9f5c-9075d5508f0a_story.html.

22.  Sabrina Erdely, "A Rape on Campus: A Brutal Assault and Struggle for Justice at UVA," *Rolling Stone*, December 19, 2014, http://www.rollingstone.com/culture/features/a-rape-on-campus-what-went-wrong-20150405.

23.  Brendan O'Neill, "The Real Problem with Rolling Stone's Campus Rape Fiasco," *Reason*, April 12, 2015, https://reason.com/archives/2015/04/12/campus-rape.

24.  Rebecca Quick, "CNBC Full Transcript: CNBC's 'Your Money, Your Vote: The Republican Presidential Debate,'" CNBC, October 28, 2015, http://www.cnbc.com/2015/10/29/cnbc-full-transcript-cnbcs-your-money-your-vote-the-republican-presidential-debate-part-2.html.

25.  Hannah Rosin, "The Gender Wage Gap Lie," Slate, August 30, 2013, http://www.slate.com/articles/double_x/doublex/2013/08/gender_pay_gap_the_familiar_line_that_women_make_77_cents_to_every_man_s.html.

26.  Felicia Schwartz, "In a First, Two Women to Graduate from Army's Ranger School," *Wall Street Journal*, August 18, 2015, http://www.wsj.com/articles/first-female-soldiers-to-graduate-from-armys-ranger-school-1439920871.

27.  Harvey C. Mansfield, *Manliness* (New Haven: Yale University Press, 2007).

28.  Stephanie Coontz, "The Myth of Male Decline," *New York Times*, September 29, 2012, http://www.nytimes.com/2012/09/30/opinion/sunday/the-myth-of-male-decline.html?_r=0.

29.  Helen Smith, *Men on Strike: Why Men Are Boycotting Marriage, Fatherhood, and the American Dream—and Why It Matters* (New York: Encounter, 2013).

30.  Mansfield, *Manliness*, 240–41.

31.  James Carville, quoted in Eric Lach, "Carville: If Hillary Gave Obama One of Her Balls, 'He'd Have Two,'" *Talking Points Memo*, November 18, 2010, http://talkingpointsmemo.com/dc/carville-if-hillary-gave-obama-one-of-her-balls-he-d-have-two.

## CHAPTER 7

1.  Perez Hilton, "Perez Hilton Calls Miss California A 'Dumb Bitch,'" YouTube video, 2:25, *TheRightWingNet*, April 21, 2009, https://www.youtube.com/watch?v=NMYP9opfMfI.
2.  Jeffrey Toobin, quoted by Connor Williams, "CNN's Toobin: Parallel Between Oppostion to Interracial Marriage and Gay Marriage is 'Precise,'" *NewsBusters*, June 29, 2015, http://newsbusters.org/blogs/connor-williams/2015/06/30/cnns-toobin-parallel-between-opposition-interracial-marriage-and.
3.  Joel B. Pollak, "Boies, Olson Predict Gay Marriage Nationwide," Breitbart News, June 27, 2014, http://www.breitbart.com/california/2014/06/27/boies-olson-predict-gay-marriage-nationwide/.
4.  Meghan Daum, "Carrie Prejean vs. Perez Hilton," *Los Angeles Times*, April 25, 2009, http://articles.latimes.com/2009/apr/25/opinion/oe-daum25.
5.  Carrie Prejean, quoted in Eric Ditzian, "Perez Hilton Was 'Shocked' by Miss California's Gay-Marriage Answer," MTV, April 21, 2009, http://www.mtv.com/news/1609672/perez-hilton-was-shocked-by-miss-californias-gay-marriage-answer/.
6.  Hilton,"Perez Hilton Calls Miss California a "Dumb Bitch."
7.  Fox News and Associated Press, "Carrie Prejean Says Answer to Gay Marriage Question Cost Her Miss USA Crown," FoxNews.com, April 20, 2009, http://www.foxnews.com/story/2009/04/20/carrie-prejean-says-answer-to-gay-marriage-question-cost-her-miss-usa-crown/.
8.  *Baker v. Nelson*, 291 Minn. 310 (1971).
9.  Pew Research Center, "Gay Marriage Around the World," *Pew Forum*, June 26, 2015, http://www.pewforum.org/2015/06/26/gay-marriage-around-the-world-2013/.
10. Commonwealth of Massachusetts, "Legal Impediments to Marriage," accessed November 20, 2015, http://www.mass.gov/eohhs/docs/dph/vital-records/legal-impediments-marriage.pdf.
11. *In re Marriage Cases*, 43 Cal. 4th 757, (2008).
12. Dale Carpenter, "On to Polygamy?," *The Volokh Conspiracy blog*, May 20, 2008, http://www.volokh.com/posts/1211292450.shtml.

13. *Loving v. Virginia*, 388 U.S. 1, 12 (1967).

14. *Hollingsworth v. Perry*, 570 U.S. 12-144 (2013).

15. *U.S. v. Windsor*, 570 U.S. 12-307 (2013).

16. Ibid., Kennedy, J.

17. *Obergefell v. Hodges*, 576 U.S. 14-556 (2015).

18. Mark Joseph Stern, "'Same-Sex Attracted Men and Their Wives' Ask SCOTUS to Rule against Marriage Equality," Slate, April 13, 2015, http://www.slate.com/blogs/outward/2015/04/13/same_sex_attracted_men_and_their_wives_asks_scotus_to_rule_against_marriage.html.

19. *Elane Photography, LLC v. Willock*, 309 P.3d 53, at 80 (N.M. 2013).

20. John Nolte, "WA State Sues Florist for Refusing to Service Gay Wedding," Breitbart News, April 10, 2013, http://www.breitbart.com/big-government/2013/04/10/wa-state-sues-florist-for-refusing-to-service-gay-wedding/.

21. Noel Sheppard, "Anti-Bullying Activist Dan Savage Curses at Christian High School Students, Calls Them 'Pansy-A—ed,'" *NewsBusters*, April 28, 2012, http://newsbusters.org/blogs/noel-sheppard/2012/04/28/sex-advice-columnist-and-anti-bullying-advocate-dan-savage-curses-hig#sthash.eDIIroIKf.dpuf.

## CHAPTER 8

1. Thurgood Marshall, "The Bicentennial Speech," Remarks at the Annual Seminar of the San Francisco Patent and Trademark Association, Maui, HI, May 6, 1987, http://thurgoodmarshall.com/the-bicentennial-speech/.

2. Byron Williams, "Constitution Is Clearly a Living Document," Huffington Post, April 16, 2012, http://www.huffingtonpost.com/byron-williams/same-sex-marriage-constitution_b_1429064.html.

3. Barack Obama, "Sprint to Election Day; Obama Addresses Supporters in Missouri" (speech, University of Missouri, Columbia, MO, October 30, 2008).

4. Rahm Emanuel, quoted in Gerald F. Seib, "In Crisis, Opportunity for Obama," *Wall Street Journal*, November 21, 2008, http://www.wsj.com/articles/SB122721278056345271.

5. David Axelrod, quoted in Robert Creamer, *Listen to Your Mother: Stand Up Straight! How Progressives Can Win* (Santa Ana: Seven Locks Press, 2007).

6. Ibid., 539.

7. Derrick Bell, *Faces at the Bottom of the Well: The Permanence of Racism* (New York: Basic Books, 1992).

8. Charles C. Johnson, "Obama Assigned Bell at University of Chicago Law School," Breitbart News, March 8, 2012, http://www.breitbart.com/big-government/2012/03/08/obama-made-bell-required-reading-chicago/.

9. Joel B. Pollak, "The Vetting—Exclusive: Obama Letter to Bell to Blurb 'Dreams from My Father,'" Breitbart News, April 26, 2012, http://www.breitbart.com/big-government/2012/04/26/the-vetting-obama-letter-derrick-bell-blurb-dreams-from-my-father/.

10. Sonia Sotomayor, "Judge Mario G. Olmos Memorial Lecture," Berkeley, CA, 2001, reprinted as "Lecture: 'A Latina Judge's Voice,'" *New York Times*, May 14, 2009, http://www.nytimes.com/2009/05/15/us/politics/15judge.text.html.

11. Barack Obama, interview by Marc Maron, "Episode 613—President Barack Obama," *WTF with Marc Maron*, June 22, 2015, http://www.wtfpod.com/podcast/episodes/episode_613_-_president_barack_obama.

12. Barack Obama, "Obama 2001: Scrap the Constitution, Spread the Wealth," American Thinker, October 27, 2008, http://www.americanthinker.com/blog/2008/10/obama_2001_scrap_the_constitut.html.

13. Ibid.

14. *Lochner v. New York*, 98 U.S. 45 (1905).

15. *West Coast Hotel Co. v. Parrish*, 300 U.S. 379 (1937).

16. *Wickard v. Filburn*, 317 U.S. 111 (1942).

17. Charles Fried, quoted in Avik Roy, "Harvard Law's Fried: A Broccoli Mandate *Is* Constitutional," *Forbes*, February 2, 2011, http://www.forbes.com/sites/aroy/2011/02/02/harvard-laws-fried-a-broccoli-mandate-is-constitutional/.

18. David E. Bernstein, *Rehabilitating Lochner: Defending Individual Rights against Progressive Reform* (Chicago: Chicago University Press, 2011).

19. Eric A. Posner, "Why Originalism Is So Popular," *New Republic*, January 13, 2011, https://newrepublic.com/article/81480/republicans-constitution-originalism-popular.

20. *Hamdi v. Rumsfeld*, 542 U.S. 507 (2004) (O'Connor, J).

21. *Hamdi v. Rumsfeld*, 542 U.S. 507 (2004) (Scalia, J., dissenting).

22. Martin Feldman, quoted in Laurel Brubaker Calkins, "U.S. in Contempt over Gulf Drill Ban, Judge Rules," *Bloomberg Businessweek*, February 3, 2011, http://www.bloomberg.com/news/articles/2011-02-03/u-s-administration-in-contempt-over-gulf-drill-ban-judge-rules.

23. Lana Shadwick, "Federal Judge Orders Top Obama Officials to Court for Possible Contempt Action," Breitbart News, July 8, 2015, http://www.

breitbart.com/texas/2015/07/08/federal-judge-orders-top-obama-officials-to-court-for-possible-contempt-action/.

24. *NFIB v. Sebelius*, 567 U. S. 11-393 (2012).

25. David Nakamura, "Obama Remains Confident Supreme Court Will Uphold Health Care Law," *Washington Post*, April 2, 2012, https://www.washingtonpost.com/politics/obama-remains-confident-supreme-court-will-uphold-health-care-law/2012/04/02/gIQA9HIOrS_story.html.

26. *King v. Burwell*, 576 U.S. 14-114 (2015).

27. Barack Obama, "State of the Union Address" (speech, White House, Washington, D.C., January 27, 2010).

28. *Bush v. Gore*, 531 U.S. 98 (2000).

29. Paul Kane and Ed O'Keefe, "Senate Reaches Tentative Deal on Filibuster Rules," *Washington Post*, July 16, 2013, https://www.washingtonpost.com/politics/senate-poised-to-take-up-key-rule-changes/2013/07/16/167045da-ee1d-11e2-9008-61e94a7ea20d_story.html?hpid=z1.

## CHAPTER 9

1. Eric Holder, "Address to Department of Justice African American History Month Program" (speech, Office of Public Affairs, Washington, D.C., February 18, 2009).

2. Quentin Tarantino, interview by Lane Brown, "In Conversation: Quentin Tarantino," *Vulture*, August 23, 2015, http://www.vulture.com/2015/08/quentin-tarantino-lane-brown-in-conversation.html#.

3. Barack Obama, interview by Marc Maron, "Episode 613—President Barack Obama," *WTF with Marc Maron*, June 22, 2015, http://www.wtfpod.com/podcast/episodes/episode_613_-_president_barack_obama.

4. Martin Luther King Jr., "I Have a Dream" (speech, Lincoln Memorial, Washington, D.C., August 28, 1963).

5. John McCain, "McCain's Concession Speech" (speech, Biltmore Hotel, Phoenix, AZ, November 4, 2008).

6. CNN, "Most Blacks Say MLK's Vision Fulfilled, Poll Finds," CNN, January 19, 2009, http://www.cnn.com/2009/POLITICS/01/19/king.poll/.

7. David Ehrenstein, "Obama the 'Magic Negro,'" *Los Angeles Times*, March 19, 2007, http://www.latimes.com/la-oe-ehrenstein19mar19-story.html.

8. Eduardo Bonilla-Silva, "Eduardo Bonilla-Silver: The Problem with Obama!!!" (lecture, Association of Humanist Sociologists' Meeting, Boston, MA, November 7, 2008).

9.    Shelby Steele, *A Bound Man: Why We Are Excited About Obama and Why He Can't Win* (New York: Free Press, 2008), 8.

10.   Ibid., 14.

11.   Ibid., 18.

12.   Ibid., 44.

13.   Ibid., 71.

14.   Frank Newport, David W. Moore, and Lydia Saad, "Long-Term Gallup Poll Trends: A Portrait of American Public Opinion through the Century," Gallup, December 20, 1999, http://www.gallup.com/poll/3400/longterm-gallup-poll-trends-portrait-american-public-opinion.aspx.

15.   Frank Newport, "In U.S., 87% Approve of Black-White Marriage, vs. 4% in 1958," Gallup, July 25, 2013, http://www.gallup.com/poll/163697/approve-marriage-blacks-whites.aspx.

16.   Justin McCarthy, "Americans Less Positive about Black Civil Rights Progress," Gallup, August 7, 2015, http://www.gallup.com/poll/184523/americans-less-positive-black-civil-rights-progress.aspx.

17.   Frank Newport, "Gallup Review: Black and White Attitudes toward Police," Gallup, August 20, 2014, http://www.gallup.com/poll/175088/gallup-review-black-white-attitudes-toward-police.aspx.

18.   Peter Arcidiacono, et al., "The Effects of Proposition 209 on College Enrollment and Graduation Rates in California," Duke University, December 2011, http://public.econ.duke.edu/~psarcidi/prop209.pdf.

19.   Jack Martinez, "Princeton Protestors Demand Removal of Woodrow Wilson's Name," *Newsweek*, November 20, 2015, http://www.newsweek.com/princeton-woodrow-wilson-protest-black-students-396717.

20.   "Oxy United for Black Liberation," List of Demands, accessed December 5, 2015, http://www.documentcloud.org/documents/2515492-demands-final.html.

21.   Joel B. Pollak, "Black Students Burn Paintings of Whites at South Africa Protest," Breitbart News, February 18, 2016, http://www.breitbart.com/national-security/2016/02/18/black-students-burn-paintings-of-whites-in-south-africa-protest/.

22.   "Students Are Throwing 'Colonial' Art on the Pyre," *Economist*, February 20, 2016, http://www.economist.com/news/middle-east-and-africa/21693278-students-are-throwing-colonial-art-pyre-whiteness-burning.

23.   L. Gordon Crovitz, "Rhodes Must Not Fall," *Wall Street Journal*, January 24, 2016, http://www.wsj.com/articles/rhodes-must-not-fall-1453670305.

24. Tamerra Griffin, "College Protests over Racial Discrimination Spread Across U.S.," Buzzfeed, November 12, 2015, http://www.buzzfeed.com/tamerragriffin/college-protests-over-racial-discrimination-spread-across-us#.vwVmoVMaPO.

25. Frederick Douglass, "What The Black Man Wants" (speech, Annual Meeting of the Massachusetts Anti-Slavery Society, Boston, MA, April 1865).

26. *Fisher v. University of Texas*, Supreme Court cause 04-981, oral argument, transcript pg. 67, lines 10–23, December 9, 2015, http://www.supremecourt.gov/oral_arguments/argument_transcripts/14-981_4h25.pdf.

27. Dan McLaughlin, "This Dumb, Dishonest Attack on Justice Scalia Takes the Cake," Federalist, December 10, 2015, http://thefederalist.com/2015/12/10/this-dumb-dishonest-attack-on-justice-scalia-takes-the-cake/.

28. Joel B. Pollak, "How Jake Tapper Tricked Donald Trump into Bashing Scalia," Breitbart News, December 13, 2015, http://www.breitbart.com/big-government/2015/12/13/how-jake-tapper-tricked-donald-trump-on-scalia/.

29. Joe Biden, "Obama Campaign Rally" (speech, Institute for Advanced Learning and Research, Danville, VA, August 14, 2012).

30. Trinity United Church of Christ, "About Us," https://web.archive.org/web/20050901170910/http://www.tucc.org/about.htm.

31. Biran Ross and Rehab El-Buri, "Obama's Pastor: God Damn America, U.S. to Blame for 9/11," ABC News, March 13, 2008, http://abcnews.go.com/blotter/democraticdebate/story?id=4443788&page=1.

32. Barack Obama, "A More Perfect Union" (speech, National Constitution Center, Philadelphia, PA, March 18, 2008).

33. Geoffrey Dickens, "Chris Matthews Hails Obama Speech As 'Worthy of Abraham Lincoln,'" *Newsbusters*, March 18, 2008, http://www.newsbusters.org/blogs/geoffrey-dickens/2008/03/18/chris-matthews-hails-obama-speech-worthy-abraham-lincoln.

34. Maureen Dowd, "Black, White & Gray," *New York Times*, March 19, 2008, http://www.nytimes.com/2008/03/19/opinion/19dowd.html.

35. Charles Krauthammer, "The Speech: A Brilliant Fraud," *Washington Post*, March 21, 2008, http://www.washingtonpost.com/wp-dyn/content/article/2008/03/20/AR2008032003017.html.

36. Ta-Nehisi Coates, *Between the World and Me* (New York: Spiegel & Grau, 2015), 8.

37.  Ibid., 10.

38.  Ibid., 11.

39.  U.S. Department of Justice, *Department of Justice Report Regarding the Criminal Investigation into the Shooting Death of Michael Brown by Ferguson, Missouri Police Officer Darren Wilson*, March 4, 2015, https://assets.documentcloud.org/documents/1681212/doj-report-on-shooting-of-michael-brown.pdf., 82.

40.  Ibid., 31.

41.  Ibid., 87.

42.  Thomas Chatterton Williams, "My Black Privilege," *Los Angeles Times*, January 3, 2016, http://www.latimes.com/opinion/op-ed/la-oe-0103-williams-black-victim-self-definition-20160103-story.html.

43.  Ibid., 55.

44.  Mark Memmott, "15 Years Later, Tawana Brawley Has Paid 1 Percent Of Penalty," National Public Radio, August 5, 2013, http://www.npr.org/sections/thetwo-way/2013/08/05/209194252/15-years-later-tawana-brawley-has-paid-1-percent-of-penalty.

45.  Byron Tau, "Obama: 'If I Had a Son, He'd Look Like Trayvon,'" *Politico*, March 23, 2012, http://www.politico.com/blogs/politico44/2012/03/obama-if-i-had-a-son-hed-look-like-trayvon-118439#ixzz3tWMJkSQx.

46.  Barack Obama, "Remarks by the President in Eulogy for the Honorable Reverend Clementa Pinckney" (speech, College of Charleston, Charleston, SC, June 26, 2015).

47.  Dylann Roof, quoted in Brendan O'Connor, "Here Is What Appears to Be Dylann Roof's Racist Manifesto," *Gawker*, June 20, 2015, http://gawker.com/here-is-what-appears-to-be-dylann-roofs-racist-manifest-1712767241.

48.  Jennifer Agiesta, "Under Obama, 4 in 10 Say Race Relations Worsened," CNN, March 13, 2015, http://www.cnn.com/2015/03/06/politics/poll-obama-race-relations-worse/. See also "50% Say Race Relations in America Getting Worse," *Rasmussen Reports*, January 19, 2016, http://www.rasmussenreports.com/public_content/lifestyle/general_lifestyle/january_2016/50_say_race_relations_in_america_getting_worse.

## CHAPTER 10

1.  Seth McFarlane, quoted in Mandy Bierly, "Seth MacFarlane Likens Arizona's Immigration Law to Nazi Germany," *Entertainment Weekly*, May 4, 2010, http://www.ew.com/article/2010/05/04/seth-macfarlane-arizona-immigration-law-nazi-germany.

2. Barack Obama, "Remarks by the President at Town Hall on College Access and Affordability" (speech, North High School, Des Moines, IA, September 14, 2015).

3. Joe Biden, quoted in Mark Knoller and Catherine Cannon, "Biden Slams Trump on Immigration," CBS News, September 15, 2015, http://www.cbsnews.com/news/biden-slams-trump-on-immigration/.

4. Jeffrey M. Jones, "In U.S., 65% Favor Path to Citizenship for Illegal Immigrants," Gallup, August 12, 2015, http://www.gallup.com/poll/184577/favor-path-citizenship-illegal-immigrants.aspx.

5. Dana Banton, "Fox News Poll: Majority Says Legal Immigration Should Be Reduced," Fox News, April 23, 2013, http://www.foxnews.com/politics/2013/04/23/fox-news-poll-majority-says-legal-immigration-should-be-reduced.html.

6. Fred Barnes, "The Amnesty Next Time," *Weekly Standard*, May 20, 2013, http://www.weeklystandard.com/the-amnesty-next-time/article/722057.

7. Michelle Moons, "Women Busted in 'Birth Tourism' Raid Vow to Stay in U.S. and Fight," Breitbart News, March 14, 2015, http://www.breitbart.com/national-security/2015/03/14/women-busted-in-birth-tourism-raid-vow-to-stay-in-usa-and-fight/.

8. Joel B. Pollak, "Supremes Uphold Substance, Strike Down Form of AZ Immigration Law," Breitbart News, June 25, 2012, http://www.breitbart.com/big-government/2012/06/25/breaking-supreme-court-upholds-substance-strikes-down-form-of-az-immigration-law-sb-1070/.

9. Barack Obama, "Remarks by the President on Comprehensive Immigration Reform" (speech, Del Sol High School, Las Vegas, NV, January 29, 2013).

10. Barack Obama, "Remarks by the President on Immigration–Chicago, IL" (speech, Copernicus Center, Chicago, IL, November 25, 2014).

11. Barack Obama, "Remarks by the President at Town Hall on College Access and Affordability" (speech, North High School, Des Moines, IA, September 14, 2015).

12. Joe Biden, quoted in Mark Knoller and Catherine Cannon, "Biden Slams Trump on Immigration," CBS News, September 15, 2015, http://www.cbsnews.com/news/biden-slams-trump-on-immigration/.

13. Ann Coulter, interview by Jorge Ramos, "Jorge Ramos Spars with Ann Coulter over Her Comparison of Immigrants to ISIS," *Fusion*, May 26, 2015, http://fusion.net/video/139852/jorge-ramos-ann-coulter-interview/.

14. Mark Salter, "Obama's Immigration Reform Vision: Clouded by Cynicism," RealClearPolitics, May 12, 2011, http://www1.

realclearpolitics.com/articles/2011/05/12/obamas_immigration_reform_vision_clouded_by_cynicism_109830.html.

15. Luis Gutierrez, quoted in Joel B. Pollak, "Using Rich People's Guilt to Sell Immigration Reform," Breitbart News, April 23, 2013, http://www.breitbart.com/blog/2013/04/23/using-rich-people-s-guilt-to-sell-immigration-reform/.

16. Mark R. Levin, *Plunder and Deceit: Big Government's Exploitation of Young People and the Future* (New York: Threshold, 2015), 97.

17. Barack Obama, "Remarks by the President on Comprehensive Immigration Reform" (speech, El Paso, Texas, May 10, 2011).

18. Robert Farley, "Obama Says the Border Fence Is 'Now Basically Complete,'" *PolitiFact*, May 16, 2011, http://www.politifact.com/truth-o-meter/statements/2011/may/16/barack-obama/obama-says-border-fence-now-basically-complete/.

19. Ana Gonzalez-Barrera, "More Mexicans Leaving Than Coming to the U.S.," Pew Research Center, November 19, 2015, http://www.pewhispanic.org/2015/11/19/more-mexicans-leaving-than-coming-to-the-u-s/.

20. Daniel Horowitz, "Appallingly Dishonest Pew Study on Immigration Trend from Mexico," Conservative Review, November 22, 2015, https://www.conservativereview.com/commentary/2015/11/appallingly-dishonest-pew-study-on-immigration-trend-from-mexico.

21. Matt Wolking, "22 Times President Obama Said He Couldn't Ignore or Create His Own Immigration Law," *Speaker of the House blog*, November 19, 2014, http://www.speaker.gov/general/22-times-president-obama-said-he-couldn-t-ignore-or-create-his-own-immigration-law.

22. Julia Preston, "Program Benefiting Some Immigrants Extends Visa Wait for Others," *New York Times*, February 8, 2014, http://www.nytimes.com/2014/02/09/us/program-benefiting-some-immigrants-extends-visa-wait-for-others.html.

23. Hillary Clinton, quoted in Ryan Lovelace, "Hillary Clinton: I Would 'Go Even Further' than Obama on Immigration," *Washington Examiner*, May 5, 2015, http://www.washingtonexaminer.com/hillary-clinton-i-would-go-even-further-than-obama-on-immigration/article/2564050.

24. Michelle Moons, "Pro-Amnesty Crowd Burns American Flag at Murrieta on 4th of July," Breitbart News, July 4, 2014, http://www.breitbart.com/california/2014/07/04/american-flag-burned-at-murrieta-protests-on-4th-of-july/.

25.   Joel B. Pollak, "The Hateful Side of Immigration Reform," Breitbart News, August 6, 2013, http://www.breitbart.com/big-government/2013/08/06/the-hateful-side-of-immigration-reform/.

26.   Francisco Rivera, quoted in Michelle Moons, "WATCH: Latino Immigrant Blasts City over Illegal Aliens," Breitbart News, August 18, 2015, http://www.breitbart.com/big-government/2015/08/18/watch-latino-immigrant-blasts-city-over-illegal-aliens/.

27.   Ibid.

## CHAPTER 11

1.    Elizabeth Warren, "Elizabeth Warren on Debt Crisis, Fair Taxation," YouTube video, 2:05, *LiveSmartVideos*, September 18, 2011, https://www.youtube.com/watch?v=htX2usfqMEs.

2.    Alan Grayson, "Alan Grayson on the GOP Health Care Plan: 'Don't Get Sick! And if You Do Get Sick, Die Quickly!,'" YouTube video, 2:27, September 29, 2009, https://www.youtube.com/watch?v=-usmvYOPfco.

3.    Barack Obama, "Statement by the President on the 50th Anniversary of the War on Poverty" (speech, White House, Washington, D.C., January 8, 2014).

4.    Barack Obama, Text of President-elect Obama's Economic Speech" ABC News, January 8, 2009, http://abcnews.go.com/Politics/Business/story?id=6603716&page=1.

5.    Christina Romer and Jared Bernstein, "The Job Impact of the American Recovery and Reinvestment Plan," January 10, 2009, https://otrans.3cdn.net/45593e8ecbd339d074_l3m6bt1te.pdf.

6.    Terence P. Jeffrey, "U.S. Has Record 10th Straight Year without 3% Growth in GDP," CNSNews, February 26, 2016, http://www.cnsnews.com/news/article/terence-p-jeffrey/us-has-record-10th-straight-year-without-3-growth-gdp.

7.    Bill Clinton, "Address Before a Joint Session of the Congress on the State of the Union," The American Presidency Project, January 23, 1996, http://www.presidency.ucsb.edu/ws/?pid=53091.

8.    Barack Obama, quoted in "Obama Jokes at Jobs Council: 'Shovel-Ready Was Not as Shovel-Ready as We Expected,'" Fox Nation, June 13, 2011, http://nation.foxnews.com/president-obama/2011/06/13/obama-jokes-jobs-council-shovel-ready-was-not-shovel-ready-we-expected.

9.    Lydia Saad, "Cost Is Foremost Healthcare Issue for Americans," Gallup, September 23, 2009, http://www.gallup.com/poll/123149/cost-is-foremost-healthcare-issue-for-americans.aspx.

10. Grace-Marie Turner, "Part D Can Be a Model for Medicare Reform," *The Hill*, March 14, 2013, http://thehill.com/blogs/congress-blog/healthcare/288147-part-d-can-be-a-model-for-medicare-reform.

11. Barack Obama, "36 Times Obama Said You Could Keep Your Health Care Plan | SuperCuts #18," YouTube video, 2:52, Washington Free Beacon, November 5, 2013, https://www.youtube.com/watch?v=qpa-5JdCnmo.

12. Peter H. Schuck, *Why Government Fails So Often and How It Can Do Better* (Princeton: Princeton University Press, 2014).

13. Ibid., 353.

14. Ibid., 354.

15. Ibid., 365.

16. Ibid.

17. Paul Roderick Gregory, "The Timeline of IRS Targeting of Conservative Groups," *Forbes*, June 25, 2013, http://www.forbes.com/sites/paulroderickgregory/2013/06/25/the-timeline-of-irs-targeting-of-conservative-groups/.

18. Kim Barker and Justin Elliott, "IRS Office That Targeted Tea Party Also Disclosed Confidential Docs From Conservative Groups," ProPublica, May 13, 2013, https://www.propublica.org/article/irs-office-that-targeted-tea-party-also-disclosed-confidential-docs.

19. John D. McKinnon, et al., "Higher-Ups Knew of IRS Case," *Wall Street Journal*, May 17, 2013, http://www.wsj.com/articles/SB10001424127887324767004578488833834357540.

20. James Taranto, "President Asterisk," *Wall Street Journal*, May 17, 2013, http://www.wsj.com/articles/SB10001424127887324082604578489171510582616.

21. Barack Obama, quoted in "Barack Obama's IRS statement (transcript, video)," *Politico*, May 15, 2013, http://www.politico.com/story/2013/05/barack-obama-irs-statement-transcript-091445.

22. Barack Obama, quoted in Brendan Bordelon, "Obama Dismisses IRS Targeting of Conservatives: 'They've Got a List, and Suddenly Everybody's Outraged,'" Daily Caller, December 6, 2013, http://dailycaller.com/2013/12/06/obama-dismisses-irs-targeting-of-conservatives-theyve-got-a-list-and-suddenly-everybodys-outraged/.

23. Adam Liptak and Coral Davenport, "Supreme Court Deals Blow to Obama's Efforts to Regulate Coal Emissions," *New York Times*, February 9, 2016, http://www.nytimes.com/2016/02/10/us/politics/supreme-court-blocks-obama-epa-coal-emissions-regulations.html?_r=0.

24.    Laurence H. Tribe, "The Clean Power Plan is Unconstitutional," *Wall Street Journal*, December 22, 2014, http://www.wsj.com/articles/laurence-tribe-the-epas-clean-power-plan-is-unconstitutional-1419293203.

25.    L. Gordon Crovitz, "Obamanet Is Hurting Broadband," *Wall Street Journal*, September 13, 2015, http://www.wsj.com/articles/obamanet-is-hurting-broadband-1442183370.

26.    F. A. Hayek, *The Constitution of Liberty: The Definitive Edition, The Collected Works of F. A. Hayek*, (Chicago: Chicago University Press, 2011), 165.

## CHAPTER 12

1.    Christopher Dodd, "Beyond Iraq and into an Era of Bold Engagement" (address, U.S. Center for Citizen Diplomacy, Des Moines, IA, April 12, 2007).

2.    Nobel Prize Committee, "The Nobel Peace Prize for 2009," October 9, 2009, http://www.nobelprize.org/nobel_prizes/peace/laureates/2009/press.html.

3.    John Kerry, interview by Bob Schieffer, "Face the Nation Transcripts March 2, 2014: Kerry, Hagel," CBS News, March 2, 2014, http://www.cbsnews.com/news/face-the-nation-transcripts-march-2-2014-kerry-hagel/.

4.    Shepard Smith, *Shepard Smith Reporting*, Fox News Channel, December 1, 2015.

5.    Douglas J. Feith, *War and Decision: Inside the Pentagon at the Dawn of the War on Terrorism* (New York: Harper, 2008), 66, 183.

6.    Ibid., 212.

7.    Ibid., 224.

8.    Barack Obama, quoted in "Part 1: Obama Talks War on Terror, Iran, and Pakistan in First-Ever Interview with O'Reilly," *The O'Reilly Factor*, Fox News, September 5, 2008, http://www.foxnews.com/story/2008/09/05/part-1-obama-talks-war-on-terror-iran-and-pakistan-in-first-ever-interview-with.html.

9.    Jim Rutenberg, "Finding Archives Lacking, Obama Returns to 2002," *New York Times*, October 12, 2007, http://www.nytimes.com/2007/10/12/us/politics/12obama.html.

10.    Paul Starobin, "A Moral Flip-Flop? Defining a War," *New York Times*, August 6, 2011, http://www.nytimes.com/2011/08/07/opinion/sunday/harold-kohs-flip-flop-on-the-libya-question.html.

11.    Barack Obama, "Letter from the President on the War Powers Resolution" (speech, White House, Washington, D.C., June 15, 2011).

12.    Hillary Clinton, interview by Bob Schieffer, *Meet the Press*, CBS News,
       March 27, 2011, http://www.cbsnews.com/htdocs/pdf/FTN_032711.pdf.

13.    Samantha Power, interview by Steve Inskeep, "U.S. Ambassador Samantha
       Power Presses for Strikes On Syria," National Public Radio, September 9,
       2013, http://www.npr.org/2013/09/09/220586231/u-s-ambassador-susan-
       rice-makes-case-for-strikes-on-syria.

14.    Barack Obama, interview by Lester Holt, *NBC Nightly News*, November
       2, 2015.

15.    Barack Obama, Democratic Presidential Debate, CNN/YouTube, July 24,
       2007, http://www.cnn.com/2007/POLITICS/07/23/debate.transcript/.

16.    Barack Obama, "Remarks by the President on the Iran Nuclear Deal"
       (speech, American University, Washington, D.C., August 5, 2015).

17.    Barack Obama, interview by Fareed Zakaria, *GPS with Fareed Zakaria*,
       CNN, August 9, 2015, http://www.cnn.com/2015/08/07/politics/obama-
       iran-gop-comparison/.

18.    Barack Obama, quoted in David Nakamura and Juliet Eilperin, "Obama
       Calls GOP Rhetoric on Syrian refugees a 'potent recruitment tool for
       ISIL,'" *Washington Post*, November 17, 2015, https://www.
       washingtonpost.com/news/post-politics/wp/2015/11/17/obama-calls-gop-
       rhetoric-on-syrian-refugees-a-potent-recruiting-tool-for-isil/.

19.    Barack Obama, "Press Conference by the President at the Nuclear Security
       Summit" (speech, White House, Washington, D.C., April 13, 2010).

20.    John McCain, quoted in "Obama: America a Superpower 'Whether We
       Like It or Not,'" Fox News, April 15, 2010, http://www.foxnews.com/
       politics/2010/04/15/obama-america-superpower-like.html.

21.    John McCain, quoted in Mike Glover, "McCain Says Pundits Being
       Fooled, Promises Victory," Associated Press, October 28, 2008, http://
       www.boston.com/news/politics/2008/articles/2008/10/28/mccain_targets_
       rural_pennsylvania/.

22.    Barack Obama, "Remarks by the President at the Acceptance of the Nobel
       Peace Prize" (speech, Oslo City Hall, Oslo, Norway, December 10, 2009).

## CHAPTER 13

1.     Barack Obama, interview by Matthew Yglesias, "Obama: The Vox
       Conversation. Part Two: Foreign Policy," *Vox*, February 9, 2015, http://
       www.vox.com/a/barack-obama-interview-vox-conversation/obama-
       foreign-policy-transcript.

2.     John Kerry, "Remarks to the Staff and Families of U.S. Embassy" (speech,
       U.S. Embassy, Paris, France, November 17, 2015).

3.    Tom Fuentes, interview by Jake Tapper, *The Lead with Jake Tapper*, CNN, December 2, 2015, http://transcripts.cnn.com/TRANSCRIPTS/1512/02/cg.01.html.

4.    Ibid.

5.    Ryan Grenoble, "Financial Times' Europe Editor Calls Charlie Hebdo 'Stupid,' Accuses Paper of 'Muslim Baiting,'" Huffington Post, January 7, 2015, http://www.huffingtonpost.com/2015/01/07/financial-times-charlie-hebdo-stupid-muslim-baiting_n_6430242.html.

6.    Obama, interview by Matthew Yglesias, "Obama: The Vox Conversation."

7.    Hillary Clinton, interview by George Stephanopoulos, *This Week with George Stephanopoulos*, ABC, December, 6, 2015, http://abcnews.go.com/Politics/week-transcript-hillary-clinton-jeb-bush/story?id=35596885.

8.    Brandeis University, "Statement from Brandeis University," April 8, 2014, http://www.brandeis.edu/now/2014/april/commencementupdate.html.

9.    Ayaan Hirsi Ali, quoted in Bill Kristol, "Ayaan Hirsi Ali Speaks," *Weekly Standard*, April 9, 2014, http://www.weeklystandard.com/blogs/ayaan-hirsi-ali-speaks_786719.html

10.   Ayaan Hirsi Ali, "Here's What I Would Have Said at Brandeis," *Wall Street Journal*, April 10, 2014, http://www.wsj.com/articles/SB100014240527023045125045794934102876639O6.

11.   Barack Obama, "Speech to the United Nations General Assembly" (speech, United Nations Headquarters, New York, NY, September 25, 2012).

12.   Ibid.

13.   Loretta Lynch, "Remarks at Muslim Advocates Dinner" (speech, Muslim Advocates Annual Dinner, Washington D.C., December 3, 2015).

14.   George W. Bush, "Address to a Joint Session of Congress and the American People" (speech, United States Capitol, Washington, D.C., September 20, 2001).

15.   Barack Obama, "Remarks by the President at Cairo University" (speech, Cairo University, Cairo, Egypt, June 4, 2009).

16.   Barack Obama, "Remarks by the President at the Closing of the Tribal Nations Conference" (speech, White House, Washington D.C., November 5, 2009).

17.   Barack Obama, "Remarks by the President at National Prayer Breakfast" (speech, Washington Hilton, Washington, D.C., February 5, 2015).

18.   Abdel Fattah al-Sisi, "Remarks at Al-Azhar University" (speech, Al-Azhar University, Cairo, Egypt, January 1, 2015).

## CHAPTER 14

1.  Barack Obama, "Remarks by the President at a Discussion with Ohio Families on the Economy" (speech, White House, Washington, D.C., August 18, 2010).

2.  Obama, "Weekly Address: Celebrating Fifty Years of Medicare and Medicaid" (speech, White House, Washington, D.C., August 1, 2015).

3.  Robert Creamer, *Listen to Your Mother: Stand Up Straight! How Progressives Can Win* (Santa Ana: Five Locks, 2007), 17.

4.  Dan Bilefsky and Landon Thomas Jr., "The Bitter Pills in the Plan to Rescue Greece," *New York Times*, April 30, 2010, http://www.nytimes.com/2010/05/01/business/global/01euro.html.

5.  Paul Krugman, "We're Not Greece," *New York Times*, May 30, 2015, http://www.nytimes.com/2010/05/14/opinion/14krugman.html.

6.  Krugman, "Fiscal Scare Tactics," *New York Times*, February 4, 2010, http://www.nytimes.com/2010/02/05/opinion/05krugman.html.

7.  Krugman, "We're Not Greece."

8.  Federal Reserve Bank of St. Louis, "Federal Debt: Total Public Debt as Percent of Gross Domestic Product," Economic Research, December 2, 2015, https://research.stlouisfed.org/fred2/series/GFDEGDQ188S.

9.  Wade Pfau, "Potential Directions for Social Security," *Forbes*, December 8, 2015, http://www.forbes.com/sites/wadepfau/2015/12/08/potential-directions-for-social-security/.

10. Barack Obama, "Remarks at a Campaign Event," (speech, Fargo, ND, July 3, 2008).

11. Barack Obama, "Second Presidential Debate" (debate, Belmont University, Nashville, TN, October 7, 2008).

12. Obama, quoted in Michael D. Shear, "Obama Pledges Reform of Social Security, Medicare Programs," *Washington Post*, January 16, 2009, http://www.washingtonpost.com/wp-dyn/content/article/2009/01/15/AR2009011504114.html.

13. Obama, "Weekly Address."

14. Barack Obama, quoted in Yuval Levin, "The Great Reformer," *National Review*, July 11, 2014, http://www.nationalreview.com/corner/271603/great-reformer-yuval-levin.

15. Steny Hoyer, "Keynote Address on Entitlement and Health Care Reform," Bipartisan Policy Center, May 6, 2009, http://www.democraticwhip.gov/content/hoyer-delivers-keynote-address-entitlement-and-health-care-reform.

16. Creamer, *Listen to Your Mother*, 17.

17. Ibid., 15.

18. Carl Hulse, "Lesson Is Seen in Failure of Law on Medicare in 1989," *New York Times*, November 17, 2013, http://www.nytimes.com/2013/11/18/us/politics/lesson-is-seen-in-failure-of-1989-law-on-medicare.html?pagewanted=all.

19. Erica Payne, interview by Neil Cavuto, "'Grandma' Thrown off Cliff in New Anti-GOP Ad," Fox News, transcript, May 18, 2011, http://www.foxnews.com/transcript/2011/05/18/grandma-thrown-cliff-new-anti-gop-ad/.

20. "Geithner to Ryan on Debt: We Don't 'Have a Definitive Solution to Our Long-Term Problem,'" transcript of House Budget Committee Hearing on the President's Fiscal Year 2013 Revenue and Economic Policy Proposals, RealClearPolitics, February 16, 2012, http://www.realclearpolitics.com/video/2012/02/16/geithner_to_ryan_on_debt_we_dont_have_a_definitive_solution_to_our_long-term_problem.html.

21. Ibid.

22. Bernie Sanders, "It's Time to Make College Tuition Free and Debt Free," BernieSanders.com, January 4, 2016, https://berniesanders.com/issues/its-time-to-make-college-tuition-free-and-debt-free/.

23. Benjamin VanMetre, "Illinois Drowning in Debt: $127 Billion and Counting," Illinois Policy Institute, January 7, 2014, https://www.illinoispolicy.org/illinois-drowning-in-debt-127-billion-and-counting/.

24. Elizabeth Campbell and Tim Jones, "Rauner Seeks Cuts to Close $6 Billion Illinois Deficit," *Bloomberg Politics*, February 18, 2015, http://www.bloomberg.com/politics/articles/2015-02-18/illinois-governor-rauner-seeks-cuts-to-close-6-billion-deficit.

25. Barack Obama, "Remarks by the President on Fiscal Policy" (speech, White House, Washington, D.C., April 13, 2011).

26. Mike Mullen, quoted in "Mullen: Debt Is Top National Security Threat," CNN, August 27, 2010, http://www.cnn.com/2010/US/08/27/debt.security.mullen/.

## CHAPTER 15

1. Andrew Leonard, "Why Do Republicans Hate Poor, Hungry People?," Salon, January 11, 2012, http://www.salon.com/2012/01/11/why_do_republicans_hate_poor_hungry_people/.

2. Barack Obama, "Remarks by the President at a Campaign Event" (speech, University of Vermont, Burlington, VT, March 30, 2012).

3.   David Corn, "More Evidence of Paul Ryan's 'Inner Cities' Problem," *Mother Jones*, March 27, 2014, http://www.motherjones.com/politics/2014/03/paul-ryan-inner-cities-problem.

4.   Newt Gingrich, "Speech to Georgia Republican Party" (speech, Georgia Republican Party convention, Macon, GA, May 13, 2011).

5.   Suzanne Gamboa, "Gingrich to Black People: Paychecks, Not Food Aid," Associated Press, January 6, 2012, http://tinyurl.com/jpg3kb7.

6.   U.S. Department of Agriculture, "Supplemental Nutrition Assistance Program," December 11, 2015, http://www.fns.usda.gov/sites/default/files/pd/34SNAPmonthly.pdf.

7.   Brooks Jackson, "Fact Check: Gingrich's Faulty Food-Stamp Claim," *USA Today*, February 6, 2012, http://usatoday30.usatoday.com/news/politics/story/2012-01-18/fact-check-gingrich-obama-food-stamps/52645882/1.

8.   Franklin D. Roosevelt, "Eighth Annual Address to Congress" (speech, White House, Washington, D.C., January 6, 1941).

9.   House Budget Committee, "The War on Poverty: 50 Years Later," March 3, 2014, http://192.168.1.1:8181/http://budget.house.gov/uploadedfiles/war_on_poverty.pdf.

10.  World Bank, "Measurement Is Fundamental for Ending Extreme Poverty, but Must Be Done Better, Says World Bank Report," press release, October 9, 2014, http://www.worldbank.org/en/news/press-release/2014/10/09/measurement-fundamental-ending-extreme-poverty-world-bank-report.

11.  Mark J. Perry, "It's the Greatest Achievement in Human History, and One You Probably Never Heard About," American Enterprise Institute, November 3, 2014, http://www.aei.org/publication/greatest-achievement-human-history-one-probably-never-heard/.

12.  Ayn Rand, *Atlas Shrugged* (New York: Signet, 1957), 76, 125.

13.  Barack Obama, "Remarks by the President at a Campaign Event."

14.  Barack Obama, "The American Promise" (speech, Acceptance Speech at the Democratic Convention, Mile High Stadium, Denver, CO, August 28, 2008).

15.  *Lochner v. New York*, 198 US 45 (1905).

16.  *Lochner*, Holmes, J., dissenting.

17.  Noah Berlatsky, "Is Racism Slowing Job Recovery?," *Pacific Standard*, March 11, 2015, http://www.psmag.com/business-economics/public-sector-jobs-recovery-african-americans.

18.  Igor Volsky, "Paul Ryan Blames Poverty on Lazy 'Inner City' Men," ThinkProgress, March 12, 2014, http://thinkprogress.org/economy/2014/03/12/3394871/ryan-poverty-inner-city/.

19. Jason L. Riley, "A Black Conservative's War on Poverty," *Wall Street Journal*, April 18, 2014, http://www.wsj.com/articles/SB100014240527023 04441304579481593325577488.

20. Peter Schweizer, quoted in Wynton Hall, "Boomtown 2: Fast Food Giant Lobbied to Get into Food Stamp Game," Breitbart News, April 5, 2013, http://www.breitbart.com/big-government/2013/04/05/boomtown-2-fast-food-giant-lobbied-to-get-into-the-food-stamp-game/.

21. Robert Creamer, *Listen to Your Mother*: *Stand Up Straight*! *How Progressives Can Win* (Santa Ana: Five Locks, 2007), 545.

22. Chris Matthews and Barbara Boxer, quoted in Geoffrey Dickens, "Matthews Joins Barbara Boxer in Dismissing 'Brooks Brothers' Protestors," *NewsBusters*, August 4, 2009, http://www.newsbusters.org/blogs/geoffrey-dickens/2009/08/04/matthews-joins-barbara-boxer-dismissing-brooks-brothers-protestors.

23. Joel B. Pollak, "Was Democrats' Health Care Strategy Written in Federal Prison?," Breitbart News, December 7, 2009, http://www.breitbart.com/big-government/2009/12/07/was-democrats-health-care-strategy-written-in-federal-prison/.

24. Robert Reich, quoted in Joel B. Pollak, "Ryan on Poverty: 'A Reform Debate, Not a Funding Debate,'" Breitbart News, July 30, 2014, http://www.breitbart.com/big-government/2014/07/30/ryan-on-poverty-a-reform-debate-not-a-funding-debate/.

25. Arne Duncan, quoted in "Activists Protest Obama Administration's Spending Cuts to D.C. Voucher Program," Fox News, September 10, 2009, http://www.foxnews.com/politics/2009/09/08/activists-protest-obama-administrations-spending-cuts-dc-voucher-program.html.

26. Caitlin Emma, "Jindal Scores a Win with Appeals Court Voucher Ruling," Politico, November 10, 2015, http://www.politico.com/story/2015/11/louisiana-school-voucher-case-doj-setback-215720.

27. Arthur C. Brooks, "Making a Moral Case for Capitalism," American Enterprise Institute, October 21, 2012, https://www.aei.org/publication/making-a-moral-case-for-capitalism/.

## CHAPTER 16

1. Barack Obama, interview by Bret Baier, "President Barack Obama Talks to Bret Baier about Health Care Reform Bill," Fox News, March 17, 2010, http://www.foxnews.com/story/2010/03/17/president-barack-obama-talks-to-bret-baier-about-health-care-reform-bill.html.

2.  Demonstrators, recorded by Joanna Schuth, "Madison Chant: 'Tell Me What Democracy Looks Like! / This Is What Democracy Looks Like!'" February 16, 2011, https://vimeo.com/17461565.

3.  Peter Orzsag, "Too Much of a Good Thing," *New Republic*, September 13, 2011, https://newrepublic.com/article/94940/peter-orszag-democracy.

4.  Gary Washburn and Jon Hilkevitch, "Daley Rips Up Meigs Runways in Surprise Raid; Terror Concerns Prompt Closing, Irate Mayor Says," *Chicago Tribune*, April 1, 2003, 1.

5.  Richard M. Daley, "Meigs Field Press Conference: Edited Transcript of Daley Comments," *Chicago Tribune*, April 1, 2003, 18.

6.  Eric Zorn, "X's Mark Spot Where Daley Went Too Far," *Chicago Tribune*, April 1, 2003, 1.

7.  Barack Obama, "President Barack Obama Talks to Bret Baier."

8.  David Axelrod, "A Well-Oiled Machine: A System That Works?," *Chicago Tribune*, August 21, 2005, C1.

9.  Woodrow Wilson, "What Is Progress?," 1912, reprinted at Heritage, http://www.heritage.org/initiatives/first-principles/primary-sources/woodrow-wilson-asks-what-is-progress.

10. Saul Alinsky, *Rules for Radicals: A Pragmatic Primer for Realistic Radicals* (New York: Knopf Doubleday Publishing Group, 2010).

11. Barack Obama, *Dreams from My Father: A Story of Race and Inheritance* (New York: Crown, 1995), 230.

12. Luis Gutierrez, *Still Dreaming: My Journey from the Barrio to Capitol Hill* (New York: W. W. Norton, 2013).

13. Obama, *Dreams*, 231.

14. Ken Klukowski, "Another Appeals Court Rules Obama Recess Appointments Unconstitutional," Breitbart News, May 23, 2013, http://www.breitbart.com/big-government/2013/05/23/another-appeals-court-says-obama-s-appointments-unconstitutional/.

15. *NLRB v. Noel Canning*, 571 U.S. 12-1281 (2014).

16. *NLRB v. Noel Canning*, 571 U.S. 12-1281 (2014), Scalia, J., concurring.

17. John Kerry, quoted in Ian Hanchett, "Kerry: US Not Negotiating 'Legally Binding' Iran Deal," Breitbart News, March 11, 2015, http://www.breitbart.com/video/2015/03/11/kerry-us-not-negotiating-legally-binding-iran-deal/.

18. John Kerry, quoted in Patrick Goodenough, "Kerry: Iran Deal Not a Treaty 'Because You Can't Pass a Treaty Anymore,'" CNSNews, July 29, 2015, http://www.cnsnews.com/news/article/patrick-goodenough/kerry-iran-deal-not-treaty-because-you-cant-pass-treaty-anymore.

19. U.S. Congress, "Treaty Documents," accessed January 4, 2016, https://www.congress.gov/treaties?q=%7B%22treaty-status%22%3A%22Approved%22%7D.

20. Suzanne Goldenberg, "How US Negotiators Ensured Landmark Paris Climate Deal Was Republican-Proof," *Guardian* (UK), December 13, 2015, http://www.theguardian.com/us-news/2015/dec/13/climate-change-paris-deal-cop21-obama-administration-congress-republicans-environment.

21. Stephen Montemayor, "Protesters Call for Justice in March to State Fair," *Minneapolis Star-Tribune*, August 31, 2014, http://www.startribune.com/st-paul-braces-for-state-fair-protest-march-today/323310741/.

22. Josh Earnest, "Press Briefing by Press Secretary Josh Earnest, 11/9/15" (press briefing, James S. Brady Press Briefing Room, White House, Washington, D.C., November 9, 2015).

## CHAPTER 17

1. Barack Obama, "Call to Renewal's Building a Covenant for a New America" (keynote address, Washington, D.C., June 28, 2006).

2. Sam Harris, *Letter to a Christian Nation* (New York: Knopf, 2006), xi.

3. Peter Manseau, "America Is Not a 'Christian' Nation," FoxNews, March 6, 2015, http://www.foxnews.com/opinion/2015/03/05/america-is-not-christian-nation.html.

4. Barack Obama, "Remarks by the President at National Prayer Breakfast" (speech, Washington Hilton, Washington, D.C., February 5, 2015).

5. Barack Obama, "Remarks at Easter Prayer Breakfast" (speech, East Room, White House, Washington, D.C., April 7, 2015).

6. William Bigelow, "Vandals Deface Junipero Serra Mission," Breitbart News, November 3, 2015, http://www.breitbart.com/california/2015/11/03/vandals-deface-junipero-serra-mission/.

7. Pew Research Center, "Latest Trends in Religious Restrictions and Hostilities," February 26, 2015, http://www.pewforum.org/2015/02/26/religious-hostilities/.

8. Ta-Nehisi Coates, "The Foolish, Historically Illiterate, Incredible Response to Obama's Prayer Breakfast Speech," *Atlantic*, February 6, 2015, http://www.theatlantic.com/politics/archive/2015/02/the-foolish-historically-illiterate-incredible-response-to-obamas-prayer-breakfast-speech/385246/.

9. Arthur Koestler, *Darkness at Noon*, trans. Daphne Hardy (New York: Bantam, 1966), 128.

10.     Thomas Jefferson, "Notes on the State of Virginia," The Avalon Project, http://avalon.law.yale.edu/18th_century/jeffvir.asp.

11.     Christopher Hitchens, *God Is Not Great: How Religion Poisons Everything* (New York: Twelve, 2007), 192.

12.     Ibid., 230.

13.     *Engel v. Vitale*, 370 U.S. 421 (1962).

14.     *Roe v. Wade*, 410 U.S. 113 (1973).

15.     Max Weber, *The Protestant Ethic and the Spirit of Capitalism* (New York: Penguin, 2002).

16.     Rand Paul, (Fourth Presidential Debate, Milwaukee, WI, November 10, 2015).

17.     Barack Obama, "Remarks at News Conference" (speech, Strasbourg, France, April 4, 2009).

18.     Peter Manseau, "We are Not a Christian Nation: Ronald Reagan, John F. Kennedy and the Eternal Lie of the 'City upon a Hill,'" Salon, February 14, 2015, http://www.salon.com/2015/02/14/we_are_not_a_christian_nation_ronald_reagan_john_f_kennedy_and_the_eternal_lie_of_the_city_upon_a_hill/.

## CHAPTER 18

1.      Bob Herbert, interview by Melissa Harris-Perry, *The Melissa Harris-Perry Show*, MSNBC, April 27, 2013, http://www.nbcnews.com/id/51703290/ns/msnbc/.

2.      Christopher Hayes, interview by Trevor Noah, *The Daily Show with Trevor Noah*, November 11, 2015, quoted in Jeffrey Meyer, "MSNBC's Chris Hayes Denies Existence of Liberal Media Bias," *NewsBusters*, November 12, 2015, http://www.newsbusters.org/blogs/nb/jeffrey-meyer/2015/11/12/msnbcs-chris-hayes-denies-existence-liberal-media-bias.

3.      David Brock, *Killing the Messenger: The Right-Wing Plot to Derail Hillary and Hijack Your Government* (Grand Central Publishing, Kindle Edition, 2015), 191.

4.      Andrew Breitbart, *Righteous Indignation: Excuse Me While I Save the World* (New York: Grand Central, 2011).

5.      Kelly Riddell, "Republicans' Media Bias Claims Boosted by Scarcity of Right-leaning Journalists," *Washington Times*, November 8, 2015, http://www.washingtontimes.com/news/2015/nov/8/republicans-media-bias-claims-boosted-by-scarcity-/.

6.      Tom Stocky, Facebook post, May 10, 2016, https://www.facebook.com/tstocky/posts/10100853082337958.

7. Sam Thielman, "Facebook Relies on Editors' Judgment for Trending News Feed, Documents Show," *Guardian* (UK), May 12, 2016, https://www. theguardian.com/technology/2016/may/12/facebook-trending-news-leaked-documents-editor-guidelines.

8. Michael Nunez, "Want to Know What Facebook Really Thinks of Journalists? Here's What Happened When It Hired Some," Gizmodo, May 3, 2016, http://gizmodo.com/want-to-know-what-facebook-really-thinks-of-journalists-1773916117.

9. Tim Groseclose, *Left Turn: How Liberal Media Bias Distorts the American Mind* (New York: St. Martin's Press, 2011).

10. Ibid., ix.

11. Ibid.

12. Ibid.

13. Ibid., x.

14. Ibid., 134.

15. Brock, *Killing the Messenger*, 274.

16. Ibid.,191.

17. Groseclose, *Left Turn*, 151.

18. Chris McGreal, "Are These Photos Racist?," *Guardian* (UK), February 28, 2000, http://www.theguardian.com/media/2000/feb/28/mondaymediasection.pressandpublishing2.

19. Matthew Boyle, "Emails Reveal Justice Dept. Regularly Enlists Media Matters to Spin Press," Daily Caller, September 18, 2012, http://dailycaller.com/2012/09/18/emails-reveal-justice-dept-regularly-enlists-media-matters-to-spin-press/.

20. Andrew Breitbart, "The White House Guess List: How Obama Pulled a Fast One on the American People—in the Name of 'Transparency,'" Breitbart News, March 22, 2011, http://www.breitbart.com/big-government/2011/03/22/the-white-house-guess-list-how-obama-pulled-a-fast-one-on-the-american-people-in-the-name-of-transparency/.

21. Hayes, *The Daily Show*.

22. Joel B. Pollak, interview by Soledad O'Brien, CNN, March 8, 2012, http://transcripts.cnn.com/TRANSCRIPTS/1203/08/sp.02.html.

23. Erik Wemple, "CNN's O'Brien Goes for a Do-Over," *Washington Post*, March 12, 2012, https://www.washingtonpost.com/blogs/erik-wemple/post/cnns-obrien-goes-for-a-do-over/2012/03/12/gIQAFEVY7R_blog.html.

24. Tim Graham, "Study Reveals Republicans Lie More ... or That PolitiFact Has a Serious Liberal Bias Problem," *NewsBusters*, May 29, 2013, http://

www.newsbusters.org/blogs/tim-graham/2013/05/29/study-reveals-republicans-lie-moreor-politifact-has-serious-liberal-bias. See also Eric Ostermeier, "Selection Bias? PolitiFact Rates Republican Statements as False at 3 Times the Rate of Democrats," Smart Politics, February 10, 2011, http://editions.lib.umn.edu/smartpolitics/2011/02/10/selection-bias-politifact-rate/.

25. John Nolte, "Embattled Washington Post Fact Checker Admits Pinocchio Ratings 'Are Subjective,'" Breitbart News, September 30, 2015, http://www.breitbart.com/big-journalism/2015/09/30/embattled-washington-post-fact-checker-admits-pinocchio-ratings-are-subjective/.

## CHAPTER 19

1. Robert Kuttner, "Can Liberal Democracy Survive?," *American Prospect*, March 6, 2015, http://prospect.org/article/can-liberal-democracy-survive.

2. Matthew Yglesias, "American Democracy Is Doomed," *Vox*, October 8, 2015, http://www.vox.com/2015/3/2/8120063/american-democracy-doomed.

3. James Carville, *40 More Years: How the Democrats Will Rule the Next Generation* (New York Simon & Schuster, 2009).

4. Joel Kotkin, "How Liberals Are the New Autocrats," Daily Beast, January 3, 2016, http://www.thedailybeast.com/articles/2016/01/03/how-liberals-are-the-new-autocrats.html.

5. Kuttner, "Can Liberal Democracy Survive?"

6. Christopher Chantrill, "Liberals Say U.S. Is Ungovernable. Again," American Thinker, February 16, 2010, http://www.americanthinker.com/articles/2010/02/liberals_say_us_is_ungovernabl.html.

7. Tina Nguyen, "In Shocking Twist, Donald Trump Says He's Running for President," *Vanity Fair*, June 16, 2015, http://www.vanityfair.com/news/2015/06/donald-trump-running-for-president.

8. Richard Riordan, "GOP Donors Wrestle with Possibility of Trump Nomination," *The Hill*, November 29, 2015, http://thehill.com/blogs/ballot-box/261227-gop-donors-wrestle-with-possibility-of-trump-nomination.

9. Bret Stephens, "The Donald and the Demagogues," *Wall Street Journal*, August 31, 2015, http://www.wsj.com/articles/the-donald-and-the-demagogues-1441064072.

10. Peggy Noonan, "The First Amendment Needs Your Prayers," *Wall Street Journal*, December 4, 2015, http://www.wsj.com/articles/the-first-amendment-needs-your-prayers-1449187707.

11. Andre Vergara, "Missouri Protest: List of Demands Issued to University," Fox Sports, November 8, 2015, http://www.foxsports.com/college-football/story/missouri-protesters-issue-list-of-demands-to-university-110815.

12. Erika Christakis, quoted in Roger Kimball, "The Rise of the College Crybullies," *Wall Street Journal*, November 13, 2015, http://www.wsj.com/articles/the-rise-of-the-college-crybullies-1447458587.

13. "Oxy United for Black Liberation," Final List of Demands, December 22, 2015, http://www.documentcloud.org/documents/2515492-demands-final.html.

14. Roger Kimball, "The Rise of the College Crybullies," *Wall Street Journal*, November 13, 2015, http://www.wsj.com/articles/the-rise-of-the-college-crybullies-1447458587.

15. Peter Beinart, "Players' Physical Abuse, Sandusky Case Show Little Honor Left in Football," Daily Beast, November 21, 2011, http://www.thedailybeast.com/articles/2011/11/21/players-physical-abuse-sandusky-case-show-little-honor-left-in-football.html.

16. Peter Beinart, "The Questionable Ethics of Teaching My Son to Love Pro Football," *Atlantic*, January 16, 2014, http://www.theatlantic.com/entertainment/archive/2014/01/the-questionable-ethics-of-teaching-my-son-to-love-pro-football/283119/.

17. Barack Obama, quoted in Matt Ford, "President Obama on Political Correctness," *Atlantic*, September 14, 2015, http://www.theatlantic.com/notes/2015/09/president-obama-on-political-correctness/405328/.

18. President Barack Obama, "Remarks by the President at Howard University Commencement Ceremony" (speech, Howard University, Washington, D.C., May 7, 2016).

19. Charlie Spiering, "Obama Takes Shot at Washington Redskins for Native American 'Stereotypes,'" Breitbart News, November 5, 2015, http://www.breitbart.com/big-government/2015/11/05/obama-takes-shot-washington-redskins-native-american-stereotypes/.

20. Barack Obama, quoted in Mayhill Fowler, "Obama: No Surprise That Hard-Pressed Pennsylvanians Turn Bitter," Huffington Post, May 25, 2011, http://www.huffingtonpost.com/mayhill-fowler/obama-no-surprise-that-ha_b_96188.html.

21. Charles Krauthammer, *Fox News Special Report*, Fox News, September 27, 2014.

22. Mark R. Levin, quoted in Newsmax, "Commentator Mark Levin Slams Boehner's Lawsuit Against Obama," July 11, 2014, http://www.newsmax.com/Headline/Boehner-lawsuit-Obama-Levin/2014/07/11/id/582148/.
23. U.S. Constitution, Article V.
24. Pablo Guzmán, WCBS-TV, September 16, 2001, https://www.youtube.com/watch?v=3auKMHkZJnQ.
25. Wendy Kaminer, "The Progressive Ideas behind the Lack of Free Speech on Campus," *Washington Post*, February 20, 2015, https://www.washingtonpost.com/opinions/the-progressive-ideas-behind-the-lack-of-free-speech-on-campus/2015/02/20/93086efe-b0e7-11e4-886b-c22184f27c35_story.html.
26. Joel B. Pollak, "Buzzfeed Effectively Bans Pro-Donald Trump Opinions from Site," Breitbart News, December 9, 2015, http://www.breitbart.com/big-journalism/2015/12/09/buzzfeed-bans-pro-donald-trump-opinions-from-site/.
27. John Nolte, "The Polls Were Right, We Were Wrong, and That's the Good News," Breitbart News, November 8, 2012, http://www.breitbart.com/big-government/2012/11/08/polls-right-we-wrong/.
28. Nate Silver, "The Polls Were Skewed Toward Democrats," FiveThirtyEight, November 5, 2014, http://fivethirtyeight.com/features/the-polls-were-skewed-toward-democrats/.

# INDEX

# Performance-Based Certification

# Performance-Based Certification

How to Design a Valid, Defensible, Cost-Effective Program

*Judith Hale*

San Francisco

ISBN: 0-7879-4640-0
Library of Congress Catalog Card Number 99-006896

**Library of Congress Cataloging-in-Publication Data**

Hale, Judith A.
  Performance-based certification : how to design a valid, defensible, cost-effective program / Judith Hale—1st ed.
      p.     cm.
Includes index.
  ISBN 0-7879-4640-0
  1. Occupations—Certification.   2. Professions—Certification.   I. Title.
  HD3629 .H35 2000
  658.3'124—dc21

                                                                99-006896

Printed in the United States of America

Published by

**JOSSEY-BASS/PFEIFFER**
A Wiley Company
350 Sansome St.
San Francisco, CA 94104-1342
415.433.1740; Fax 415.433.0499
800.274.4434; Fax 800.569.0443

www.pfeiffer.com

Acquiring Editor: Matthew Holt
Director of Development: Kathleen Dolan Davies
Developmental Editor: Joan Kalkut
Senior Production Editor: Xenia Lisanevich
Manufacturing Manager: Becky Carreño
Interior Design: Joseph Piliero
Jacket Design: Laurie Anderson
Illustrations: Kathie Tyler

Printing 10  9  8  7  6  5  4  3  2

# Contents

# Preface

........................... *T*his book is based on my nearly thirty years of experience designing certification programs for corporations and professional associations. Since I began this work in 1971, I have seen a significant increase in the number of certifications available. The computer industry, for example, now uses certification to promote brand recognition among consumers, to qualify individuals as expert users of specific products, and to officially recognize preferred distributors. The medical profession has led the way in setting standards for credentialing agencies and in defining new measures of competence for practitioners. Professional societies are certifying their members and others who meet their criteria. Corporations are certifying their employees, their suppliers, their vendors—even their customers—to demonstrate competence in discrete areas.

In each of these situations, certification fulfills a legitimate need. Each need for certification is unique, however, and thus there is some confusion about what it means to be certified and about the best way to design a certification program. My hope is that this book will clear up that confusion and clarify what it takes to design and implement a certification program that is defensible, effective, and fair.

Over the last twenty-five years I have met many capable people charged with creating certification programs. They wanted to know what worked, what didn't work, and why. They wanted to know what to do, what to watch out for, and what to avoid. They wanted examples of what organizations have done well and what they have not done so well. Over the years, various clients have asked for a straightforward set of guidelines for designing, developing, and implementing a useful, sustainable certification program. Thus I wrote this book, because I have found that when people have a set of guidelines and a few examples to refer to, they can develop certification programs that meet their organization's needs.

The primary audience for this book is human resource and training professionals whose organizations want to certify employees, suppliers, third-party service providers, and customers. The principles and guidelines also apply to professional and trade organizations that certify people working in newly evolving fields.

## ACKNOWLEDGMENTS

A lot of people helped make this book possible. The following individuals described their experiences during certification and what they learned from the process: Don Kirkey, manager of certification, Johnson Controls, Inc.; Dick Hibbard, vice president of education and training, ABB Automation; Lee Forrest, manager of certification and academic affairs, International Facility Management Association; Lynne Goede, corporate merchandising and global product training, Amway Corporation; Todd Bostick, executive director, National Council of Interior Design Qualification; Herb Canfield, manager of computer services, Boeing; Kathie K. Holland, management consultant, Certified Management Consultants; Cheryl Mounts, executive director, American Board of Oral and Maxillofacial Surgery; Tom Norfleet, manager associate, training and development, Subaru-Isuzu Automotive, Inc.; and Kandetta Raether, manager of training, Enerpac.

Other people served as content experts. They were diligent readers and contributed numerous ideas and examples. Special thanks goes to Dean Larson, department manager, safety and industrial hygiene, US Steel (Gary Works); Odin Westgaard, consultant, Heurists; Peter Dodson, delivery systems certification and training, Boeing; Cordell Hauglie, organizational adviser, delivery systems certification and training, Boeing; Frank Hatcher, director, Assessment Systems, Inc., southeast region; Marcia Jaquith, consultant; Lynn Anderson, executive director, Joint Commission on Allied Health Personnel in Ophthalmology; Marie Raines, Electronic Data Systems; Ray Halagera, vice president of operations and finance, Strategic Management Group, Inc; Annemarie Laures, manager of corporate performance and training, Walgreens; Jamie R. Mulkey, certification program manager, Hewlett Packard; Jim Momsen, manager of technical training, Rockwell Automation; and Michael Tapia, vice president, ABN AMRO. Behind the scene were Carla Williams, a consultant who contributed a critical eye based on her extensive experience in the health care field, and Joan Kalkut of the Empire Communications Group, who worked hard to keep the discussion consistent and readable. I was fortunate to have the confidence of Kathleen Dolan-Davies, Matt Holt, and Jamie Corcoran of Jossey-Bass/

Pfeiffer, whose support made this book possible. Special thanks goes to my friend Sue Simons, who encouraged me to be true to my style of simplicity and directness.

*September 1999*                                                                 Judith Hale
*Downers Grove, Illinois*

# Introduction

*cer•ti•fy 1: to attest authoritatively as meeting a standard*
—WEBSTER'S NINTH NEW COLLEGIATE DICTIONARY

*T*o become certified, a person must fulfill a set of requirements or satisfy a set of standards. These might include achieving a certain level of education, completing a training curriculum, or gaining some specific experience; passing a test, performing a task, or accomplishing a goal; committing to a code of conduct, paying a fee, being recommended by someone who is already certified, or having one's work reviewed. What is required depends on the motives of the people involved in the certification—both those who bestow the credential and those who want to obtain it. The certification standards spell out how much and what type of education, training, and experience a person must have to become certified and on what basis his or her knowledge, ability, or work will be judged. The rigor of the standards depends on the promises made by those who bestow the credential.

The traditional approach to designing a certification program presumes that there is a codified body of knowledge relevant to the person, position, or activity being certified that people can acquire through an accredited academic program. This approach often does not work for corporations or evolving professions, however, either because no specific body of essential knowledge has been defined for the position or activity to be certified or because formal academic programs do not exist to teach such knowledge. Thus corporations use certification programs, instead, to define required knowledge and skills and establish common performance standards. This helps them quickly identify and deploy competent workers anywhere in the world. Professional associations, too, develop certification programs in the absence of relevant accredited academic programs or because industry or professional standards are lacking.

## THE ELEMENTS OF A CERTIFICATION PROGRAM

A well-designed certification program starts with an analysis that identifies and describes the market for the program, the drivers or business needs behind it, and the stakeholders associated with it. Included in this analysis are estimates of the initial and long-term investments required to implement the program and an estimate of the potential gains from it. Because certification programs are usually created in response to a specific problem, making a business case for a certification program involves comparing the costs of the program with the costs of alternative solutions to the problem. Once a certification program has been identified as the most economical and viable intervention, then the organization can develop the elements of it. Following are the key elements that must be defined and developed for any certification program:

- *Certification requirements:* what people must do to become certified under the program

- *Program standards:* the program's assessment criteria, derived from job or task analyses and from input from key stakeholders

- *Program tests:* the assessment methods that will be used to determine whether candidates have met the program standards, and how those methods will be created, administered, maintained, and evaluated

- *Preparation and remediation options:* the opportunities for training, education, apprenticeships, on-the-job experience, and so on that will be provided to help candidates meet the program's standards and fulfill its requirements

- *Governance body:* the group of individuals, such as a board of directors, that will provide oversight and stewardship; set policy on issues like appeals, recertification, grandfathering, and information disclosure; and evaluate the program's effectiveness

- *Administrative practices:* how the program's assessment, record-keeping, and reporting processes will be administered to eliminate bias, preserve confidentiality, and prevent misuse of test results

- *Public relations and communications plans:* how information about the purpose, operating specifics, results, and impact of the certification program will be disseminated to management, customers, employees, and suppliers

## OBJECTIVES OF THIS BOOK

Through explanations, examples, and guidelines, this book will describe how to define and design the program elements just described as well as how to

- Determine the need for and goals of a certification program

- Define requirements for recertification (such as reassessment and continuing education)

- Define competence in a job or task by analyzing the job or task, specifying required outcomes for it, and developing criteria-based performance statements for it
- Assess competence with performance tests, skill tests, knowledge tests, customer satisfaction surveys, productivity indicators, portfolio reviews, and peer reviews
- Describe standards in sufficient detail to support curriculum development and assessment
- Define requirements for administration, marketing, communications, records management, and assessment
- Market and deploy certification programs within individual organizations as well as across different companies or constituents, nationally and internationally
- Maintain "exclusivity" of credentials
- Measure the impact of a certification on individual and organizational performance and on customer confidence
- Set processes in place to ensure that a certification program continues to meet the needs of all stakeholders

## HOW THIS BOOK IS ORGANIZED

This book is organized around the key phases in developing and implementing a cost-effective, legally defensible certification program, from defining a program's goals to evaluating its effectiveness. The sequence of the chapters in between is not prescriptive (that is, it's not essential to do these things in this exact order) but is intended to provide an understanding of all that is involved. Figure I.1 provides a flowchart of the process.

Each chapter explains a major phase in the process of designing and implementing a certification program:

- Chapter One, "The Driver," explains both the traditional and more current reasons why organizations (profit and not-for-profit) certify people. It discusses the important stakeholders and describes their role in the process.
- Chapter Two, "The Requirements," describes what people are typically required to do to become certified and how to select the appropriate set of requirements for your program.
- Chapter Three, "The Standards," explains the role standards play in certification programs and describes how to develop standards. This chapter describes the process for conducting a job or task analysis.
- Chapter Four, "The Business Case," goes into why building a business case for certification is important and how to develop one.

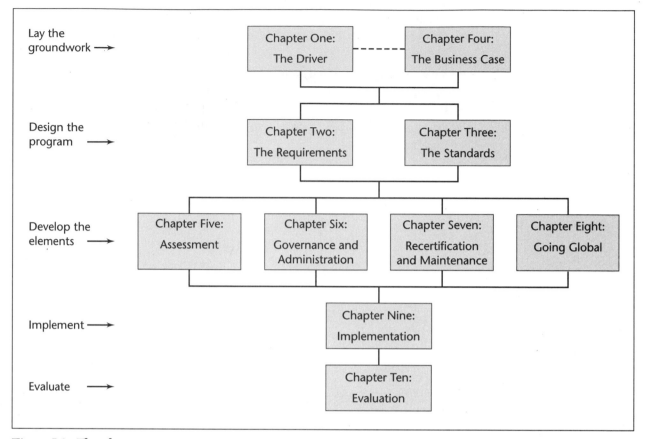

**Figure I.1. Flowchart of the Program Development Process**

- Chapter Five, "Assessment," describes the different ways organizations assess people's knowledge, skills, and ability to perform.

- Chapter Six, "Governance and Administration," describes the importance of setting up a management structure to provide oversight, and the issues it should be prepared to address, such as appeals, recertification, and disclosures.

- Chapter Seven, "Recertification and Maintenance," explains the difference between recertification and maintenance and describes ways to ensure that both candidates and the program's requirements stay current and live up to stakeholder expectations.

- Chapter Eight, "Going Global," describes how to modify or develop new standards and assessment processes so they can be used internationally.

- Chapter Nine, "Implementation," describes how to market, communicate, launch, and implement a certification program.

- Chapter Ten, "Evaluation," describes how to measure the impact of your certification program.

Every chapter has guidelines, tips, and checklists for how to execute the phase, examples of what other organizations have done well, and a section called Missteps and Oversights that explains common mistakes. The examples describe what others have done to certify field sales support personnel; technical support staff who install, repair, and maintain one or more multigenerational products; customer and sales support staff who take orders, handle customer complaints, track order status, and schedule customer service for one or more product lines and customer groups; trainers and computer technicians who support field staff, product launches, and so on; production, manufacturing, and distribution staff who build, assemble, test, package, and ship products; and third parties (such as independent contractors, distributors, and resellers) who work in product support areas, such as sales, customer support, and maintenance.

Each chapter has a section called Where to Learn More that lists references, and endnotes that contain many useful facts. The accompanying disk contains the guidelines and checklists for your use in developing and evaluating your program.

The book's organization is linked to its objectives as follows. Given a request for a certification program or a program to qualify people's ability at some level, you will be able to

- Define the target audience, the stakeholders, and identify the drivers or expectations of the certification program (Chapter One)
- Establish business measures to evaluate the effectiveness of the certification (Chapters Four and Ten)
- Determine the requirements (Chapter Two)
- Conduct a job or task analysis (Chapter Three)
- Develop the performance standards (Chapter Three)
- Develop the elements required to support the certification program: assessment (Chapter Five), governance and administration (Chapter Six), maintenance and recertification (Chapter Seven), adaptation for international markets (Chapter Eight)
- Market and implement the program (Chapter Nine)
- Evaluate the program's effectiveness and revise the process or standards as needed (Chapter Ten)

## KEY DEFINITIONS

One of the problems people experience when they begin to develop a certification program is the lack of a shared understanding of what "to certify" means. Long-established credentialing agencies have developed a vocabulary that is not generally understood or used in the same way by corporations. Here are definitions of key terms used in this book:

- *Credential.* A credential is a designation, mark, or stamp given to a person, organization, or program that has satisfied a set of standards. The more common credentials are education degrees, certifications, licenses, accreditations, and endorsements or approvals. These credentials are similar in that they are intended to qualify the recipient, control practice, and protect the public. They qualify through the standards they impose. They control because they affect people's opportunity to work, participate in a discipline or profession, or use a name or title. They protect by ensuring that only qualified people practice.

- *Educational degree.* A degree is a credential awarded by an academic institution. Receiving a degree infers one has successfully completed a curriculum that covers a specific body of knowledge. There are academic degrees and professional degrees. An academic degree is concerned with general education and the liberal arts and sciences. A professional degree is concerned with the skills and knowledge of a specific profession. This book is concerned with degrees when they are required for certification or are used to replace experience.

- *Certification.* A certification is a credential awarded by an employer, a vendor, or an association or independent agency. A certification is also a designation given to people, products, and processes that have satisfied a set of standards. Business and government use performance standards to certify their employees, contractors, suppliers, third-party providers, and customers. Vendors use product and performance standards to certify customers, third parties, and contractors to train others in how to use and support their products. Professional and trade associations use professional or industry standards to certify people in those professions or trades. Associations may establish separate boards to certify members of their profession (for example, the twenty-four medical boards that certify people who practice in specialized medical disciplines).[1] The American National Standards Institute (ANSI) and the American Society for Quality Control (ASQC) certify processes. The focus of this book is on certifications of individuals by employers, vendors, and professional and trade associations.

- *License.* A license is a credential awarded by a state government or its authorized agent. Licenses permit individuals to practice a profession or use a title in association with their work. Not all professions or titles are licensed; government agencies license only those professions where there is a need to protect the public. Examples of professions that are licensed are medical doctors, dentists, dental hygienists, nurses, nurse anesthetists, dieticians, beauticians, barbers, real estate brokers, cosmetologists, and interior designers. To be licensed, people may be required to pass a test, complete some amount of formal education, or have a minimum amount of experience. This book does not deal with licensing except in instances where certification requires it.

The licensing of institutions or organizations is not the same as the licensing of individuals. Organizations license other enterprises—that is, grant them the right to produce, use, or sell products, intellectual property, and brand names. For example, Microsoft licenses users of its software. Argonne National Laboratories and the University of Chicago, through their joint subsidiary the ARCH Development Corporation, license the use of inventions developed by professors. Corporations license the use of their brand names and products to franchisees. Examples include restaurant and hotel chains like McDonald's and Hilton; branch banks like Harris Bank; service providers like Mail Boxes, Etc.; and automotive service shops like National Tire and Battery and Jiffy Lube. Some professional associations are experimenting with licensing their certifications as a way to deploy their credential internationally (for example, the International Facility Management Association). This book does not discuss the licensing of brand images, intellectual property, or business operations.

- *Accreditation.* An accreditation is a credential awarded by a nongovernmental association that regulates academic programs, specialized education, and training offered by universities, colleges, trade schools, and vendors. For example, the North Central Association for Colleges and Schools accredits colleges and schools in nineteen states.[2] North Central also accredits private colleges such as Hamburger U, operated by McDonald's. Professional associations like the American Medical Association and the American Bar Association accredit medical and law schools, respectively. Examples of other programs that are accredited by professional associations include education, engineering, interior design, psychology, property management, and social work. Training programs offered by vendors and corporations can also be accredited. This book does not deal with accreditation except in the case where graduation from an accredited program is a requirement for certification.

- *Approvals and endorsements.* Approvals, recognitions, endorsements, registrations, and charters are credentials awarded by independent organizations. For example, Underwriter's Laboratories bestows a credential when it allows organizations to affix the UL trademark on their product materials. Product ratings by *Consumer Reports* could be considered a type of approval or endorsement in that the ratings influence consumer buying decisions. The International Standards Organization (ISO) authorizes other agencies to certify organizations whose processes meet ISO 9000 or 14000 standards. The Illinois Occupational Skills Standards and Credentialing Council (IOSSCC) endorses standards developed by industry groups. Professional associations recognize and endorse academic programs. This book does not discuss these types of credentials.

Figure I.2 provides an at-a-glance summary of the different types of credentials.

| | Degrees | Certification | Licenses | Accreditation | Endorsements |
|---|---|---|---|---|---|
| Awarded by | Universities, schools | Employers, vendors, independent agencies | Government agencies and their agents | Nongovernmental associations | Any organization |
| Awarded to | People | People, products, processes | People | Universities, schools | People, products, processes |
| Standards used | Academic and professional | Performance, professional, industry, trade | Safety, professional | Academic | Product, industry, professional |

**Figure I.2.**
**Types of Credentials**

It is important to understand that degrees, certifications, licenses, accreditations, and approvals exact some degree of control over people's right to work. How much control depends on the motive behind the credential, the criteria used to judge compliance with the standard, and the consequences of not meeting the criteria. Licenses control whether or not people can work in a field. Certifications offered by credentialing agencies, such as those bestowed by the twenty-four medical boards, are voluntary, in that people can practice medicine without being certified. Yet, not being certified can prevent them from working in certain hospitals. Certifications offered by employers may or may not be voluntary; that is, they may be required for employment or advancement. Certifications bestowed by external agencies, such as certification by the Red Cross in cardiopulmonary resuscitation (CPR), may or may not be required, depending on the person's job. Accreditation is voluntary in the United States; however, this statement is somewhat misleading, since universities that are not accredited risk low enrollment, the loss of state or federal funding, and rejection of their graduates' education by business and industry. Some approvals and endorsements are necessary for businesses to operate; for example, some businesses may not be able to sell their products without getting their products approved by Underwriter's Laboratories.

**NOTES**

1. The twenty-four medical specialty boards that certify medical practitioners are Allergy and Immunology, Anesthesiology, Colon and Rectal Surgery, Dermatology, Emergency Medicine, Family Practice, Internal Medicine, Medical Genetics, Neurological Surgery, Nuclear Medicine, Obstetrics and Gynecology, Ophthalmology, Orthopaedic Surgery, Otolaryngology, Pathology, Pediatrics, Physical Medicine and Rehabilitation, Plastic Surgery, Preventive Medicine, Psychiatry and Neurology, Radiology, Surgery, Thoracic Surgery, and Urology (*Annual Report & Reference Handbook* [Evanston, IL: The American Board of Medical Specialties Research & Education Foundation, 1994]).

2. The nineteen states accredited by the North Central Association of Colleges and Schools are Arizona, Arkansas, Colorado, Illinois, Indiana, Iowa, Kansas, Michigan, Minnesota, Missouri, Nebraska, New Mexico, North Dakota, Ohio, Oklahoma, South Dakota, West Virginia, Wisconsin, and Wyoming. North Central also accredits the American Dependents' Schools operated overseas for the children of American military and civilian personnel, and the Navajo Nation schools.

*What it is!*
*What we are!*
*What it is not!*

# Performance-Based Certification

# Chapter 1

# The Driver

*why implement?*

*T*he driver is the impetus behind an organization's decision to become involved in certification. Some certifications are created in response to an event, like a lawsuit or the loss of a major customer. Others are implemented to gain a competitive advantage or to prevent employee disputes by helping managers make better personnel decisions. Many certification programs are the result of external pressures on organizations to ensure that their people perform to standard. It's important to be clear and in agreement on just what the driver is, because the driver is the platform on which everything else to do with the certification program will be based. The driver shapes the program's design and determines the requirements candidates must satisfy to earn the credential. The design, in turn, determines what the program will cost to implement and maintain. The driver also provides the criteria against which the program will be evaluated and revised.

*Know the driver*

One of your first tasks in designing a certification program, then, is to find out if there is a valid driver—a problem worth solving—for it and if a certification program is indeed the appropriate solution. Based on that information, you can design the certification program so that it will fulfill stakeholder expectations. Once the program is designed, you can plan how it will be managed, marketed, and implemented so that it will continue to add value to the organization.

## WHY ORGANIZATIONS CERTIFY

The main driver behind organizations' either adopting an external certification or developing their own is to protect the safety, health, and welfare of their workers or the public. Examples of external certifications include those offered by the Board of Certified Safety Professionals, the American Board of Industrial Hygiene, and the Board of Certification in Professional Ergonomics. Both external and internal certifications force organizations to be more disciplined in

*1*

confirming that their people have or can get the knowledge and skills required to do their jobs safely, efficiently, and effectively. Other reasons organizations implement certification programs are to enhance the stature of a role or position, to promote continuous improvement, to increase productivity, and to maintain employee skills and knowledge.

These reasons focus attention on recognizing people's accomplishments and improving organizations' work processes. Some certifications are created because there is a market for them—that is, there are enough people who will seek the designation that it becomes profitable for an organization to offer it. Indeed, the driver behind most certifications is economic, whether this fact is stated or not. Businesses want to leverage their investments in research and development and in training and technology, and they want to reduce or avoid unnecessary costs. Recently, many companies have sought to protect and enhance their investments in redesigning processes, outsourcing noncore functions, expanding globally, and automating tasks to increase productivity. As a result, more organizations are turning to certification programs as a way to help them compete for and retain competent staff; establish uniform performance standards so they can rapidly deploy workers; outsource work to capable contractors and third-party providers; raise the level of core competencies across the organization; apply a multidisciplined approach to solving complex problems; better integrate products, supply chains, and processes; and comply with local and international regulations. The following paragraphs discuss these goals in greater detail.

## Attracting and Retaining Staff

To help organizations attract and retain competent workers, certifications are being designed to identify qualified job candidates, to promote career development, and to recognize employee achievement. Businesses are looking to educational institutions and industry associations to better define and develop technical job competencies and workplace social skills among potential job candidates, and certification helps businesses identify candidates that have acquired these attributes. Businesses and organizations are also investing considerable amounts to develop and maintain technical and professional staff themselves, and certifications are one way to leverage that investment. Consider these examples:

- Amway, a firm based in Michigan, certifies trainers employed by affiliates in forty-nine countries. The certification is designed to help the affiliates attract and retain trainers and to ensure that the trainers they hire meet performance standards for product knowledge, product merchandising, and delivery of training.

- To support employee retention, an automobile manufacturer certifies its dealers' technicians and sales staff and its own production crews.

- The Illinois Occupational Skill Standards and Credentialing Council (IOSSCC) was created to develop standards that can be used by private and public educational institutions to develop the workforce and make it more employable. The standards are used by third parties to certify graduates of these educational programs. The IOSSCC works with fourteen industry subcouncils to develop and market industry-recognized skill standards.[1]

## Establishing Uniform Performance Standards

Uniform standards enable organizations to hire capable workers and more rapidly deploy people to different work sites locally, nationally, and internationally. Common job descriptions, hiring criteria, and training are not enough to ensure that staff will possess the same level of competency or can perform to the same standard throughout a national or multinational company. When employees are relocated, whether from southern to northern California or from Germany to Portugal, they often encounter differences in work processes and equipment, tolerance for error, customers' performance expectations, available support and technology, and management expectations between the two locations. These differences affect their ability to perform their tasks; therefore, companies are using certifications to establish common standards and work practices across work sites and even countries. For example:

- Asea, Brown, Bovari (ABB) is a Swedish-Swiss conglomerate of over one thousand companies. The driver behind its certification program is its need to quickly deploy workers anywhere in the world. Its certification is designed to create uniform standards that reduce differences in performance among people doing the same tasks in different locations around the globe; to gain the confidence of product managers by proving that employees can properly sell, service, and maintain products; and to demonstrate to the customer that ABB is seriously committed to continually raising the quality of its people.

- A firm that manufactures HVAC (heating, ventilation, and cooling) systems has to quickly deploy technical and professional staff nationally and internationally. Its certifications are designed to ensure that staff can perform tasks to the same level of proficiency no matter where they are assigned.

## Facilitating Outsourcing

To control costs, many organizations outsource tasks to outside individuals and firms. Many companies outsource even key functions such as billing and collections, purchasing, and human resources. (The work may or may not be performed off-site: increasingly, "outsourcing" means hiring independent contractors to perform work on-site.) At the same time, companies are relying on third parties—independent distributors and dealers—to sell and service their products, to provide field and customer support, and to operate the after-market business (repairs, upgrades, and add-on features). The performance of the contractor or third party reflects directly on the brand image of the company and affects its customer relations. As a result, companies are qualifying their contractors and third parties or requiring them to put a quality system in place that includes earning an external credential. For example:

- ARAMARK, a large multinational firm, is hired by other organizations to manage their facilities. ARAMARK is getting its facility managers certified by the International Facility Management Association to demonstrate its commitment to ensuring the capability of its staff.

- Enerpac, a manufacturer of hydraulic pumps, relies on a network of independent service centers to service and repair its pumps. Enerpac wants to certify the service centers and their technicians to make sure its network is capable of servicing its products.

- A manufacturer of doors, windows, and other home improvement products wants the independent contractors who install their products to be certified. Improper installation results in leaks, which leads to customer demands for replacements from the manufacturer. The American Architectural Manufacturers Association is developing a certification program for the company so it can certify contractors competent to install its products.

## Raising the Level of Core Competencies

Organizations have discovered that people in different positions and at different levels fulfill many similar roles and perform many similar tasks, such as managing teams, building project plans, and formulating business cases. Similar roles and tasks require the same core competencies, such as good communication skills, leadership ability, and a knowledge of planning. The lack of such competencies limits people's ability to perform common roles effectively, which has a negative impact on productivity and costs. Certification is being used to specify job requirements, identify skill gaps, and develop individual performance improvement plans. For example:

- A major credit card company certifies its customer service representatives, corporate account managers, and service managers. Training people for these jobs is a costly process. The certifications are used to recognize those who have achieved a certain level of competence and are a requirement for promotion. The program's driver was the need to identify people who perform well and are capable of moving into positions of greater responsibility.

- A large manufacturer certifies its information services (IS) personnel. The initial driver was to satisfy internal customers' demand for qualified staff to service the company's computer infrastructure. The program assures management that the company's IS staff are as qualified as outside contractors certified by Novell and Microsoft. The program also allows management to track the skill mix, proficiency levels, and training gaps in the company's IS staff.

- A manufacturer of HVAC systems determined that project management skills were needed by people throughout the organization and that the lack of competency in this area negatively affects cost containment and customer satisfaction. It now certifies people to serve as project leaders.

- An automobile manufacturer certifies supervisors and team leaders who have acquired specified management, interpersonal, and leadership skills.

- An international pharmaceutical company certifies its scientists, engineers, and administrative staff in computer applications such as word processing because they prepare the documentation required for governmental approval of new drugs.

- The external certifications offered by software companies like Microsoft and Novell and by hardware manufacturers are being used by organizations to ensure minimum capability among staff and contractors.

## Creating Multidisciplined Jobs

Today, many jobs require people to be competent in more than one area or knowledgeable about more than one discipline (due partly to an increasing need for an interdisciplinary approach to solving problems in business). Therefore, for many employees companies are requiring either cross-training or additional training in new areas. In addition, organizations are providing new development pathways to certify people whose jobs require these multidisciplined competencies. For example:

- The Board of Registered Polysomnographic Technologists, Inc., certifies technicians who work in sleep disorder clinics. This is a newly evolving field, and currently available educational programs do not address the need for competence in multiple disciplines related to the study of sleep disorders, specifically respiratory care and neurodiagnostics. The board wants the professionals who conduct sleep disorder studies and the clinics that hire them to understand the legitimate need for cross-discipline training. The board also wants to distinguish professionals who are qualified to conduct sleep disorder studies from professionals trained only in a single discipline.

- The Association for Worksite Health Promotion represents people who manage on-site company fitness centers that have exercise equipment, gymnasiums, swimming pools, and locker rooms and offer change-of-lifestyle programs such as smoking cessation courses and fitness counseling. Employers want people with abilities beyond facility management to manage these types of centers. They are looking for individuals with degrees in health and fitness and skills in management and marketing. The association is designing a certification that reflects this multidisciplined set of competencies.

### Integrating Products, Supply Chains, and Processes

Integrating products, supply chains, and processes is a very sophisticated cost management strategy. It gives organizations better control over their supply chains, distribution channels, and internal processes, but it requires a more complex set of competencies among organization personnel. Specifically, it requires expertise in relationship management, process redesign, activity-based costing, and measurement. It also requires a different approach to problem solving. Managers still have to apply algorithms to diagnose problems, but they must also look at situations more holistically, noting in particular the impact on internal and external relationships. They have to facilitate the use of cross-functional teams in redesigning processes and develop measurement systems that track and quantify improvements. They also have to develop incentives that support better cost management through integration. For example:

- An international retail chain contracts with suppliers all over the world. Its product managers are expected to work with their supply chain members to identify and eliminate inefficient processes, unnecessary requirements, and excess capacity. The managers are assessed on their ability to maintain and influence business relationships through a sophisticated combination of incentives and their ability to develop and consistently implement interventions that improve the performance of their supply chains. Managers that achieve these outcomes are certified.

- An automobile manufacturer is designing a certification program to shift its purchasing personnel's perception of their work from "buying parts" to "managing supply chains."

- A pharmaceutical firm is certifying its professional staff to diagnose team effectiveness, identify barriers to performance, design innovative solutions, and successfully implement those solutions.

## Complying with Local and International Regulations

Both government and industry impose regulations on companies and other organizations, and companies must comply with them if they want to sell products or provide services, locally or internationally. For example, being certified by the International Standards Organization (ISO) is a requirement for many companies to compete internationally. Firms must qualify their employees and suppliers for ISO certification by some means such as training, experience, or testing. Organizations are experimenting with certifications to help them comply with ISO, local government, and internal regulations. For example:

- Florida's Small Business Development Centers require certification for all of their business analysts. The driver behind this certification requirement was qualification for federal funding from the Small Business Administration (SBA) and matching funds from the state.

- The National Council for Interior Design Qualification (NCIDQ) was set up to develop a certification program and create model statutory guidelines for interior designers, since their work affects public health and safety. Interior designers are regulated in twenty-one states. Those states use the NCIDQ exam to test interior designers' ability to specify products and design interiors that meet local fire and safety codes and comply with the Americans with Disabilities Act. The American Society for Interior Design (ASID) and the International Interior Design Association (IIDA) require members to be NCIDQ certified before they can be designated "professional" members. The inference is that NCIDQ certification distinguishes interior designers from interior decorators as more qualified and capable of performing more duties. The drivers behind the related design societies' support for the NCIDQ certification were to establish one set of standards for the profession, to increase employment opportunities for interior designers, and to build consumer demand for interior designers' services.

In each of these examples, organizations have chosen certification as a way to respond to internal and external pressures. Some certifications focus on ensuring the people have the required skills to perform a job. Other programs are designed to influence educational curricula. Still others are meant to influence consumers' buying behavior.

## WHO TO INVOLVE

Two groups are key to successfully designing and implementing an effective certification program: the target audience and the stakeholders. The following paragraphs discuss these groups in detail.

### Target Audience

These are the people to be certified—the candidates. Obviously, they have a vested interest in decisions about certification requirements and about what will be made available to help them satisfy those requirements. Candidates for a particular certification may work at the same or different sites and perform the same or different jobs, depending on the driver behind the certification. For example, some certifications are designed for a narrowly defined group who perform a discrete set of tasks, such as product installation, inventory analysis, customer service, or emergency medical assistance. Such certifications are usually based on the target audience's meeting standards unique to the task. Other certifications are for people who serve in different roles yet require the same level of competence in core tasks, such as team leaders, supervisors, and customer and sales support staff. When this is the case, the certifications are usually based on candidates' meeting a common set of standards in areas such as leadership, meeting management skills, interpersonal skills, communication skills, and product knowledge.

The target audience for a certification may all work in the same building, at external customers' sites, from their cars, or even for different employers. They may work independently or as part of a team. It is important to fully define the target audience, in terms of why they would want to be certified (especially if the credential is voluntary), what they already know, what they can do, other credentials they may have, and their work conditions. It is equally important to define the size of the target audience and where they are located. You will use this information to identify incentives necessary for them to support certification, determine how to best reward them once they attain the credential, and decide just what to require of candidates (such as training, an external credential or minimum experience, or passing a test).

### Stakeholders

The stakeholders are those individuals or groups who have a vested interest in ensuring that the certification's standards or results are appropriate. They are often key decision makers, persons who determine whether or not a program gets implemented. Because the stakeholders are the ones who will define success for the certification program, it is important to identify and define them. Ask such questions as Who are the stakeholders? How many are there? Where are they located? What role must they play for the program to be successful?

You will also want to identify the incentives for stakeholder support for the certification. You will use this information to prove a need for the program and to further define the requirements. Stakeholders include sponsors; customers and consumers; supervisors; providers of educational and training programs; the public and regulatory agencies; human resources staff, legal personnel, and internal auditors; and internal or contracted support personnel, such as administrative and information technology staff. The following paragraphs discuss these different types of stakeholders in detail.

*Sponsors* are those individuals or departments that will fund the certification effort. Consequently, they usually have the greatest economic stake in the program. They have to see a clear link between the certification program and the business or societal need behind it. There may be multiple sponsors, depending on the size and scope of the program. For example, one sponsor might fund a feasibility study and the design and development phases, whereas the costs of implementing and maintaining the program might be borne by a different sponsor. Sponsors' expectations concerning the use of their investment help determine how costs are recovered (through departmental chargebacks or fees) and what the baseline economic measures for the program as a whole are.

*Customers and consumers,* whether internal or external, are the groups that depend on the competency of the target audience. For example, when the target audience performs one phase of a larger process (like sales), the internal customers are those groups that perform the next phases of the process (like billing, shipping, and installation). If the target audience is supervisors, then the customers are the people who report to those supervisors, as well as the supervisors' bosses. There is almost always more than one set of customers for a certification program, and each has a different set of expectations concerning the target audience. Customer buy-in is essential for the long-term success of any certification program; therefore, it may be necessary to first define a set of shared expectations among the program's customers before designing the program. You will use information from customers and consumers to help set expectations for the certification program, define its standards, and identify potential areas of resistance to it.

*Supervisors* should have a vested interest in the competency of the workforce they oversee. Thus they generally have a great deal of influence over the implementation and final standards of a certification program. Supervisors must support and reward the behaviors and outcomes the certification is designed to achieve. Some programs even require supervisors to become certified themselves, so they will be qualified to judge other people's performance. Knowing the number of supervisors involved, what their expectations are for the target audience, and to what degree they agree on what competence is will help you set standards they will support. It is also important to create ways to reward or recognize supervisors who hire certified people or support their employees' becoming certified.

*Providers of educational and training programs* are the groups that offer the education and training required to achieve the credential. Some may even administer and manage the program. They include universities, community colleges, private schools, vendors of training programs, professional and trade associations, and internal training departments. You want to know what role they will play, how supportive they are of the standards, and to what degree their programs impart knowledge and build skills. You will use this information, along with a profile of the target audience, to identify which programs to use and whether or not the programs should be modified.

*The public and regulatory agencies* are concerned with public health and safety, so organizations that claim their certifications are designed to protect the health and safety of the public should in some way incorporate its voice. Naturally, the public has an interest in the technical competency of the groups or individuals being certified. It also has other expectations, however, such as being kept informed and being treated in a respectful manner. Regulatory agencies are interested in the target audience's technical competence, in how the certifying organization will define and measure that competence, and in how its methods will correlate with accident prevention and threats to public safety and health. You will use information about what the public and regulators expect to develop the standards for the certification.

*Human resources staff, legal personnel, and internal auditors* want a voice in the design and implementation of any internal certification program, since they have to deal with employee relations, lawsuits, and compliance issues. Internal auditors emulate the process they expect external auditors to follow, so they can uncover and correct problems in advance of formal compliance reviews. Therefore, you want to know who the auditors are, what criteria they use to judge compliance, and what they expect of the certification. Consider how you will involve human resources (HR) staff, legal personnel, and your internal auditors when developing the certification's standards.

*Internal or contracted support staff,* such as administrative and information technology staff, are the ones who will design and manage the program's database. For example, records should be maintained documenting what each member of the target audience has done to satisfy the standards, who has been certified, and when they should be recertified. Computer software used for general training is sometimes used for certification programs as well. Some organizations use HR data tracking systems for certification programs. Computer systems are also used to administer tests, to register candidates for training and testing sessions, and even to deliver training and testing on-line. You will use information about your program's target audience and standards to define your need for support staff.

Following are examples of the stakeholders of various programs I've observed:

- At ABB, every employee that supports one or more products—such as engineering, sales, service, and training staff—is a member of the target audience. The main customers are the product managers. The training department is a stakeholder because it must provide programs for all six thousand employees, since the required skills and knowledge are not available from any other source. The supervisors are stakeholders because they do the actual assessment. The information systems (IS) department is a stakeholder because it supports the worldwide intranet, where all employees can access their certification status and find out what is required of them. The manager of the certification program includes the target audience, the product manager, a supervisor, and someone from training to set performance standards and develop the assessment criteria.

- An automobile manufacturer certifies its maintenance crews and team leaders. The main customers are the plant manager and production schedulers. Shift supervisors have to judge the competency of the crews and team leaders. The training department manages the certification, administers the assessment, and provides courses to upgrade skills. The IS department created the database to track the certification status of crews and team leaders. The auditing department monitors compliance with policy. All of these stakeholders influence the success of the certification.

- NCIDQ's stakeholders are the associations that provide professional development programs for interior designers, state licensing boards who want designers to be more knowledgeable about fire and safety codes, colleges and universities with interior design programs, manufacturers of furniture and finishes who want designers to recommend their products, and the consumers who rely on designers to create functional and esthetically pleasing interiors.

## BENEFITS OF CERTIFICATION

A well-designed certification program meets the needs of the public, the organization that maintains it, the target audience, and the stakeholders. The public benefits when people perform work in ways that protect consumers, workers, and the environment. The certifying organization benefits when the program fulfills its mandate, whether that be to deliver qualified people, to improve performance, or to satisfy an expectation of customers or the public. The target audience benefits when it has a credential that distinguishes it from others in the workforce. Stakeholders benefit when the credential satisfies their specific needs for prudent operations and competent workers. You should identify not only the expectations of the certifying organization and all the vested parties but also what they see as the potential benefits. Knowing this will help you build a business case for supporting the credential and help you evaluate the program's effectiveness.

## MISSTEPS AND OVERSIGHTS

When organizations begin developing a certification program, they frequently make three mistakes:

1. *They fail to identify the business driver.* This is a crippling error, because understanding the driver behind a program is what enables you to measure its effectiveness and to identify what has to be in place to produce the expected results.

2. *They fail to appreciate the level of discipline required of the organization.* Organizations often fail to realize that certification programs require greater discipline on the part of the certifying organization than they do from the people being certified. Before you can certify that someone possesses a particular set of competencies or can execute a procedure to a certain standard, the stakeholders have to agree on those competencies or that standard. A major portion of a certification program manager's job is to secure agreement among stakeholders on the goals and standards of certification. Another important task is to identify what organizational support systems have to be in place for a program to be effective. For example, if a certification is intended to confirm that people know a particular set of rules and can perform their tasks according to those rules, then the organization should reward compliance with the rules. There are a lot of factors that interfere with people's ability to perform their job well. Most of those factors are within the control of the organization and are not due to deficiencies in people's skills and knowledge.

3. *They fail to establish reasonable expectations.* Another oversight is the failure to establish reasonable expectations among *all* of the stakeholders concerning what the program can and cannot accomplish. Therefore, before going forward, make sure that the stakeholders agree with the stated reasons for the program and that you understand what each stakeholder hopes to accomplish. The public, in particular, might interpret or assign mean-

ing to the credential beyond what it is designed to accomplish. Over time these expectations can become what I call "public promises." For example, public promises happen when

- Sponsors who are asked to fund a certification expect a return on their investment.

- Managers assume that certified employees perform better than non-certified employees, with little or no support from them.

- Candidates come to believe that attaining a credential will result in job advancement or help them compete in the marketplace.

- Consumers are led to believe that work performed by someone who is certified is better than work performed by someone who is not.

These expectations may be reasonable or unrealistic. It is easy to understand how customers could assume that people who are certified are better skilled at what they do than those who are not and that their work meets higher standards. Unfortunately, the design of a particular certification may not support these assumptions. For example, training departments may promote certifications simply so they can require people to attend courses, rather than to help the organization identify and eliminate actual barriers to performance. Professional societies may promote certifications to get additional revenues from application fees and the sale of training manuals, rather than to promote standards that protect public safety and welfare. There is nothing wrong with wanting people to enroll in training courses or buy publications; however, you have to be sensitive to the possibility that people may assign greater value to a certification program than it can deliver, and any organization that offers a certification cannot ignore the fact that it has made promises, either directly or indirectly.

---

My brother wanted to hire a technical writer to generate documentation covering equipment specifications and work procedures. One of the people who applied for the contract attached his business card, which read "Certified Document Specialist." My brother concluded that this man had subjected himself to some degree of professional scrutiny, that he took pride in what he did, and that his work complied with professional standards. The certified document specialist got the contract, and the quality of his work met my brother's expectations.

**TIPS**

Here are some tips to help you and your team avoid some of the pitfalls other organizations have experienced:

1. *Define the customers.* Take the time to carefully identify exactly who the target audience's customers are. If you are designing an internal certification, find out where the target audience falls on the organization's value chain or the part it plays in the process of producing the organization's products or services. Pay attention to the people who are upstream and downstream of the target audience's place in the organization. These customers have expectations. They have modified their work processes to accommodate the target audience's current capability. Improving that capability may affect them positively or negatively. Depending on what the impact will be, they might either champion the certification program or put up barriers to implementing it.

2. *Educate the team.* Learn everything you can about how to design and implement a certification program. Find out what others have done, why they did it that way, and how well their program is working. Consider becoming a member of the National Organization for Competency Assurance or another organization whose members administer certification programs.

3. *Set standards for the process.* Just as you would for any major project, develop a set of standards for how you and your team will operate. For example, how will you define consensus? How will you resolve disputes within the team and between key stakeholders? Create a vision and mission for the project. Periodically check to see how well you are living up to the vision and accomplishing your mission.

 **GUIDELINES**   **Driver**

Here are some guidelines to help you lay the groundwork for an effective program:

A. Put together a three- to five-member cross-functional team. Together answer the following questions:

   • What is the driver behind the certification? What problem are you trying to solve?

   • What do you hope the certification will accomplish?

   • What might happen if you do nothing?

   • What evidence, both initially and over time, will demonstrate that the program is accomplishing what was promised?

B. What do you know about the target audience (their number, their responsibilities, their position in the organization, and so on)?

- How will becoming certified affect the target audience?
- What kinds of decisions will be made on the basis of their becoming or not becoming certified?
- What criteria are currently being used to select and evaluate them?
- Why do you think certifying this group will add value or solve the problem?
- What evidence will the certification program team want to show that the certification program has somehow positively affected the target audience, the stakeholders, and the organization?

C.  Who are the other stakeholders?

- How many stakeholders are involved?
- Where are they located?
- How will they benefit if the certification is successful?
- How will they be affected if it is not successful?
- What role do you want them to play?
- How do they have to change for the program to be successful?
- Who would be an effective, credible representative of each stakeholder?

D.  Meet with the stakeholders and find out

- If they share your understanding of the problem
- What they expect the program to accomplish
- How they envision certification better enabling the target audience to do their job
- Their views on other possible effects of the program, such as forcing managers to agree on a common set of standards, providing additional training or developmental opportunities, and so on
- How willing they are to change and to live up to their commitments to make the program successful
- Which issues they agree on and where they disagree

E.  Prepare a short presentation on certification programs that paints a larger picture of what they do, what makes them effective, what other organizations are doing and why, and what you hope to accomplish through your program.

## SUMMARY

When you start the process of certifying any group, you set in motion a whole series of events that may have some unexpected fallout. The organization will have to define and agree on its expectations and its commitment to rewarding and supporting the desired behaviors and outcomes. If you want to certify people so you can deploy them as needed, then you will have to get supervisory support for a common set of procedures and performance measures across the organization. If you want people to more accurately represent and service your products, then besides certifying their knowledge and skills you will have to provide them with accurate information in a timely manner. One of the more powerful outcomes from the process of developing and implementing a certification is the pressure it will place on the organization to align its human resource systems (that is, its selection, placement, and promotion criteria). Another unanticipated outcome is that the process will reveal just how capable (or incapable) supervisors are at recognizing and reinforcing competent performance.

During the design process, identify what the organization has to do or change to fully realize the desired outcomes of the program. For example, certifications cannot compensate for inadequate educational and training systems, incompetent or uncaring supervisors, insufficient equipment, poorly designed information systems, or inappropriate criteria for merit rewards. However, if well designed, a certification program will raise everyone's awareness of relevant deficiencies, whether in academic programs, organizational leadership, or the design of work processes. The ultimate goal of every internal certification should be to support human performance by aligning industry standards, organizational HR systems, and management practices. The ultimate goals of external certifications offered by professional associations or their credentialing boards are to protect the health and safety of the public and to enhance the stature of the profession they represent.

It is important to remember that with certifications come public promises; that is, certifications raise expectations. Sometimes those expectations are warranted; other times they are not. Once you determine why you want to certify a group of people, be sure to consider what others might conclude about your program and about the people you certify.

##  CHECKLIST

### Driver

Here is a checklist you can use to evaluate your certification program.

|  |  | YES | NO |
|---|---|---|---|
| A. | There is a clear statement of the goal or purpose of the certification. | ☐ | ☐ |
| B. | There is a description of who will benefit from the program and how. | ☐ | ☐ |

|  | YES | NO |
|---|---|---|
| C. There is a description of the target audience, including who is eligible, the number of potential candidates, where they are located, and why they should care about being certified. | ☐ | ☐ |
| D. There is a description of the stakeholders, noting their expectations (both of the program and of the people who will be certified), how they will benefit from the program, and what role they will play in the design and implementation. | ☐ | ☐ |

**WHERE TO LEARN MORE**

Browning, A. H., Bugbee, A. C., Jr., and Mullins, M. A. (eds.). *Certification: A NOCA Handbook* (Washington, DC: National Organization for Competency Assurance, 1996). This book describes the criteria for voluntary certification. It also describes the criteria that independent nongovernmental credentialing agents must satisfy to have their programs accredited by the National Commission for Certifying Agencies.

Lenn, M. P., and Campos, L. (eds.). *Globalization of the Professions and the Quality Imperative: Professional Accreditation, Certification, and Licensure* (Madison, WI: Magna Publications, 1997). This book presents a series of articles explaining how trade agreements such as the North American Free Trade Agreement (NAFTA, 1993) and the World Trade Organization's General Agreement on Trade in Services (GATS, 1994) have encouraged "the development of common educational standards, mutual recognition and the liberalization of processes by which professionals are allowed to practice. Among nations whose education and regulatory systems vary significantly, it falls to educators and professional accrediting agencies to establish review procedures that will ensure the quality of professionals licensed to practice" (p. 2).

**NOTE**

1. The National Skills Standards Council was created to promote the identification and definition of skills and standards for growing occupations in the United States. The Illinois Occupational Skills Standards Act established the Illinois Occupational Skill Standards and Credentialing Council (IOSSCC) in 1992. Illinois is one of three states engaged in identifying and developing skill standards for occupations that offer strong local employment and earnings opportunities. (The other two states are Indiana and Texas.) What is noteworthy about the IOSSCC's work is that it requires standards developed by industry subcouncils to be sufficiently detailed to support the development of educational and training curricula and assessment. The IOSSCC has three major functions: to recognize and develop skills standards and credentialing systems, to market and promote the application of these systems in the private sector, and to work with state councils and agencies to promote the application of standards and credentials in all approved and funded workforce development programs.

# Chapter 2
# The Requirements

$O$nce the program designers and stakeholders have agreed on why they want to certify and how either the public, the organization, or the target audience will benefit, you can then begin to look at what you want the program to entail. For programs that will certify people, one of the first questions to consider is what to require of candidates for them to gain the certification. Should you require them to complete a training program, pass a test, or do something else? To answer this question, you must first decide what role certification will play in the larger process of qualifying people for jobs.

I want my backyard certified as a bird sanctuary by the National Wildlife Federation.[1] The requirement for the credential is to provide year-round water, food (seed for birds and nectar for butterflies), cover, and nesting places for birds to raise their young.

## DISTINCTIONS BETWEEN ELIGIBILITY, QUALIFICATION, AND CERTIFICATION

The terms *eligible, qualified,* and *certified* are all used to describe people who possess a minimum required level of education, a certain set of skills, or specific work experience required to be considered for a position or to be allowed to compete for one. The terms take on different meanings, however, when used to describe different points in the process of becoming fully capable of performing a task or job. For example, many organizations have a formal process that begins with an initial assessment, to confirm that a candidate has the required skills and knowledge to perform a job, and ends with another assessment, to determine if he or she can perform a task to a specific standard. Often candidates are deemed "qualified" once they successfully complete the first assessment and "certified" after completing the second. Still other organizations defer calling people certified until they have demonstrated that they can perform a task consistently under real working conditions. Here are some examples to help illustrate how the terms are used to indicate where a person is in the process of becoming proficient:

- Athletes are *eligible* to try out for an Olympic team if they meet certain requirements, such as having amateur status, having a record of competing in previous events, and demonstrating a minimum capability for the event in which they wish to compete. They may *qualify* for the team if under controlled conditions they demonstrate even greater capability or achieve scores that are higher than the other eligible athletes. They can be thought of as *certified* once they are actually chosen to compete during the Olympics.

- To professional societies and credentialing agencies, practitioners are *eligible* or *qualified* to apply for a designation if they meet specific minimum requirements, such as a certain level of education or experience, payment of a fee, and commitment to a code of ethics. They are *certified* only after successfully satisfying an additional set of requirements, like passing a test.

- In business, the distinctions are closer to those in the example of the Olympic athlete. Think about the job posting process. People are *eligible* to apply for a job if they satisfy a minimum set of requirements, such as already being employed by the company, having been in their current job for a minimum amount of time, getting the approval of their current supervisor to apply, and so on. They are considered *qualified* for the job if they did something similar in the past, completed a relevant course of training, or worked under someone's supervision. They become *certified* only after they have proven their ability to perform a task to a specific standard.

## ROLES CERTIFICATION PLAYS

Before deciding what the requirements for becoming certified should be, you have to decide what role certification (and, later, recertification) will serve in your organization. Certifications can be designed to serve as a gate or a screen (that is, qualify people), confirm that people can perform to a certain standard, distinguish different levels of capability, and recognize or reward demonstrated performance.

### Gatekeeping or Screening

When certifications are designed to serve as gates, attaining the credential is usually required before people are allowed to perform a task or function or advance to a higher job. This type of certification is usually created in response to a safety issue and is intended to reduce risks to workers and the public. Typically candidates have to first satisfy some prequalification criteria, such as having a certain type or amount of education, appropriate experience, and a positive work record. This step is usually accomplished by having the candidate complete a job application and an interview. The next step is usually training. The training can be quite extensive, lasting for weeks or even months. When the training plays a key role in the process, candidates are usually tested to see if they have achieved the training objectives. Then, if they perform successfully on the test, they are certified. When safety is a major concern, there may be a third step, in which candidates have to demonstrate that they can perform the tasks correctly under controlled or simulated conditions or work under the direct supervision of someone who is qualified or certified (see Figure 2.1).

**Figure 2.1. Gatekeeping or Screening Certifications**

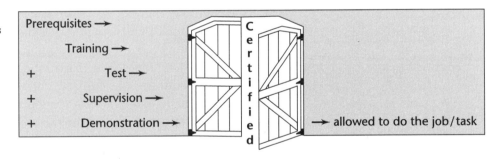

Examples of jobs and tasks for which certification acts as a gate or screen include operators at nuclear power plants, airplane mechanics, cheerleading coaches, and midwives. All of these individuals have to be certified to participate in these occupations, even moms who volunteer to help their high school's cheerleading squad. Eligibility requirements range from passing a physical to being willing to take training and passing a test to successfully completing an accredited educational program. For example:

- Business analysts who work for Florida's Small Business Development Centers must satisfy specific requirements for certification within six months of being hired, and they must be recertified every three years.

They must complete training on professional conduct before seeing their first client and training on counseling techniques and cross-selling services within thirty to sixty days of their employment. The rest of the sixty to ninety days is used to satisfy the remaining nine competencies required for certification. Until they are certified they work under the direction of a manager who is certified, and this manager must attest that they have successfully satisfied the remaining criteria before they can become certified.[2]

- Asea, Brown, Boveri (ABB), a multinational conglomerate, has multiple levels of assessment and certification. There is a pathway for every job that explains what people have to do to become certified and how they can obtain the required skills and knowledge. For example, the pathway for trainers requires them to successfully achieve a minimum of four certifications to be eligible to train others on a product. The first certification is granted for acquiring "basic trainer skills" (in, for example, presentation, classroom management, and class time management). The second certification, "ABB terminology," is required for everyone in every job in the company. People must demonstrate that they can define the common terms used companywide (such as *business unit, segment, area,* and so on), in all of the different countries where ABB operates. The third certification, "product knowledge," requires trainers (and everyone else who supports a particular product, such as sales, sales support, installation, and maintenance personnel) to demonstrate that they can explain how that product works—how it is put together, what it does, how to read the maintenance flowchart, and so on. The fourth certification requires trainers to demonstrate that they can deliver the course materials for a particular product. They are not allowed to actually train until they complete all four certifications. Trainers are assigned to a product group, and most are certified to train for at least four to five products in that group (there are two hundred to three hundred products overall); a typical trainer has from ten to twelve certifications.

- Interior designers who work in one of the twenty-one states that require interior designers to be licensed may not refer to themselves as interior designers until they pass the exam offered by the National Council for Interior Design Qualification (NCIDQ). Once they pass this test they may refer to themselves as "interior designers" or "registered interior designers," depending on the state.

- A major catalog merchandiser requires managers to pass the same test given to qualify inventory analysts before they are eligible for a promotion.

- The Hoffman Estates, Illinois, Athletic Department requires parents who want to help coach the town elementary school's cheerleading squad to become certified before they can coach. The requirements for certification are attending a lecture and passing a test on the choreographed movements cheerleaders are and are not allowed to do.

In each of these situations, the difference between being eligible, qualified, and certified is minimal, but these organizations choose to use the term *certified*. Therefore, being certified means a person has successfully satisfied a basic set of requirements.

## Recognizing Demonstrated Performance

Another role certifications fulfill is to recognize people who have demonstrated their competence through their on-the-job performance. This type of certification requires people to prove that they can perform a task to a standard under regular working conditions. This type of certification is used when an organization relies on other controls to protect people, assets, and relationships until candidates are certified. For example:

- The manufacturer of HVAC systems (discussed earlier) certifies its technicians who work in field offices. Technicians are only certified after they demonstrate that they can perform a core set of tasks under real working conditions, to a specific standard, consistently. On average it takes a couple of years to earn the certification. Technicians can develop their competencies through training, on-the job coaching, or a combination of both. The method technicians use to develop their competencies has no bearing on whether or not they are considered to have fulfilled the certification requirements.

- To be eligible for certification by the American Board of Oral and Maxillofacial Surgery (ABOMS), candidates must already have a degree from an accredited dentistry school and be licensed to practice. To be certified by ABOMS, they must first pass a written qualifying exam. Approximately twelve months later, they are eligible to take the oral certifying examination, which requires them to submit surgical case documentation and, when given surgical scenarios, explain to peers how they would treat those patients.

## Recognizing Different Levels of Accomplishment or Different Capabilities

Certifications also serve to recognize people with different levels of accomplishment or different capabilities. For example, people can receive an initial certification once they demonstrate a basic level of proficiency. They are eligible to receive another, more advanced certification after they gain an additional skill set or have successfully applied what they have learned on the job for a pre-determined period of time. They may even be eligible for a third level of certification after completing additional training, successfully performing new tasks, or meeting a higher set of performance goals. For example:

- A major credit card company has two levels of certification. Customer service representatives are certified after completing training and passing a test on understanding product features, updating customer records on-line, verifying customer data, and so on. After three months on the job they are eligible to take training that ends with a test on cross-selling. Once they have successfully sold a predetermined amount of additional services, they are certified at the second level.

- Amway ranked what it expects its trainers to know and be able to do into three levels of expertise: beginner, intermediate, and advanced. Demonstration of the skills and knowledge at each level results in a new, more prestigious certification. It takes a trainer approximately one year to earn each certification.

## TYPICAL REQUIREMENTS FOR CERTIFICATION

Here are some of the typical things organizations require of candidates for them to become certified and the types of questions you should answer before considering any of these requirements for your own program. You should also revisit this list when you are deciding what to require for people to maintain their credentials or to be recertified.

- *Education, training, and development.* Should education, training, or development be required? If so, how much should be required? When should it be required (how recently)? What topics should it cover? What objectives should it fulfill? Who should provide it?

- *Tests.* Will there be one, several, or no tests? If tests are used, what should they assess—knowledge, skills, application, or performance? Who should administer them? How frequently should they be offered? Who will score them? What criteria will they use?

- *Experience.* Should it be a requirement? If so, how much experience should be required, and how recent should it be? What type of experience (doing what) will be required, and under what circumstances?

- *Work samples.* Should they be required? If so, how many should be required? How recent should they be? What type should they be? What criteria will be used to judge them? Who will do the judging?

- *Work or personal records.* Do you have access to them? What part (attendance, performance reviews, scope of duties, and so on) is relevant to this credential? Will they be used to confirm application of what was learned in training? As proof of experience? Or will they become a source of data to prove eligibility for the new credential?

- *Endorsement.* Should candidates be endorsed by someone? If so, should that person be certified? Be a peer? Be the boss?

- *External credentials.* Should candidates be required to have a credential beyond the one you bestow? If so, should it be from a nationally recognized group, a vendor, or a licensing agency?

- *Code of conduct.* Should a code of conduct be included? If so, is there a standard for ethics? What will the code include? How will it be enforced, and what will be the consequences if it is violated?

- *Maintenance or recertification.* Will anything be required to maintain the credential, such as agreeing to a certain amount of continuing education, taking another assessment, staying active in the field, regularly performing the task on the job, or paying an annual fee?

- *Fees.* Should candidates have to pay to be certified (or to participate in the program)? If so, what will it cost to apply, to have work samples judged, to enroll in training, to take the test, and to maintain the certificate?

The combination of these requirements that will be appropriate for your situation depends on what you care about—development, experience, proof of ability, and so on. Each one of these requirements serves a different purpose. Training and education develop skills and knowledge; tests judge knowledge, skills, and performance; experience provides opportunities to perfect skills and knowledge; work samples demonstrate capability; and work records, endorsements, and external credentials demonstrate past successes. Codes of conduct, maintenance and recertification requirements, commitments to future development, and fees are used mostly by professional societies to distinguish people who are committed to their profession. Here is a description of the benefits, limitations, and implications of each of these requirements.

## Education, Training, and Development

In some organizations, a person can become certified by earning a degree or completing a training and development program. There may also be a test for the certification, but how well a person performs on it is often inconsequential; the real requirement is participation in some type of development program. Education plays a major role when degree programs exist for the relevant field or discipline. Training plays a greater role when required skills and knowledge are not easily obtained through formal education programs. Other organizations require candidates to participate in some form of development to become certified.

Still other organizations do not require any education, training, or development to become certified. They don't care how a candidate acquires the knowledge, skills, or competence needed, only that he or she can demonstrate it. For example, Amway, ABB, and the manufacturer of HVAC systems discussed previously all have extensive job training programs. Yet none link completion of their training program with their certifications. They certify people based on their ability to perform a task on the job. It doesn't matter that people have to go through training to learn to do their jobs. These companies see two benefits to keeping training separate from certification: impartiality and cost containment. When training is not part of the certification requirements, the certification manager can be more impartial when identifying when people are not prepared for the job. Cost containment occurs because people take only the training they need, based on an assessment of their performance.

However, not requiring education, training, or development for certification is rare, as there are benefits to having people complete an approved series of courses. A certification that requires training

- Exposes everyone to the same content, rules, principles, and procedures in the same way. It reduces the likelihood that people will learn different methods of accomplishing the same tasks.

- Allows you to assess how well everyone has learned the content presented in the training program. It gives you an indication of what people know and what they can do under simulated conditions.

- Allows you to correlate performance in training with performance on the job.

- Allows you to evaluate how well your training prepares people for the job.

- Demonstrates that you have exercised some prudence before allowing people to do a job.

However, when training is the only requirement, then all you can claim is that certified people have completed training. *You cannot generalize beyond the objectives of the training program.*

## Tests

A test is any tool or event designed to help you judge people's knowledge, skills, abilities, or attitudes. Tests come in many forms: multiple choice questions, practical skill-based tasks, in-basket exercises, performance checklists, simulations, and so on. Whatever the form of the test, its purpose is to discriminate between those people who know the material (or can do the job) and those who don't know the material (or can't do the job). Testing has several benefits:

- Everyone is subjected to the same measurements under the same conditions.
- Tests can help you identify gaps in knowledge, skills, and performance that might signal a trend.
- Tests can identify the need for remediation.
- The process of building tests exerts discipline on you, because you have to define what candidates must know and be able to do under specific circumstances.
- Testing can be an effective alternate means of assessing employees when on-the-job assessment puts people or property at risk.

Organizations use tests in their certification programs for different reasons. For example, candidates might be tested before beginning training either to confirm that they are eligible to attend the training (that is, that they have the required enabling skills and knowledge) or to determine how much they already know about the topic. People may be excused from training if they can pass a test on the course objectives. Organizations retest people at key points during training to measure whether or not they are learning, and at the end of training to measure the amount of growth and learning that occurred. Once on the job, people may be tested again on their ability to apply what was learned during training. Other tests are given independent of training to determine if people know or can do what their job requires.

Organizations also use tests to discover or measure different things. Some tests are used to assess people's knowledge (that is, that they know certain facts, definitions, rules, principles, and so on). I call this *knowledge-based assessment.* Other tests are used to assess skills and are usually administered under controlled conditions (like in a training program) or simulated work conditions. I refer to this type of testing as *skill-based assessment.* A third type, *performance-based assessment,* requires people to demonstrate that they can do a job or produce a piece of work that meets certain standards consistently under real working conditions (see Figure 2.2).

**Figure 2.2. Knowledge-Based, Skill-Based, and Performance-Based Assessment Compared**

| *Knowledge-based* | *Skill-based* | *Performance-based* |
|---|---|---|
| Knows the terms, rules, principles, concepts, and procedures | Can apply the terms, rules, principles, concepts, and procedures under controlled conditions, such as in a simulation | Can apply the terms, rules, principles, concepts, and procedures consistently under real working conditions |

Certifications for which training is the primary requirement frequently assess retention of the material discussed in the training program. These assessments may combine knowledge-based and skill-based tests. The first three certifications developed by ABB for trainers combined knowledge-based and skill-based assessments, requiring candidates to know and be able to explain ABB company terms, how the company is organized, and features of the company's products. The fourth certification, for which candidates must demonstrate that they can deliver the course materials, is performance-based. Enerpac's certification program requires technicians to pass a skill-based test. Skills are assessed by sending technicians a broken hydraulic pump and having them repair it. The reason Enerpac's test is skill-based rather than performance-based is that the cause of the broken pump is known, and every technician is presented with a problem of the same level of complexity. The broken pump only simulates the kinds of problems technicians will face on the job. The certifications used by the manufacturer of HVAC systems are performance-based, as people's abilities are assessed under normal rather than controlled work conditions.

Knowledge, skill, and performance can be demonstrated in ways other than testing, such as through observation, review of work experience, or evaluation of work samples. Tests play such an important role in certifications that this book devotes an entire chapter (Chapter Five) to them.

### Experience

Professional associations usually require people to have some amount of experience to qualify for their certifications. Businesses, by contrast, usually do not require a minimum amount of experience for their certifications. Both businesses and professional associations may accept experience as a substitute for education or training. Substituting experience for another requirement is called *grandfathering*. Grandfathering is an appropriate short-term solution for new certification programs when the workforce is experienced and education or training were not readily available in the past. For example:

- When the International Facility Management Association (IFMA) started its certification program, it had two paths to certification. One path required candidates to have two to five years of experience, depending on their level of education, and to pass a test. The other path, which the association called certification through "equivalency," allowed people to submit a detailed report explaining how through their work they had satisfied each of the competency requirements. Those who achieved certification through equivalency did not have to take the exam. However, after the program was in place for one year, the equivalency path was eliminated.

- The State of California grandfathered all of the state's pharmacy technicians (based on their experience) when it first instituted a requirement for certification of pharmacy technicians. If it had not done so, the state's pharmacies would not have been able to meet the demand for new and refilled prescriptions.

- Florida's Small Business Development Centers' certification program is based on a point system. Analysts must achieve one hundred points to become certified. When the program started, business analysts were given four points for every year of experience, and a degree was not required. Over time the number of points allowed for experience was reduced and the number of points for education was increased. Today, business analysts must have a four-year college degree.

- The HVAC systems manufacturer's certification is not based on experience or education. Everyone, no matter how many years of experience they have, must demonstrate their ability to meet the standards through their work performance. However, very experienced workers can frequently meet the standards in less time than it takes employees with less tenure.

A more difficult decision is whether to require depth of experience or breadth of experience. Some organizations want candidates for certification to demonstrate depth of experience, or time spent doing similar tasks within a narrow range of responsibility. Others want candidates to demonstrate breadth of experience, or experience with a diversity of assignments and responsibilities. For example:

- IFMA is more interested in managers' having experience across a range of responsibilities that parallel its standards than in their having a lot of experience in particular areas. Experience that is limited to fewer responsibilities has to be supported by education to make up the difference. Facility managers must have three to five years of experience as a facility manager, depending on their level of education. They still have to pass a test to receive the credential "certified facility manager."

- Interior designers can practice anywhere in the country without being certified. However, before they are allowed to take a certification exam, they must have at least six years of combined education and experience in interior design, two years of which must be in education in interior design or a related field.

- To become a certified safety professional in the United States, candidates are required to study and pass an exam in those areas where they lack experience.[3]

If you want to recommend that experience be a requirement or be accepted as a substitute for education or testing in your certification program, then you must first define the extent of the experience you will require or accept. For example, specify a level of responsibility the candidate must have attained (in terms of number of people, size of budgets, or scope of projects managed) and tasks the candidate must have performed (hiring, firing, building a budget, installing a 3500 machine, calibrating an XX gauge, and so on). Then when you or others review a person's experience, you will know in advance what you are looking for and can better judge if his or her experience satisfies the requirement.

## Work Samples

You might require candidates to submit a sample of their work to determine if they are eligible for certification, to assess their skills, or as a substitute for experience, training, or testing. Requiring a work sample is a form of testing. Unlike a simulation or case study, a work sample is not created in a controlled setting or within a fixed time period. Work samples are used to judge skill when time is not a criterion, when observing performance in a controlled environment is too costly or inappropriate, and when there are other requirements for certification. For example, if you wanted to certify a Webmaster, one requirement might be to submit samples of Web pages the candidate created, either as part of a school assignment or for a client. Here are some other examples:

- The Embroiderer's Guild of America, Inc., requires work samples as part of its process to qualify its master judges. Judges decide whether or not needlework can be accepted for display at local, state, regional, national, and international exhibitions. They judge the needlework based on whether or not it meets the standards for execution, design, color, and so on. To become a judge, people have five years to satisfy six requirements, one of which is to exhibit eight pieces of their own embroidery. The fact that their work was accepted for exhibition means it was juried; that is, it met the minimum standards for execution, design, color, and so on. In other words, judges not only have to recognize quality work, they have to be able to produce works that meet the standards for being exhibited.

- The pharmaceutical manufacturer described in Chapter One requires candidates for its HR certification to prepare a business plan and a change strategy. Candidates have thirty-six months to satisfy these as well as other requirements. The plan and strategy must be based on their business unit needs, and they must use information about their own work area—they can't make it up.

You should define the attributes work samples should demonstrate for them to be accepted as fulfilling the requirement. For example, the Embroider's Guild has very specific criteria for pieces to be accepted for exhibition.

## Work or Personal Records

In the past, certifiers were more likely to use work or personal records to qualify people to apply for a credential than they are today. Today, such records are used to corroborate experience and "professional behavior." Behavior usually comes up when there is a requirement related to conduct, customer satisfaction, safety, conflict of interest, or susceptibility to blackmail or bribery. For example, one organization requires its employees to achieve a minimum customer satisfaction rating to receive and maintain their certification. Another organization qualifies its people based on capability but only certifies them after a financial audit that shows them to be financially solvent (and therefore less likely to accept kickbacks or bribes).

## Endorsements

Some professional societies and credentialing boards require candidates to have an endorsement. They might specify that the endorsement must be from someone in the field, someone who is certified, or a member of the association. For example, you must be recommended by a certified safety professional to become one. Businesses might require candidates to be approved or nominated by their current or previous supervisor. Endorsements are also used to confirm that people are active in their field and that their behavior is acceptable.

## External Credentials

Sometimes organizations want candidates for certification to have an external credential in addition to meeting other requirements. The external credential might be used to exempt candidates from taking a test or meeting an experience requirement. For example, if candidates are Certified Industrial Hygienists (CIHs), they are excused from taking the first of two tests required to become a Certified Safety Professional (CSP). Having an external credential may also exempt candidates from meeting significant education or experience requirements if it means they have already satisfied an educational, experience, or assessment requirement. The types of external credentials that are more frequently required are licenses from state agencies and certifications in a discipline related to health and safety.

### Acceptance of a Code of Conduct

Codes of conduct and ethics statements are rarely required for certifications from businesses. Ensuring ethical behavior is usually handled in other ways, such as by corporate policy. Businesses also rely on supervisors to ensure that people's actions are in keeping with local laws and corporate policy. However, the State of Illinois conducts background checks on pharmacy technicians before they can be licensed, and Walgreens requires its pharmacists and pharmacy technicians to sign an ethics statement. Agreeing to a code of conduct or statement of ethics is more frequently required by professional societies and credentialing agencies as part of their certification requirements. Some codes of ethics list expected behaviors; others list responsibilities. Listing responsibilities gives you an opportunity to include obligations to the organization, the public, and the profession, such as paying dues, reporting misconduct, following procedures, and so on. Specified behaviors may include both acceptable and unacceptable activities. Figure 2.3 provides a code of ethics for management consultants as an example.

The dilemma that a code of conduct presents to professional societies is how to deal with enforcement. Some societies only ask candidates to sign a statement indicating that they have read and agree with a code of ethics. The National Board of Certified Counselors (NBCC) has developed an effective protocol for dealing with ethical and legal charges against its members. The NBCC's process is based on three elements: a certification attestation agreement, a set of procedures for dealing with ethical cases, and a code of ethics. To be certified, candidates must sign the attestation agreement, by which they agree to voluntarily abide by the code of ethics and the procedures for dealing with ethical cases, to disclose information about any criminal and professional behavior, and to cooperate fully should they be investigated. The procedures describe the investigation, review, decision, and appeals processes. The NBCC's code of ethics addresses both professional and personal behaviors. Independent credentialing boards rely on other groups, such as commissions on professional conduct, to respond to charges of misconduct or malpractice.

If you want to include a code of ethics or conduct as part of your certification requirements, try to link that requirement to any current organizational policies governing behavior such as theft, sexual harassment, and so on. If those provisions do not exist or are inadequate, then work with your stakeholders, including legal counsel and human resources personnel, to develop them.

### Maintenance and Recertification

Maintenance and recertification are not exactly the same thing. Maintenance refers to requiring candidates for certification to commit to doing something in the future, at some predetermined point after they receive the credential,

**Figure 2.3. Code of Ethics for Management Consultants**

*Clients*

- We will serve our clients with integrity, competence, and objectivity.

- We will keep client information and records of client engagements confidential and will use proprietary client information only with the client's permission.

- We will *not* take advantage of confidential client information for ourselves or our firms.

- We will *not* allow conflicts of interest which provide a competitive advantage to one client through our use of confidential information from another client who is a direct competitor without that competitor's permission.

*Engagements*

- We will accept only engagements for which we are qualified by our experience and competence.

- We will assign staff to client engagements in accord with the experience, knowledge, and expertise.

- We will immediately acknowledge any influences on our objectivity to our clients and will offer to withdraw from a consulting engagement when our objectivity or integrity may be impaired.

*Fees*

- We will agree independently and in advance on the basis for our fees and expenses and will charge fees and expenses that are reasonable, legitimate, and commensurate with the services we deliver and the responsibility we accept.

- We will disclose to our clients in advance any fees or commissions that we will receive for equipment, supplies, or services we recommend to our clients.

*Profession*

- We will respect the intellectual property rights of our clients, other consulting firms, and sole practitioners and will not use proprietary information or methodologies without permission.

- We will *not* advertise our services in a deceptive manner and will *not* misrepresent the consulting profession, consulting firms, or sole practitioners.

- We will report violations of this Code of Ethics.

---

*Source:* Reprinted with permission of the Institute of Management Consultants, a division of the Council of Consulting Organizations, Inc.

with the understanding that failing to honor that commitment will result in their losing the credential. The most common requirement is to earn a minimum number of continuing education credits every year. Professional societies also give points for staying actively involved in the field, such as by teaching, writing, and serving on committees. The assumption is that by earning continuing education credits or staying active in their field, people are also staying current with changes in technology, laws, and so on. For example, IFMA requires holders of its certification to earn 120 points every three years to maintain the credential. They can earn points through a combination of professional and educational activities. Therefore, when you require maintenance you are asking people for a commitment; you are not asking them to redemonstrate a capability or knowledge.

Recertification refers to situations in which a certifying organization puts a time limit or some other restriction on its credential, at which point the credential expires. To become recertified—that is, to earn the credential again—people have to demonstrate that they can still satisfy the original requirements or a new set of requirements. For example, people who are certified in cardiopulmonary resuscitation (CPR) must be recertified every year. The requirements for CPR recertification are the same as for the initial certification: candidates have to take a written test and demonstrate that they know how to administer the technique. Another example is driver's licenses that expire after a preset period of time. To reinstate his or her license, a driver has to demonstrate all or a subset of the original requirements, like parking a vehicle or passing a vision test, and pay a fee. Some organizations do not put time limits on their certifications but maintain the right to stop recognizing them when there are changes in technology, laws, product features, customer expectations, and so on that invalidate the original requirements. The manufacturer of HVAC systems, for example, retains the right to announce new requirements every six months. Everyone affected by the change must be recertified. An automobile manufacturer recertifies its maintenance crews whenever work processes, procedures, rules, and technology change enough to render the original requirements invalid. Therefore, if you foresee the need to impose new or more difficult standards in response to changing technology, customer expectations, laws, procedures, and so on, then you will want to require that people be recertified. The subject of maintenance and recertification is so important to maintaining the credibility of credentials that an entire chapter (Chapter Seven) is devoted to the topic.

## MISSTEPS AND OVERSIGHTS

Here are descriptions of one common misunderstanding and one common mistake organizations make when they start to design their certification programs:

1. *Avoiding the word* certification. A common misconception held by businesses is the notion that if they avoid using the word *certified*, they won't get sued. Organizations use all sorts of words to label the people who have demonstrated an ability to meet a set of minimum requirements. The label doesn't matter; what matters is the rigor used in developing the criteria for judging proficiency and the fairness with which the program is administered. Anytime you put a process in place whose purpose is to distinguish some people from other people, you have to prove that the criteria are relevant to safety, performance, and so on. Choosing to say that people are "eligible," "qualified," "proficient," or "capable" instead of "certified" *does not release you from the responsibility of being prudent.*

2. *Failing to plan for change.* Organizations do not always think through how they will handle changes that might affect the people they certify. If you are certifying people in a task or role in which staying up-to-date is essential to honor the credential's public promises, then you should put a time limit on the credential and require people to demonstrate their currency at a specified point in the future. If actually demonstrating their currency is unnecessary, then you should consider requiring people to commit to maintaining and expanding their knowledge, skills, and so on. Maintenance and recertification are not mutually exclusive: you can require both.

**TIPS**

Here are some tips to consider when deciding what the requirements for certification should be:

1. *Have more than one requirement.* Training, testing, experience, and work samples, by themselves, give you only one source of measures. When your certification is based on only one requirement, such as training, it is much more difficult to generalize its significance beyond "the person completed the training." Success on a test is just that, nothing more. Similarly, you cannot infer that because someone has experience he or she will perform to the same level in another setting. However, training, testing, and experience in combination can give you a greater sense of confidence about a person's ability. Relying on one source of data about an individual overly burdens that source.

2. *Involve the target audience in defining the requirements.* When you are in the process of deciding what and how much to require, involve representatives of the target audience. Frequently they will come up with innovative alternatives that strengthen the credential and deal with the concerns of older, more experienced candidates. They can also help you come up with a plan to migrate to a more stringent set of requirements over time.

## GUIDELINES

### Requirements

Here are some guidelines to help you and your team decide what the requirements should be for your certification. Meet with your team and stakeholders and answer the following questions:

A.  Eligibility. What do you want people to have to be able to do, or what requirements do you want them to meet just to be eligible to begin the certification process?

B.  Certification

- Once they are eligible to apply for certification, what do people have to do to become certified? And how do these requirements differ from those for eligibility?

- If you want to require candidates to pass a test to gain certification, what do you want the test to confirm?

- If you want to require training or education, how many credit hours or courses do you want candidates to have to earn? What content must they cover? Does it matter where or how long ago candidates received their training or education?

- If you want to require experience, how many months or years do you want? What has to be part of the experience in terms of tasks, duties, scope of responsibility, and so on? How recent must the experience be? Does it matter where the experience was gained? How will you confirm the experience (that is, that the candidate really has it)?

- How will you handle grandfathering?

- Would requiring candidates to get an endorsement add value to the credential? Who should be allowed to do the endorsing?

- Would asking candidates to gain an external credential be beneficial? What would the credential have to be in? From whom would they have to get it? Would an external credential allow candidates to be exempted from another requirement? Which one?

- Will the requirements stay the same, or do you see them evolving over time? If so, how will they change?

- Do you want people to commit to some continuing education or other activity to stay current? Or will you want to put limitations on the credential so you can change the requirements?

- What will the requirements mean to the target audience and the other stakeholders?

- How will these requirements help solve the problem or meet the needs of the organization?

**SUMMARY**

When most people hear the word *certification* they think about training and tests. Training and tests certainly play a significant role in many certifications. However, much more can be involved. You have to decide what role the certification will serve: will it screen, confirm capability, distinguish levels of competence, or recognize competence? When coming up with a set of requirements for the credential, you should also revisit the driver behind the certification program and any promises made to stakeholders. You have to determine the feasibility of managing a program with multiple requirements and compare that to the anticipated benefits. The checklist and guidelines in this chapter (also on the accompanying disk) will help you determine what set of requirements is best for your program.

 **CHECKLIST**

### Requirements

Here is a checklist you can use to evaluate your requirements. There exists a description or statement of

|  |  | YES | NO |
|---|---|---|---|
| A. | The intent, purpose, or need the certification is expected to satisfy | ☐ | ☐ |
| B. | What candidates can say or declare about themselves after having achieved the certification | ☐ | ☐ |
| C. | Who is eligible to apply for the credential | ☐ | ☐ |
| D. | The rules for when and how many times a candidate can apply for certification | ☐ | ☐ |
| E. | What experience or education can be substituted for another requirement | ☐ | ☐ |
| F. | What attributes the experience or education must possess to be considered an acceptable substitute | ☐ | ☐ |
| G. | What is required for certification (*Note:* more than one requirement is recommended): | | |
| | • Education, training, or development | ☐ | ☐ |
| | • Test | ☐ | ☐ |
| | • Experience | ☐ | ☐ |
| | • Work samples | ☐ | ☐ |
| | • Work or personal records | ☐ | ☐ |
| | • Endorsement | ☐ | ☐ |
| | • External credentials | ☐ | ☐ |
| | • Code of ethics | ☐ | ☐ |
| | • Maintenance | ☐ | ☐ |
| | • Recertification | ☐ | ☐ |
| | • Fees | ☐ | ☐ |

**WHERE TO LEARN MORE**

American Board of Industrial Hygiene (ABIH), 6015 West St. Joseph Street, Lansing MI 48917, 517-321-2638.

American Society of Safety Engineers, 1800 East Oakton Street, Des Plaines IL 60018, 847-699-2929.

Board of Certification in Professional Ergonomics (BCPE), P.O. Box 2811, Bellingham WA 98227, 360-671-7601.

Board of Certified Safety Professionals (BCSP), 208 Burwash Ave., Savoy IL 61874, 217-359-9263.

Guilbert, Douglas E., Ph.D., NCC, LPC, ethics officer, NBCC; and Richard A. Goldberg, attorney, at 2897 Main Street, Lawrenceville NJ 08648-1046, 609-896-1543, to learn more about the ethical practice standards of the National Board for Certified Counselors (NBCC) and its process for dealing with ethical issues.

Hale, J., and Westgaard, O. *Achieving a Leadership Role for Training* (New York: Quality Resources Press, 1995). This book describes how training and human resource departments can apply the Baldrige criteria and the ISO standards to their own functions. The book illustrates how different types of requirements are used and how organizations satisfy them.

Institute of Management Consultants, 521 Fifth Avenue, 35th floor, New York NY 10175, 800-221-2557, www.imcusa.org.

International Association of Emergency Managers, 111 Park Place, Falls Church VA 22046-4513, 703-538-1795 (voice), 241-5603 (fax).

**NOTES**

1. The National Wildlife Federation hopes to double its twenty-two thousand certified backyard habitats by the year 2000. To learn more, contact the National Wildlife Federation at 8925 Leesburg Pike, Vienna VA 22184-0001, 703-790-4434, www.nwf.org/habitats. The National Wildlife Federation's goal is to increase the number of safe havens for birds and butterflies. My goal is to support the environment. I also enjoy watching wildlife and want to attract them to my backyard. If I can reduce the amount of yardwork that I have to do without risking ostracism from my neighbors, that will be nice, too. Hopefully my neighbors will see my backyard as a friendly and safe place for wildlife and thus something that enhances their property value.

2. The business analysts who are certified by Florida's Small Business Development Centers (SBDCs) must complete twelve training modules, covering counseling skills, public speaking, cross-selling SBDC's services, specialty programs, government requirements, market research and planning, financial statement analysis, sources and requirements for financing, business plans, how to start a business, human resources management, and the SBDC's code of professional conduct.

3. The Board of Certified Safety Professionals (BCSP) provides certification testing for the following credentials: Certified Safety Professional (CSP), Associated Safety Professional (ASP), Occupational Safety and Health Technologist (OSHT), Construction Safety and Health Technologist (CSHT), and Safety-Trained Supervisor in Construction (STS). Recertification is required every five years. The American Board of Industrial Hygiene (ABIH) provides certification testing for the following credentials: Certified Industrial Hygienist (CIH), Occupational Safety and

Health Technologist (OSHT), Construction Safety and Health Technician (CSHT), and Safety-Trained Supervisor in Construction (STS). The STS test is the same one offered by the BCSP. Recertification is required every five years. The Board of Certification in Professional Ergonomics (BSPE) offers certification testing for the following credentials: Certified Professional Ergonomist (CPE), which can be designated Certified Human Factors Professional (CHFP) instead at the candidate's option, and Certified Ergonomics Associate (CEA). The International Association of Emergency Managers offers two credentials: Certified Emergency Management (CEM) and Associate Emergency Management (AEM). Candidates do not have to be association members. The certification is based on a peer review process. The requirements are experience, education, three references, one hundred hours of classroom training in emergency management, one hundred hours of general management, and contribution to the profession. The assessment involves writing an essay in response to a scenario and passing a one-hundred-question multiple choice test.

# Chapter 3
# The Standards

Not too long ago I was scheduled to fly on an airplane for business. When I went to the ticket counter to check in, the ticket agent asked to see some photo identification. I handed her my Sam's Club membership card. She protested, saying that I had to submit an official identification card. I reminded her that all that was required was an identification card with my photograph on it. I didn't tell her that because of a speeding ticket, my driver's license was in the hands of the state's attorney office and that I'd left my passport at home. After reviewing the requirement, she gave in and gave me a seat assignment. A few weeks later I heard an announcement at the same airport that passengers must present an "official, government-issued" photo identification to check in. The standard was the same, but the criterion had changed.

**A** frustrating yet exhilarating part of developing a certification program is the process of setting standards and criteria. The confusion surrounding this task is the frustrating aspect, because it makes it difficult to explain just what is expected of candidates. The exhilarating aspect is the debate that occurs as people challenge one another's assumptions about what, exactly, the organization wants to certify and "how much is good enough" in terms of requirements. The debate starts over the role of the certification. Which of the following will the certification accomplish?

- *Develop people*—help people acquire required knowledge, skills, and abilities

- *Qualify people*—confirm that people have required knowledge, skills, and abilities

- *Distinguish people*—differentiate between people with different levels of proficiency

- *Recognize people*—acknowledge people who consistently perform to standard

A certification may accomplish one or a combination of these objectives.

After the certification's role has been decided, the debate soon moves to what evidence stakeholders will accept as proof that people have learned, know, can do, or have done well whatever it is that is required. The outcome of these debates drives the creation of standards and criteria to evaluate proficiency, learning, experience, work samples, and so on.

## COMPETENCIES, STANDARDS, AND CRITERIA

The terms *competency, standards,* and *criteria* are bantered about whenever the subject of certification comes up. However, not everyone understands the role each plays and how they differ. The term *competency* is used as a label for those areas in which performance matters, such as communication, project planning, strategic thinking, and so on. Competencies, therefore, tell you what organizations value. For example, a company may consider its core competencies to be designing, planning, consulting, problem solving, communication, interpersonal relations, leadership, teamwork, and strategic thinking. The organization may add a brief definition after each label; for example:

- *Designing:* conceiving and developing systems, programs, and processes that meet identified requirements and specifications

- *Planning:* establishing priorities, setting courses of action, and determining what resources are required to achieve desired results

- *Consulting:* providing experience and expertise as a resource to help resolve individual and organizational issues

These core competencies are generic (that is, they can apply to almost any job or role), and the level of detail in these descriptions is not sufficient to judge whether or not people in a particular job or role can be said to possess them to an adequate degree. In other words, they lack standards.

*Standards* describe a task in enough detail to support the development of tools that will enable an organization to fairly judge people's proficiency at performing that task. The description is usually in three parts:

1. The *conditions* describe the context in which the work being described is performed. Conditions include things like what triggered the task, what equipment and materials are available, and any training that may have been completed.

2. The *performance* specifies the tasks, behaviors, and thinking that make up the job or duty.

3. The *criteria* define the actions (behavior or thinking) or outcomes required for the performance to be considered done "to standard."

Collectively, the conditions, performances, and criteria define proficiency of performance or sufficiency of skills and knowledge in a way that can be measured. Here are some examples of performance standards with conditions, performances, and criteria.

---

### PERFORMANCE STANDARD: HYDRAULIC PUMP TECHNICIAN

**Conditions**

The technician is given a hydraulic pump turned in for repair, a working test bench with calibrated gauges, a set of recommended tools, and a copy of the manufacturer's specifications for the pump being worked on.

**Performances**

The technician will do the following:

1. Determine the type and model of pump, based on either the date code or the description on a parts sheet

2. With the aid of a test bench, simulate the conditions under which the pump would be expected to work, to see if it attains and holds pressure, leaks, works, and so on

3. Visually identify cracks or dents that would make the pump nonrepairable

4. Visually or tactically identify if foreign material is in the oil (grit, metal shavings, and so on)

5. Visually check for leaks

6. Diagnose the cause of the problem

7. Determine if any costs to repair are covered under warranty

8. Determine whether or not the pump is worth fixing

9. Inform the customer of the findings and recommendations

### Criteria

The technician will perform the aforementioned tasks so that

1. Failures due to abuse of the pump (versus normal wear and tear) will be noted.
2. The recommendation to the customer will consider the cost of the repair (parts and labor), the estimated useful life of the pump once it is repaired, the customer's intended use of the pump, and the price of a new pump.

### Conditions

The technician has decided that it is feasible to repair the pump, and the customer has approved the repair.

### Performances

The technician will do the following:

1. Locate the appropriate documentation (specification sheet)
2. Locate or order the appropriate parts kit
3. Select the appropriate tools
4. Take the pump apart using the appropriate tools
5. Replace all parts in the parts kit
6. Explain why any parts were not used
7. Reassemble the pump
8. Test the pump, using a test bench, to confirm that it performs to the specification
9. Complete a work-order form, checking off what was wrong with the pump and what was done to fix it.

### Criteria

The technician will perform the aforementioned tasks so that, once the pump is returned to the customer, it will operate to specification.

## PERFORMANCE STANDARD: PLANNING A PRODUCT LAUNCH

### Conditions

A new product is scheduled to launch. The planner has a description of the product's features and benefits, a description of the target market, and a competitive analysis.

### Performances

The planner will develop a plan to support the launch that includes

- The name of the agency to be used to develop the advertising campaign (such as newspaper, radio, and television advertising)
- The name of the agency to be used to design and produce promotional items (such as mailers, trade show giveaways, banners)
- The expected deliverables and budget for each agency
- The timeline, with milestones for the launch
- Key dates for approvals, production, and distribution
- Names of people who have to approve all copy and promotional materials

### Criteria

The planner will include these things in the plan so that

- Deliverables and expectations can be communicated to all vested parties in sufficient time for them to honor their commitments
- All elements will establish a brand image and reinforce the targeted market position of the product

## PERFORMANCE STANDARD: ETHICAL CONDUCT

### Conditions

Interior designers' integrity and ethics are manifested in their behaviors, specifically through their recommendations and choices.

### Performances

Interior designers will

- Make recommendations regarding interior space and elements such as furniture, fixtures, and equipment
- Make recommendations regarding the need for and use of other contractors and suppliers

### Criteria

They will do these things in such a way that

- The health and safety of the environment are not compromised.
- The well-being (financial, psychological, and physical) and image of the client are not compromised.
- The client is kept informed of the interior designer's financial relationships with suppliers and contractors related to the project.
- The designer does not represent himself or herself as capable or knowledgeable, or offer information under the guise of being an expert in a discipline outside of the discipline of interior design.

When a certification has requirements other than performance, such as training, experience, or submitting work samples, the standard similarly defines how these requirements will be satisfied (by attending class, completing class assignments, passing tests, being on the job for a minimum amount of time, contributing to the organization, and so on). For example:

- The pharmaceutical firm that certifies its HR generalists (described previously) requires candidates to complete four approved courses.
- The International Facility Management Association (IFMA) requires candidates to have at least four years of experience in facility management. The criteria are that 75 percent of the manager's time had to have been spent on tasks that fall under at least six of the following eight competency areas: operations and maintenance, human and environmental factors, facility function, quality assessment and innovation, real estate, planning and project management, finance, and communication.

## DEFINING THE SCOPE OF THE EFFORT

When I begin the process of designing a certification program, I present clients with a simple exercise that helps them decide what part of the job to focus on and helps them understand why they should do a job or task analysis before deciding what the standards should be. The exercise also lays the groundwork for a conversation about what role they see the requirements (training, experience, work samples, and so on) playing in the process (see Figure 3.1). The premises behind the exercise are as follows:

1. Success, in whatever the scope of work (occupation, job, role, or task), requires a combination of skills.
2. At a minimum, that combination includes three sets of abilities:
   a. *Technical or professional knowledge and skills:* the ability to perform those activities that are unique to the occupation, job, role, or task
   b. *Interpersonal skills:* the ability to get along with, work with, and relate to others
   c. *Work management skills:* the ability to be self-disciplined, set priorities, think through implications, and organize work
3. The proportion or ratio of these skills to one another depends on the work to be performed and the amount and type of support the organization can provide.

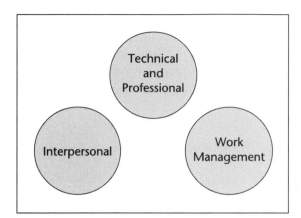

**Figure 3.1.  Skills Required for Success**

What falls under the *technical and professional* cluster are the knowledge and skills that make up the work. For example:

- Accountants have to know the organization's financial goals and practices and know and be able to apply accounting principles.
- Sales support staff have to be able to apply knowledge of the products, the customers, and the business agreements.

This cluster also includes the ability to use specific equipment, such as computer software, laboratory instruments, machine shop tools, and so on. This cluster takes on particular importance when the skills are not easily acquired or their absence affects product performance, safety, or customer relations.

The skills that fall within the *interpersonal* cluster include the ability to recognize and interpret social and cultural cues, to establish a rapport, to engage people, to be a part of the team, and so on. Competencies like consulting, communication, and selling are included in this cluster. The interpersonal cluster increases in importance when the work requires interacting with people of a different culture or people who do not have the same values and goals as the organization.

The skills included in the *work management* cluster relate to organizing tasks, setting priorities, meeting commitments, foreseeing consequences, and planning. This cluster takes on greater importance when the work requires people to perform with minimal direction or with few organizational cues as to what to do, when to do it, and how to do it.

The specific skills within each of these three clusters vary for different types of work. For example:

- It might seem that a night security guard position would require few interpersonal skills. However, with the increasing potential for violent situations today, the job of night security guard may increasingly require superior skills at diffusing emotionally charged situations and the ability to manage one's own reactions. The required technical skills are specific to the scope of responsibilities, such as locking up facilities, checking personnel badges, using electronic surveillance equipment to monitor movements, and so on.

- HR generalists need to have sophisticated interpersonal skills such as consulting, negotiating, and mediating. Their work management skills include the ability to manage projects and to weigh the consequences of policies on employee relations. Their technical or professional skills relate to employee relations, staffing and hiring, performance management, compensation, benefits, and so on.

Skills within all three clusters are present, to some degree, in every task or job. The exercise does two things:

1. It reveals people's expectations concerning the certification. For example, is its purpose to attest to people's ability in just one cluster, like the required technical or professional skills, or their ability in two or all three clusters?

2. It shifts the debate to a focus on the role the requirements play in developing, qualifying, distinguishing, or recognizing people's abilities in one or more of the clusters. For example, is the role of the requirements to

   - Develop people's interpersonal skills, technical or professional skills, work or self-management skills, or some combination of them all?

   - Confirm the presence of skills or knowledge in one or more of the areas?

   - Confirm (by evaluating experience, work samples, and work records) that people have sufficient ability in one or more of the three areas? That they are eligible to apply for the credential? That they are ready to receive the certification? That they can be exempted from other requirements?

For example:

- Enerpac decided to focus its certification for field technicians only on those skills that fall under the technical-professional cluster. It relied on the service centers to ensure the presence of skills in the interpersonal and work management clusters.

- The pharmaceutical firm that certifies its HR generalists focuses on those skills that fall under the interpersonal and work management clusters. It relies on its HR policies and procedures and on requiring degrees in human resources or organizational development to cover the skills under the technical-professional cluster.

The exercise opens the door to discussing the idea that although a lot is known about the task or job in question, thoughts about what people have to know and be able to do are either conjecture or based on old data. This last insight creates enough dissonance for clients to become receptive to doing a job or task analysis to confirm just what abilities are really required.

## THE JOB OR TASK ANALYSIS

The Civil Rights Act of 1964 and the Uniform Guidelines on Employee Selection Procedures are very specific about what organizations must do if they use tests to screen or qualify people or in any way judge people's capability. Figure 3.2 summarizes the key points of the procedures.

A job analysis is a formal process for determining or verifying what people do, under what working conditions they do it, what they must know to do it, and the skills they must have to do it. The analysis can be applied to a set of duties, a group of tasks, a job, a role, or an occupation, but most people just refer to the process as a job or task analysis. The purpose of the analysis is to get enough data to support the development of performance standards, tests, training, and criteria to judge experience, work samples, ethics, and so on.

> - Tests must be based on a thorough job analysis.
> - Test content must be linked to the job analysis.
> - The validity of the test content must be determined based on the relative importance of the job behaviors.
> - There must be agreement among the raters.
> - The ratings must be based on performance dimensions.

**Figure 3.2. Summary of Title VII of the Civil Rights Act of 1964 and the Uniform Guidelines on Employee Selection Procedures**

There are a number of proven processes for conducting a job or task analysis, but any analysis should include the following phases:

1. *Phase One* involves generating a list of tasks or behaviors that describe what people do, the conditions under which they do it, and the skills and knowledge required to do it. Some of the methods used to generate the initial list of tasks are to

   - Convene a panel of experts—representatives from the target audience (in person or electronically)—to describe the job or task

   - Convene the stakeholders (in person or electronically) to describe their expectations of people in the job

   - Interview experts and stakeholders to elicit what is done, why it is done, and what is important

   - Observe one to three experts performing the task being studied to identify what is done and under what conditions

   - Survey experts and stakeholders to identify trends affecting the job and future skills

   - Conduct literature reviews and document searches to identify the results of other studies about the job

2. *Phase Two* involves (a) verifying the degree to which a larger group agrees with the initial description and (b) rating or ranking the specific tasks or behaviors according to their importance, frequency, and difficulty. The typical methods used to do this are to survey (by phone, by mail, in person, or electronically) the target audience, survey (by phone, by mail, in person, or electronically) the stakeholders, and interview (in person or by phone) the target audience and stakeholders.

3. *Phase Three* involves converting the list of tasks into performance standards that include

   • The conditions and constraints under which people are expected to demonstrate knowledge, skills, or performances

   • What they have to work with (tools, equipment, information, relationships)

   • What triggers the tasks

   • The tasks or behaviors encompassed in the performance

   • The criteria used to judge adequacy or proficiency

The goal of the first two phases is to build as complete a picture as possible of the task, the environment in which it is performed, and the stakeholders' expectations. The goal of the third phase is to describe the organization's expectations in sufficient detail to support assessing candidates' ability to satisfy the standards.

For example, Enerpac began by interviewing experts and stakeholders at its corporate office (Phase One). It validated the results of those interviews by conducting field visits to five major service centers. The field visits included interviews with the owners and technicians as well as an opportunity to see the conditions under which the technicians worked and the resources they had available (Phase Two). The results were then converted into a set of requirements and performance standards (Phase Three).

## CONTROLLING BIAS

A major error made by many organizations is the failure to control the three main sources of bias or distortion when doing a job or task analysis. These are

1. *Sampling error,* caused by the failure to poll either enough stakeholders or people who truly represent the stakeholders

2. *Design error,* exemplified by using an insufficient number of sources or inappropriate methods to get the data

3. *Administrative error,* caused by inconsistent implementation and a failure to control the environment in which the data gathering occurs

*Sampling errors,* also called alpha or Type I errors, occur when the group being polled doesn't properly or adequately represent either the population you are studying or the organization's expectations of that population. *Design and administrative errors,* sometimes called beta or Type II errors, occur when the group being polled is somehow manipulated during the process. To control all three sources of bias,

- Use proper sampling techniques, so the people you involve will adequately represent the larger population and the needs of the sponsoring organization.

- Use more than one method to gather the data, so you will get a more complete picture of the task and work environment and can cross-validate your findings.

- Select methods that by their design help control environmental factors such as group dynamics and distractions.

- Document your procedures, so you and your team will be consistent in how you interview, conduct groups, observe, and analyze the data.

- Pilot-test your questions and other data-gathering techniques to find out if they elicit the types of responses you require.

The International Facility Management Association (IFMA) followed this process when it conducted its job analysis. For Phase One, a panel of experts was appointed to oversee the project, which included

- A review of the available documentation on facility management practices and trends.

- Seven nominal group technique (NGT) sessions: one with the panel of experts, five with facility managers, and one with educators. The NGT is a structured data-gathering process designed to control the bias that normally occurs as a result of group dynamics. The process is described in greater detail later in the chapter.

Phase Two included

- Structured phone interviews with 181 facility managers from the United States and Canada who were nominated by local IFMA chapter presidents.

- On-site observations of thirty-eight facility managers from the United States and Canada at work, to determine what they do, how they do it, and who they interact with. The managers were nominated by local IFMA chapter presidents.

- A written survey sent to a random sample of 1,380 facility managers to determine the importance and frequency of their job functions.

For Phase Three, the results were summarized. From them, performance standards and a test were developed.

### Sampling Error

All three phases in the job or task analysis process require you to observe or poll the opinions of others. Whom you choose to poll or observe will influence what you learn. Rarely can you poll everyone in the target audience, every customer, every supervisor, every regulatory body, and so on. Organizations often make the mistake of basing their analysis on one voice, whether it be experts or incumbents. One voice only gives you part of the picture. Therefore, understanding sampling theory can increase the chances that the people you include will adequately represent the target audience and other stakeholders.

Sometimes you are lucky enough to know how many people are in the target audience—that is, how many security guards you employ or how many HR generalists you have working for you—and you can get a list of their names. When you know how many there are and you can get to them, you can either poll all of them or a subset (that is, take a sample).

Other times you don't know how many there are in a population, because it is hard to identify them. This was the problem faced by Enerpac, NCIDQ, and IFMA:

- Enerpac knew how many service centers it had, but it didn't know how many technicians the centers employed.

- NCIDQ had a list of certified interior designers and had access to non-certified interior designers who were members of the major professional associations. Yet it had no way of getting the names of those interior designers who were neither certified nor members of an association.

- IFMA knew how many members it had, but it didn't know how many facility managers there were in the United States and Canada who were not members.

When you don't have access to everyone in the target audience, you define that audience according to the group you do have access to. Based on that definition, you can choose to select that entire group or a smaller subset, or sample.

There are three ways to select people to be in a sample. You can appoint people, pull a random sample, or do both. Over the course of the job or task analysis, you will probably use all of these methods.

*Appointed representatives* are the people who have been nominated to represent the target audience, their supervisors, their customers, and other stakeholders. You are more likely to begin your job or task analysis with people who are nominated, because you want knowledgeable experts, key customers, and main sponsors. However, whenever you choose to appoint people, there should be a reason for why some get chosen and some do not. For example, most job or task analyses use "high" performers or experts as a major source of data. These experts are almost always nominated. The question you must be prepared to answer is "Experts according to whom?" Do you deem them experts based on supervisor ratings, productivity ratings, awards they've won, customer satisfaction ratings, or something else? The same is true for the other appointed stakeholders. Do you choose customers who buy the most, customers who are ISO registered, or customers who participate on special councils? Do you choose supervisors based on seniority, proximity, history of resistance to change, or some other criterion? It is important to document the criteria used to select the representatives.

*A random sample* is a group of people you want to pick at random to represent the target audience and the key stakeholders. A sample is random when everyone in the population has an equal opportunity to be selected or left out. When you pull every third name from a list, the sample is *not* random, because anyone who had a number other than 3, 6, 9, and so on never had a chance to be selected. But if you gave everyone in the population a three-digit number from 001 to 900 and used a set of randomly generated three-digit numbers to select people, then everyone would have an equal opportunity to be included or excluded. Random samples are more typically used in Phase Two, when you are validating what people do, how they do it, and what constitutes acceptable performance. Comparing what the experts say they do with what the representatives from the larger population say they do is the primary function of Phase Two.

The size of the sample depends on the size of the population, the number of data-gathering methods you are using, and how you plan to analyze the data. For example, the size of the sample is very important when you only use one data-gathering method, such as a survey. Figure 3.3 suggests how many people you should survey for the sample to adequately represent the larger population. The use of multiple data-gathering methods reduces the need for large samples because you can cross-validate your data through the different sources.

| Size of the population | Percent used in the sample |
|---|---|
| 1–50 | 100 percent |
| 51–100 | 50 percent |
| 101–250 | 25 percent |
| 251–500 | 10 percent |
| 501–1,000 | 5 percent |

*Source:* Reprinted from Westgaard and Hale, *Measuring Productivity* (Western Springs: Hale Associates, 1986), with permission of the authors.

**Figure 3.3. Suggested Sample Sizes**

A *stratified sample* is a random sample including the voices of specific sub-groups, such as the people who work the second shift, those who handle national accounts, customers who order over $100,000 worth of product annually, and so on. In this case you identify the subgroups you want to sample and pull a random sample for each one. Figure 3.4 provides an example of a stratified random sample where you are only doing a survey and you want to make sure that three audiences from two different locations are equally represented. It doesn't matter that a different number of people work in each location, only that the sample size is appropriate.

**Figure 3.4. Stratified Random Sample**

| Areas | Total Population | Sample Size | Location A | Location B |
|-------|------------------|-------------|------------|------------|
| Technicians | 244 | 62 or 25 percent | 25 percent | 25 percent |
| Engineers | 76 | 38 or 50 percent | 50 percent | 50 percent |
| Scientists | 76 | 38 or 50 percent | 50 percent | 50 percent |

## Design Error

A second source of bias occurs when your data-gathering methods do not capture the information you require to determine what the standards should be. The techniques commonly used to do job and task analyses include convening groups, eliciting information from individuals (by conducting interviews and observations or distributing surveys), doing literature reviews, and conducting document searches. All of these methods have value, and limitations.

***Convening Groups.*** Almost all job and task analyses involve getting a group together to either generate or evaluate data. The groups may include the target audience (also called subject matter experts), supervisors, customers, and others who have a vested interested in the task's being done well. All of the group processes are more or less effective, depending on how they are used.

The *focus group,* also called an open panel discussion, is a qualitative research technique. It is less structured than other group process techniques. Focus groups are often used for market research, but they can be used for parts of a job or task analysis as well. People are selected to participate in a focus group because they have shared some experience that is the subject of the focus group (for example, they went to the same training, serviced the same customer, or did the same task). Traditionally, participants are asked to focus on their feelings about the shared experience.

Focus groups are an effective way to generate hypotheses that you will want to test (for example, that candidates with four-year degrees reach proficiency faster than others), to help analyze the results from other methods (such as why there are discrepancies in what people say about what they do or how a task is done), and to test a group's reaction to a set of requirements (such as taking training, passing a test, or being observed). They are less effective at controlling group dynamics, generating a comprehensive set of facts, or determining the frequency, weight, or criticality of a task. Also, focus groups require a highly skilled facilitator. The procedure for designing and conducting a focus group is included in the Guidelines section of this chapter and on the accompanying disk.

Here is an example of how the pharmaceutical firm used a focus group to determine if employee expectations regarding benefits were making the HR generalists' jobs harder and perhaps affecting their skill set. It conducted three focus groups. Seven people were invited to participate in each of the sessions. Two of the sessions included six HR generalists and one employee relations specialist. The benefits manager was added to the third session. The same facilitator was used. Two people were assigned to record the discussion. Figure 3.5 shows the questions the facilitator prepared prior to holding the sessions.

**Figure 3.5. Focus Group Process and Questions**

> Estimated time: 15–20 minutes
>
> 1. Over the past three years, has your job gotten easier or harder?
> 2. What caused it to become easier (or harder)?
>
> (Probe if there was no mention of benefits)
>
> 3. Who do you rely on to keep you up-to-date regarding employee benefit issues?
> 4. Are there any organizations in particular that you rely on?
> 5. What about publications?
> 6. How have changes in some of the extra benefits or coverages affected your job?
>
> (Probe for specifics)
>
> 7. How have changes in dental benefits affected your job? Vision benefits? Flexible spending plans? Medical deductions?
> 8. What would make this part of your job easier?
>
> (Probe for specific expectations)
>
> 9. Are there any resources that would help?
> 10. In what ways might training help you in this aspect of your job?
> 11. Do you feel there are skills that, if you were to improve them, it would help?

The *nominal group technique (NGT)* was developed to improve group decision making, specifically by reducing powerful personalities' influence over the group's ability to generate and impartially examine ideas. As the word *nominal* implies, the people in the group are a group in name only; they do not work together or otherwise function as a group outside of this particular situation. The NGT is an effective technique for generating a comprehensive set of facts and weighing those facts according to some variable, like importance or frequency. Because responses are assigned points, you can identify those responses that are statistically significant. The NGT is also an effective technique for analyzing trends or the results from other sources of data. For example, you might ask

- What might be the cause of this trend?
- What effect will the trend have on the organization (or some other group)?
- What do think is the most problematic trend facing the discipline today?

This process requires less skill on the part of the facilitator. Briefly, the process is to ask participants to privately generate a list of responses to a question. The facilitator then asks members to give one answer at a time in a round-robin style until everyone has exhausted his or her list. Next, the participants privately pick the five responses, from all of the ones generated, that they feel are the most important and assign them points. Finally, the points are tallied for those responses that received points (see Figure 3.6). (A more detailed description of the process appears in the Guidelines section at the end of this chapter and on the accompanying disk.)

For example:

- NCIDQ began its occupational analysis by conducting seventeen NGT sessions in fifteen cities across North America. Fifteen of the groups consisted of interior designers, one consisted of educators, and one consisted of outside voices (major clients and safety experts). Both designers and educators were asked the same five questions, in the same order (see Figure 3.7).

The responses were analyzed, classified by theme—such as "user-oriented" (an attribute), "design principles" (a sphere of knowledge), and "develops contents" (a skill)—and compared. According to the interior designers, the factor that most distinguishes them from others working in the field is their education in interior design; however, the group that represented customers and safety experts rated the designers' being user-oriented significantly higher than their having a certain level of education. Figure 3.8 provides one example of how raw data from an NGT

---

1. Ask the question.
2. Generate responses.
3. Report out responses.
4. Discuss responses.
5. Combine and eliminate responses.
6. Rank top five responses.
7. Assign values to top five.
8. Attach values to the responses.
9. Discuss the results.
10. Proceed to the next question.

**Figure 3.6. NGT Steps**

**Figure 3.7. Examples of NGT Questions Asked of Interior Designers and Educators**

1. What distinguishes professional interior designers from others who practice interior design?
2. What do professional interior designers do that other professionals who contribute to the environment don't typically do?
3. What important knowledge base do interior designers draw on to do their work?
4. What skills are required for interior designers to accomplish their work?
5. What should those who contract for interior design services expect from a certified interior designer?

**Figure 3.8. Example of NGT Data and Analysis**

One NGT group's responses to Question No. 2 (sorted by order of importance, based on points awarded). *Note:* Only those responses that received points are listed.

| No. | *What do professional interior designers do that other professionals who contribute to the environment don't typically do?* | Class | PTS |
|---|---|---|---|
| 21 | Use existing conditions to create a new environment | SD | 15 |
| 7 | Listen | SC | 12 |
| 9 | Add impact to productivity and bottom line | AUP | 12 |
| 1 | More intimate relationship with client | AUO | 10 |
| 16 | We serve as coordinator for large groups of unrelated professionals | ABI | 10 |
| 25 | Concentrate on ergonomics and human dimension issues | KHE | 10 |
| 11 | Interpret the client's personality | SDN | 10 |
| 12 | Psychology of enclosed environment | KPS | 9 |
| 20 | Solve problems created by other professionals | STP | 7 |
| 24 | Deal with individual preferences | AU | 7 |
| 3 | They "give a damn" | AU | 5 |
| 22 | Accept more responsibility for outcomes | AIN | 4 |
| 28 | Relates to space: traffic pattern and spatial perception | KPS | 3 |
| 29 | Ask the right questions | SDN | 3 |
| 30 | Humanize, using scale and proportion | KPS | 3 |
| 33 | Can make client succeed or fail | AUP | 1 |
| 31 | Details, details, details | AOD | 1 |

| | |
|---|---|
| Mean | 7.18 |
| Standard deviation | 4.23 |
| Total of mean and standard deviation (to identify responses that are statistically significant—that is, that exceed this total) | 11.41 |

session can be displayed and analyzed. The first column is the sequence in which the response was given. The second column contains the response. The third column shows how each response was classified by theme. The first letter of the theme code indicates whether the response was about knowledge (K), skills (S), or a personal attribute (A). The second and third letters allow for further classification, such as business, design, aesthetics, health, and so on. The last column shows the number of points the response received.

Defining *outcome-based competencies* is another process you can use. I developed this process to help experts more rapidly identify the typical tasks or behaviors that make up a job or task, the skills and knowledge required to perform it, and the results that could be used to judge proficiency in it. It is an effective and efficient process for generating an initial set of data that can be used later in surveys and interviews to validate what the experts think. It is also an effective process for controlling group dynamics, because it focuses the group's attention on being comprehensive instead of on whose opinion is right. The process calls for displaying the group's work throughout the meeting, so the members can add to or modify their thinking at any time. Figure 3.9 briefly describes the process. (A more detailed set of procedures is provided in the Guidelines section at the end of this chapter and on the accompanying disk.)

For example:

1. Display sample chart.
2. Generate a list of the job components (tasks).
3. List what people must know.
4. List the skills people must have.
5. List how performance might be measured.
6. Validate what was captured, by surveying a larger group of stakeholders and candidates.
7. Compile the results.
8. Convert the results into performance statements.

**Figure 3.9. Defining Outcome-Based Competencies**

- The pharmaceutical firm had already developed a set of core competencies for HR generalists. It even had some brief descriptions of how the competencies might be defined for people at different levels in the organization. However, it had not done a task analysis. The head of the project asked senior managers to nominate respected HR generalists from a manufacturing plant, a field sales office, the corporate offices, and an international office to work on the project. Five people were nominated. They followed the process for defining outcome-based competencies. They met for two days, during which they identified the major functions of a generalist—that is, organizational effectiveness, employee relations, training and development, staffing and recruiting, benefits, health, and safety. Next they listed the typical tasks that make up each function, identified the required skills and knowledge, and listed what could reasonably be used as evidence of competence for each. Figure 3.10 shows the tasks, skills, knowledge, and measures the group came up with for staffing and recruiting.

Recruiting/staffing: facilitating the process of sourcing and selecting employees whose competencies are aligned with the business need, so that we have and maintain an employee profile with the skills and behaviors required today and in the future

| Knowledge required | Skills required | Typical tasks | Possible measures |
|---|---|---|---|
| 1. The job you are trying to fill (part-time, full-time, contract) | 1. Communication (verbal, listening, and written) | 1. Get more than one person's perception of the job | 1. Number of requests |
| 2. Who knows the job best and can help you design interview questions | 2. Interview: staying focused, purposeful | 2. Educate managers on their role in the process | 2. How long it takes to fill jobs |
| 3. What the company is about: its products, place in the market, competition, and so on | 3. Analyze data and compare it to the skills profile | 3. Develop an interview strategy, behavioral questions with criteria | 3. Responsiveness at each step |
| 4. How to source—when internally and when externally | 4. Behavioral interviewing | 4. Give advice on internal equity | 4. Number of qualified candidates |
| 5. The human and business dynamics of the work environment | | 5. Interview | 5. Number of internal qualified candidates |
| 6. How to create and close a requisition | | 6. Write and place ads | 6. Cost of recruiting |
| 7. The job posting process | | 7. Choose the media (newspaper, headhunter) | 7. Cost of the job's being vacant |
| 8. Legal issues and illegal questions | | 8. Do background checks | 8. Success of the employee in the job or role |
| 9. When and how to prequalify external candidates (for example, drug screening) | | 9. Schedule drug screening | 9. Retention rate |
| 10. Compensation ranges, variances, negotiations, promotional guidelines, equity issues, and so on | | 10. Review resumes | 10. Ratio of acceptance to offers |
| | | 11. Design interviews | |
| | | 12. Compile results | |
| | | 13. Do a phone screening | |
| | | 14. Do college recruiting | |
| | | 15. Set up, arrange, coordinate, do product displays for career fairs | |
| | | 16. Participate in manpower planning and forecasting | |

**Figure 3.10. Example of Outcome-Based Competency Data**

The *Delphi technique*—the most structured of the group processes—was developed to do forecasting. It is less likely to be used by a business as part of its job or task analysis; however, it can be used effectively to forecast training needs, identify trends that might affect job performance standards, and predict trends in a profession. The Delphi technique is named after the oracle at Delphi, whom the ancient Greeks sought out to predict the future. What distinguishes the Delphi technique from the other group processes is that participants never meet; they do not even know who the other members are. Members are sent a problem or question (either by mail or electronically) and given a specific amount of time to respond. Once the responses are returned, they are sorted by theme and then presented (by mail or electronically) to everyone who participated in the first round. Participants then evaluate their own position compared to everyone else's and either modify their position or adopt another one. The process is repeated, usually three times, until everyone's responses coalesce around specific themes. Figure 3.11 briefly describes the steps in the technique. (A more detailed description appears in the Guidelines at the end of this chapter and on the accompanying disk.)

Even though the Delphi technique effectively prevents powerful group members from overly influencing others, it is much more time-consuming than the other group processes. Figure 3.12 has some examples of Delphi technique questions that can be used to help forecast the need to add or modify current performance standards.

**Figure 3.11.
The Delphi Technique**

1. Select the panel.
2. Get agreement from the panel on the process and rules.
3. Round 1, present the question.
4. Interpret and arrange the data.
5. Round 2, return to panel for study.
6. Analyze and rank responses.
7. Round 3, share and ask for critiques.
8. Analyze and share the results with the panel.
9. Repeat steps 7 and 8 to get consensus.

***Gathering Data from Individuals.*** Other data-gathering tools are designed to elicit opinions or actions from individuals rather than groups. These include interviews, surveys, and observations. You might interview experts and supervisors to get an initial list of the behaviors that make up a task. You might interview, observe, or survey experts to confirm what they do. As with group processes, there are a number of ways to effectively get information from individuals.

**Figure 3.12. Examples
of Delphi Technique
Questions**

1. How might changes in technology (or government standards, customer requirements, and so on) affect our field technicians in the next three to five years?
2. Do you foresee customers' expectations changing in the next three years in ways that will affect how we qualify our sales force? If so, how do you see them changing?
3. How might marketplace pressures affect how we qualify and prepare our engineering staff?

In an *open interview,* you encourage people to say anything they wish in response to a question. You record their answers verbatim for later analysis. Open interviews are best done early in the process, particularly to get stakeholder's expectations. The advantage of open interviews is that they can reveal details and insights that other methods fail to uncover. The disadvantage is the time it takes to record and analyze people's responses.

Enerpac conducted open interviews with technicians who were assigned to the corporate help desk set up to support field technicians. Interviews were also done with the trainer and technical writer and the directors of after-market sales, parts, and services. Everyone was asked the same set of questions, and their responses were recorded and compiled (see Figure 3.13). Collectively, their responses began to capture what a technician does and has to know to meet these stakeholders' expectations.

**Figure 3.13. Examples of Open Interview Questions**

1. In general, what do technicians do?
2. How many models of pumps do they have to deal with? How many would you expect them to be able to handle?
3. Talk me through the steps that a technician goes through to repair or refurbish a pump.
4. What tools would you expect a technician to have and be able to use to repair a pump?
5. What resource materials (equipment manuals, specification sheets, and so on) are available to the technician to use when repairing a pump?
6. What does a technician have to know to do the job?
7. If you could watch a technician, what would you look for as evidence that he or she was doing the job well?

*Structured interviews* are meant to validate what others have already said. The questions in a structured interview are like those used in an open interview and are asked in exactly the same manner, but instead of recording the interviewee's answers verbatim, the interviewer categorizes them based on a predetermined list of possible answers. The list of possible answers comes from what was learned in earlier interviews and group sessions conducted in Phase One. The advantage of structured interviews is that it is much easier to analyze the responses than it is to analyze the responses of an open interview. However, the interviewer must carefully listen to each answer and determine which one on the list of possible responses it most closely matches (new responses can be added if necessary). Figure 3.14 presents two of the twenty-five structured interview questions used by IFMA in its job analysis and the anticipated responses that were most frequently given by the 181 people who were interviewed.

| | |
|---|---|
| **Figure 3.14. Examples of Structured Interview Questions** | What is the most important role facilities managers play in their corporation? |

| What is the most important role facilities managers play in their corporation? | When it comes to budgets and finance, what do you have to do to be an effective facilities manager? |
|---|---|
| Highest-ranked anticipated answers:<br><br>1. Plan for new space, facility, and equipment.<br>2. Maintain the current facility.<br>3. Coordinate changes with vendors and tenants.<br>4. Protect and make wise use of assets.<br>5. Communicate current rules, policies, and changes. | Highest-ranked anticipated answers:<br><br>1. Prepare budgets<br>2.5 Use available assets wisely.°<br>2.5 Project cost accounting.°<br>4. Financial analysis.<br>5.5 Know inventory space and costs.°<br>5.5 Cut costs.°<br>°Received equal rankings. |

The *critical-incident interview* technique is designed to identify appropriate and inappropriate behavior in defined situations. The process can only be used with people who have directly observed someone else's behavior. The word *incident* refers to any observable behavior. The incident is considered critical if the intent behind the behavior is clear to the observer and the observer has "little doubt" about the consequences of the behavior. The results can be used to develop assessment instruments, particularly performance checklists. One disadvantage of critical-incident interviews is that they require people to recall what they observed, and depending on the amount of time that has passed since their observations, their recollections could be faulty. Therefore, critical-incident interviews are best used when people are asked to recall a recent incident. Another disadvantage is that it is very difficult to generalize about behaviors others should emulate or avoid based on what a few people did well or poorly. Therefore, you should validate the desirable and undesirable behaviors through another process. Critical-incident interviews can be done with individuals or with groups; however, when used with groups, people should be allowed time to privately recall their observations. In either case, specially prepared forms should be used for recording the data. Figure 3.15 has examples of critical-incident questions.

*Observations* are the *only way* to confirm what the work environment is and how it might influence what people do and how they do it. However, not all tasks or jobs lend themselves to being observed. An observation is an effective method for identifying the steps that make up a procedure or the activities that make up a discrete task; however, it is not an effective method for getting good data about a larger process, such as project management, that might span weeks or even months. Here are some examples in which observations worked well:

**Figure 3.15. Sample Critical-Incident Questions**

1. Think about a manager you've seen in action. Recall an incident that you thought that person did not handle as well as he or she should have. You should have directly observed both the way the manager handled the situation and the consequences or results of his or her actions.

2. What did that person do that made you think he or she was not good at what he or she was doing?

3. How did he or she do it?

4. What were the consequences or results of the person's actions?

5. Think about a manager you've seen in action. Recall an incident that you thought that person handled very well. You should have directly observed both the way the manager handled the situation and the consequences or results of his or her actions.

6. What did that person do that made you think he or she was very good at what he or she was doing?

7. How did he or she do it?

8. What were the consequences or results of the person's actions?

9. Think about specific examples of when you've seen a salesperson be very effective. Write down what you observed and what the outcome of the performance was. Write out as many scenarios as you remember. Limit your stories to what salespeople do.

10. Now think about specific examples of when you've seen a salesperson be ineffective. Write down what you observed and what the outcome of the performance was. Write out as many scenarios as you remember. Limit your stories to what salespeople do.

- A pharmaceutical firm was required to qualify its people who manufactured liquid drugs. Observations were done on each part of the manufacturing process, from line setup to line clearance. The observations were very effective at identifying the constraints under which people worked and exactly what had to be done, how it had to be done, when it had to be done, and in what order it had to be done.

- Enerpac sent observers to five service centers. The observers were able to see the tools and equipment technicians had to work with and what technical specifications were available. Observing a technician repair a pump was less feasible since the process requires putting a pump on a test bench to see if it holds pressure for eight or more hours. Enerpac supplemented the observations with interviews with the technicians and their bosses.

- IFMA observed thirty-eight facility managers. The observations focused on the amount of time spent on each activity and the frequency of the activity. The observations were one day in length. Figure 3.16 shows the type of form the observers used to record their observations.

**Figure 3.16. Sample Observation Form**

Observation Log

| When (Time) | What's the Person Doing? (Activity) | What's It About? (Subject) | Who's Involved? (People) | What's the Result? (Outcome) |
| --- | --- | --- | --- | --- |
| | | | | |

*Print, phone, and electronic surveys* can be an effective and efficient way to reach a large audience. They can be used in Phase One to determine the degree to which a larger audience sees a need for certification, standards, training, and so on, and they can be used in Phase Two to verify what people do and what they think is important. They are best used to support or validate the results from other methods. The problem they present is how to get people to fill them out and return them. There is the chance that you will get responses only from those people who are interested in the project, and they may not be truly representative of the larger group. For this reason it is best to use a cover letter to encourage people to participate and later follow-up with nonrespondents through postcards or phone calls. Another way to increase the chances of getting an excellent return is to ask managers or supervisors to be responsible for having people complete and return the survey. For example:

- The pharmaceutical firm used the outcome-based competency definitions it compiled to build two surveys: one to be sent to a larger sample of HR generalists and one to be sent only to supervisors. The first survey asked the generalists how frequently they did each task, how important and difficult each was, and how skilled they were at doing it. The second survey asked the supervisors how often generalists did the same set of tasks, how important they were, and how skilled the generalists were at doing them. The survey data showed that the generalists' jobs differed significantly depending on where they worked. The project manager could also correlate the common skill deficiencies with those tasks considered most important by both groups. Figure 3.17 is an excerpt from the survey sent to HR generalists.

*DACUM* (**D**eveloping **A** Curricul**UM**) is a well-documented process for doing a job or task analysis. The process was developed by Robert Norton, senior research and development specialist at Ohio State University. The DACUM

**Figure 3.17. Sections of a Survey**

*Professional profile section*:

1. Your name:_____

2. Your job title: _____

3. How many years of experience do you have in human resources?

    _____ Less than 2 years

    _____ More than 2 years but less than 5 years

    _____ More than 5 years but less than 7 years

    _____ More than 7 years

4. Your educational background:

    _____ 0– 2 years of college

    _____ 3– 4 years of college

    _____ Undergraduate degree

    _____ Graduate degree

5. Look over the following job responsibilities.

    a. Put the percentage of time you dedicate to each responsibility in the space provided.

    b. Rank the responsibility on a scale from 1–7 to indicate how important each one is to your job effectiveness (1 = most important).

| *Major Responsibility* | *Percent of Time* | *Importance* |
| --- | --- | --- |
| Organizational Effectiveness | | |
| Employee Relations | | |
| Recruiting/Staffing | | |
| Compensation | | |
| Training | | |
| Benefits | | |
| Employee Health and Safety | | |
| Other: | | |
| _____ mailroom | | |
| _____ receptionist | | |
| _____ cafeteria | | |
| _____ security | | |
| _____ other, please specify_____ | | |

**Figure 3.17. Sections of a Survey,** *cont'd.*

| How often do you participate in the following activities? | Almost always | A lot | About half | Rarely | Never |
|---|---|---|---|---|---|
| External recruiting | ☐ | ☐ | ☐ | ☐ | ☐ |
| Initially screening job candidates (reviewing resumes) | ☐ | ☐ | ☐ | ☐ | ☐ |
| Deciding how to best recruit (headhunter, newspaper ads, ads in professional journals, and so on) | ☐ | ☐ | ☐ | ☐ | ☐ |
| Selecting a headhunter | ☐ | ☐ | ☐ | ☐ | ☐ |
| Writing job ads | ☐ | ☐ | ☐ | ☐ | ☐ |
| Doing background checks on candidates | ☐ | ☐ | ☐ | ☐ | ☐ |
| Setting up job fairs | ☐ | ☐ | ☐ | ☐ | ☐ |
| College recruiting | ☐ | ☐ | ☐ | ☐ | ☐ |
| Scheduling drug screenings | ☐ | ☐ | ☐ | ☐ | ☐ |
| Helping managers identify the best candidate(s) | ☐ | ☐ | ☐ | ☐ | ☐ |

process uses direct observations, interviews, and surveys to generate data for training materials and competency tests. The process is based on three premises: expert workers can describe or define their job better than anyone else can, any job can be described in terms of the tasks that successful workers perform, and all tasks depend on workers' possessing a specific body of knowledge and attitudes. The process effectively identifies job duties and task statements that describe what a successful person does in a particular job. The tasks can be further ranked according to which ones are important and difficult to learn. The results are used to develop learning materials. Once you have an itemized list of tasks, the next step is to verify that list with a larger group from the target audience. A disadvantage of the DACUM process is that it does not always incorporate the voices, or needs, of other stakeholders. It does tell you what successful people do; however, without adding the other voices, it will not tell you what successful people *should* do. A significant outcome of the DACUM process is a chart that describes all the tasks, in sequence, required to carry out a job duty. For example:

- A manufacturer used DACUM to develop performance standards and curricula for its hourly production crew. Crew members were observed and interviewed. The process identified twenty job duties and the tasks that were involved. Figure 3.18 presents a section of the task chart dealing with one duty.

| Duties | Tasks |
|--------|-------|
| Stage the Job | 1. Assign job priorities (scheduler) |
| | 2. Obtain job folder |
| | 3. Review all paperwork |
| | 4. Audit job parts |
| | 5. Verify accuracy of shortage sheets |
| | 6. Notify planner or expediter of parts shortages |

**Figure 3.18. Example of a DACUM Task Chart**

Once the tasks were identified, the manufacturer developed standards for each one. The next step was to assess workers' ability to perform them to standard. Training was then developed to support any gaps in performance.

***Document and Literature Searches.*** Frequently overlooked resources include internal historic documents, training task analysis data, and industry or professional research papers. If the research is relatively current and was done with some rigor, you can use it as a starting point for defining what the target audience does or should do. For example:

- When Amway wanted to certify its trainers, it based its certification on the professional standards developed by the International Board of Standards for Training, Performance and Instruction. Representatives from Amway's corporate training and marketing departments modified the professional standards based on the company's goals and requirements. Their recommendations were then sent to all of the company's U.S. field trainers for their review and to be sorted based on whether they applied to beginner, intermediate, or advanced trainers.

### Administrative Error

Administrative errors happen when the people carrying out a study are not consistent in conducting it or do not control environmental factors that might cause people to restrict their responses or not fully disclose their opinions.

***Inconsistency.*** To be consistent when conducting interviews, introduce the purpose of the interview in the same way to all interviewees; ask the same questions, in the same order, to all interviewees; and allow all interviewees the same amount of time to respond. Inconsistency is easily avoided by preparing a script, a set of protocols that explains the purpose of the interview, and answers to frequently asked questions like "Why me?" "Who will see my answers?" "How did other people answer the question?" "How long will this take?" and so on. It also helps to use a preprinted form containing the interview questions, to ensure that you ask them in the same sequence for all interviewees.

To be consistent when conducting observations, figure out what you are going to look for in advance, record your observations at the same times, record your observations in the same way, and sketch the layout of the work area in advance for referencing. Avoiding inconsistency in observations is best achieved by practicing observing before actually doing it. Decide in advance what behaviors or events you want to track, at what times you want to record what is happening, and how you are going to record what you see or hear.

To reduce administrative error when analyzing data, decide *in advance* how you are going to classify responses, compile or group responses, and statistically analyze the data. Errors in analyzing data are best avoided by thinking through in advance how you want to examine data, calculate results, identify trends, and determine significant differences. For example, IFMA used graduate students to do its observations. Every student was sent a letter of agreement asking them to commit to doing the following:

- Prepare for the observations by using the training materials sent to them
- Contact the facility manager to arrange for the observation and to get preliminary information about the facility (size, type, number of employees, organizational chart, and so on)
- Conduct the observations within a specific time frame
- Record the facility manager's activities in ink on the observation forms provided
- Return the observation forms, videotape, and summary of their impressions by a specific time
- Contact the coordinator if any difficulties or questions arose
- Use the training materials, consisting of a videotape demonstrating how to conduct the observation and a job aid
- Use the observation forms for recording their observations

The people who were selected to be observed were sent a cover letter explaining the purpose of the observation, how it would be done, how the results would be recorded, and how the results would be used.

**Environmental Influences.** Distractions, lack of privacy, and group dynamics can cause people to censor or restrict their responses.

*Distractions* can be caused by the people conducting the study, by interruptions, and by lack of privacy. For example, interviewers introduce bias if they inadvertently reveal to interviewees that their responses are different from or agree with what others have said, and observers introduce bias if they draw attention to themselves by fidgeting or coughing or otherwise distract the people they are observing. Distractions are best avoided by developing a clear set of guidelines explaining what interviewers and observers can and cannot do and then training all participants in those procedures.

*Lack of privacy* is best controlled by arranging in advance to meet, interview, or observe at a time and place that is less susceptible to casual interruptions or being easily overheard.

*Group dynamics* are a factor whenever you ask people to provide input in a group setting. Participants with strong personalities or high status within the organization might overly influence the others, and shy or low-status participants might censor their remarks, withhold their opinions, or appear to agree when they don't. For example, when a group contains people of different status, those of lower status will usually delay speaking until after those of higher status have spoken and will rarely disagree or offer a contradictory opinion. This type of bias is best controlled by imposing structure on the process, which is what the NGT and the Delphi technique do. Another technique is to focus people's attention on being comprehensive rather than on coming to consensus, which is what the DACUM process and the process of defining outcome-based competencies do.

## MISSTEPS AND OVERSIGHTS

The most frequent oversight is the failure to conduct a thorough job or task analysis. An analysis validates what people actually do and the skills and knowledge required to do it. Not performing an analysis of the job or task puts the organization legally at risk. Frequently the people who are championing a certification or have the most to gain from its being implemented believe that they already know what people do and thus what constitutes doing it well. But what they believe does not matter; what will matter is whether or not they can follow (and document) a valid process for *verifying* what they believe. A job or task analysis verifies just exactly what people have to do, under what conditions, and at what level to be considered proficient or competent. Neglecting it has particular ramifications if a requirement involves some type of assessment, such as passing a test.

## TIPS

Here are some tips for when you conduct a job or task analysis:

1. *Control group dynamics.* Whenever you want to engage a group to generate an initial set of expectations or to validate the results from another source and the group is made up of people of different status within the organization, follow a more structured process. If the people don't know one another and are of the same status, you can use a less structured process.

2. *Use more than one method, and incorporate more than one voice.* If at all possible, use more than one method to get the data, and incorporate more than one voice. At a minimum, involve people who do the job and people

who depend on the job's being done well. If the job or task is regulated or puts people or property at risk, also include safety or external experts.

3. *Avoid emotionally laden words and complex structures in your interviews and surveys.* When developing your interviews and surveys, avoid emotion-laden words, compound questions, and complex sentences. Emotion-laden words in a question distract people and are likely to inspire a response to the word rather than to the question. Compound questions confuse people. The more complex the question, the more the respondent has to work at understanding the question. Technical writers or individuals skilled at developing surveys and interview questions can help you formulate effective questions. Westgaard's *Tests That Work* (San Francisco: Jossey-Bass/ Pfeiffer, 1999) has a nice section on how to develop questions (see Where to Learn More at the end of this chapter).

4. *Use computer software and electronic information systems.* Consider using electronic information tools to conduct a job or task analysis. For example, Delphi studies, interviews, and surveys can all be done using e-mail, intranets, and the Internet. Software is now available to analyze responses. If you already have the software and hardware in place, it can save time and be less costly.

5. *Maintain the standards.* Job and task analyses cost time and money. Based on the amount of change the target audience has to accommodate by adding to their knowledge or skill base, consider doing a Delphi study or hosting focus groups to identify trends that might signal the need for you to update or expand your curricula and standards.

 **GUIDELINES**

## Job or Task Analysis

Here are some suggestions to guide you in performing job or task analyses:

A. If you have very limited time and dollars, use the following guidelines for Phase One:

1. Set up a cross-functional team of six to eight people who represent the target audience (ideally, high performers) and stakeholders (a customer group, management group, opinion leaders, or others who have a vested interest).

2. Put together three to five questions similar to these:

- What does this group do that is of value to the organization?
- What do they have to know to do it?

- What distinguishes high performers from others who do a similar or the same job or task?
- What are the typical tasks or activities that a person in this group does to accomplish the job or task?
- How do you know when a person in this group is doing the job or task well?
- How does performance of the job or task affect you when it is done well? When it is done poorly?

3. Schedule a meeting and use the NGT to elicit people's answers. You can cover three to five questions in about half a day.

4. Validate the results of your Phase One efforts:

   - Distribute a survey to a larger sample (ideally at least twenty-six people) from the target audience, picked at random.
   - Conduct phone interviews with a representative sample from the other stakeholder groups (ideally at least six of each).
   - Observe three people performing their job or task. If the job or task does not lend itself to being observed because it involves a larger process like project management, then, at a minimum, go look at where the work occurs.

5. Summarize the results, and develop a set of standards for the job or task.

6. Submit the standards to the first group who participated in the NGT, and get their input and agreement. You can distribute this to a larger group, if you wish.

7. With your certification program in mind, review your list of requirements and set standards for each one (that is, training, experience, work samples, and so on).

8. With your steering committee, set some milestones for the certification, and test the standards. Based on what you learn, you may or may not need to further develop or expand the standards.

B. If members of the group you want to certify work in very different environments, then

   1. Add another method to the suggestions above to build on the list of activities, knowledge, and expectations.

   2. Submit the proposed tasks, knowledge, and so on to a larger group to validate them.

   3. If possible, observe at least three people at work who work in different environments, to determine how much variance there is in the work environment.

### Standards

Once you know what people do and know, the skills they have to have, and what stakeholders expect of them, you are in position to develop a set of standards. Here is a process for developing and describing standards:

A. List what you learned about what initiates the activity, what equipment and information is available to the person doing the task, and the physical environment (the *conditions*).

B. Take what you learned from the job or task analysis and list the steps or activities that make up the task (the *performances*).

C. List what the expected outcome is or what attributes will be used to judge proficiency (the *criteria*).

D. Submit the standards to representatives from the target audience and key stakeholders to confirm that they adequately represent the task.

### SUMMARY

Standards that are based on a well-designed job or task analysis are fundamental to developing a valid certification program. You have available a number of proven methods for getting information about what people do, how they do it, and what they should have to do it well. The data-gathering techniques and the results from the job or task analysis will provide you with information you can use for other applications, such as developing training programs, hiring, awarding promotions, and conducting self-assessments. The following checklist and the previous set of guidelines (also provided on the accompanying disk) are intended to help you define the standards and conduct a job or task analysis. There are guidelines with detailed instructions on how to use the various data-gathering methods.

 ### CHECKLISTS

### Job or Task Analysis

Use the following checklist to evaluate your job or task analysis:

|  |  | YES | NO |
|---|---|---|---|
| A. | A job or task analysis was done. | ☐ | ☐ |
| B. | The job or task analysis included getting input from |  |  |
|  | • The people who do the job or task | ☐ | ☐ |
|  | • Supervisors | ☐ | ☐ |
|  | • Customers | ☐ | ☐ |
|  | • Others dependent on or vested in the quality of the job's or task's output | ☐ | ☐ |

|  | YES | NO |
|---|---|---|
| C. The process is documented. | ☐ | ☐ |
| D. The documentation includes | | |
|    • The basis on which people were selected to participate in the process | ☐ | ☐ |
|    • When the job or task analysis was done | ☐ | ☐ |
|    • Which tasks out of all of the tasks will be assessed as part of the certification | ☐ | ☐ |
|    • The people who decided which tasks were to be included | ☐ | ☐ |
|    • How the data were gathered (that is, what methods were used, such as NGT, DACUM, surveys, and so on) | ☐ | ☐ |
|    • What steps were taken to control | | |
|       Sampling error | ☐ | ☐ |
|       Design errors | ☐ | ☐ |
|       Administrative errors | ☐ | ☐ |
|    • Documents and records searched and verified | ☐ | ☐ |
|    • How many people were observed | ☐ | ☐ |
|    • The basis on which they were selected | ☐ | ☐ |
|    • How many people were interviewed | ☐ | ☐ |
|    • Which stakeholders they represent | ☐ | ☐ |
|    • The basis on which they were selected | ☐ | ☐ |
|    • How many people were surveyed | ☐ | ☐ |
|    • Which stakeholders they represent | ☐ | ☐ |
|    • How the data were analyzed | ☐ | ☐ |
|    • The basis on which tasks were rated (importance, difficulty, frequency) | ☐ | ☐ |
|    • The results and recommendations | ☐ | ☐ |

## Standards

Use the following checklist to evaluate how your standards were developed:

|  | YES | NO |
|---|---|---|
| A. There is documentation that describes how the data from the job or task analysis were converted into standards. | ☐ | ☐ |

|  | YES | NO |
|---|---|---|

B. There is a list of performances, including

- The conditions, or givens, based on

  Inputs, requests, directives, and so on ☐ ☐

  Desired business outcomes or the desired end state ☐ ☐

  Availability and access to aids, equipment, information, and so on ☐ ☐

- The criteria, or what will be accepted as evidence of proficiency (at different levels if appropriate) ☐ ☐

C. There is a list of who participated in the development of the task statements or descriptions, performance criteria, and performance levels (if appropriate):

- Authorities in the discipline ☐ ☐
- Exemplary practitioners ☐ ☐
- Clients, customers, or users of outcomes ☐ ☐
- Technical staff (experts in developing performance statements) ☐ ☐

D. The basis on which the people were selected is described. ☐ ☐

E. There is a process to review and validate the standards. ☐ ☐

 **PROCEDURES**

Here are some procedures for conducting a focus group, using the NGT, defining outcome-based competencies, and conducting a Delphi study:

### Focus Group

1. Determine the purpose of the focus group. What kind of information do you want to get? Why do you want it? Do you expect it to add clarity to other projects or initiatives?

2. Involve the target audience and other key stakeholders in developing the questions and identifying the types of people who should participate. (However, they should not be participants in the actual focus groups.)

3. Determine the number and size of the groups.

- One to four groups are usually sufficient for initial exploratory work.
- Six to eight groups are better for a more complete content analysis.
- Have six to twelve people in a group. Small groups' input may be biased due to existing relationships between participants. Very large groups make recording and controlling side conversations more difficult.

4. Determine the groups that you want the participants to represent (the same or different departments).

5. Set up a schedule, allocating time for developing questions, preparing the room, getting authorization for people to participate, briefing observers and recorders, conducting the sessions, compiling the results, analyzing the results, and drafting the report.

## The NGT

The NGT is a proven process for generating and ranking variables. It is designed to help achieve a consensus among experts without sacrificing individual ideas to "groupthink." It solicits input from a group of experts, who contribute ideas individually. The group then discusses, ranks, and weights each submitted idea. The process is structured to encourage participants to articulate a large number of responses (opinions) while reducing inhibitions about expressing unusual or uncommon ideas. The process accommodates and integrates diverse opinions held by experts from related disciplines and interests. It enables representatives to work together so they can pool their knowledge. The process allows for equal participation by all members. Since the process can build on the experience, research, and knowledge of both academics and practitioners, the results will have greater value. Here are some guidelines for using the process:

1. *Introduce the process.* Describe the purpose of the study and how the session will be structured. Explain that the process is designed to minimize group dynamics. Ask the first question.

2. *Generate answers.* Ask each person to privately generate and write down six to ten answers to the first question. Tell participants that answers should be in the active voice and no longer than five words. Each answer should follow the form *verb*-plus-*object*. Give the group five minutes to answer the question.

3. *Report out.* Ask each person to read one answer, in round-robin style. Write each response on a flipchart. If a person's answer has already been given, that person should supply a new answer. Continue the round-robin until everyone has read all of his or her answers.

4. *Discuss.* Ask the group if they would like to discuss, clarify, or explain any of their answers. Keep the discussion to a minimum.

5. *Combine.* Ask the group to identify any answers they feel could be combined or eliminated because of duplication. *Do not eliminate any answer without the expressed permission of the person who generated it.*

6. *Rank.* Ask each person to privately select, write down, and rank the five most important answers from all the ones that have been given.

7. *Assign values.* Ask each person to assign values to his or her five answers: 5 points to the most important, 4 points to the next important, and so on. Allow five minutes for this.

8. *Accumulate values.* Read the responses one by one and ask the group how many points they gave to each. Total the points for every response. Record and maintain all responses.

9. *Discuss the results.* Review the scores with the group and make any further adjustments.

10. *Proceed.* When the group is ready, proceed to the next question.

## Outcome-Based Competency Session

1. Display a sample of the chart (see Figure 3.19).

2. Ask the group to privately come up with a list of the typical tasks that make up a job or role.

3. Next, ask the group to share their lists, and record their responses on a flipchart. After everyone has exhausted his or her list, ask if there are any additions.

4. Repeat the process, asking the group to privately generate a list of what people have to know to do these tasks, what skills are needed, and what they would want as evidence that the tasks had been done well.

5. Take all of the information for each task or functional area, and summarize it into one or two sentences that describe what the task is, why it is done, and how it is done.

6. Validate the results with a larger population, including stakeholders other than the target audience.

7. Once the information is validated, use the information to develop assessment instruments.

## Delphi Study

1. Select a panel of experts. The panel should be made up of people who are knowledgeable about the issue but not in constant contact with one another. The size of the panel should be at least six but no more than twenty-five.

2. Confirm that group members are willing to participate in the process. Explain the protocols, including not contacting one another, remaining anonymous, and so on. If the group members represent different geographic areas, educational backgrounds, or some other variable you are interested

in, ask them to complete a form requesting demographics or their area of expertise.

3. Round One: present the question to everyone (this can be done at the same time as Step 2). The question should be open-ended. Explain how they are to get their answers back to you.

4. Have three people analyze the data independently, and then compare the results of their analyses. This minimizes having bias introduced by the people doing the analysis. In the analysis, eliminate redundancies and combine responses that reflect similar positions. If appropriate, arrange the responses along a spectrum or continuum.

5. Round Two: send the results of the analysis back to the panel for its assessment. Ask the panel to react privately to the modified position statements. Their reactions can be in the form of a positive or a negative response, a ranking of the statements on a scale, or a modification to the statements.

6. Reanalyze the panel's input by calculating the distribution of their responses. You should determine which responses received a mean (average) number of statements or indications of agreement, which fell in the top and lower quartiles, and which were one or more standard deviations above or below the mean.

7. Round Three: send your analysis and how the responses compare, and ask the panel to reassess their position based on the group's responses. Ask those panelists whose position varies significantly from the group's to provide a rationale in support of their view.

8. Analyze the responses and share the results, including the supporting statements for any minor opinions, with the whole panel.

9. Round Four: repeat steps 7 and 8 if necessary.

**Figure 3.19. Generic Outcome-Based Competency Chart**

*Definition: What is done, why it is done, and how it is done.*

| Tasks | Knowledge | Skills and Behaviors | Expected Results |
|---|---|---|---|
| The group of related activities required to accomplish the task, role, or function | The information people draw on to perform the task, role, or function | The intellectual, emotional, and physical behaviors required to perform the task, role, or function | The outputs, or work produced<br><br>The outcomes, or business impact of what was produced |

**WHERE TO LEARN MORE**

To learn more about defensible job or task analyses and job testing, get a copy of Title VII of the Civil Rights Act of 1964, Section 2000e-2, Unlawful Employment Practices, paragraph (h), and the Uniform Guidelines on Employee Selection Procedures. Sections 1607.5 through 1607.10 and section 1607.14 deal with validity. Section 1607.14 lists the technical standards for validity studies, including the standard that studies should be based on information about the job, technical standards for criterion-related validity studies, technical standards for content validity studies, and technical standards for construct validity studies.

Delbecq, A. L., and Van de Ven, A. H. *Group Techniques for Program Planning: a Guide to Nominal Group and Delphi Processes* (Glenview, IL: Scott, Foresman, 1975). This is the seminal research on these methods. It is also excellent reading.

Flanagan, J. C. "The Critical-Incident Technique," *Psychological Bulletin,* 1954, *51,* 327–358 (published by the American Psychological Association, 750 First Street, NE, Washington, DC 20002-4242).

Fowler, F. J., Jr. *Survey Research Methods* (Thousand Oaks, CA: Sage, 1984).

Mager, R. F. *Preparing Instructional Objectives* (Belmont, CA: Pitman Learning, 1984). A basic "how to" book everyone should have.

Norton, R. E. "DACUM: A Proven and Powerful Approach to Occupational Analysis." Paper presented at the 1192 Mid-America Competency-Based Education Conference, June 14–17, 1992, Chicago. Available through the Ohio Center on Education and Training for Employment, The Ohio State University, 1900 Kenny Road, Columbus, OH 43210-1260. This paper describes the DACUM process and includes an example of a DACUM chart listing duties and tasks. It also includes guidelines called conventions or standards that should be followed for the process to be labeled a DACUM occupational analysis.

Toseland, R. W., Rivas, R. F., and Chapman, D. "An Evaluation of Decision Making Methods in Task Groups," *Social Work,* July-August 1984, pp. 339–346 (published by the National Association of Social Workers).

Westgaard, O. *Tests That Work* (San Francisco, CA: Jossey-Bass/Pfeiffer, 1999). This book has excellent guidelines for writing questions, defining competence, and developing performance criteria.

# Chapter 4

# The Business Case

Ordinarily you will want to build a business case for a certification program before deciding on the requirements for the credential or conducting a job or task analysis. You might even develop a series of business cases, one for each of the major steps in creating a certification program. That is, you might want to develop a separate business case for

- Conducting a feasibility study to determine if there is a need or market for the program
- Determining if a certification program is an economically optimal solution to a problem
- Conducting a job or task analysis and developing the standards
- Developing and validating the assessment component
- Developing the required training or other prerequisite for the credential
- Implementing and administering the program

A business case presents a justification for why scarce funds should be allocated to developing a certification program and not to other competing projects. A business case requires you to examine and compare different alternative solutions or approaches to a problem. Some business cases argue for using funds to take advantage of an opportunity. Others argue for investing money in one specific solution to a problem versus another solution. A good business case explores the impact of pursuing different alternatives (doing nothing versus doing A, doing B, and so on). Every action has some financial effects; the reason you compare alternatives is to make sure you identify and implement the one that will have the greatest positive or least negative impact on the organization.

Thus a business case for a certification program must convince the reader that the organization should allocate resources (funds and people) to creating and deploying the program instead of doing something else with those resources. It should *not* answer the question "Should people be qualified to do the job?" Instead, it should answer questions like "Is certification the best way to make sure people are qualified or can perform to the same standard anywhere in the world?" or "Is certification the best way to confirm that people are performing to standard consistently?" or "Is certification the best strategy for accomplishing our goals?"

Management, whether in a business, a government agency, or a professional association, decides how to allocate funds. Some funds are already dedicated to covering fixed costs, such as facilities, depreciation, and salaries. Other funds are earmarked to cover the costs of making the product, such as raw materials, supplies, sales and marketing, product and customer support, packaging, and shipping and handling. Everything else (research and development, training, and programs like certification) competes for the remaining funds. A business case

- Increases the chance that the program can successfully compete for limited funding
- Reduces the likelihood of your having to ask for additional funding later (because writing a business case makes you think through what the direct and hidden costs will be to develop, implement, and support the program over time)
- Provides you and future certification managers with a reference point or history for use in evaluating the program so that you can improve and sustain it

## WHAT GOES INTO A BUSINESS CASE

What goes into a business case depends on what information management values when making their funding decisions. Therefore, the first thing to do is to build a relationship with the finance department and enlist their help in building a business case. Figure 4.1 lists what you might be asked to include. You may have to add or substitute other elements, depending on the specific decision-making or funding protocols of your organization.

**Figure 4.1. Items to Include in a Business Case**

A. A description of the problem or situation, including
  - The background and rationale for taking action, making a change, adopting a new strategy, and so on
  - What the problem costs now (expressed in terms meaningful to your management, such as lost time accidents, lost sales, cost of turnover, low productivity, cost of overtime due to lack of skills, overruns due to inadequate project management, and so on)
B. A description of the proposed solution (that is, the certification program)
C. An assessment of what the certification program will cost in terms of staff hours; equipment and materials; and external resources, for each major component, needed to
  - Design the component
  - Implement the component
  - Operate the component annually
  - Disengage the component if it fails to accomplish the intended goal or is replaced with an alternative
D. A description of what value or benefit will be gained by incurring these costs and an estimate of when those benefits will materialize or outweigh the costs you identified when describing the problem
E. A timeline for the necessary investments and expenditures
F. A description of the alternatives you considered and an explanation of why you rejected them
G. A description of what the major deliverables are
H. An overall timeline for the program, from development to implementation, with milestones
I. A description of barriers you identified and an explanation of how you intend to address them
J. A list of what your financial measures of success will be, indicating to whom they apply; for example:
  - Net present value or internal rate of return
  - Reduced costs (indicate for whom)
  - Reduced waste of time and materials
  - Decreased required working capital (indicate from whom)
  - Increased asset utilization (indicate by whom)
  - Cost savings or avoidance (indicate by whom)
  - Increased revenue (indicate for whom)
K. A list of other key success indicators that will be used; for example:
  - Rate of adoption
  - User acceptance
  - Impact on compliance
  - Time savings
  - Improved response time
  - Customer confidence
  - Customer retention
L. An explanation of how the certification program might leverage or optimize other investments

## HYPOTHESES, PREMISES, AND BEST GUESSES

Your argument for funding your certification program should be based on specific hypotheses. For example, one hypothesis might be that confirming that people can perform to standard is a more effective way (compared with the alternatives) for your organization to

- Secure or strengthen its market position
- Conceive, design, and introduce to market new products faster
- Improve investor, customer, or employee satisfaction
- Improve vendor alliances
- Eliminate or reduce fixed and variable costs, or avoid costs
- Improve the performance of a product, a process, or people
- Ensure some level of readiness for the future, through the continual development of people skills
- Comply with regulatory requirements

The alternatives might be to invest in well-thought-out employee selection criteria and screening tools, to add training programs, to identify and leverage the organization's core competencies, to develop detailed performance criteria, or to implement an apprenticeship program. Your recommending a certification program, then, would be based on the hypothesis (whether explicit or inferred) that supporting $X$ (certification) will result in $Y$ (getting a pool of people who can perform to standard faster and at less cost), and $X$ is a better choice than $M$, $N$, or $O$. You want to prove that certification is the best strategy, knowing that it isn't the only viable strategy. Your goal is to show through your business case that a certification program offers additional net benefits compared with those other choices. For example, you might want to show that a certification program can

1. Integrate human resource criteria (for hiring, selection, promotion, development, and retention) with the performance management process
2. Help you identify the performance criteria that best correlate with
   - Business economics (costs, revenues, and profit)
   - Performance (product, process, and people)
   - Satisfaction (investor, customer, and employee)
   - Employee development (number and quality of employees prepared for today and the future)

3. Promote membership growth, increased sales of ancillary services (such as books and training), and increased attendance at regional and national conferences

Therefore, your hypothesis is that certification is the best alternative.

## METRICS, OR KEY SUCCESS INDICATORS

Every good business case is based on metrics, the factors that will be used to compare the different strategies and determine the probability that a program will live up to expectations. Some metrics are financial; others have financial implications but are more likely couched in language about safety, customer satisfaction, market edge, improved performance, and so on. For example:

- Enerpac's hypotheses were that certification would

  - Increase revenues—that is, increase the sale of parts and the company's share of the after-market business. The metrics were the number of parts sold and their dollar value.

  - Increase customer satisfaction. The metrics were ratings on customer satisfaction surveys.

  - Reduce the cost of service—that is, lower the internal costs to support field technicians. The metrics were the number of support center calls and the time spent handling those calls.

  - Ensure continuous improvement—that is, provide a way to continuously improve the service centers' and technicians' competencies. The metrics were the number of calls to the support center and the number of technicians that completed the training.

- The Florida Small Business Centers' hypothesis was that certified business analysts (versus noncertified ones) would increase small business owners' use of the Centers' resources and that this, in turn, would result in economically stronger businesses. The metrics included the number of small businesses that took advantage of the Centers' services, the number of services those businesses used, and how those numbers correlated with business failures and improved economic position among Florida small businesses.

- The Association for Worksite Health Promotion's hypothesis was that certification would become the preferred criteria for employers. The metric would be the number of times the words *certified preferred* appeared in job announcements.

- ABB's hypotheses were that

  - Certification was a cost-effective way to create uniform standards. The metrics included the number of standards developed, the number of people certified, and the time (in months) that it took to get people certified.

  - Uniform standards would positively impact profits. The metrics included the correlation between the number of people certified and pretax profit.

- The American Architectural Manufacturers Association's central hypothesis was that certification would reduce the number of complaints against manufacturers. The metrics were the number of complaints, correlated with the number of certified contractors.

- Amway's hypotheses were that certifying trainers would increase the retention of trainers and distributors and support sales. The metrics were the time (speed) it took to get at least 50 percent of the trainers certified, the number of trainers certified by country, and how those numbers correlated with retention of trainers and distributors, sales, and the success of product launches.

- The IFMA's goals were to ensure professional excellence, to establish standards for professional practice, to increase recognition for the profession in the organization and community, and to influence the direction of the profession. Underlying these goals were the hypotheses that certification would attract members, increase participation at regional and national conferences, increase revenues through the sale of educational programs and publications, and position the association to become the "official voice" of the profession. The metrics used to evaluate the success of the program were

  - The number of members who joined because of the certification

  - Attendance at conferences

  - Sales volume of educational programs and materials

  - The number of educational programs that sought IFMA's endorsement

  - The number of program providers (manufacturers of furnishings, speakers, and chapters) that wanted to be registered by IFMA

  - The percent of facility managers who became members

  - The number of other nations that wanted to adopt IFMA's standards for their own certifications

## Economic Metrics

The two economic metrics most often used to evaluate the worth of a proposed program are costs and cash flow (also referred to as return on investment, or ROI).

***Costs.*** Certifications are frequently put into place based on the argument that they will help the organization reduce or avoid costs. For example, organizations implement certifications to reduce the costs of sales and service, of producing a product or service, of recruiting and retention, of bringing people to a certain level of proficiency, of bringing a product to market, of continuous improvement, and of regulatory agencies' fines.

When you base your business case primarily on the potential to control costs, it is important to understand the difference between eliminating, reducing, and avoiding costs: an organization eliminates or reduces current costs and avoids future costs. Figure 4.2 shows the difference.

**Figure 4.2. Differences Between Eliminating, Reducing, and Avoiding Costs**

| *Current costs* | *If you do nothing* | *If you certify* | *If you do something else* |
|---|---|---|---|
| Cost A. | Cost A stays the same. | Cost A is eliminated. | Cost A is reduced. |
| Cost B. | Cost B goes up. | Cost B is reduced. | Cost B is reduced. |
| Cost C. | Cost C stays the same. | Cost C is the same. | Cost C is the same. |
| | Cost D (a new cost) is added. | Cost D is avoided. | Cost D is partly avoided. |
| | | Cost E (a new cost) is added. | Cost E is avoided. |
| | | | Cost F (a new cost) is added. |

For example, if you want to argue that certification will cause the cost of service to go down, then you should show first what makes up the cost of service and second how each of those cost components will be affected by doing nothing, by implementing certification, and by doing something else. You should also compare the new costs that will be added or avoided for each alternative. If you want to argue that certification will reduce the cost of sales or increase revenues, begin by showing a breakdown of the costs required to generate the revenues and of how and by how much certification will affect those costs. Next, you can present your logic for why certification will increase revenues. Remember to include any new costs (fixed, startup, and ongoing) that will be incurred to actualize each alternative; otherwise you will have an incomplete picture.

***Cash Flow, or Return on Investment.*** Discounted-cash flow (DCF) is an approach to capital budgeting that focuses on cash inflows and outflows and the time value of money. According to Horngren, Sundem, and Selto, approximately 85 percent of the large industrial firms in the United States use DCF models to compare potential investments—that is, to determine the return on investment (ROI). Whenever a program affects more than one year's budget, the initial investment is often referred to as a capital outlay. All programs that require capital outlays involve risk, because the organization cannot accurately forecast the net return or the cost of money over the life of the program. Thus if a proposed certification program requires a capital outlay, your organization will weigh the financial risks if the hypotheses do prove true and the risks if they do *not* prove true. Finance departments use one of two DCF formulas; both are based on the theory of compound interest.

*Net present value* and *internal rate of return* are two robust ways of determining return on investment (ROI). Each method uses a formula that treats tomorrow's dollars as equivalent in value to today's dollars. Net present value is the difference between the *present* value of a project's expected *future benefits* compared with the *present* value of its expected *future costs.*

Internal rate of return is the discount rate that exactly equates the project's *present* value of the *expected benefits* to the *present* value of its *expected costs.* Both formulas factor in the rate of inflation, the cost of money, depreciation schedules, marginal tax rates, and labor rates. Both models require a considerable amount of information and judgment to implement. Here is the kind of information that an information systems group would have to provide to justify any investment, including a certification program:

- A clear purpose statement and an explanation of the group's basic assumptions about the implications of doing nothing versus those of doing something. The group cited the cost of errors and downtime, risks to data, and lost productivity due to system failures. You might cite lost opportunities, lost sales, cost of sales, cost of service, and so on.

- A description of feasible alternatives, such as buying standardized tests versus developing performance tests, delivering training on-line versus delivering it in the classroom, developing performance checklists to be used by supervisors versus conducting testing on-line, and so on.

- A projection of benefits (in terms of revenues or cost savings) for each year for each alternative. The number of years you should include depends on your rollout plan, key milestones, the expected life of each alternative, and your organization's financial protocols. Usually three years is sufficient. Sometimes you are asked only to supply what will be gained, such as less time to get people to proficiency and a reduced sales cycle. Your finance department will convert those gains to dollars.

- Cost projections in dollars for each year and each alternative, including
  - Any initial capital expenditures to buy software and equipment to support an intranet (or any other system) that will be used to track candidates' progress, register candidates, do on-line testing, deliver training, and so on
  - An estimate of developer time (in hours, for the first year and for subsequent years) to develop and maintain tests, develop the training, and so on

- An estimate of the project manager's time (in hours or a percentage of time, for the first year and for subsequent years) to coordinate meetings, conduct the job or task analysis, do acceptance testing, and so on

- Any preparation costs, such as for training or expert help, to bring the team up to speed on what it has to know and do to ensure program success

- The risks associated with each alternative, such as people's unwillingness to be trained or assessed on-line, increased travel costs if classroom and on-site assessment are used, and so on.

## Noneconomic Metrics

Most proposed certification programs are promoted based on anticipated noneconomic benefits, such as safety, image, customer satisfaction, retention of employees and customers, due diligence, and so on. Noneconomic metrics can be quantified, but usually not in economic terms. For example:

- Organizations usually measure safety in terms of the number of reported accidents. This measure has economic value an organization may take for granted; that is, the organization may decide to track only the *number* of accidents and lost days and compare these numbers to what happened in previous years, versus calculating the *cost* of accidents and lost days.

- Organizations measure the capability of third parties, contractors, and employees in terms of number of training days, number of credentials earned, productivity, performance, and customer satisfaction. It is in an organization's best interests to (1) demonstrate due diligence or prudence by showing that it took steps to ensure that only qualified people perform certain tasks, (2) improve productivity or performance by confirming that only capable people perform certain tasks, and (3) support sales and marketing by earning customers' confidence through assurances that they will be serviced only by qualified people. An economic value can be determined for each of the following examples but is usually inferred:

  - *Prudence* is measured in terms of estimates of avoided lawsuits and complaints, reduced insurance claims, and reduced regulatory fines. All of these can be expressed in dollar terms if management requires it.

  - *Productivity* is measured in terms of the time it takes to produce or service a specific number of units (products or customers).

  - *Performance* is measured in terms of compliance with a standard. It is possible to calculate the dollar value of noncompliance; however, this is usually difficult for most organizations to do.

  - *Customer confidence* is measured in terms of the number of repeat customers, customer loyalty, and customer satisfaction scores.

**THE REQUIREMENTS**

When developing your business case, you have to decide what you want to fund as part of your certification program and what should be funded as part of other initiatives. Usually the business case will include the costs to do a job or task analysis; the costs to develop the standards; the costs to develop the assessment instruments and procedures; the costs to purchase any electronic systems to help administer the program, do testing on-line, and so on; the costs to staff the effort; and the costs to secure expert advice.

However, if your certification program requires candidates to complete training, gain experience, or earn an external credential, then you must decide if you want to include these costs. If the training will be developed and delivered whether or not people are certified, then you should not include them as part of your costs; instead, focus on how the certification will leverage that investment. Mentoring and apprenticeship programs, job rotations, and special assignments designed to accelerate people's opportunity to gain experience may also be funded either separately or as part of your program.

**MISSTEPS AND OVERSIGHTS**

Here are two common mistakes people make when building a case for a certification program:

1. *Overreliance on a champion's support.* It is a mistake to rely too heavily on one champion to support a certification program. You must have a champion to get initial funding and support for adoption and deployment, but you must also have a powerful business case to sustain the investment. Indeed, a powerful business case will back up your champion's support and actions. Many programs are established because a powerful leader wants a certain program as a personal legacy—a way to be remembered over time. Unfortunately, champions get distracted by newer initiatives or leave, only to be replaced by other powerful personalities. Eventually, their programs must compete with newer ones (perhaps initiated by younger champions for similar reasons) for funds. Programs that are legacies of powerful leaders instead of viable strategies in their own right will find themselves underfunded, understaffed, and floundering. A business case establishes a certification program as a viable strategy, not just the pet project of an individual.

2. *Failure to involve the finance department early on.* Another common mistake is failing to involve up front the people who understand the organization's economics. People who understand the organization's finances and business drivers can help quantify the dollar value of the current problem and come up with viable economic measures for showing how a certification program is the best strategy for solving it. Most human resource and training professionals lack skills in business economics or are not perceived as

credible when it comes to financial issues. Between their lack of financial skills and their image as "people people," they risk having their arguments discounted from the beginning. To construct a successful business case, involve the finance department and key stakeholders right from the start. Finance people know the organization's business goals and issues in dollar terms, its accounting practices, how resources are valued, and how to structure a business case that meets management's decision-making criteria.

**TIPS**

Here are some tips for how to build an effective business case:

1. *Involve the finance department.* Involve a respected member of the finance or accounting department early in the process. Keep him or her informed of what you want to accomplish, how you are going about designing the program, what you learned as a result of your job or task analysis, and what key customers expect. Seek his or her advice on how to translate your findings into economic or financial metrics that management can relate to.

2. *Define and quantify the problem early on.* Tell people in the beginning what the problem is, what it is costing the organization, and what a certification program will do to solve it (for example, "A certification program will provide a process to ensure that our people are qualified" or "Certification will confirm that everyone in a job category can perform to the same standard"). If you assume that your audience already knows what you are talking about (that is, the problem), then you risk their not paying attention to your presentation. If they don't understand the basic problem, they'll be wondering "What is this about?" or continually interrupting you with questions.

3. *Include alternatives in your business case.* There is a natural tendency to present only the features and benefits of the program you are proposing and not to mention alternative strategies for solving the problem at hand. However, by fairly describing other choices, you will come across as an objective team player interested in the greater good of the organization, not just a zealot for certification. You will also be in a better position to respond to counterproposals. So, describe the pros and cons of just relying on a curriculum, or just adding tests to training, or holding managers accountable for their people's performance, and so on. These recommendations have merit; however, they have not always been successful in and of themselves.

4. *Learn about activity-based costing and cost drivers.* You will find it easier to understand and discuss the economics of your case if you have some basic knowledge of activity-based costing and cost drivers. Activity-based costing is an accounting system designed specifically to identify costs and support

cost management. Organizations engage in activities to create products and deliver services. Activity-based costing helps you identify those activities and their associated costs. Cost drivers are operating practices (activities) that cause an organization to consume too many resources or very costly ones. The major cost drivers are poorly designed processes (because they use resources inefficiently), people who lack the appropriate skills for the task (because they are inefficient, cause rework, or require extra supervision), and not fully understanding customer and product requirements (which results in rework).

5. *Include the cost of disengaging from financial commitments should it become necessary.* Sometimes your plan calls for you to make a significant financial commitment, such as to purchase or lease equipment, contract for training, and so on. Include in your plan the cost to extricate yourself from such commitments, in case you find the resource or service less than effective or you want to take advantage of more effective resources that become available later.

6. *Involve your key stakeholders.* Stakeholders either vote or influence those who do. They are the closest to the problem; they know what good performance looks like and what happens when it is present and absent. They know the implications downstream for customers, service, and costs when people lack the capability to perform to standard. Therefore, it only makes sense to solicit their help when you build your business case.

7. *Keep the language of your business case specific and to the point.* Here are some suggestions to increase the chances that your business case will be read and understood:

   - Use the active voice, not the passive voice.
   - Use second person (you), not third person (we or they).
   - Use the language of your audience, not HR's language.
   - Include examples.
   - Be specific.
   - Keep sentences short and to the point. Your word processor can give you the reading level of your report. A lower reading level helps people get through the report faster and reduces the chances of misunderstanding. Aim for an eighth-grade reading level.
   - Use numbered or bulleted points or lists. Solid blocks of text are harder to read and comprehend when time is limited.
   - Information Mapping[1] is a style proven to help both the writer and the reader. It helps you write more clearly and the reader understand the content.

8. *Use visual aids to present your business case.* Use overheads or slides as part of your presentation. They help communicate concepts and relationships. When creating your visual aids,

- Limit the number of lines per visual aid to no more than six
- Limit the number of words per line to six to ten
- Limit the text to the main points; add detail through your oral remarks
- Use colors that are easy to read, such as medium blue for the background and dark yellow for the text

9. *Practice your delivery.* Here are some suggestions to help focus your audience's attention on your argument and not on your delivery skills:

- Establish eye contact at least once with everyone in your audience.
- Repeat any questions asked, to confirm your understanding and to make sure everyone in the room heard the question.
- Practice to minimize any physical or verbal distracting mannerisms.
- Minimize any physical barriers between you and your audience.
- If you use visual aids, do not block their projection.
- Pace your presentation so that you can move through all of the content in the time allocated.
- Speak loudly and clearly to ensure you are heard and understood.

 **GUIDELINES**    **Business Case**

A business case can take many forms and be presented in many ways. For example, you can use slides, present the case in an executive meeting, or submit a written proposal. Whatever form it takes, it should be accompanied by supporting detail. Here are some guidelines for presenting your business case:

A.  Begin with an overview. Consider the possibility that this will be the only section people will read; thus they should get a decent sense of what the case is about and what you want from them.

1. If you are preparing a written report, the overview should be about one page long and contain

- The purpose of the report.
- What the mandate is and what problem certification will solve.
- What certification means or entails.
- Why the readers should care and what's in it for them.
- Your recommendations or conclusions.

- How the report is organized.
- What you expect of the readers (approval, funding, and so on).
- A brief description of the work you did to come to your conclusions or recommendations; include the dollar values of the cash flow method you used.

2. If you are making an oral report, the overview should cover

- What you are and are not going to discuss.
- What certification means and what it entails.

**Figure 4.3. Sample Cost Breakout for a Certification Program**

| *Year One* | *Year Two* |
|---|---|
| *Staff time (in hours)*<br>Lead coordinator: _____<br>Job/task analysis: #_____ @ _____<br>Train observers: _____<br>Develop standards: _____<br>Graphic artist: _____<br>Develop the test: _____<br>Pilot the test: _____ | *Staff time (in hours)*<br>Lead coordinator: _____<br>Trainer: _____ |
| *Equipment*<br>Software: _____<br>Computer terminals: _____<br>Scanner: _____ | *Equipment*<br>Computer terminals: _____<br>Sample products for the simulation: _____ |
| *Materials and other resources*<br>PR materials: $ _____ | *Materials and other resources*<br>Off-the-shelf training materials: $ _____<br>Standardized tests: $ _____<br>External credentials: $ _____ |
| *Consulting services*<br>Job/task analysis: $ _____<br>Standards: $ _____<br>Training developer: $ _____<br>Test developer: $ _____<br>Self-assessments: $ _____ | *Consulting services*<br>Trainers: $ _____<br>Facilitators: $ _____<br>Psychometrician: $ _____ |

- Why the listeners should care and what's in it for them.

- Whether or not you will use visual aids, handouts, or other supporting documents.

- Whether you want questions during your presentation or at the end.

- How your report is organized. Number your points, alternatives, or main sections (for example, "There are three reasons for supporting certification; the first reason is $x$, the second is $y$, and the third is $z$").

B.  Next, repeat the same information, but in greater detail.

1.  This is the body of the report or presentation. This is the part where you give your facts, arguments, evidence, and details.

2.  Begin with the general and support it with specifics (deductive), or go from the specific to the general (inductive), *but don't mix the two approaches.*

- The inductive approach begins with the details that constitute the problem (point 1, point 2, point 3, and so on) and then presents the conclusion (that a certification program is the best way to solve the problem just discussed).

- The deductive approach begins with the conclusion (what certification is and why it is the best alternative) and then presents the supporting evidence that supports that conclusion (detail 1, detail 2, detail 3, and so on). The deductive approach is usually best when time is limited. It also keeps your audience focused on your argument instead of wondering what certification is.

3.  Use the same numbering or sequence of topics you used in the overview.

C.  Summarize the main points.

1.  Recall or restate the main points.

2.  Close with a statement that says *what you want from them.*

D.  Finally, add a section that contains the details, such as the names of the people who provided input or helped develop the business case, where the data came from, a cost breakout for each alternative, and so on (see Figure 4.3).

## SUMMARY

The business case is an often overlooked key ingredient to getting support for a certification program. It has particular importance when the goal is to institutionalize the certification—that is, to make it *"the* way" that the organization prepares and qualifies people or recognizes people who have satisfied a set of requirements. Therefore, you must fully understand the driver behind the certification program and what you want it to affect. The best way to gain this understanding is by involving the people who have the most to gain from your program's success. Make it a point to better understand your organization's financial models and the programs your proposal will be competing against. Demonstrate sensitivity to the organization's issues and way of doing business, to increase your credibility and to encourage others to help you be successful. Get your facts (or at least your assumptions) together. Many organizations do not know their costs or even their cost drivers, which is why certification programs prove to be effective vehicles for measuring performance and correlating the results with other variables. The following checklist and previous set of guidelines (both also on the accompanying disk) are provided to help you work with finance and other stakeholders to build an effective argument for a certification program.

## CHECKLIST

### Business Case

Here is a checklist to help you evaluate your business case:

|  | YES | NO |
|---|---|---|
| A. The business case includes | ☐ | ☐ |
| • A description of the problem or situation | ☐ | ☐ |
| • A description of the solution (that is, the proposed certification program) | ☐ | ☐ |
| • A discussion of how certification relates to an organizational initiative | ☐ | ☐ |
| • A discussion of the probability of negative impact if nothing is done | ☐ | ☐ |
| B. The negative impact of doing nothing is described in terms of | | |
| • Costs, such as the costs to recruit, staff, develop, retain, and so on | ☐ | ☐ |
| • Safety, either of people or of other assets | ☐ | ☐ |
| • Public image (community or investor) | ☐ | ☐ |
| • Compliance | ☐ | ☐ |
| C. There is a list of required expenditures and commitments to move forward, such as | | |
| • Estimated staff hours | ☐ | ☐ |
| • Estimated budget | ☐ | ☐ |
| • Estimated need for other resources, such as technology, expert help, and so on | ☐ | ☐ |
| • When organizational commitment to proceed is needed | ☐ | ☐ |

| | YES | NO |
|---|---|---|
| D. The business case lists alternatives and | | |
| • The reason for their rejection | ☐ | ☐ |
| • What factors were used to compare them | ☐ | ☐ |
| E. There is a cost projection that covers the cost to | | |
| • Design the program | ☐ | ☐ |
| • Implement the program | ☐ | ☐ |
| • Sustain the program | ☐ | ☐ |
| • Disengage, if projections fail to materialize or the need is eliminated | ☐ | ☐ |
| F. The case details | | |
| • The value to be gained if it is carried out (the measures of achievement) | ☐ | ☐ |
| • The amount of time it will take to realize the gain | ☐ | ☐ |
| • Any identified barriers to success, including any vested interests that might be against certification | ☐ | ☐ |
| • How those barriers will be addressed | ☐ | ☐ |
| • The economic and noneconomic measures of success | ☐ | ☐ |
| G. There is a project plan that includes | | |
| • Major tactics | ☐ | ☐ |
| • Milestones | ☐ | ☐ |
| • Deliverables | ☐ | ☐ |
| • A timeline | ☐ | ☐ |
| • Resources needed, by type and volume | ☐ | ☐ |
| H. Finance has been consulted. | ☐ | ☐ |

**WHERE TO LEARN MORE**

The first three books helped me better understand business economics.

Cokins, G., Stratton, A., and Helbling, J. *An ABC Manager's Primer: Straight Talk on Activity-Based Costing* (Montvale, NJ: Institute of Management Accountants, 1992).

Droms, W. G. *Finance and Accounting for Non-Financial Managers* (Reading, MA: Addison-Wesley, 1990).

Hawkins, P. *The Ecology of Commerce* (New York: HarperCollins, 1993). Just read Chapter Nine, "The Opportunity of Insignificance."

Stalk, G., and Hout, T. *Competing Against Time* (New York: Free Press, 1990). Pay attention to pages 76 and 77.

Horngren, C. T., Sundem, G. L., with Selto, F. H. *Introduction to Management Accounting, Ninth Edition* (Englewood Cliffs, NJ: Prentice Hall, 1993).

Hale, J. A., *The Performance Consultant's Fieldbook: Tools and Techniques for Improving Organizations and People* (San Francisco: Jossey-Bass/Pfeiffer, 1998). The chapters on costs and measurement add to what is covered in this book.

Any of the "Finance for Non-Finance Managers" booklets provided by professional associations.

**NOTE**

1. Information Mapping is a registered service mark and Info-Map® is a registered trademark of Information Mapping, Inc., 300 Third Avenue, Waltham MA 02154 (617-890-7003).

# Chapter 5

# Assessment

Although it is true that passing a test is often the main requirement for certification, this does not mean it is necessarily the best prerequisite for your credential. Before choosing to require a test, you should first agree on why you want the certification program and what the requirements and standards should be. Otherwise a test could be nothing more than an arbitrary hurdle people have to clear. Defining the need, deciding on the requirements, and developing the standards will help you justify your decision to require or not require a test and, if you do require one, determine what the test will cover and how you will administer it.

Not all certifications use tests. For example, if your certification program only calls for candidates to complete a training course or curriculum, then all that will be required is a record of their attendance. In other situations, certification programs may incorporate tests as a part of their training, but the test results are used to evaluate the training, not candidates' knowledge or ability. For example, a major automobile manufacturer requires all of its employees to be certified. The certification is based on employees' completing three training programs:

- A self-administered unit on the history and philosophy of the company. After completing this course, employees take an on-line multiple choice test. The system records who took the test and when. The system also tells the employee which items were answered correctly and incorrectly and where to find the correct answer in the training materials.

- A self-administered unit on the cars the company manufactures. This training emphasizes product features, benefits, and how the company's cars compare to the competition's. A self-scored test is included to reinforce the content.

- A unit on handling customers. This unit emphasizes the company's philosophy concerning customer relations, including procedures for complaint resolution and where to direct customers who need information or have a problem. The classroom version uses role-plays; the self-study version has scenarios or descriptions of customer situations, followed by multiple-choice questions.

In all three training programs, the test results are used to evaluate the training, not the candidates' knowledge or ability. If people tend to misunderstand certain points, then the certification manager improves or eliminates the misleading questions or works with the training department to enhance or supplement the materials.

For many people, assessment means testing—they are one and the same thing. Yet, tests are only one form of assessment. Most certifications involve assessments other than or in addition to tests.

## DEFINITIONS

*To assess* is to determine value or worth. Assessing is judging; it is evaluating whether something or someone met a standard. Therefore, assessments apply to all of your requirements, not just candidates' skills, knowledge, and performance. For example, depending on your requirements, you could assess candidates' experience, education, ethics, and work samples. Many years ago I managed a certification program. Two of the requirements were sound financial practices and ethical business practices, because one of the job duties was handling other people's money. My job was to confirm whether or not candidates met these requirements. The process required each candidate to undergo an audit by a certified public accountant and submit a statement from the accountant attesting to the candidate's sound accounting practices. I contacted the relevant local Better Business Bureau, state's attorney's office, and state licensing boards to see if candidates had any record of criminal complaints, civil lawsuits, or professional censure. The criteria were that candidates could not receive the certification if they had been found guilty or liable for fraudulent business practices. I didn't care about traffic citations, domestic disputes, or other charges not related to business. I did look for indications of questionable business and ethical practices, however (specifically, fraud, embezzlement, and theft).

Associations, in particular, typically include education and experience requirements in their certification programs. This means they have to assess, or judge, the worthiness of candidates' education and experience. Associations assess education by whether or not it was obtained at an accredited institution or a program approved by them. They can even specify the amount of credits that must be earned in a specific discipline or in specific courses. Evaluating people's experience, particularly the quality of their previous work, is more difficult without direct access to their work records. Therefore, associations tend to allow candidates to substitute experience for education and vice versa (*x* years of experience equals *y* years of schooling). They may require a detailed description of the work experience, though, with a definition of duties and, perhaps, the level of responsibility or decision authority.

Businesses, too, judge whether or not candidates' experience and training satisfy their certification requirements. However, businesses are in a better position than are associations to judge the quality of candidates' experience, because they have access to work records and performance reviews. Businesses can require that experience include specific levels of responsibility in addition to specific duties, such as approval of budgets, headcounts, business agreements, and so on. Like associations, they tend to assess education based on whether or not it was obtained at an accredited institution or through an approved program.

Judging the adequacy or appropriateness of your certification requirements depends on the goal of the program and the standards candidates have to satisfy. If the goal is to ensure that candidates went through a particular process in earning their degree or were exposed to a particular body of knowledge, then the requirement might be to submit a transcript from an accredited school that shows a minimum number of credits in a specific discipline. You might also accept a certificate from an approved program.

If the goal is to ensure that candidates have demonstrated some level of proficiency in their past positions, then the assessment will require a review of their work history (specifically, the duties they performed or responsibilities they had). You might also accept a record of volunteer work. You might even insist that candidates have an external credential such as Certified Public Accountant or Certified Safety Professional.

The point is that to assess education and experience fairly, you have to agree on why they are important, what you want to learn about the candidate, what you will accept as evidence of his or her satisfying the criteria, and what you are going to do with the information. For example:

- NCIDQ requires a combination of education and experience before a candidate is eligible to take its exam. Candidates can have less experience if they have completed an accredited program in interior design or a related field. The accepted related fields are defined and include disciplines like architecture and art. The experience, too, is defined, as full-time work with an interior design or architectural firm. NCIDQ requires transcripts and signed affidavits attesting to the relevance of the candidate's experience.

- IFMA also requires a combination of education and experience. Again, candidates can have less experience if they have earned a degree from an approved program. To meet the experience requirement, candidates complete a very detailed work history to prove that they have performed specific tasks or had certain responsibilities. Initially the results of the assessment were used to exempt candidates from taking the exam; now they are used to confirm a minimum level of proficiency in at least six of the required competency areas. IFMA does not require copies of transcripts or signed statements attesting to the accuracy of the work profile; however, it does check candidates' references.

- An automobile manufacturer requires its dealers' automotive technicians to have a minimum of sixty months of experience and to complete a university or other advanced educational program in automotive mechanics to be eligible for the company's master technician certificate. The manufacturer requires a signed statement from the dealership, attesting to the accuracy of the candidate's work record. The manufacturer also has on file a history of candidates' previously earned certifications and education records.

The most-used and most-expected type of assessment is the test. A test is any device or method used to judge if people possess or can apply (or both) a body of knowledge or set of skills. What exactly the test determines depends on the goal of the program and what the standard for "passing" the test is. For example:

- If the goal of the certification program is to develop people, then the test should assess whether or not people have learned—that is, whether they know or can do more after completing a development program than they knew or could do beforehand. This is usually done by giving a pretest and a posttest.

- If the goal of the certification program is to confirm that people possess certain knowledge or can perform certain tasks, then the test should directly assess their knowledge or their ability to do those tasks. The test may or may not be done in conjunction with training.

- If the goal of the certification program is to determine if people's work meets a standard, then the assessment should compare candidates' work samples (or observations of how they did the work) to that standard.

- If the goal of the certification program is to recognize people whose work consistently meets a standard, then the assessment should compare a historical series of work samples or observations to that standard.

The point to remember is that whenever tests are used to judge people's knowledge or ability, it is important to link the test to the job or task analysis and performance standards.

## RIGOR AND VALIDITY

Rigor and validity are considerations no matter what form an assessment takes. How rigorous you should be depends on what you plan to do with the results. If the assessment will be used to make decisions affecting a candidate's employability, opportunities, or compensation, then you must ensure (and be able to prove) that the test or the criteria used to judge experience, ethics, and so on are valid. There is one way to prove validity—show that people who pass the test (or satisfy the criteria) can perform the task and that those who don't, can't. Tests are valid when scores correlate positively with people's ability to perform the job or task (that is, when performance on the test predicts performance on the job). Therefore, the more the test looks like the task, the easier it is to prove the test's validity. Since performance tests, by design, emulate the actual task, it is easier to prove their validity than it is to prove the validity of knowledge and skills tests.

Proving the validity of knowledge and skills tests is a two-step process. First you have to prove that the knowledge or skill is required to do the job or task (that is, that people who have the knowledge perform much better than those who don't); second you have to prove that your test actually assesses that knowledge or skill and not something else, like reading or test-taking ability.

The same three sources of bias that affect job and task analyses—sampling error, design error, and administrative error—apply to assessment design and development as well. Failure to control these sources of bias can undermine the validity of a test or assessment. In a test, *sampling error* occurs when test items do not adequately sample the required body of knowledge, the objectives of the training, the activities that make up the task, or the criteria used to judge the adequacy of a product or performance. *Design error* occurs when the test items are inappropriate for what you want to discover or confirm. *Administrative error* occurs when you are not consistent in how you deliver or score the test.

### Sampling Error

Sampling, in terms of designing a test, means choosing what performances, training objectives, or elements of a task you want to test. Sampling errors happen when your test either underrepresents the knowledge, skill, or performance required or focuses on extraneous abilities instead of what the job or task analysis discovered was important or critical.

***Underrepresentation.*** Underrepresentation occurs when you generalize that candidates know or can do something based on testing only a small subset of the important knowledge or skills required. This is a major problem for organizations that want to certify people in jobs where the required knowledge is not stable, such as in the computer and telecommunications industries. It is very difficult to sample content that is constantly changing. For example, field technicians service equipment and systems that use a wide range of technologies, vary in age, and are built by different manufacturers. This presents a problem for utilities and manufacturers of heavy equipment that want to certify their employees.

To avoid underrepresentation, the test developer has to be reasonably sure of what content to test (that is, what to sample), at what level to test it, and how to test it. If your test is made up of performance items, then one approach is to select samples that exemplify a basic set of operating principles or represent the most common or problematic models. Another approach is to test candidates' knowledge of fundamental operating principles (and perhaps train them on those principles as well). Here is how some organizations decided what to test:

- Enerpac has hundreds of different types of hydraulic pumps in the field. The pumps last a long time. Customers use them in widely diverse settings, such as shipping (where they are subjected to salt water), mining (where they are subjected to extreme heat), and automotive manufacturing (where they are an integral part of a larger system). It is not feasible to test technicians on all of the pumps they might possibly have to service, much less on their individual applications. So Enerpac decided to combine a performance test with training on the principles of hydraulics. The pumps selected for performance testing represent widely used models. Technicians are sent a pump to repair. They have access to the manuals, gauges, and other equipment they would normally use when repairing pumps. The technicians can even check their own work before returning it to be judged.

- A major utility's training center simulates the hybrid switching systems technicians are likely to find in the field. The hybrid switching systems are used both in training and for testing. The field technicians service and repair switches of different ages, so the center's switches must represent both out-of-date and newer technologies. Technicians also have to use whatever computer is on-site, so the center also has different brands of computers with different operating systems.

- The manufacturer of HVAC systems cannot predict the models or even the brands of equipment its technicians will have to service and repair. Its technicians service building control systems for all types of businesses, including health care centers, warehouses, research laboratories, power plants, freestanding retail stores, shopping malls, office complexes, even nurseries and wineries. The systems they service may have equipment from different manufacturers that use different technologies. There are also regional differences that require different system capabilities. In addition, earthquakes, tornadoes, hurricanes, floods, drought, high humidity, heavy snow, and so on challenge the equipment. Technicians have to know how the environment affects the equipment and how to install or replace it so it will be less susceptible to environmental damage. It is critical that the technicians be able to quickly restore the systems and prevent future breakdowns, as some of the equipment is used to maintain carefully controlled environments; slight differences in temperature and humidity can put inventory or people's health at risk. To meet these challenges, the manufacturer chose to develop different levels of certification. The first level assesses technicians' ability to perform a core set of procedures that apply to most equipment. The next level assesses technicians' knowledge of specific product lines. Performance tests are used for both levels of certification. They are administered in the field by supervisors.

***Extraneous Abilities.***   Similarly, you should not generalize that candidates are proficient at a task when the test items predominantly cover skills and knowledge that are outside of what is required to perform the task to standard. This mistake happens when stakeholders impose an attribute they admire on an assessment. For example:

- *Cleanliness of an employee's work area.* Cleanliness is certainly a desirable trait. However, cleanliness should not be tested unless it correlates with an important measure such as safety and productivity. If the job or task analysis shows that high performers do not always keep their areas clean and poor ones sometimes do, then cleanliness is not essential for effective performance and so should not be assessed. It is wiser to encourage and reward cleanliness in other ways.

- *Interpersonal skills.* If employees who are consistently rated as exceeding expectations on their performance reviews have very poor interpersonal skills, then it would be very difficult to prove the validity of a test on interpersonal skills. Even if the assessment effectively measured interpersonal skills (which could be difficult to do), the results would not correlate with performance. Until you can prove that interpersonal skills correlate with performance, these skills should be developed and encouraged through other means. Such skills can become an added requirement in the future if the organization can show that an absence of interpersonal skills somehow puts the organization or its relationship with customers at risk.

***Test Specifications.*** You can control sampling error by creating a test specification ("spec") or blueprint. A test spec helps you make sure every test question is relevant to a training objective, the results of the job or task analysis, or a standard. To build a test spec, create a matrix or grid. On one axis, list the knowledge, skills, or performances you want to include in each version of the test. On the other axis, indicate what type of items will be used, at what level the skill or knowledge will be tested, and how often it will be tested. For example:

- If you want to test knowledge, then list the definitions, rules, or symbols people must know (as indicated by the job or task analysis) on one axis. On the other axis, note the type of test item that will be used to assess each knowledge element and how often each element will be tested.

- If you want to test candidates' ability to apply certain knowledge, list the knowledge they must apply on one axis. Record when, how, and how often candidates must demonstrate their ability to apply the knowledge on the other axis.

- If you want to test candidates' ability to perform a task, list the tasks on one axis. On the other axis, note how the performance will be tested and how many opportunities a person will have to demonstrate he or she can do it.

You should create a test spec for every test you create to assess knowledge or skills. This will help you confirm that your tests adequately sample the important content or activities, that your pretests and posttests cover the same content in the same ways, and that subsequent tests cover the same content in the same ways as earlier tests.

## Design Error

Design error happens when one or more test items is inappropriate for what you want to discover or confirm or is poorly constructed, and thus elicits the wrong type of information or performance from the candidate. The performance standards should direct you to the type of test item to use, and there are rules for constructing test items that can help you when developing questions. Here are two factors to consider when designing a test.

***Domains of Knowledge or Ability.*** Most psychologists and educators agree that there are three domains of knowledge or ability: the cognitive domain, the affective domain, and the psychomotor domain. The *cognitive domain* encompasses intellectual skills and is the domain most tests focus on. The *affective* *domain* encompasses people's values and emotions and is what determines the choices they make when they are confronted by dilemmas. The *psychomotor domain* entails people's physiological abilities and is measured in terms of strength and coordination; visual, audio, and olfactory acuity; dexterity and physical speed, and so on. Some tests require the test taker to manipulate data (cognitive); some ask the test taker to make choices (affective); others ask the test taker to do something physical (psychomotor). Most performance standards involve all three domains. For example:

- Hematology technicians have to interpret equipment specifications and printouts (cognitive), visually compare specimens to controlled substances (psychomotor and cognitive), and decide whether or not to replace or refurbish parts (affective and cognitive).

- Hydraulic pump technicians have to locate the right specifications (cognitive and affective); take the pump apart, feel for foreign debris in the oil, and look for signs of cracks (psychomotor and cognitive); and consider the cost of repair compared to the expected shelf life of the pump (cognitive).

- HR generalists have to know personnel laws and corporate policies (cognitive), decide when to inform people of employee relations issues and who to try to influence (affective and cognitive), and use computers and word processors to create presentations and reports (cognitive and psychomotor).

- Warehouse workers have to have good depth perception (psychomotor) to place pallets on high shelves using a forklift.

***Levels of Knowledge or Ability.*** Level of knowledge or ability refers to the relative complexity of a specific skill and the difficulty of acquiring it. Figure 5.1 has the terms commonly used to describe the increasing levels of difficulty of knowledge and abilities in the cognitive domain.

**Figure 5.1. Levels in the Cognitive Domain**

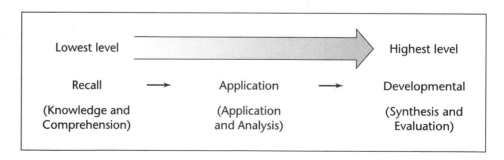

For example, to test cognitive skills you can ask people to

- Recall information (considered the lowest level), such as
  - "What are our three top-selling models?"
  - "Paraphrase the benefits of each model."
- Apply information (more complex), such as
  - "Calculate the profit margin if we sell one thousand units at $x$ price."
  - "Contrast the benefits of each model."
- Use the information to develop new ideas or solutions (the most complex), such as
  - "Put together a package of accessories that gives us a higher margin, distinguishes us in the marketplace, and reduces our fixed costs."
  - "Critique the two proposed marketing plans."

When testing the affective domain (that is, the choices people make), the complexity of the dilemma the people face defines the level. The simpler the dilemma, the lower the level. Figure 5.2 lists the terms frequently used to classify the levels of complexity for the affective domain.

**Figure 5.2. Levels in the Affective Domain**

Some jobs require people to work through complex ethical problems or conflicting issues where there is no one clear path or right answer. When this is the situation, the test should emulate those dilemmas. Such a test might present candidates with a situation that requires them to weigh the consequences of different actions. For example, the candidate would have to work through issues like protecting the company, being honest with the client, maintaining the loyalty of coworkers, meeting personal financial commitments, winning a contest, and so on. You want to be sure your test discriminates between candidates who make appropriate choices when confronted with feasible dilemmas and those who do not. Case studies, action mazes, in-basket exercises, and role-plays can effectively assess higher-level cognitive and affective skills.

Skills in the psychomotor domain also have levels. For example, the skills required to play basketball in the neighborhood are not at the same level as those required to play on a professional team. Some tasks require highly sophisticated psychomotor skills, like directing surgical lasers, adjusting microscopes to study microorganisms, manipulating dials or wheels to coordinate robots, visually checking circuit boards, tasting food or wines, and so on. When psychomotor skills are key to performance, the test should demand that candidates demonstrate them.

### Administrative Error

Administrative error is best avoided by conducting tests consistently; requiring jurors to use performance checklists when evaluating candidates' answers, performances, or work samples; and qualifying your jurors. You can reduce administrative error for both juried and nonjuried tests (discussed later) by allowing the same amount of time for all candidates to take the test; providing consistent instructions or information to all candidates; providing an equal testing environment for all candidates, by making sure all candidates have the same amount and type of space, materials, tools, and job aids; and limiting distractions.

To control bias when you administer juried test items (that is, items someone will have to judge the accuracy or adequacy of; see next section), do the following:

- Before candidates are tested, show them the checklist with the steps or criteria that will be used to judge their answers or performance. If possible, candidates should use the same checklist to assess their own performance prior to their formal evaluation.

- Document the evaluation session and the results.

- Provide each juror with a script. This is particularly important if the juror presents the problem orally.

- Train each juror to use the checklist.

- If the score will be considered in personnel decisions, arrange for at least two independent evaluations or other corroborating evidence. For example, you can look at documents or records of the number of assignments completed, time records, accuracy records, complaints, and so on.

## TYPES OF TEST ITEMS

There are two commonly used types of test items: items where several alternate responses are supplied and the test taker must pick the right one, and items were no response is supplied and the test taker has to create one.

### Response-Supplied Items

Items where the test taker must choose from provided responses are the easiest and fastest to score and lend themselves to computer testing and self-scoring. The two most frequently used examples of this type are multiple choice and matching questions.

***Multiple Choice Questions.*** Multiple choice items are very versatile. People are used to them, they are easy to score, and they can effectively measure knowledge and some cognitive and affective skills at the recall and application levels. The test taker is given a question and four or five possible alternative answers, from which they must select the correct or most appropriate one. A variation of this format is when the candidate is given a case study followed by a series of multiple choice items. Candidates have to interpret information in the case study to appropriately answer the questions. Another variation is the action maze, which is a collection of multiple choice questions based on a complex problem. This type of test was developed to assess people's leadership and supervisory skills. Every alternative takes the candidate to a new set of information, similar to computerized tests that branch. The candidate is presented with having to make new choices based on the consequences of earlier choices. Case studies and action mazes can be used to effectively assess candidates' higher-level cognitive and affective skills. See Figure 5.3 for uses of multiple choice items.

| Multiple choice items are used to test | |
| --- | --- |
| *Knowledge of* | *The ability to* |
| Terminology | Apply facts and principles |
| Specific facts | Justify methods and principles |
| Principles | Discern cause-and-effect relationships |
| Methods or processes | |

**Figure 5.3. Uses of Multiple Choice Test Items**

***Matching Questions.*** Matching questions are a special type of multiple choice test item in which there are usually two columns and people are asked to match the terms or symbols in the first column with the definitions or examples in the second column (see Figure 5.4).

| *This item type is used to test people's ability to match* | |
| --- | --- |
| Terms with their definitions | Types of equipment with their uses |
| Symbols with their proper names | Organisms with their classifications |
| People with their achievements | Causes with effects |
| Principles with situations | |

**Figure 5.4. Uses of Matching Test Items**

### Response-Not-Supplied Items

What distinguishes this type of item from the types just discussed is that the test taker must supply his or her own answer. When a candidate has to supply an answer instead of pick one out of a list, the item has to be juried, meaning someone has to judge the adequacy and correctness of the response. Ideally, the criteria for judging are predetermined and documented on a checklist.

***Essay, Short Answer, and Fill-in Items.*** Essay, short answer, and fill-in items require people to respond either in writing or orally. These types of items require someone to read, listen to, or watch the answer and judge the adequacy of the response. Figures 5.5 and 5.6 show the typical uses of these items.

Essay items are used to test

- Reasoning or logical ability
- Problem-solving skills
- Presentation skills
- Knowledge and skills in the affective domain (that is, the ability to make choices well)
- Language ability

**Figure 5.5. Uses of Essay Test Items**

Short answer and fill-in items are used to test

- Recall of facts, terms, symbols, and classifications
- Ability to apply rules and interpret data
- Use of symbols and equations
- Ability to solve scientific and mathematical problems

**Figure 5.6. Uses of Short Answer and Fill-in Test Items**

***Performance Items.*** Performance items require the test taker to demonstrate his or her ability to do something, such as solve a problem or perform a task. Performance items are used to test both people and the work they produce:

- They are used to test whether a person can perform a procedure or task to some standard, either in a simulated environment or their actual job environment. The person is observed by qualified jurors, who compare what he or she does with criteria on a checklist. In-basket exercises, role-plays, and simulations can be performance items. Someone must judge the adequacy of the response. In the case of an in-basket exercise, someone must judge the candidates' ability to set priorities and organize work. In the case of a role-play, a qualified juror must observe and look for the presence or absence of specific behaviors. Depending on the simulation, a juror may have to judge interpersonal, supervisory, managerial, or problem-solving skills. In-baskets exercises, role-plays, and simulations can effectively assess higher-level cognitive, affective, and psychomotor skills.

- They are also used to test whether work produced (output) meets some standard. In this case the jurors judge the product instead of how the person produces it and decide whether or not it meets the minimum requirements.

People tend to automatically link checklists with performance items. You will want to use performance items with checklists when the act you are measuring is something that cannot be evaluated easily using multiple choice or other objectively scored items. However, you can test performance using the other test item types as well. For example:

- Many cognitive and affective tasks can be tested by presenting a case study, a scenario, or a problem statement and then asking an essay question or a series of multiple choice or short answer questions about it.

- Procedures can also be tested using a series of multiple choice questions or an essay question.

## COMPUTER-BASED TESTING

Because many workforces are scattered and managers want to avoid the costs of convening people, organizations are looking for better ways to deliver training and administer tests than in the classroom. They are particularly interested in using computers and the Internet to deliver training and assess people's knowledge and skills. Here are some examples of how organizations are using computers to administer tests:

- *Computer adaptive testing.* In this method, the computer presents candidates with increasingly hard (or easy) questions based on the accuracy of their previous answers. Candidates who answer a series of questions correctly are presented with harder questions. Candidates who answer a series of questions incorrectly are presented with easier questions. The intent is to more accurately assess candidates' capability. The technology allows candidates who answer increasingly more difficult questions correctly to answer fewer questions (because they have already proven they know the concepts, principles, and so on). Candidates who answer easier questions correctly are presented with more opportunities to demonstrate that they know the concepts, principles, and so on.

- *Branching.* Branching is an electronic version of an action maze. The computer presents the candidate with a situation, which is followed by a multiple choice or fill-in question. Depending on the answer the candidate selects or provides, the computer presents him or her either with additional information followed by a question or with just another question. What information and questions the computer presents depends on the answers given to previous questions.

- *Hot spot identification.* Sometimes you want to test people's ability to accurately locate a spot, and precision is important. In this model, the computer presents candidates with an image, such as a still photograph. It the asks them to locate the best or most appropriate spot on the image, using the mouse, to perform a step in a task. For example, you could use this method to test whether or not acupuncturists know the correct spot to insert a needle to treat a particular ailment. You can even score this type of question by assigning points based on the proximity of a candidate's answer to the correct location.

- *Scenario.* A computer equipped to display full-motion video with audio can show a person performing a task, carrying out a procedure, or following a set of guidelines for handling a customer complaint. In this method, candidates are asked to stop the video whenever they see an error in how a task is being performed, a violation of an established procedure, or a deviation from a set of guidelines. When they stop the video, candidates are presented with a series of multiple choice questions about what is amiss.

If they fail to stop the video at the right times, they could lose points for not recognizing poor practices.

- *Simulated assembly.* A computer can display a series of parts used in assembling a piece of equipment and ask candidates to click on the parts and drag them to their correct positions.

- *Problem solving or judgment.* The computer can present candidates with a problem or dilemma (using either video or text) and ask them to pick the best solution to it. Computer technology allows you to assign points in decreasing order based on whether candidates select the best, next best, least best, or worst alternative. This type of test can even allow for negative scoring if a selected answer would produce a less-than-neutral result. For example, selecting the wrong tool (next best) might only mean a task will take longer; however, selecting the wrong tool (worst) could damage a system.

Computers let you simulate equipment breakdowns, sophisticated installation procedures, emotionally charged situations, and cultural stumbling blocks. These are situations that lend themselves to computerized training and testing. Computerized testing will increasingly be used as the technology grows in sophistication, its costs go down, and people's access to and familiarity with computers increase.

## DETERMINING THE PASSING SCORE

One of the more difficult decisions you will have to make when designing assessments is "How much is good enough?" or "How many questions can a person miss and still pass?" The passing score is that point where you can say a candidate knows enough or can do the task well enough to be certified. There are three recognized methods for determining where that point is: the informed judgment method, the contrasting-group method, and the conjecture, or Angoff-Nedelski, method.

### Informed Judgment Method

This method is appropriate for both performance and skill-based tests. To use it, poll expert performers and those stakeholders who are most dependent on candidates' satisfying the performance standards, and ask them the number of questions candidates should answer correctly or what other criteria they should satisfy to pass the test. You can also ask them how many times candidates should be allowed to retake the test. For example:

- To qualify its laboratory technicians, a pharmaceutical firm has them analyze the contents of three vials. The technicians have to accurately analyze the contents of all three vials to pass the test. If they are wrong on even one vial, they have to repeat not only the test but also the entire training program. The organization decided to use the informed judgment method to determine the criteria for passing the test, and stakeholders based their decision on requiring 100 percent accuracy because of the criticality of the technicians' job (analyzing specimens).

- The manufacturer of HVAC systems uses performance tests. Technicians are certified only after they have performed the tested task to standard at least six times. The decision to require six demonstrations of accuracy was made by high performers, their bosses, and product managers, who all agreed that customers expect accuracy. An inability to properly install, calibrate, service, and repair systems puts clients' assets at risk. Also, there are processes in place (like job aids, manuals, and access to experts) to help ensure exactness.

- The oral certifying examination conducted by the American Board of Oral and Maxillofacial Surgery (ABOMS) is analogous to an essay exam. Candidates are presented with a surgical scenario (slides containing dental and medical information) and are asked how they would approach the procedure. Examiners meet prior to the examination to calibrate the examination process. They reach consensus on the elements that must be present in a candidate's oral response for him or her to pass. Each candidate verbally presents his or her response to two jurors, who independently score the response.

## Contrasting-Group Method

This method is effective for both performance tests and knowledge and skill tests. To use it, have two groups take the test at the same time. It is called the contrasting-group method because one group is made up of people who are known to be competent, perhaps experts or high performers, and the second group is made up of people who are known to be incompetent. The second group are as much like the first group as possible, but they are known to lack education or experience specific to the body of knowledge or task being tested. Compare the scores of the two groups; they should be significantly different. If they are similar, then your test does not discriminate between people who know the content or can do the task from those who don't know the content or can't do the task. The contrasting-group method is the most defensible method for setting a passing score. The scores of the competent group are compared with those of the other group, and the passing score is usually placed somewhere between the mean scores of both groups (specifically, one standard deviation below the mean score of the competent group and one standard deviation above the mean score of the second group). Figure 5.7 illustrates how the scores of the two groups compare. The left-hand column lists the scores of the competent group. Their mean (average) score is 25. One standard deviation below the average score is 21. Three people from this group scored below 21. Such people are sometimes referred to as "false negatives," since they are known to be able to do the task or to have the knowledge or skill. The right-hand column lists the scores of the other group. Their average score is 11; one standard deviation above their average is 15. Two people from this group received scores above 15; they represent "false positives" because they are known to not be able to do the task. The pass score is usually set somewhere below 21 and above 15. If the organization wants to reduce the likelihood of passing "false positives," it will set the passing score at or close to 21. If it wants to reduce the chance of failing "false negatives," it will set the passing score at or close to 15.

**Figure 5.7. The Contrasting-Group Method**

| | Competent Group | Incompetent Group |
|---|---|---|
| 32 | / | |
| 31 | | |
| 30 | / | |
| 29 | /// | |
| 28 | // | |
| 27 | // | |
| 26 | ///// | |
| 25 | //// Mean | |
| 24 | | |
| 23 | /// | |
| 22 | //// | |
| 21 | //            −s | |
| 20 | ------------------------------------------------------ | |
| 19 | //     Zone of | |
| 18 | acceptance | / |
| 17 | /     for passing score. | |
| 16 | ---------------------------------------------/-------- | |
| 15 | | /        +s |
| 14 | | / |
| 13 | | // |
| 12 | | /// |
| 11 | | //// Mean |
| 10 | | ///// |
| 9 | | // |
| 8 | | //// |
| 7 | | |
| 6 | | // |
| 5 | | |
| 4 | | |
| 3 | | / |
| 2 | | |

For example:

- NCIDQ and a credit card company that certifies its customer service representatives both used the contrasting-group method to set their passing scores.

- IFMA brought together twenty-two facility managers who were considered competent and twenty-two other people who lacked experience and education in facility management (schoolteachers, car salesmen, social workers, beauticians, and secretaries). The test was administered to both groups at the same time. The test was divided into four parts to reduce the likelihood of fatigue's affecting the scores. Two parts each consisted of one hundred multiple choice questions. The other two parts had fewer questions, as they required the test taker to answer questions about technical documents and case studies. The scores of the facility managers were very close together and clustered near the maximum number of points possible. The other group's scores clustered too, but they were significantly lower. The passing score was placed between one standard deviation below the mean score of the facility managers and one standard deviation above the mean score of the other group.

### Conjectural (Angoff-Nedelsky) Method

This method is used mainly for knowledge and skills tests. The passing score is determined by estimating, or conjecturing, the probability that a minimally competent candidate would answer each question correctly. The procedure is as follows:

- Convene three to five judges who are familiar both with the performance standards being tested and with how competent members of the target audience have scored on the test.

- Have the judges independently estimate the probability that a minimally competent person will get the right answer for each question. A probability of 1 means the question is so easy that any candidate is almost certain to get it right. A probability of .5 means a candidate has a 50-50 chance of getting it right. A probability of less than .5 means that the question is harder, and thus the probability of getting the right answer is less than 50-50. The highest possible probability estimate (indicating that candidates will answer the question correctly) is 1. The lowest possible probability estimate depends on the number of alternatives in the question: for multiple choice questions with three alternatives, the lowest possible estimate is .33; for questions with four alternatives, it is .25; for questions with five alternatives, it is .20; and so on.

- To calculate the passing score, average the sums of each judge's probability estimates. For example, assume that three judges are asked to estimate the probability that a minimally competent candidate will correctly answer each and every item on a one-hundred-item test. Assume the sum of Judge 1's estimates is 84.2, the sum of Judge 2's estimates is 79.4, and the sum of Judge 3's estimates is 81.3. Then the sum of the three judges' probability estimates is 244.8 (84.2 + 79.4 + 81.3 = 244.8) for the one-hundred-item test. Therefore, candidates would need to score 82 on the test to pass (244.8 ÷ 3 = 81.9).

## ISSUES IN ASSESSMENT AND TESTING

There are some major issues surrounding assessment and testing that apply to all types of organizations. Organizations have to show that candidates have been given a reasonable opportunity to learn the required skills and knowledge and an adequate amount of time to demonstrate what they know and that they can perform to standard. The test design must appear valid to the target audience and stakeholders, and the organization must document its rationale for using whichever testing method it selects.

### Opportunity to Learn

One issue all organizations face is to avoid discriminating against people because they did not have an adequate opportunity to acquire needed skills and knowledge. This is why many organizations require training as part of their certification programs. Professional disciplines like medicine, accounting, and architecture can rely on the formal education system to equip candidates. However, the educational system is not always equipped to fully support newly evolving fields or jobs within business and industry. Thus companies have learned that they must provide opportunities for workers to learn jobs and develop new capabilities. Requiring education and training becomes an issue of validity when workers can do a job or task but have not had any formal training for it. They learned on the job. It is likely they don't even fully appreciate what it is they know that contributes to their success; moreover, it is probably not documented. A well-designed task analysis will uncover their skills and knowledge, and this will enable others to learn more efficiently. However, you still have to prove that those who can pass a test on the job or task (whether they completed the training for it or not) can perform it to the level of those who learned on the job.

### Adequate Time and Resources

Another issue is the need to give people enough time and the right resources to demonstrate that they know the content and can do the task. One organization only allows fifty-nine minutes for training and testing. This may not be enough time to demonstrate proficiency. For organizations with workers all over the world, it may be too costly to set up simulations to adequately test skills, particularly problem-solving or troubleshooting skills; an alternative is to use computer-based testing. Organizations are increasingly deploying training and testing through their intranets. The challenge is to show that performance on a computerized test correlates with performance on the job. The computer can increase the psychological distance between the real task and the candidates' thinking processes (unless, of course, the task being tested involves using a computer). Another alternative organizations with a very dispersed workforce use is to qualify their supervisors to assess workers' abilities. This alternative requires a fair amount of trust in the supervisors, and well-designed performance checklists. Preparing supervisors to judge workers' performance can also put in place a system to keep skills current as products, regulations, customer expectations, and technology change. Because the test and job performance are one and the same, the organization can easily prove the validity of its assessments.

## Face Validity

"Face validity" occurs when the test format and method make sense to the target audience and key stakeholders. A swimming test is a simple example. It makes sense on the face of it that for such a test candidates would have to get in the water and swim some distance. How far they would have to swim, what the temperature of the water would be, whether or not hazards (like an undercurrent) would be present, and whether candidates would be expected to swim unhampered (hands not tied or not towing an unconscious person) would depend on the performance criteria and on how the tests results will be used. It would not make sense, on the face of it, for a summer camp's basic swimming test to require the candidate to swim a long distance in ice-cold water with his or her hands tied; such a test would not have face validity.

It is easy to assume that the cost of creating a simulation would be greater than the cost of developing a computer-based test of multiple choice questions. However, costs can be affected by face validity. When a test format does not make sense to the target audience or key stakeholders (even though you can show a correlation between test scores and performance), you may have increased instead of reduced costs. When a test does not make sense to the people who must support it, you inevitably have to expend more effort (and more money) on communications, public relations, preparation, and test maintenance. Therefore, make sure your decisions on how to test are in the best interests of all the parties involved, not just those of a few.

### Documentation

Documenting who participated in deciding what to test, how to test it, and what constitutes passing is very important. Not only does it provide you with an audit trail, it also allows you to evaluate and improve your internal processes. The main reason for documenting your decisions is to demonstrate that you exercised prudence when making those decisions. Documentation helps you show that your decisions were not arbitrary. Documentation also helps you demonstrate that your tests discriminate appropriately. (Yes, tests are supposed to discriminate—that is, they are supposed to distinguish people who know or can do something from those who don't know or can't do something. They are not supposed to be discriminatory, however; that is, they should not favor one group of individuals over another group for reasons unrelated to knowledge or performance. The difference matters.)

**MISSTEPS AND OVERSIGHTS**

Here are two common oversights made by organizations when they decide to require testing as part of their certifications:

1. *Overlooking job or process redesign.* Sometimes organizations fail to distinguish between skills that are really essential for a job and skills that could be made less critical by redesigning the job, providing job aids, or offering different incentives. Rather than testing candidates' ability to handle complex situations or conflicting issues, organizations could choose to implement controls or redesign their processes to reduce the conflicts. The same principle is true for processes: instead of developing a complex simulation to test ethics or honesty, for example, organizations could require candidates to submit to a personal financial audit. Some jobs historically required specific physical abilities, such as olfactory or visual acuity (like the ability to discriminate subtle tastes and colors), manual dexterity, or fine motor skills. These types of jobs may lend themselves to being redesigned or supported with job aids. Sometimes higher-level skills continue to be required; other times they can be supported with aids or a redesign of the job. You want to be sure that your test discriminates based on the abilities that are actually required, not just the old way of doing business.

2. *Use of dichotomous test items.* Dichotomous test items require people to pick one of two answers. The most popular example is the true-false test question. Dichotomous items are not recommended simply because people have a 50-50 chance of getting the right answer just by guessing. Therefore, you must assume that anyone can get 50 percent right, which

leaves only the other 50 percent on which to base your passing score. For example, if you have a ten-item test and you set your passing score at 60 percent, it means a person only has to actually get one item right (and simply guess right on five items) to pass. Another problem with dichotomous test items is that there are very few situations or problems for which there are only two alternatives or choices, so performance on them is very removed from most real-world tasks. For example, one state certified its high school wrestling officials by giving them a two-hundred-item true-false test, but it would be very difficult accurately to predict a coach's ability to fairly judge a match based on this test.

**TIPS**

Here are some suggestions on how to avoid some of the common pitfalls of testing:

1. *Continually reassess the capabilities of computer technology.* New developments in computer technology are happening every day; therefore, yesterday's decisions about their use should be revisited periodically. Computerized testing presents you with a special set of challenges, primarily test security and ensuring that only legitimate candidates take the tests. Therefore, unless you are very sophisticated in the use of Internet and intranet technology and computer-based testing, work with organizations that specialize in these fields. Many have well-developed security systems and test-authoring software to help you.

2. *Select a set of standards for test items, and use them.* There are standards for multiple choice, matching, fill-in, short answer, and performance test items. Many people feel that learning about test items is unnecessary since they have had years of experience taking tests. They know what tests are and what they look like. Unfortunately, what many people learned was bad habits and bad examples instead of how to design tests that truly discriminate as intended (see the accompanying box). Therefore, find a set of standards and follow them. Document the source of the standards you are using. (See Where to Learn More at the end of this chapter.)

3. *Figure in all of the costs.* When developing the business case or budget, be sure to include all of the direct and indirect costs of the program. The method you choose for testing will directly affect the cost of training (or preparation), prequalification, remediation, and public relations.

4. *Build a test spec or blueprint.* It doesn't matter what form the test spec or blueprint takes. It is a job aid to help you be rigorous in deciding what to

test, when to test it, and how many times to test it. The test spec will help you prove that subsequent tests are equally difficult, easy, or thorough as the initial test. It can help you consider just what it is you want to test and if your test really verifies that candidates can satisfy the performance standards.

## EXPERIENCE IS NOT ALWAYS THE BEST TEACHER

- I received the second-highest score, 98 out of 100, when I took my high school chemistry class's final exam. My score presented my teacher with a serious dilemma. He knew and I knew that my score did not reflect my comprehension of chemistry. It showed I'm an excellent test taker. So I presented him with a solution: "Give me a *B*, and I'll promise never to enter a chemistry lab again or represent myself as knowing anything about chemistry." We struck a deal.

- The final grade for a five-credit college geology course was based solely on one exam that consisted of five fill-in questions. One question was "The name of the man whose picture appears on page 323 is _____?" The other four were equally irrelevant to geology. To get an *A*, you had to answer all five questions correctly. If you missed one you got a *B*, two you got a *C*, and so on. I got a *B*, and still to this day I cannot distinguish rocks from cement. Unfortunately, I had classmates who knew considerably more than I did but did very poorly on the test.

**Figure 5.8. Example of a Test Spec**

| *Objective* | *Method and Frequency* | *Level* |
|---|---|---|
| Interpret the terms and symbols. | Matching (1) | Application |
|     Term 1 | | |
|     Term *n* | | |
| State the rules. | Multiple choice (1) | Recall |
| Read the specifications. | Performance (1) and multiple choice (3) | Application |
| Take the equipment apart. | Performance (1) | Application |
| Identify worn parts. | Performance (1) and multiple choice (3) | Application |
| Insert the correct replacement parts. | Performance (1) | Application |

## GUIDELINES

### Assessing Education and Experience

Here are some guidelines for when you begin the process of designing assessments:

To assess education or experience

A. List the attributes that must be present for the education or experience to be accepted (specific approved courses, employment in a specific type of business, and so on).

B. Determine how you will verify the education (transcripts, certificates, and so on).

C. Determine how you will verify the experience (resumes, endorsements by employers or supervisors, a portfolio or work samples, attainment of an external credential, and so on).

D. Decide if you will accept substitutions (that is, experience for education, test scores for experience, external credentials for training, and so on). If so, what can be substituted for what, how much of the substitute item will be needed, and how recent must it be?

E. If you require work samples, define the attributes that must be present for the work to be considered acceptable (how recent must they be, how many of them does the candidate have to submit, do they have to have seals of authenticity, should they have been reviewed by quality assurance people, must they have been juried and found to meet the qualifications to be accepted for exhibit, and so on).

F. Let candidates know in advance how your organization will judge whether or not they have satisfied the requirements for certification.

### Selecting Test Items

When deciding on the type of questions you want to ask, begin with the performance standard, and answer the following questions:

A. What verbs are you using to describe what you want candidates to know or do (that is, to describe the desired performance)?

B. Based on those verbs, what is the domain or combination of domains involved in the job or task?

C. How difficult, or at what level, is the performance?

D. What kind of response will give you confidence that candidates know it or can do it?

E. Would multiple choice items present the kinds of questions or situations that would generate the responses you want?

F. Would matching items?

G. Would a written or verbal response?

H. Are the required responses something you could watch or listen to?

I. Could the candidate generate a piece of work that would require him or her to use the knowledge and skills you think are important?

J. Are there constraints you have to consider, such as time, lack of access to equipment or computers, lack of qualified jurors, and so on?

## Building a Test Spec

Here are some guidelines to help you build a test specification or blueprint:

A. List the performances that make up the objective you want to test.

B. Decide how to best test them (multiple choice items, matching items, or a juried process) and how many times you want to test them.

C. Based on the importance or complexity of the performance, decide at what level you want to test it.

D. Create and fill in a matrix similar to the one in Figure 5.8.

## Qualifying Jurors

Whenever candidates' performance or response will be judged by someone, it is important to qualify the person who will do the judging. At a minimum, it must be someone who will be perceived as credible. Here are some guidelines to help you qualify jurors or observers:

A. Meet with stakeholders, including representatives from the candidate group, and jointly identify the attributes a person should have to be qualified to judge candidates' responses, performances, or work.

- Judges should be certified. That is, a judge should be someone who has already earned the same designation candidates are trying to earn or who has credentials relevant to the job, such as vendor certification.

- Judges should have performed the same job previously (but not so long ago that they may not remember or the standards they followed no longer apply).

- Judges should be responsible for quality assurance. That is, a judge should be someone who, by virtue of his or her position, is responsible for attesting to the capability of processes and products.

- Judges should have experience as managers or supervisors (that is, they should have the same experience as someone who currently judges the work being tested).

B. Train the jurors prior to asking them to judge candidates' responses or performance.

- Have them practice reading, listening, or observing and completing the checklist.

- At the same time, have a master juror (someone who is already qualified) do the observation and complete the checklist.

- Have the master juror review and confirm the decisions of the candidate juror.

C. Be sure the juror is free of any conflict of interest or bias (either negative or positive) toward the candidate. For example, the juror should not get rewarded for getting people certified, nor should there be any history of conflict or a personal relationship between the juror and a candidate.

D. Remove any information about the candidate that is not relevant to the performance being evaluated. The juror should not be given information such as what other people think of the candidate or if the candidate has failed in the past, is nervous, has won an award, is a party to a class action suit pending against the organization, and so on.

E. Have detailed criteria for evaluating and scoring.

F. Have each juror score the performance independently.

## Using Tests

Here is a set of guidelines you can use when developing tests for your certification program. They assume that the stakeholders are in agreement concerning the goal of the test and what you will do with the results and that you have conducted a job or task analysis and converted the data from it into a set of performance standards.

A. Determine when you will use tests: at the time of enrollment in the certification program, at the start of training, at the end of training, or after some period of time on the job.

B. Determine how you will use the results. Will they help you determine people's eligibility to do a task, compete for a position, or participate in some way? Will they qualify people to use a designation? Will they be used to evaluate a training or development program?

C. Determine what you want the test to measure:

- Development—if people learned something

- Knowledge—if people possess a body of knowledge

- Performance—how well people can perform a task

D. If the test is intended to measure development or knowledge, decide on what level you want to test: recall or application.

E. If the test is meant to measure skills, decide what domain and what level you want to test: cognitive, affective, psychomotor, or some combination.

F. If the test is to measure performance, either through simulations or on the job, identify the behaviors or outcomes you will use to judge proficiency.

G. Based on the goal and the standard, decide on the type of items you want to use:

- Multiple choice
- Matching
- Juried

    Essay or oral

    Fill-in or short answer

    Performance

H. Build a test spec showing how each item links to a performance standard, the training content, or the job or task analysis to confirm that you are adequately sampling the content, skills, or tasks.

- If the knowledge is volatile or the range of application is unpredictable, document your reasoning for what you plan to do and why you plan to do it.

- If the test measures problem-solving or troubleshooting skills and candidates will be presented with a unique problem every time the test is offered, then

    Set criteria for the problem (that is, the number of variables, level of complexity, required enabling knowledge, and so on).

    Have the jurors take the test and agree on what candidates must demonstrate or score to pass.

I. Develop the items.

J. Have subject matter experts or high performers confirm the accuracy of the items, the correctness of the answers, or the correctness of the behaviors or attributes on the performance checklists.

K. Decide who will decide what the minimum score must be for candidates to pass, and describe how that decision was made.

L. Pilot the tests to determine if they discriminate between candidates as intended.

M. Document the decisions you made, the standards you used, and the people involved in the process.

## SUMMARY

Tests are frequently an integral part of a certification. When well designed, they are excellent tools for confirming that candidates have fulfilled the objectives of the certification. However, your program will not be effective if you do not put policies and systems in place to ensure that your tests discriminate between candidates as intended. The checklists on the following pages are designed to help you select the best method of testing and to ensure that your tests serve the purpose you intended.

 **CHECKLISTS**

Here is a series of checklists you can use to evaluate your tests and testing process:

### Assessment

If the certification requires successful completion of a test, either as a prerequisite or as part of the certification, then the test should match the test specifications.

| | YES | NO |
|---|:---:|:---:|
| A. The test specifications | | |
| • List the performances or content areas to be tested | ☐ | ☐ |
| • State at what level the performances are to be tested: | | |
|    Knowledge level | ☐ | ☐ |
|    Application level | ☐ | ☐ |
|    Developmental level | ☐ | ☐ |
| • Indicate the sequence in which the performances or content areas will be tested | ☐ | ☐ |
| • State how many opportunities (by performance and level) each exam will give candidates to demonstrate proficiency | ☐ | ☐ |
| • State how each performance will be tested: | | |
|    Multiple choice items | ☐ | ☐ |
|    Matching items | ☐ | ☐ |
|    Juried items, such as | | |
|       Essay with checklist | ☐ | ☐ |
|       Short answer with checklist | ☐ | ☐ |
|       Performance with checklist | ☐ | ☐ |
|       Portfolio or work sample with checklist | ☐ | ☐ |
| • State how many parts there are to the test | ☐ | ☐ |

|                                                                                                                      | YES | NO |
|----------------------------------------------------------------------------------------------------------------------|:---:|:--:|
| • Describe the recommended or required order of each part                                                            | ☐ | ☐ |
| • Specify the amount of time the candidate has to complete the test or each part of the test                        | ☐ | ☐ |
| • Indicate how many questions have been or are targeted to be developed for each content area, performance, and level | ☐ | ☐ |
| • State who developed the test specifications and on what basis those people were selected                          | ☐ | ☐ |

B.  The test design indicates

|                                                                                                                      | YES | NO |
|----------------------------------------------------------------------------------------------------------------------|:---:|:--:|
| • The rationale for the type of testing procedure selected                                                          | ☐ | ☐ |
| • What information, guidelines, equipment, or materials the candidate will have access to and can use during the test | ☐ | ☐ |
| • The procedures for administering and scoring the test                                                             | ☐ | ☐ |
| • What standards were used for                                                                                      |   |   |
|     Multiple choice items                                                                       | ☐ | ☐ |
|     Matching items                                                                              | ☐ | ☐ |
|     Juried items                                                                                | ☐ | ☐ |
| • Who has sign-off authority and accountability for the design of the test and for ensuring that the test specifications and format reflect the results of the job analysis | ☐ | ☐ |

C.  Each question is coded to

|                                                                                                                      | YES | NO |
|----------------------------------------------------------------------------------------------------------------------|:---:|:--:|
| • Reflect the content area, performance, and level                                                                  | ☐ | ☐ |
| • Reference the material that confirms the correct response                                                         | ☐ | ☐ |
| • Reflect when and how often it has been used                                                                       | ☐ | ☐ |
| • Show the correct answer                                                                                           | ☐ | ☐ |

D.  The test includes

|                                                                                                                      | YES | NO |
|----------------------------------------------------------------------------------------------------------------------|:---:|:--:|
| • A segment to orient the candidate to the requirements of the test                                                 | ☐ | ☐ |
| • A description of the purpose and objectives of the test                                                           | ☐ | ☐ |
| • A summary of the scoring procedures                                                                               | ☐ | ☐ |
| • Instructions for the test taker                                                                                   | ☐ | ☐ |

## Test Analysis

Tests should be piloted to confirm that the instructions, test items, and checklists work as designed. An item analysis should be done after the pilot and each offering to identify any items that need to be reviewed, modified, or eliminated. (The procedure for doing an item analysis is discussed in Chapter Six.)

|  | YES | NO |
|---|---|---|
| A. The test and its administration were piloted. | ☐ | ☐ |
| B. Documentation of the pilot includes | | |
| • The criteria used to select candidates for the pilot | ☐ | ☐ |
| • A description of who decided who would make up the pilot group and on what basis they made this decision | ☐ | ☐ |
| • The number of people who participated in the pilot | ☐ | ☐ |
| • The pilot group's test scores | ☐ | ☐ |
| • A list of who observed and debriefed the pilot group after they completed the test | ☐ | ☐ |
| • The composition of the people used to set the passing score | ☐ | ☐ |
| C. Passing scores were set. | ☐ | ☐ |
| D. Documentation regarding passing scores describes | | |
| • What the passing score is | ☐ | ☐ |
| • How the passing score was determined | | |
| Expert opinion method | ☐ | ☐ |
| Contrasting-group method | ☐ | ☐ |
| Conjecture (Angoff-Nedelski) method | ☐ | ☐ |
| E. An item analysis was performed. | ☐ | ☐ |
| F. Documentation of the item analysis describes | | |
| • How the item analysis was performed | ☐ | ☐ |
| • Who performed the item analysis | ☐ | ☐ |
| • Who has sign-off authority and accountability for ensuring the test is and remains valid and reliable | ☐ | ☐ |

## Performance Items

When the certification requires demonstration of job performance, either on the job or in a simulated environment, the observer who attests to the adequacy of the performance should be qualified to do so. The documentation should include the following:

|  | YES | NO |
|---|---|---|
| A. The standards used for developing performance items: | | |
| • Item directions are clear. | ☐ | ☐ |
| • Actions are observable. | ☐ | ☐ |
| • All required steps are listed. | ☐ | ☐ |
| • Critical and sequential steps are identified. | ☐ | ☐ |
| • If a process, the activities are in the order in which they must occur. | ☐ | ☐ |
| • If the candidate is required to draw or label items, the items are clearly identified, with only one correct term for each item to be labeled. | ☐ | ☐ |
| • If the candidate must draw a path, there is only one correct path. | ☐ | ☐ |
| B. The performance checklists used to score performance | ☐ | ☐ |
| C. The minimum criteria required to be considered proficient, such as those for adherence to procedures, time to complete the test, accuracy, and completeness | ☐ | ☐ |
| D. A description of how people were qualified to be jurors | ☐ | ☐ |
| E. An explanation of how jurors' work is reviewed to ensure consistency | ☐ | ☐ |
| F. A description of what process is followed when a juror decides the performance criteria were not met | ☐ | ☐ |
| • Is there a second blind review? | ☐ | ☐ |
| • Does it require confirmation by another juror? | ☐ | ☐ |
| G. A description of who has sign-off authority for ensuring that the performance checklists match the results of the job analysis and the performance statements | ☐ | ☐ |

## Juried Items

Juried items include both oral and written responses to questions and work samples that have to be evaluated. Juried items should be linked to the job analysis. The documentation should indicate the following:

|  | YES | NO |
|---|---|---|
| A. The standards used for developing juried items: | | |
| • Items are clearly stated (so it will not be a reading test). | ☐ | ☐ |
| • The main ideas precede the blank to be filled in. | ☐ | ☐ |
| • The questions or requests directed to the candidate are clear. | ☐ | ☐ |
| • Items are constructed so there is only one correct, brief answer. | ☐ | ☐ |

|  | YES | NO |
|---|:---:|:---:|
| B. The checklists used to score the response | ☐ | ☐ |
| C. The minimum criteria required to be considered proficient, such as adherence to procedures, time, accuracy, and completeness | ☐ | ☐ |
| D. How people are qualified to be jurors | ☐ | ☐ |
| E. How jurors' work is reviewed to ensure consistency | ☐ | ☐ |
| F. What process is followed when a juror decides the performance criteria were not met | | |
|    • Is there a second blind review? | ☐ | ☐ |
|    • Does it require confirmation by another juror? | ☐ | ☐ |
| G. Who has sign-off authority for ensuring the checklists match the results of the job analysis and the performance statements | ☐ | ☐ |

## Multiple Choice Items

When the certification includes multiple choice questions, the questions should be well designed and linked to the job analysis. The documentation should include all of the following:

|  | YES | NO |
|---|:---:|:---:|
| A. The standards used for developing multiple choice items: | | |
|    • The questions are easy to read. | ☐ | ☐ |
|    • Negatives are underlined or bolded. | ☐ | ☐ |
|    • Each item is in the form of a question, not an open-ended statement. | ☐ | ☐ |
|    • The questions do not call for opinions. | ☐ | ☐ |
|    • The information necessary to select a correct response is provided. | ☐ | ☐ |
|    • The concept being measured is relevant to doing the job. | ☐ | ☐ |
|    • Each question measures only one concept. | ☐ | ☐ |
|    • The stem contains only relevant information. | ☐ | ☐ |
|    • There is only one correct answer. | ☐ | ☐ |
|    • There are a consistent number of alternatives. | ☐ | ☐ |
|    • Alternatives appear plausible. | ☐ | ☐ |
|    • Alternatives are of similar length and level of detail. | ☐ | ☐ |

|  | YES | NO |
|---|---|---|
| • Use of "all" and "none of the above" has been avoided. | ☐ | ☐ |
| • The position of the correct answer varies. | ☐ | ☐ |
| • The alternatives appear in some logical order. | ☐ | ☐ |
| • Responses are not revealed by other questions. | ☐ | ☐ |

B.   Evidence that the process used to code and select items ensures each test offering will be equivalent     ☐ ☐

C.   Who has sign-off authority for ensuring the multiple choice items match the results of the job analysis and the performance statements

## Matching Items

When a certification test uses matching questions, the questions should be well designed and linked to the job analysis. The documentation should include all of the following:

|  | YES | NO |
|---|---|---|
| A.   The standards for developing matching items: | | |
| • The number of premises (column A) and responses (column B) are unequal. | ☐ | ☐ |
| • The instructions state how many times a response can be used. | ☐ | ☐ |
| • The number of premises (column A) is seven or less. | ☐ | ☐ |
| • The items in both columns are arranged in some logical order (alphabetical, chronological, big to small, and so on). | ☐ | ☐ |
| • The items in both columns are homogeneous (of the same class of things), unless the task is to classify items. | ☐ | ☐ |
| • All of the items in both columns are on the same page. | ☐ | ☐ |
| • Specific determiners have been removed. | ☐ | ☐ |
| B.   Clear directions indicating how the candidate is to respond | ☐ | ☐ |
| C.   Analysis: | | |
| • The source of the correct answer is cited. | ☐ | ☐ |
| • The level being tested is noted. | ☐ | ☐ |
| • The items are matched to the test specification. | ☐ | ☐ |

**WHERE TO LEARN MORE**

Westgaard's and Shrock and Coscarelli's books should be required reading for anyone who buys or develops tests. The books complement each other, and both contain useful guidelines and recommendations.

Shrock, S. A., and Coscarelli, W. C. *Criterion-Referenced Test Development* (Reading, MA: Addison-Wesley, 1989). This book is now available through the International Society for Performance Improvement (ISPI), Washington DC.

Westgaard, O. *Tests That Work* (San Francisco: Jossey-Bass, 1999). This book has a detailed set of guidelines for developing multiple choice and performance items and is available through ISPI, Amazon.com, and the publisher.

The Council on Licensure, Enforcement, and Regulation (CLEAR), c/o the Council on State Governments, P.O. Box 11910, 3560 Iron Works Pike, Lexington KY 40589-1910, 606-231-1892. This organization has some publications that are a must for any organization planning to incorporate tests as part of its certification program; in particular are "Principles of Fairness: An Examining Guide for Credentialing Boards" (1993) and "Development, Administration, Scoring and Reporting of Credentialing Examinations: Recommendations for Board Members" (1993).

The National Organization for Competency Assurance (NOCA) holds national conferences and regional workshops on subjects related to certification, particularly testing. It also has among its members companies that specialize in computer-based testing. You can contact NOCA at 1200 19th Street NW, Suite 300, Washington DC 20036-2422, 202-857-1165.

A new set of standards is being developed by the Joint Committee on the Standards for Educational and Psychological Testing. The joint committee is made up of representatives from the American Educational Research Association, the American Psychological Association, and the National Council on Measurement in Education. To obtain a copy of the standards, contact the American Psychological Association at 750 First Street NE, Washington DC 20002-4242, 202-336-6000.

Hale Associates. *Workbook and Job Aids for Designing Good Fair Tests* (Downers Grove, IL: Hale Associates, 1997). This workbook contains the rules and only the rules. There are some excellent job aids to help you find the language that best describes what you want candidates to know and do.

# Chapter 6

# Governance and Administration

Governance and administration of a certification program go hand in hand. Indeed, I think of them as two hands clapping. If one hand fails to join in enthusiastically, the overall sound is less than robust; hearty applause requires both hands to work together, equally.

Governance is the side that provides oversight and stewardship of the program; administration is the side that manages its implementation. The governance board makes the hard decisions, armed with the program administrator's recommendations. Both roles are necessary for an effective program.

## RESPONSIBILITIES OF THE GOVERNANCE BOARD

The governance board has three major responsibilities:

1. Make policy decisions.
2. Rule on disputes.
3. Assess the effectiveness of the program.

At the outset of a new certification program, the governance board will

- Confirm the purpose of the program
- Set policies for appeals, disclosure, and grandfathering
- Establish criteria for evaluating the program
- Agree on the requirements for certification, maintenance, and recertification
- Approve the administrative guidelines

Later the board's work will shift to hearing disputes and reviewing the implications of its rulings on policy. Periodically it will revisit the standards and the certification requirements, based on its evaluations of the program or changes within the organization, the target audience, or the job or skill being certified. The board decides if and when a new job or task analysis should be done and what the requirements for recertification will be. The program administrator provides the board with information and recommendations so it can make well-informed decisions.

The bulk of the board's work is to set policy and approve operating procedures related to the design and administration of the program. For example, the board will have to develop policies for issues like the following:

- Requirements and standards—what they will be and when they will need to be updated or revalidated

- Timing—when candidates must apply for the credential and how long they will have to earn it

- Passing scores—how they will be determined

- Jurors and the judging process—who will be eligible to be a juror and how the process will work

- Disclosure—what information about tests or candidates will be documented, who will have access to it, what will get communicated, and to whom it will be communicated

- Systems—how they will be used and maintained

- Test administration—how tests will be scored and analyzed, how to comply with the Americans with Disabilities Act and other relevant regulations[1]

- Recertification—if it will be necessary, how often it will be required and available, and at what intervals

- Fees (for external candidates) and compensation (for internal candidates)—what they will be

- Appeals—what the process will be for hearing candidates' complaints or disputes about the results of the assessment; how the fairness or appropriateness of the standards or the certification process will be demonstrated

- Exemptions—what the processes will be for relieving candidates from meeting a requirement and for considering substitutions

- Government regulations—how the program will comply with the Americans with Disabilities Act, regulatory agency requirements, licensing requirements, and so on

- Language—what the policy will be regarding translations or the use of interpreters

- Opportunity—what the process will be for helping candidates gain the required skills, knowledge, and experience

### Candidate Rights

A major responsibility of the governing board is to decide what rights candidates will have in all stages of the process. Most of the questions about candidate rights deal with fairness and equal opportunity. Candidates want to know what is expected of them, what they have to do to succeed, how much help they can receive, and what will happen once they succeed (or fail). Most of these issues are related to the administration of the test; some apply to the larger process.

The Joint Committee on Testing Practices (JCTP), a consortium of professional associations that undertakes projects to improve the quality of testing practices (in the public interest), developed a set of guidelines and expectations for test takers.[2] What is interesting about these guidelines is that they allude to the responsibilities of the test administrator as well as those of the test taker. The rules apply to any assessment, not just tests. There are two parts: test taker *rights* and test taker *responsibilities* (see Figure 6.1).

### Disclosure

A number of the rights and responsibilities cited by JCTP address the question of who gets to find out what candidates' test scores are. The issue of disclosure goes beyond releasing test scores, however; it applies to any information about the test and candidates. For example:

- How many times a candidate took a test

- Who the jurors were and the names of the specific jurors who judged a candidate's work

- How a particular candidate's score compared to those of others who took the test

- Which questions a candidate missed

- What the test questions and answers were

- How many people missed a particular question

The concern over disclosure is about how to protect the integrity of the test and reduce the possibility of someone's misusing information about candidates' performance on the test.

| *As a test taker, you have a right to* | *As a test taker, you have the responsibility to* |
|---|---|
| 1. Be informed of your rights and responsibilities as a test taker. | 1. Read and/or listen to your rights and responsibilities as a test taker. |
| 2. Be treated with courtesy, respect, and impartiality, regardless of your age, disability, ethnicity, gender, national origin, religion, sexual orientation or other personal characteristics. | 2. Treat others with courtesy and respect during the testing process. |
| 3. Be tested with measures that meet professional standards and that are appropriate, given the manner in which the test results will be used. | 3. Ask questions prior to testing if your are uncertain about why the test is being given, how it will be given, what you will be asked to do, and what will be done with the results. |
| 4. Receive a brief oral or written explanation prior to testing about the purpose(s) for testing, the kind(s) of tests to be used, if the results will be reported to you or to others, and the planned use(s) of the results. If you have a disability, you have the right to inquire and receive information about testing accommodations. If you have difficulty in comprehending the language of the test, you have a right to know in advance of testing whether and what accommodations may be available to you. | 4. Read or listen to descriptive information in advance of testing and listen carefully to all test instructions. You should inform an examiner in advance of testing if you wish to receive a testing accommodation or if you have a physical condition or illness that may interfere with your performance on the test. If you have difficulty comprehending the language of the test, it is your responsibility to inform an examiner. |
| 5. Know in advance of testing where the test will be administered, if and when test results will be made available to you, and if there is a fee for testing services that you will be expected to pay. | 5. Know when and where the test will be given, pay for the test if required, appear on time with any required materials, and be ready to be tested. |
| 6. Have your test administered and your test results interpreted by appropriately trained individuals who follow professional codes of ethics. | 6. Follow the test instructions you are given and represent yourself honestly during the testing. |
| 7. Know if a test is optional and learn of the consequences of taking or not taking the test, fully completing the test, or canceling the scores. You may need to ask questions to learn these consequences. | 7. Be familiar with and accept the consequences of not taking the test, should you choose not to take the test. |
| 8. Receive a written or oral explanation of your test results within a reasonable amount of time after testing and in commonly understood terms. | 8. Inform appropriate person(s), as specified to you by the organization responsible for testing, if you believe that testing conditions affect your results. |
| 9. Have your test results kept confidential to the extent allowed by law. | 9. Ask about the confidentiality of your test results, if this aspect concerns you. |
| 10. Present concerns about the testing process or your results and receive information about procedures that will be used to address such concerns. | 10. Present concerns about the testing process or results in a timely, respectful, way, if you have any. |

*Source:* Reprinted by permission of the Joint Committee on Testing Practices.

**Figure 6.1. JCTP Guidelines on Rights and Responsibilities of Test Takers (Draft, August 1998)**

### Appeals and Exemptions

Appeals and exemptions refer to the process for hearing candidates' complaints, disputes, and requests for results in connection with the assessment, the standards, or the certification process itself. Candidates may dispute a test score or a ruling that they have failed to satisfy a requirement. An *appeal* gives them a right to a "second hearing," or an opportunity for a second opinion. *Exemptions* are about candidates' not having to satisfy a particular requirement because of relevant work experience, education, or existing credentials. As discussed in Chapter Two, people who have been doing a task or job for some time might request to be "grandfathered," exempting them from certain requirements new hires or trainees must satisfy. Thus most exemptions are about being allowed to substitute one requirement for another (education or experience in lieu of passing a test, or taking a test in lieu of training or additional experience).

Candidates may feel some requirements are unfair or inappropriate for their situation or background. The governance board should provide a set of guidelines detailing what candidates should do if they want to appeal a decision or request an exemption as well as how the board will review and respond to such requests. If your program is to certify employees, use processes that are currently in place to address employee disputes, if at all possible. For union members, collective bargaining agreements usually spell out how such disputes are to be handled. For example:

- The company that certifies its own HR generalists (described in previous chapters) has a well-established grievance process in place. If an employee feels he or she was treated unfairly or inappropriately during the certification process, he or she has to inform the certification administrator in writing within two weeks of the incident. There are three levels of appeals. The first appeal goes to the certification program administrator. The second level goes to the employee's supervisor. The third level goes to a standing committee within HR.

- NCIDQ allows candidates to appeal the three parts of its exam that are juried, but not the multiple choice sections. Candidates who fail the test are sent a form describing the appeals process with their test results. They have exactly twenty-one days after the results are issued to return the form, with a fee. Candidates then have two choices: (1) They can go to one of approximately fourteen locations where they can view their exam but not the jurors' notes. After they see the exam, candidates have twenty-five minutes to write their appeal. (2) They can appeal in absentia. In this case, they do not get to see their exam, so they write their appeal based on what they remember. All appeals go to the jury leader who was trained to jury that particular exam. The jury leader either confirms that the exam was scored properly or modifies the score. The jury leader cannot use any new information submitted by the candidate in a decision to modify the score.

- Business analysts with Florida's Small Business Development Centers send their applications to the program administrator. Accompanying each application is proof of employment, a signature attesting to what training the candidate has completed, a transcript showing his or her degree, and a recommendation from his or her director. The program director decides if the candidate has met the requirements and submits only questionable applications to the board, along with an opinion. For example, one analyst did not have the required degree but did have thirty-five years of experience; the director recommended an exception be made to the education requirement. The board convenes three times a year by phone if there is legitimate business to consider and once in person at an annual conference.

## Preparation and Remediation

Most employees get some job training even if they were hired because of their education; still, special additional training may be required for them to become certified. When this happens the issues related to governance deal with

- Whether the training must be preapproved, and if so, by whom (supervisor, program administrator, or both)
- Whether candidates can choose where and from whom they will receive training (community college, approved vendor, internal trainer, and so on)
- Whether training will be available through one or more delivery methods (classroom, self-study, on-line, and so on)
- Whether additional training will be provided if a candidate fails to satisfy the requirements, and what form it will take if offered
- Whether to make any published sources used to build the test available to candidates

For example, one company required all of its customer service representatives to pass a test on the rules for pricing its products. The job analysis showed that inability on the part of customer service reps to apply the rules regarding pricing cost the company millions of dollars in lost revenue and put it at risk of being fined by a regulatory agency for inaccurate pricing practices. The customer service reps were given three opportunities to pass the test. If they failed once, they were directed to review those areas in the training materials that covered the questions they answered incorrectly. If they failed a second time, they were given up to five hours of individual tutoring. If they failed a third time, they were removed from the position. If there was no other position in the company that required their skills, they were fired.

## Fees and Compensation

Fees are rarely an issue with internal certification programs, but they are important to external programs. It is expected that professional associations, vendors who certify, and credentialing boards will charge candidates a fee for any or all of these services:

- Taking the application
- Having someone review the application
- Providing a self-assessment test to candidates
- Enrolling candidates in a training program
- Administering the actual certification test
- Having someone review a candidate's test results
- Handling an appeal
- Awarding the certificate
- Maintaining the credential

The board's role in this area is to determine what fees will be charged, what they will be, and what accommodations, if any, will be made for cases of hardship.

Fees are not an issue for internal certification, but compensation is. There will be questions such as these:

- Can candidates take training while on the job, or must it be done on their own time? What happens if a candidate starts but does not finish training and then wants to re-enroll?
- Can candidates take a test while on the job, or must it be done on their own time? Will the rules be the same for practice tests and makeup tests?
- If candidates are involved in an educational program related to certification, will the organization offer tuition reimbursement? How about time off with pay to study for the exam?
- If candidates fail the test or are unable to satisfy the requirements and the organization provides remediation, will candidates be given time off with pay for this purpose or not?

The board's role here is to weigh the implications of paying people to qualify for certification and to determine how much leeway people should have if they are unable to satisfy the requirements the first time around and want additional time.

## Test Administration

The board's decisions concerning test administration determine when, where, how, and how often tests are given. Associations and credentialing boards usually offer their certification exams at specific times during the year. However, computer-based exams are making it easier for candidates to elect when they want to take a test. Vendors usually offer their exams whenever they conduct a training program. Depending on how their tests are designed, corporations might offer them upon request, following training, or at predetermined times. The board has to weigh what it costs each time to offer an exam with the desire to provide people with as many opportunities as possible to become certified. Performance-based tests are most easily offered on the job and on demand. Tests that have to be juried or that require elaborate simulations are more difficult and costly to administer and therefore are more likely to be offered at predetermined locations and times.

## RESPONSIBILITIES OF THE PROGRAM ADMINISTRATOR

The program administrator has five main responsibilities:

1. Council the board on issues related to the program
2. Provide documentation and information related to the effectiveness of the program
3. Identify and recommend solutions to ensure that the program continues to meet the needs of all stakeholders
4. Serve as the first point of contact for candidates and stakeholders (resolve disputes, recommend solutions, serve as spokesperson, and so on)
5. Manage the development, implementation, and maintenance of the program

One challenge the program administrator faces is how to anticipate the kinds of questions and decisions that will come up once the program is up and running. Some of the questions will be related to administrative issues; others will be about the standards and what candidates have to do to meet them. Here are examples of the types of administrative questions that might come up:

- How long do candidates have to earn the credential?
- What happens if they don't finish on time?

- What happens if they apply but don't start the process?
- What happens if they are interrupted at some point during the process (by illness, a leave of absence, deployment to a special assignment, and so on)?
- What happens if they don't satisfy the requirements?
- Are there different requirements for candidates with a mental or physical disability?
- What happens when a candidate or someone who is already certified is charged with violating the code of ethics?
- What information is kept about candidates and tests? Where is it kept? For how long? Who has access to it?
- Do employees with years of experience have to meet the same requirements as new hires or new graduates do?

The program administrator's job is to develop a set of protocols to handle these issues. The program administrator cannot run to the governing board each time something new comes up. However, I've found three techniques very helpful for anticipating the kinds of issues that might come up:

1. Draw or diagram the processes for seeking and administering the certification, first from the perspective of the candidate and then from the perspective of the administrator.
2. Convene a group made up of candidates, trainers, and HR people and ask them generate as many issues as they can.
3. Conduct an acceptance test of the process (not unlike those done to test new computer software and systems). That is, ask people to execute each step of the process to confirm how clear the directions are and to identify where they might want exceptions made.

Each of these techniques will add to your understanding of how the program works and what issues still need to be resolved.

### Establishing Administrative Support Systems

The program administrator should have a system that allows him or her to track candidates' progress and generate status reports. If candidates are dispersed, the program administrator will also want a system that lets him or her send them information periodically. Many organizations set up Web pages and intranets to keep candidates and stakeholders informed. Some organizations use their intranets to register candidates for training, conduct training on-line, and conduct on-line testing. For example:

- ABB has a very sophisticated system that not only supports training but gives managers all over the world the ability to find out how many employees are certified for any particular task or role. Employees can find out what they have to do to become certified. As a result of this system capability, only two staff are required to administer the certification worldwide.

- The manufacturer of HVAC systems also can monitor through its Web page and intranet how many employees are certified in any job category, task, or role. Because of how the program is designed and the capabilities of the data tracking and reporting system, it takes only two people to administer the program.

- NCIDQ uses its Web page to inform candidates of exam sites and key dates.

Technology will play a more and more significant role in the future in helping organizations manage and administer their certification programs. Technology can help with all of these tasks:

- Enrolling candidates in a program

- Registering candidates for training and testing

- Checking candidates' certification status (both by candidates and by management)

- Informing candidates and management about changes to the standards and availability of training

- Informing management of the program's impact on key metrics

- Allowing candidates to do self-assessments and practice exams

- Providing remediation

- Supporting teams assigned to update the standards and performance tests

### Analyzing Test Items

One very important administrative responsibility is that of analyzing test questions (items). The program administrator should perform an item analysis every time a test is offered. An item analysis is a review of how well each test question discriminates between candidates on the basis of their ability rather than their gender, race, age, ethnicity, or other irrelevant factors. It also measures the difficulty of each question and helps you identify misleading questions and answers. For example, it tells you when a multiple choice item has a

- Wrong answer choice that is rarely picked even by people who do not select the right answer choice (meaning the answer choice is so obviously wrong that it is automatically rejected).

- Wrong answer choice that is frequently picked even by people who score high on the test (meaning the question might be misleading or the right answer might be miscoded).

- Right answer choice that almost everyone picks (meaning this choice is so obviously right that it does not discriminate people who are competent from those who are not).

- Right answer that is rarely picked (meaning the question might be misleading or the right answer might be miscoded)

An item analysis also gives you information about each item's difficulty and ability to discriminate between candidates who know the material and those who do not. More difficult items are missed by most test takers, even those who do well on the rest of the test. Examine such items to see if they are misleading or irrelevant. Items that discriminate well are missed by poor candidates but answered correctly by qualified candidates.

There is testing software available that will analyze multiple choice and matching items for you; however, when analyzing matching items, treat each premise (what is listed in column A) as a separate question, with everything listed in column B (the responses) as the possible alternatives. This means every premise in column A is a separate question with the same list of answer choices.

To analyze a performance checklist, look for steps or attributes candidates tend to omit or add, and look to see if they tend to not follow the preferred sequence. You can ask your jurors if they notice any trends, too. When candidates continually omit steps, add steps, or follow an incorrect sequence, the checklist should be modified or the criteria better defined and communicated.

To ensure that the test does not discriminate on the basis of gender, race, age, or ethnicity, make sure every item is linked to the job or task analysis and that the questions are phrased in the language of the job or task, and look for patterns (who scores well and poorly on the test). If people of a specific gender, race, age, or ethnicity tend to score lower than the rest of the candidates, examine the questions they miss. Use the services of a psychometrician—a person professionally trained in test analysis—to review your test.

## MISSTEPS AND OVERSIGHTS

Here are some suggestions on how to avoid problems organizations experience because they do not fully consider administration and governance issues:

1. *Failure to shift ownership.* A mistake that some administrators of internal certification programs make is to fail to shift ownership of the program to the relevant line or function. Likewise, professional and trade associations that offer external certifications sometimes fail to shift ownership from their own staff to elected representatives of their members. Most internal

certification programs are administered by HR or the training department; however, oversight should come from the department or function whose people are being certified. If you are certifying a role or task that crosses functions, like project management, then oversight should come from senior managers who either rely on the skills being certified or direct a high percentage of the people who perform that role or task. For external certification programs, staff should administer the program, and elected leaders should be responsible for governance. Some professional associations adopt the National Organization for Competency Assurance (NOCA) guidelines and create totally separate organizations to govern and administer their certification programs.

2. *Failure to build a process to handle exceptions.* When organizations fail to anticipate the issues that surround exceptions and to put into place a process to deal with them, they risk exposing themselves to claims of unfairness. It is impossible to anticipate every situation or request; however, it is possible to establish processes and guidelines for dealing with them as they arise.

3. *Failure to decide in advance how to handle disputes.* Handling disputes over test scores can be problematic. A mistake organizations make is to allow candidates to talk to jurors directly to discuss their scores. The problem is more complicated when the test is part of a training program and the instructor both scores the test and hears appeals. Whenever a juror communicates directly with a candidate during an appeal, the juror has an opportunity to coach or influence the candidate. The problem is that other candidates do not get the same opportunity. A better process is one in which the juror (or the person who reviews tests in response to an appeal) never has contact with candidates during the appeals process.

4. *Failure to establish a process to handle incorrect or poorly worded test items.* Another problem occurs when the administrator agrees with a candidate that one or more items should not be considered when calculating the candidate's score. If an item is dropped for one candidate, it must be dropped for all others, whether they got it right or not. Those who got it right will see their test score drop, perhaps below the passing score. Test administrators must conscientiously avoid changing scores in this way, as the consequences can be unpleasant and far-reaching.

**TIPS**

Here are some tips for how to design your governance and administrative processes:

1. *Manage the governance board.* The program administrator's job is to help the governance board be successful and a help to you, not a burden.

Therefore, establish a relationship with every member of the board. When you want the board to make a very difficult decision or endorse a course of action with long-term implications, you will want a relationship that enables you to know what the vote will be before you ask members to formally decide. Do *not* ask the board to make a decision without giving them a recommendation about what that decision should be and the reasons why. Do *not* expect the board to be experts in testing, but do help them understand the principles of test design, the importance of doing a job or task analysis, and the creation of well-formed performance statements. Do position yourself as very knowledgeable about assessment, measuring performance, and managing certifications. Do *not* position yourself as just an efficient orchestrator of events; instead, position yourself as someone who understands the needs of the organization and the goals of the program and knows how to satisfy both.

2. *Design with the target audience in mind.* It helps if you think about your requirements from the perspective of the candidate. I suggest to my clients that they actually draw or diagram what a candidate must do to become certified. The first question that usually comes up is "Who makes the initial contact?" Assume that the process begins with candidates' contacting you to learn what it is all about. Figure 6.2. shows how that approach might unfold.

The process begins with the candidate's asking questions like these:

- What do I have to do to get certified?
- Do I qualify?
- Do I have to take a test?
- How can I be sure I won't fail?
- Where can I go to get help?
- How can I find out if I'll pass?
- What do I get once I'm certified?
- What happens if I fail?
- How many chances do I get?
- What else do I have to do?
- How much experience do I need?
- How do I prove what I've done in the past?

The next step candidates take is to find out how close they are to meeting the criteria. This is when they want to see just what the criteria are, take a "practice test," see how someone else explained their experience, and so

1. Learn the rules.
2. Find out how ready I am.
3. Get ready.
4. Take the test.

**Figure 6.2. Certification from the Candidate's Perspective**

on. Now is when they fill out the application and do a self-assessment to find out what they know and what they still need to do to pass. Once they know where they stand, they sign up for training, get some time with an expert, read some materials, and take another test to see if they've learned enough to pass. Then they take the "real test" to prove they can satisfy the criteria.

The process you design for your program might have more or fewer steps, or you might make the initial contact instead of the candidate. For example, your process might require candidates to complete an application to see if they are eligible even to apply for the certification. You might require candidates to have been employed for a minimum period of time, to have their application approved by their boss, to achieve an external credential, or to submit a sample of their work.

Taking the time to consider what candidates do allows you to think through the process much more carefully. It helps you identify possible decision points where guidelines would be helpful. Defining the process will also help you identify the materials that need to be developed for the program to work. For example, it is not unusual to think about developing the test and nothing else. If practice tests, prequalifying tests, alternatives to tests, minimum requirements, boss approvals, and so on are not considered, you run the risk of making exceptions and setting precedents that may compromise your program in the long run. Thinking it through puts you in a position to come across as more professional.

3. *Design with administrative reality in mind.* Once you have a picture of what the candidate will have to do, outline the process *you* will have to do. For example:

- Will you contact people and ask them to fill out an application? Or will you wait for them to call?

- Will you prepare and distribute memos, brochures, posters, and "table toppers" telling people who the program is for, what candidates have to do, and where to sign up? Or will you expect the boss, chapter presidents, or someone else to do this? Or will you have an HR or membership network that can notify candidates electronically?

- Will you give a presentation to all or some of the target audience on what is required, what candidates have to do, and where they will need to go to get their questions answered? Or will you prepare materials and have others provide the presentations?

- Will you send everyone in the target audience an e-mail telling them to sign up for training? Or will you just list the training on your Web page?

- Will you or someone else check that candidates meet some initial criteria before they can apply, like performing the task for a minimum period of time, being employed by your company, being recommended by the boss, and so on?

- Will you design and pilot the test and then publish a practice test so candidates can see if they are ready for the real test? Or will you just make the standards available?

- Will you tell candidates that there are alternatives to the test, like a minimum amount of experience or recommendations from certain types of people? Or will it be their responsibility to ask?

The reason to describe your process is to identify where guidelines or protocols would be helpful, what supporting materials you should develop, and what policies and procedures you want to recommend.

 **GUIDELINES**

Here are some guidelines you can use when designing your governance and administrative processes:

### Board Membership

The governance board ensures that the program serves the needs of all of the stakeholders (the organization, the membership, and the public), not just the organization's training or professional development departments; therefore, its members should represent senior management or the leadership of the profession, the target audience, key stakeholders (including consumers), and the person who is responsible for administering the program. Either create a special body to provide oversight and governance, or assign responsibility to a standing committee that is already in place. The important thing is to set up a structure with checks and balances.

A. If you are starting or managing an *internal certification,* then the makeup of the governance board should include

- A senior manager who is responsible for the function the target audience works in

- A senior manager from the function most dependent on the target audience's performance

- Someone from the target audience who is certified

- Someone from HR

- The person responsible for administering the certification program

B. If you are starting or managing an *external certification,* then the makeup of the governance board should include

- Someone from the public (ideally a consumer) who uses the services of the target audience

- Someone from the target audience who is certified

- A highly respected member or practitioner of the profession, such as a formerly elected officer of the society

- The staff person responsible for administering the program

- An expert or high-ranking member of a regulating body, if the field is regulated

- Someone from the academic community, if educational programs related to the field are generally available to the candidates

C. Establish procedures for how the board will conduct business (for example, "Follow Robert's Rules of Order"). Include the following:

- How often the board will meet. Most boards meet two to three times a year when a program is in the early stages of development. Later, they should be able to meet less frequently.

- How and what kind of topics get put on the agenda.

- An operating philosophy for the board (that is, what its stance is toward professional conduct, development, ethics, fairness, performance, and leadership).

- Rules for how frequently (for example, every other year) the board will address program evaluation and maintenance issues such as recertification, updating the standards, tracking how well the program is meeting organizational needs, and stakeholder expectations.

- Terms of office. Limit the terms of office of at least some of the board members, to ensure that the changing needs of the stakeholders will continue to be represented.

D. Conduct a formal orientation for new board members. In the orientation, discuss the following:

- The roles and responsibilities of the board members

- The history of the program

- The performance metrics of the program

- The board's operating procedures and any of its decisions regarding recertification, updating the standards, and keeping the program current

- The procedures for hearing appeals and considering exemptions

## Candidate Rights

Make available to candidates in a form they can easily reference and retain a list describing candidates' rights. Include the following:

A. Candidates should be informed up front of

- The application process, including any time restrictions

- Any prequalifying criteria and minimum requirements

- How to request an exemption or an extension if their ability to participate is interrupted due to illness, a career hiatus, education, deployment to a special assignment, and so on

B. Prior to taking the test, they should be told

- When the assessment will be offered, where it will be offered, what time (how far in advance) they should show up, and what the consequences will be if they fail to show up or don't show up on time

- What materials, equipment, authorizations, identification, and so on they should bring, and what the consequences will be if they fail to bring what is required

- How the test will be administered, such as whether or not it will be timed

- If materials or references will be available during the assessment and, if so, how they can be used

- How and when (how much in advance) they should let you know if they need special accommodations due to a disability recognized under the Americans with Disabilities Act or other relevant legislation and what the consequences will be if they don't

- What the purpose of the test is, how the results will be used, what the format of the test will be (multiple choice, performance, and so on), when they will see the results, and who else will see the results

- How much time after receiving their results they will have to appeal, what the appeals process is, and what the consequences will be if they fail to follow the process

- How the test will be scored and analyzed to identify scoring errors and questions that should be modified

- What references were used to develop the questions

## Disclosure

Develop a set of protocols for what information gets shared and with whom. Document those protocols, and discuss them with the governance board to ensure that the board understands and agrees with what you are proposing. The protocols should specify who has access to what information and under what conditions. They should include statements like these:

A.  The actual questions, their answers, and the results of item analyses will be known only to the test administrator and those members of the board who are responsible for the test's design and accuracy.

B.  Candidates will be told that they passed or failed, but they will not be told who else passed or failed.

C.  Supervisors and managers will be told who and how many passed (for internal certifications), but they will not be told individual scores. (Some organizations allow supervisors and managers to see the full range of test scores, without names attached. When supervisors see actual scores or where people fall in a range, the effort can too easily become a contest instead of an assessment.)

D.  Candidates will not be told the names of the jurors who will or did judge their work samples.

E.  Candidates will not be told in advance who will judge their performance but will be introduced to the juror(s) at the time of their performance.

F.  In the event of an appeal, the certification administrator will have access to all the scores for that specific offering of the test, and the results of the item analysis.

G.  In the event of an appeal, the governance board will have access to the individual's score and the results of the item analysis.

H.  If one of the goals of the certification is development, then candidates will be told which content or performance areas they should develop based on the results of the test.

I.  When a candidate fails, the test will be rescored to ensure it was scored accurately, before the failure is made known to the candidate.

J.  When a candidate fails a juried exam, a second juror will review the candidate's answers or work sample. The second juror will not be allowed to see the first juror's notes or evaluation. If the second juror does not agree with the first juror's decision, the response or work sample will be sent to a third juror or to an expert. The third juror's or expert's decision will be final. Except in the case of using an expert, the second or third juror will not be told that the exam is being judged again. (It is best if all jurors think they are the first to see a candidate's answer or piece of work.)

## Appeals and Exemptions

The board will be asked to rule on appeals and exemptions; therefore,

A. Develop a set of guidelines for who will have the authority to rule on
   - Candidate requests for exemptions or exceptions
   - Disputes over test scores
B. Inform candidates in writing
   - How and to whom they should submit their requests
   - How much time they have to request an appeal after receiving notification that they failed
   - How many levels of appeals there are and the procedures for requesting each one
C. The guidelines should include
   - Who will review requests for exemptions and appeals
   - How long the organization will have before it must respond in writing
   - Instructions to board members and jurors to not communicate directly with candidates requesting an exemption or appeal
   - The procedures for determining who is qualified to review juried items
   - How many levels of appeals there will be
   - Who will have the authority to make the final determination

## Ethics

If ethics is one of your standards, then you should develop a set of guidelines for what types of ethical issues are appropriate for the board to review, how complaints or questions should be submitted, and the process for review. At a minimum, consider the following guidelines:

A. List examples of the kinds of behaviors or actions that would be suitable for investigation.
B. Develop a procedure for receiving, reviewing, and evaluating charges or complaints.
C. Develop a process for rejecting unfounded or unprovable charges.
D. Require charges to be submitted in writing.
E. Establish a fixed amount of time the person charged has to respond or to provide information.

F.  Limit the number of appeals a person can seek.

G.  Decide in advance what possible disciplinary actions or sanctions you might recommend to the board when a person is found to have violated the code of ethics.

H.  Have the board put its decisions in writing, including the rationale behind its decisions.

## Electronic Support

The competition among providers of software and telecommunications systems is both problematic and exciting. The demand for access to information and the ability to deploy information within organizations across the country and worldwide is driving the development of new telecommunications and intranet technologies.

A.  Here are some tasks you can perform electronically:

- Keep candidates informed of their status, training, testing, and so on
- Register candidates for training, testing, and so on
- Deliver training
- Conduct testing
- Analyze test results
- Perform item analyses
- Compile test results and generate reports
- Enable supervisors and candidates to update candidate records
- Enable supervisors to check candidates' status or identify who has what certifications

B.  Define your requirements in terms of

- Information you want to disperse, and to whom you want to disperse it
- Information you want to control access to
- Data you want to capture, and in what form you want to capture it
- Who you want to be able to enter that data, where they are, and the system capability they have now
- Data you want to control access to, particularly the ability to edit it
- Reports you want to generate based on the data

C.  Establish a network of noncompeting firms so you can share and draw on their experience to identify the best combination of software and hardware for your needs.

**SUMMARY**

Governance and administration are frequently the least thought about aspects of a certification program. Unfortunately, they are the two areas that can embarrass you the most. Senior executives or other powerful organizational members who ask for information about a candidate, promise candidates an exception will be made, or assure a candidate that a test score will be overturned inadvertently set precedents that can embarrass the organization. Or worse, they can be cited as proof of favoritism if not outright discrimination. Establishing a governance process with protocols that ensure that candidates will have a fair hearing, that tests work as intended, and that confidential information will remain confidential are essential for a defensible program. You also want a board that is informed and supportive of you and the program; therefore, it is your responsibility to educate the board members so that they can make better-informed decisions and provide the leadership the program requires. The following checklists are designed to help you assess your current governance and administrative processes and determine what you can do to improve them.

 **CHECKLISTS**

Here are some checklists you can use to evaluate your governance and administrative processes:

**Governance**

|  | YES | NO |
|---|---|---|
| A. There is a governance body responsible for oversight that | | |
| • Reviews the certification standards, criteria, and administration | ☐ | ☐ |
| • Determines how frequently accumulative scores are reviewed | ☐ | ☐ |
| • Determines how frequently performance criteria are reviewed | ☐ | ☐ |
| • Determines how frequently preparation materials are reviewed | ☐ | ☐ |
| • Determines how often liability and compliance issues are reviewed and safeguards against bias are considered and implemented | ☐ | ☐ |
| • Ensures there is a link between the certification program and the performance management system or compensation system | ☐ | ☐ |

|  | YES | NO |
|---|---|---|

B.  There are operating procedures that describe

- The makeup of the board ☐ ☐
- How often the board meets ☐ ☐
- How the certification is administered (policies and procedures) ☐ ☐
- On what basis the certification program is measured and evaluated ☐ ☐
- The recertification requirements and protocols ☐ ☐
- Who has sign-off authority regarding governance issues ☐ ☐

C.  The appeals process is documented and includes or indicates

- Directions on how to appeal or request a review ☐ ☐
- How much time after taking a test a candidate can appeal ☐ ☐
- To whom candidates submit their requests ☐ ☐
- In what form they submit their requests ☐ ☐
- How many levels of appeals there are ☐ ☐
- Who makes up the appeals board ☐ ☐
- On what basis board members were selected ☐ ☐
- How long the board has to respond to a request for a review ☐ ☐
- In what form it responds ☐ ☐
- How appeals are considered by the board ☐ ☐
- Who has the final say ☐ ☐

## Administration

|  | YES | NO |
|---|---|---|

A.  Administrative procedures include informing candidates of

- The requirements and standards for certification ☐ ☐
- How candidates begin the certification process ☐ ☐
- How candidates will be kept informed about the process ☐ ☐
- How testing sites are chosen ☐ ☐
- How test materials are distributed and maintained ☐ ☐
- The testing conditions, such as time to complete, use of materials, and kinds of interactions allowed ☐ ☐
- How candidates will be notified of their score ☐ ☐
- What the policies are for when candidates fail the test ☐ ☐

|  | YES | NO |
|---|:---:|:---:|
| • How many times candidates can attempt certification | ☐ | ☐ |
| • What information (if any) from the program will be placed in candidates' personnel files | ☐ | ☐ |
| • What information will be maintained in candidates' program files | ☐ | ☐ |
| • Who will get a candidate's test results | ☐ | ☐ |
| • What decisions or actions will be taken based on the test results | ☐ | ☐ |
| • What resources are available to prepare, assess readiness, or remediate, such as training or self-assessments | ☐ | ☐ |

B. Information on test security and maintenance includes

|  | YES | NO |
|---|:---:|:---:|
| • How consistency across offerings will be maintained | ☐ | ☐ |
| • How equivalency across offerings will be maintained | ☐ | ☐ |
| • Who has access to test questions and answers | ☐ | ☐ |

## Test Administration

Documentation of the procedures used to ensure consistent and fair test administration includes or explains

| | YES | NO |
|---|:---:|:---:|

A. Prerequisites

|  | YES | NO |
|---|:---:|:---:|
| • What prerequisites (if any) the candidate must satisfy before testing | ☐ | ☐ |
| • Who decided what the prerequisites are, and on what basis the people who made this decision were chosen | ☐ | ☐ |

B. Jurors

|  | | |
|---|:---:|:---:|
| • The criteria jurors must satisfy to become jurors | ☐ | ☐ |
| • Who decided on the criteria, and on what basis the people who decided on the criteria were chosen | ☐ | ☐ |
| • How jurors are trained | ☐ | ☐ |

C. Forms and equipment

|  | | |
|---|:---:|:---:|
| • The directions that will be given to candidates prior to and during the testing process on what to do and how proficiency will be determined | ☐ | ☐ |
| • Any forms candidates must complete prior to taking the test | ☐ | ☐ |
| • The forms that will be used to record candidates' answers or responses | ☐ | ☐ |

|  | YES | NO |
|---|---|---|
| • Performance checklists to be used by jurors to score performance | ☐ | ☐ |
| • Checklists that will be used to judge short answers or oral answers | ☐ | ☐ |
| • A list of required equipment and materials | | |

D.  On-site administration

|  | YES | NO |
|---|---|---|
| • Instructions or scripts that will be used by test administrators | ☐ | ☐ |
| • Instructions that will be given to the candidate when the test is administered electronically or as part of a self-administered test booklet | ☐ | ☐ |
| • Instructions that will be given to jurors about how to complete the checklists | ☐ | ☐ |
| • Guidelines on how to accommodate disabilities | ☐ | ☐ |

E.  Test security

|  | YES | NO |
|---|---|---|
| • Who has authority to review the test items | ☐ | ☐ |
| • Who has access to the test items and item analysis results | ☐ | ☐ |
| • Who has authority to review individual and accumulative scores | ☐ | ☐ |
| • Who has sign-off authority and accountability for confirming test administration procedures have been followed | ☐ | ☐ |

**WHERE TO LEARN MORE**

Browning, A. H., Bugbee, A. C., Jr., Mullins, M. A. (eds.). *Certification: A NOCA Handbook* (Washington, DC: National Organization for Competency Assurance, 1996). The sections on policies and procedures and test administration are a must.

**NOTES**

1. There are groups specially qualified to review requests for accommodations due to disabilities. Requests from candidates asking for accommodation for learning and mental disorders are especially difficult to judge and should be reviewed by a qualified psychologist. To locate groups qualified to assist you, contact the National Organization for Competency Assurance or the American Psychological Association. Ask for recommendations for organizations with psychometricians with disability and psychological disorder experience.

2. Participating associations are the American Counseling Association, the American Psychological Association, the American Speech-Language-Hearing Association, the National Association of School Psychologists, and the National Council on Measurement in Education.

# Chapter 7

# Recertification and Maintenance

$R$ecertification can be a troublesome issue, both for professional associations that offer external certifications and for organizations that certify their own members. Problems with recertification arise from a number of factors, including

- Organizations' tendency to try to find a single solution for distinctly different problems
- Lack of agreement concerning what recertification should and will accomplish
- How jobs and professions are created and evolve in response to new technologies, theories, and applications

Some problems are best handled through recertification, others through maintenance, and still others by developing a new credential.

Recall from Chapter Two that recertification and maintenance are not exactly the same thing. *Recertification* applies to credentials that have a time limit—that is, they expire after a fixed period of time. When the credential expires, people have to reapply and be certified again. The certifying organization imposes a time limit because it believes the original standards and requirements might have to be changed in the future. Recertification gives the organization an opportunity to impose new requirements and standards. What people have to do to become recertified might resemble what they had to do to become certified originally, such as complete training, pass a test, submit a work sample, pay a fee, and commit to maintaining their credential. It frequently involves some type of reassessment.

Other certifications do not expire but instead have *maintenance* requirements. Once you have earned the designation, it is yours for life—as long as you pay an annual fee, earn a minimum number of continuing education credits, stay active in your field, or fulfill some other requirement. If you fail to fulfill the maintenance requirements, then you will lose the credential. Some organizations even allow retirees to maintain their credentials for a reduced annual fee. Maintenance rarely involves reassessment.

Still other credentials both expire after a set time *and* require maintenance. For example, a person could earn a certification that is valid for three years and then, to maintain the credential during that period, have to pay an annual fee, earn a minimum number of continuing education credits each year, and stay active in the field. Afterward, when the three years are up, he or she would have to reapply and meet the other requirements for recertification. To add to the confusion, some organizations require people to earn multiple new credentials every time they introduce a new product, product model, or procedure—sometimes instead of or in addition to being recertified or maintaining an existing credential.

## STABILITY OF ENABLING KNOWLEDGE

Whether people should be required to maintain a credential, become recertified, or earn an entirely new credential is not a simple decision. The certifying organization has to determine whether the original body of knowledge or level of performance will be adequate for continued competence into the future or if additional knowledge or skills will be needed because of new technology, research, or areas of application.

For example, computer software and hardware companies usually do not have maintenance requirements for the credentials they offer, because every year or two they release upgraded versions of their products. As a result, there is no need to continue supporting older products or systems. It would be pointless to require people to maintain their certification in version 3.0, since this version will disappear from the marketplace once version 4.0 comes out. Instead, they need to become certified in version 4.0.

Other industries and jobs depend on workers' retaining their knowledge of earlier products and developing knowledge of new ones. Manufacturers of durable goods and equipment used by the automotive, health care, utilities, and telecommunications industries rely on technicians' being able to support multiple generations of older products as well as ones built on different technologies. Hydraulic pumps, electronic and mechanical controls, diagnostic equipment, household appliances, and the like remain in service for many years. At the same time, newer models are introduced and have to be installed, operated, and serviced. The service industry has similar problems. For exam-

I recently moved my office into my home. I wanted to install the same type of computer network in my home office as I had used in my outside office and use as much of my old hardware as possible. My printers are all well over five years old. One computer has the latest operating system and one has the previous generation. My server's operating system is two generations old. The young man I hired to install the network was certified on all the generations but had not worked on the older systems for over a year and had done nothing to stay fresh. He frequently sighed over having to work with my antiquated equipment, commenting that my Internet service provider was "plebeian" by his standards, and assured me that I couldn't find *anyone* qualified to work on such old equipment. However, he proudly announced he was certified to install the latest version of Windows and a new tape backup system.

ple, the credit card, financial investment, and banking industries are still supporting products that have been around for years, such as college loans, mortgages, and passbook savings accounts. Some of those products have changed in response to new legislation, and different versions have been introduced to accommodate customer needs. Meanwhile, whole new service lines have been developed, such as debit cards, Roth IRAs, and reverse mortgages. Therefore, manufacturers of durable goods and certain service industries require people to maintain their credentials so that they can continue to support older products, to be recertified as products change, and to earn additional certifications as new products are developed.

### Distinguishing Between Knowledge Atrophy and Knowledge Evolution

How a job or professional discipline evolves over time may or may not affect its dependence on an original body of knowledge. Sometimes the evolution takes people away from the original body of knowledge; other times it requires them to apply it in new arenas. The health care field provides especially clear examples of the resulting dilemma for certifying organizations:

- A doctor graduates from an accredited institution and is licensed to practice medicine. Later she is certified in a specialty. After a few years, her practice becomes more and more specialized, and eventually it evolves into a subspecialty. If the credentialing board that certified her in the original specialty decides to require continuing education credits to maintain her credential, should the courses be in the original specialty, in the subspecialty, or both? If the credentialing board decides to require recertification, should she be recertified in the specialty, the subspecialty, or both? Or would an entirely new certification, in the subspecialty, be warranted?

- Dentists are licensed, and they can be certified in oral and maxillofacial surgery (a specialty) but limit their practice to cosmetic surgery or oncology. Frequently their licensure requires them to maintain their credentials by earning continuing professional education credits. Currently there is no certification for subspecialties. But if at some point a dentist is required to be recertified, should he or she be tested in the fundamentals of oral and maxillofacial surgery or in new developments? If the subspecialties require both the original and a new body of knowledge, should they be part of the recertification, or should a new certification be developed?

- Orthopedic specialists are licensed in medicine and certified in orthopedics, and they can even be certified in a subspecialty (hands). Is it sufficient for them to maintain one or both credentials? Should they be required to be recertified in one or both?

- The Association for Worksite Health Promotion (whose members manage health and fitness centers at the workplace) and the Association of Polysomnographic Technologists (whose members diagnose sleep disorders) decided a whole new certification was appropriate because these subspecialties require the practitioners to be proficient in more than just the original body of knowledge.

For some groups, it is important to ensure that practitioners' knowledge of fundamental principles has not atrophied because their practice or job has moved in new directions. This is true for internal as well as external certifications. Companies want to confirm that their people still know the safety principles, can service mature products, and still remember the fundamental concepts required to troubleshoot complex problems. In each of these situations, the practitioners have to draw on enabling knowledge (that is, the original body of knowledge).

Recertification and maintenance are viable methods for ensuring that people review and refresh their knowledge, particularly if they are required to pass a test or demonstrate the same level of proficiency as they did when they were originally certified. Some organizations recertify people by assessing them on the same content covered in the original test, whereas others only assess people on a subset of the original content. Recertification also allows an organization to require candidates to know or be able to apply a new body of knowledge. Maintenance may be less suitable if all people have to do is earn unspecified continuing education credits, because there is no control over what they might study. When the body of knowledge, task, role, or job being certified evolves to such an extent that a whole new body of knowledge or ability level is required, then the organization should consider developing a new credential.

### Defining the Purpose of Recertification or Maintenance

Therefore, certification program managers must decide if they want recertification or maintenance requirements to reinforce a core body of knowledge or capabilities or to encourage people to stay up-to-date with new developments. Once the purpose of the requirement is clear, the organization can decide how often recertification must occur and what form (test or continuing education) it should take. For example:

- The manufacturer of HVAC systems (described in previous chapters) reserves the right to change or add to its credential's standards every six months. Employees are informed of the new standards and what training is available. They even have immediate access to the new performance checklist. They are recertified when their supervisor attests that they can perform the task or role as newly defined. Since their certification is performance-based, the company assumes that if employees can perform the task to standard, they know what they need to know. Additional certifications, similar to certification in subspecialties in the medical field, are required as new products are developed.

- Amway does not recertify its trainers, but it makes training on new products and product applications available to everyone. It relies on the organization's incentives to encourage trainers to stay current about products.

- Enerpac retests its technicians every three years to confirm that they can do the job to standard.

### Redoing the Job or Task Analysis

The truth is that many groups that certify don't really know whether or not the field or task has changed enough to warrant new requirements or standards. They suspect. They don't know if practitioners' knowledge has atrophied for lack of use and, if so, if it might jeopardize something or someone. They don't know the degree to which changes in technology, customer expectations, or regulations have made the original standards inadequate or in need of an overhaul. And they won't know these things until they do a job or task analysis to find out.

The original job or task analysis is the most labor- and cost-intensive one; subsequent analyses can be more targeted. You may want to convene one or two groups (with representatives from the target audience and stakeholders) to generate an initial list of tasks and expectations. You can then validate their opinions by means of a larger survey of people who currently hold the credential and of key stakeholders. If educational institutions, allied fields, and vendors have done relevant market or consumer research, you might want to use their results to narrow your scope of study. If regulatory agencies and consumer groups are demanding competencies outside of what the original program covered, you can focus your study into those areas of concern. If you suspect that people are specializing in their work, you can design the study to determine to what degree they are still dependent on a core body of knowledge and to what degree a new body of knowledge or skills is required. Once you know what has changed, you will be in a position to ask the following important questions:

- Does it matter? What impact does the change have on our organization's ability to achieve its objectives? Does it create new problems?
- Does it jeopardize our position of social stewardship?
- Is this an opportunity for us to change the requirements or be more demanding?
- Will other groups come in with new credentials and take the market away from us?
- Will customers stop buying our products and services because our requirements have not kept up with change?

Go back to your original set of goals. Debate whether or not they are still appropriate. But find out what, if anything, has changed that might call for you to be more prescriptive in your maintenance requirements, require people to undergo a periodic reassessment, or change the requirements and standards.

## Timing the Requirement

One of the more frequent questions I'm asked is, "How often should we recertify?" People want to know if they should recertify every three years, every ten years, and so on. They assume recertifications are time-driven instead of need-driven. There is nothing to prevent an organization from requiring people to be recertified when a change warrants it. The automobile manufacturer recertifies all of its employees every year. The process requires everyone to complete a self-assessment on their knowledge of the company's new models. However, the company recertifies its production maintenance crews whenever a new technology (like robotics), a new safety rule, or a new environmental hazardous waste regulation is introduced. They just tell people in advance what is expected.

Organizations that offer external certifications often feel that they must require recertification at predetermined equal intervals. But why? If they require maintenance, they could announce periodically what the new requirements are to maintain the credential. They could even announce a change in the rules, such as all certifications will expire within eighteen months unless people demonstrate they can satisfy a new set of requirements. They could also require practitioners to take an approved course on a specific topic or even pass a test on the new body of knowledge, to maintain the credential. They could even follow the model of how some states renew driver's licenses: some years you take a vision test, some years you take a written test, and every three years you get your picture taken and pay a fee. What people want and deserve is fair notice and an adequate opportunity to learn required new information.

## MISSTEPS AND OVERSIGHTS

Here are some common mistakes organizations make concerning recertification and maintenance:

1. *Failing to periodically reevaluate what people do and must know to be effective.* A major mistake organizations make is that they wait too long to reevaluate their standards. They don't look for opportunities to regularly monitor changes in the profession or area of practice that might signal the need to commission smaller and more time-sensitive studies.

2. *Failing to define the purpose of maintenance or recertification requirements.* Some organizations seem unwilling to articulate what problem they want maintenance or recertification requirements to solve. For some reason they are hesitant to take a position on whether they want to ensure people's skills have stayed current or to confirm that people can still remember the old rules, principles, and so on. This hesitancy to define the purpose results in organizations' providing very little direction or guidance on how to maintain skills and knowledge. Simply requiring continuing professional education may not be enough. This becomes an even larger problem when the standards cover a professional discipline or job instead of just a task. It might be more helpful to specify percentages or a minimum number of credits in a series of specific topics rather than to allow people to earn all of their points in one subject.

## TIPS

Here are some tips for avoiding the mistakes some organizations make, either by failing to require maintenance or recertification or by not providing adequate guidance:

1. *Monitor changes in the field.* Conduct annual surveys or interviews with a random sample of people who are certified and with their employers, customers, and other vested parties. Compare the results with what was learned during the original job or task analysis. Have the governing board set parameters for when changes warrant a more comprehensive study.

2. *Track the cost to monitor compliance.* Periodically measure what it costs to remind people to renew their credential, to track compliance, and to keep the database current. Use this information to improve your internal processes and to argue for improved systems.

3. *Promote the benefits of maintenance and recertification.* Don't assume that certificate holders will remember or understand the intent behind maintenance and recertification requirements. Continually remind them of the benefits to themselves, to society, and to their job or discipline. Give them language that they can use to express those benefits to others. Don't overlook the importance of rewarding people for fulfilling maintenance requirements and becoming recertified.

4. *Develop maintenance criteria.* Most maintenance requirements are monitored using a point system: people are expected to earn a minimum number of points each year or within a period of years to maintain their credential. Consider giving points for attending continuing education, attending national conferences, publishing in professional or trade journals, serving on committees, doing community work, and training others. Whatever you decide to accept, make sure it supports the intent behind the maintenance requirement. For example, someone who teaches or does research may be contributing significantly to the profession but not maintaining his or her original skills. Put together a team with representatives from the target audience and some key stakeholders to identify the types of activities that would warrant points. Be sensitive to what opportunities people really have to earn the points. For example, you might find that some people will want to receive their training over the Internet, others will prefer to view videotapes, and still others can easily attend seminars.

 **GUIDELINES**

## Recertification

Here are some guidelines to help you design your maintenance and recertification requirements. When deciding whether or not to require recertification

A. Conduct a job or task analysis between every three and seven years. The scope of the study should be dictated by the volatility of the field, advances in the educational system, heightened stakeholder expectations, known changes in the required body of knowledge or skill set, and known changes in the business environment that affect the job or task.

B. Meet with your stakeholders and go over each of the following questions. Notice where you are apart and where you agree.

- What has changed?

- Did the change affect everyone or just some people?

- What is the magnitude of the change? Did it radically alter the way a task is done?

- Does the change require people to draw on a different body of knowledge or to develop new skills? If so, what is at risk if people do not acquire that knowledge or those skills?

- What problem are you trying to solve?

- What is driving the need for recertification?

- What costs will be added or incurred if there is recertification? If you do not recertify?

- Who will benefit the most and the least from recertification?

- Is it important to periodically reconfirm that people have retained a specific body of knowledge?

- Is it important to periodically reconfirm that people can still perform a specific task or tasks?

- If you were to test people as part of your recertification requirement, what would that test entail?

- Would you be satisfied if people just completed a training program or some form of self-assessment? Why or why not?

C. Based on your answers and your understanding of recertification, decide if you want to require

- Activities that encourage people to stay current (maintenance)

- Some form of assessment to verify that people either remember something, have learned something new, can still do something, can do it differently, or can do it in new ways or under new circumstances (recertification)

- A new credential

D. If you need a sponsor for a recertification or maintenance requirement, decide how you might build a business case for it.

E. Draw or diagram the process for getting recertified; that is, what will people seeking recertification have to do, and what will the organization do?

F. Decide what change, event, or time period you will use to signal that people should apply for recertification.

## SUMMARY

Recertification and maintenance are viable methods for encouraging and rewarding continued competence. However, it is important to be clear and in agreement about what you want these requirements to represent, particularly to the public, the target audience, and stakeholders. Recertification can represent your organization's commitment to ensuring that people stay current in their discipline, up-to-date on changes in the field, and capable of providing the level of service customers expect. Maintenance requirements, too, when designed well, can effectively encourage people to review the basics and learn about new developments. The following checklist (also on the accompanying disk) is designed to help you evaluate your process for encouraging and confirming continued competence.

 **CHECKLIST**

### Recertification

Here is a checklist you can use to assess your process for encouraging continued competence.

|  |  | YES | NO |
|---|---|:---:|:---:|
| A. | A new job or task analysis has been done. | ☐ | ☐ |
| B. | It has confirmed that | | |
|  | • A new body of knowledge is required. | ☐ | ☐ |
|  | • A new skill set is required. | ☐ | ☐ |
|  | • The old body of knowledge and skills are being applied in new ways. | ☐ | ☐ |
| C. | There is a statement that describes the reason for requiring maintenance. | ☐ | ☐ |
| D. | There is a statement that describes the reason for requiring recertification. | ☐ | ☐ |
| E. | There is a description or list of factors that indicate that the board should discuss the feasibility and viability of developing a new credential in lieu of recertification or maintenance. | ☐ | ☐ |
| F. | There is a description of what people must do to maintain the credential. | ☐ | ☐ |
| G. | If continuing education is required, there is a list of the attributes the education must satisfy to be accepted (when it was done, who offered it, whether or not it incorporated some type of assessment, what the topic was, and so on). | ☐ | ☐ |
| H. | If staying active in the field is required, there is a definition of what this means. | ☐ | ☐ |

|  | YES | NO |
|---|---|---|

I.  If recertification is required, there is a list of what people have to do to satisfy the requirement. ☐ ☐

J.  If an assessment is required, there is a description of

  • What people can do to ensure their readiness ☐ ☐

  • What the assessment will involve ☐ ☐

  • What the criteria for success are ☐ ☐

  • When people must register for the assessment and what the consequences are if they don't ☐ ☐

K.  The processes for appeals and exemptions for recertification and maintenance are defined. ☐ ☐

## WHERE TO LEARN MORE

So little has been written about recertification and the maintenance of credentials that I recommend drawing on the literature and research of the quality movement for this topic. Specifically, see books on continuous improvement, "Kaizen," and measuring customer satisfaction, including the following two titles.

Brunette, W. H. *Achieving Total Quality: Integrating Business Strategy and Customer Needs* (White Plains, NY: Quality Resources, 1993).

Hayes, B. E. *Measuring Customer Satisfaction: Development and Use of Questionnaires* (Milwaukee, WI: ASQC Quality Press, 1992).

# Chapter 8

# Going Global

*B*efore beginning work on this book I met with several corporate and association clients who have successfully launched certification programs in other countries. Early in our discussion the question of what the difference is between national, international, multinational, and global certification programs came up. We decided that the major differences, both for corporations and for professional associations, stem not from language or culture but from who participates in developing the standards and how universal the standards are.

If a local certification is truly voluntary, then the sponsoring organization can afford to be provincial in how it develops its standards. However, if the organization markets the credential abroad, either internally or externally, then it has to decide if it wants to limit the standards to those that can be universal (that is, applicable in every country or area where the certification is offered) or if it will allow countries to ignore, replace, or modify some of the standards to accommodate their local requirements or preferences.

## DISTINCTIONS BETWEEN NATIONAL, INTERNATIONAL, GLOBAL, AND MULTINATIONAL PROGRAMS

A national program is one that is developed in and for one country and is recognized by all the constituents of that country (state or provincial regulatory agencies, customers or employers, academic institutions, and candidates or practitioners). For the most part, a national program is analogous to a local program, although some national programs have found that they must either develop more than one set of standards to reflect differences in local laws or limit their standards to items that apply to all localities. This is the same issue organizations face when they want their credential recognized outside of the country of origin.

*167*

Here are some definitions, provided for the purposes of this discussion:

- An international program is based on standards that were developed and adopted by one country and later applied to other countries.

- A global program is one based on universal standards. Representatives from different nations collectively define a set of standards that they agree to apply universally.

- A multinational program is based on a combination of universal and local standards. Representatives from different nations collectively define a universal set of standards, but they reserve the right to supplement those standards with ones that reflect their local conditions.

For example:

- IFMA has an international certification. (Foreign organizations use IFMA standards yet they can modify or replace IFMA test questions with questions that reflect local regulatory requirements and can develop new scenarios that depict more realistic dilemmas for their part of the world, to better test candidates' problem-solving skills.) A northern European organization wanted to certify facility managers based on IFMA's standards. The organization brought together IFMA-certified facility managers from France, Germany, the Netherlands, and the United Kingdom to develop the first European version of the test. The committee sorted the items according to those that applied, those that did not apply, and those that could apply with minor modifications. It suggested modifications to the scenarios to better reflect real-life problems faced by facility managers working in northern Europe (they removed references to tornados and hurricanes and substituted terrorism). The committee decided that the first European offering of the exam would be in English, as this was their language of business. It recommended that future offerings be in French, German, and Dutch as the market for the credential grew in those countries. By passing this version of the test and meeting IFMA's education and experience requirements, Europeans can receive IFMA's designation.

- Amway's certification program is global. When Amway decided to certify trainers working for its affiliates in at least forty-nine countries, it created a set of universal standards—that is, standards that are relevant no matter where an employee works, anywhere in the world. It put together an international team to modify standards developed in the United States so that they would apply everywhere. The standards and training materials are in English, except for those used in underdeveloped countries where opportunities to learn English are practically nonexistent.

- ABB's certifications are both global and multinational. Some of its certifications are based on universal standards, and others are based on a combination of universal and local standards.

- The certifications offered by the manufacturer of HVAC systems (discussed in previous chapters) are based on the company's U.S. standards. When it deploys the certifications to plants located in other countries, managers from different nations can modify the standards so they reflect local regulatory requirements. This company has an international certification but is working toward making it a multinational one.

## WHY GO GLOBAL OR INTERNATIONAL?

Organizations "internationalize" their credentials for the same reasons they offer them in the first place:

- To facilitate the deployment of competent workers

- To enhance their brand image

- To establish standards that can be used by academic institutions and employers

- To enhance the current standards embraced by professions and academic institutions

- To penetrate or secure a position in a market

International certification simply extends these goals to the global arena: deploying workers across international boundaries, improving brand image abroad, establishing worldwide universal standards, enhancing current standards around the globe, and penetrating or securing foreign markets.

## DETERMINING RECIPROCITY, EQUIVALENCY, AND EXEMPTIONS

U.S. associations and corporations want their professional and industry standards to be accepted by other countries. Corporations in other countries want their product and industry standards to be accepted by the United States. Similarly, academic institutions want their degrees to be recognized and accepted around the world. Such cross-boundary recognition of standards and credentials may take the form of reciprocity, equivalency, or exemptions:

- *Reciprocity* is mutual recognition by two countries of each other's standards and academic programs.

- *Equivalency* is the determination that one country's industry standards and educational programs are essentially the same and of equal quality as those of another country.

- *Exemptions* occur when an organization allows candidates to substitute education completed in another country for its own educational requirements because the academic programs are considered equivalent.

Universal standards make reciprocity and exemptions easier. However, reciprocity and exemptions can happen only when the participating organizations and institutions acknowledge the equivalency of each other's standards and academic programs. For example:

- An automobile manufacturer might exempt from its qualification program new hires who have participated in another manufacturer's program, because it regards its competitors' programs to be equivalent to its own.

- A corporation that certifies its HR generalists worldwide might accept the change management training offered by a U.S. vendor and a Middle Eastern vendor as substitutes for its own program.

- A U.S. professional association might accept degrees earned from U.S. accredited institutions and degrees from universities in other parts of the world that are active in developing universal standards.

In the United States, organizations ensure candidates receive high-quality education by requiring them to attend accredited or approved programs. The assumption is that for a program to be accredited or approved, it has to satisfy a minimum set of standards. U.S. organizations are hesitant to accept degrees or test scores from countries where there is a lack of such universal standards. When their certifications indicate that those who have earned them possess specific knowledge or abilities, then organizations want assurance that any academic standards they rely on from foreign institutions are the same as the standards at domestic schools. What gets taught at foreign schools might reflect the local culture, not universally accepted principles. For example, medical schools in the United States teach drug therapy and consider acupuncture an adjunct treatment. Medical schools in Asia teach acupuncture as the primary medical therapy. Medical schools in other parts of the world stress the use of herbs and ointments. Medical credentialing boards in the United States and their counterparts in Asia and other parts of the world have to decide what academic degrees and coursework they will accept as meeting their standards.

Organizations are concerned by the possibility that they could be held legally liable if someone they certify jeopardizes someone else's safety or well-being. At a minimum, an accusation of incompetence directed at someone who is certified blemishes the value of the credential. Therefore, two issues organizations pay close attention to are the quality of education obtained abroad and the possibility for fraud that equivalency policies present.

## SAFEGUARDING AGAINST FRAUD AND MISREPRESENTATION

Unfortunately, some people misrepresent their education or falsify their certificates and transcripts. In the United States, organizations control these problems by requiring transcripts with an institution's official seal. Also, since U.S. academic institutions are just a domestic phone call away, transcripts can be easily and inexpensively verified. U.S. corporations that hire foreign nationals to work in their overseas plants and offices are in a better position to establish trusting relationships with universities in those countries. Their local human resource professionals also know how to screen job candidates and verify credentials. Verification gets more complicated when a transcript is in a language other than English or from a lesser-known institution. To circumvent this problem, U.S. professional associations and credentialing boards can rely on third parties who specialize in verifying academic credentials.

## CULTURAL ISSUES

When organizations develop their standards they do not always see the cultural bias in them. Standards that are less subject to cultural bias are those that deal with technical and professional principles, rules, and procedures. Standards that deal with relationships—such as standards for communication, teamwork, negotiation, collaboration, work habits, codes of conduct, and ethics—are frequently affected by cultural bias. Thus it is particularly important to involve people from other countries when drafting these types of standards.

## LANGUAGE DIFFERENCES

Language differences are a significant potential source of problems for organizations that go global. Indeed, there are subtle yet significant differences even between different regions within the United States. English in particular is a very rich language. There are many words that have completely different meanings depending on their use. For example, the following sentence uses the word *facility* in two different ways: "When I met with the facility managers to build a European version of the IFMA test, I was impressed at the group's facility with language." In addition, often there are several English words for the same basic concept, with each one connoting something slightly different.

Two little boys were learning the concept of synonyms. Their teacher asked them to come up with as many words as they could think of that mean "more than three." Here are some of the words they came up with: a *gaggle* of geese, a *pod* of whales, a *school* of fish, a *litter* of kittens, a *swarm* of bees, a *crowd* of people, a *bunch* of flowers, a *herd* of cattle, a *clutch* of chicks, a *group* of people. There are even more words that mean "more than three."

The point is that when developing marketing, learning, and assessment materials for people for whom English is a second language, you should be both careful and consistent in how you use words.

In many parts of the world, "the Queen's English," not American English, is the language of business. People in the professions are taught to read and write in English. However, some skilled, semiskilled, and unskilled workers may not have had an opportunity to study English. If you want to be fair about providing potential candidates with equal opportunities to earn your credential and you want the credential to be a valid assessment of their ability, then you should first build a profile of the target audience that includes language proficiency.

---

I once met with a group of European facility managers to help them draft a European version of the IFMA test. I was very impressed by these individuals' adeptness with languages. Some members could speak, read, and write in five languages. Whenever they came across a technical word or expression in English that they didn't understand, they asked one another what it meant. The Germans would speak French to the French, and the Dutch would speak German to the Germans, and the French would speak Italian to the Italians, and so on until everyone understood the English word or phrase in question. Then, as a group, they would come to a consensus on a substitute English word that they thought would better convey the meaning. They developed a test in what they called "European English."

---

Next, in your job or task analysis you should define what level of language proficiency will be required for competent performance on the job. When language is unique to a task, job, profession, or organization, there are even more opportunities for misunderstanding or misinterpretation. Verbal proficiency—in any language—may or may not be a measure of competence for a particular job. And literacy is more than just being able to read and write words—some jobs require workers to be literate in mathematics, the sciences, engineering, or the arts. Your materials, then, should be in the language of the job in question, and if candidates do not have an opportunity to learn the English version of that language, then you should translate your materials.

Corporations that certify their own employees could benefit from doing what Caterpillar did. Even if the process does not eliminate the need to translate materials, using language consistently makes translating them easier. Here is what other companies are doing to ease their translation burden:

A number of years ago, Caterpillar, for reasons unrelated to certification, decided that the cost to translate its service manuals was getting prohibitive. The company was translating its manuals into almost one hundred different languages. Instead of continuing this practice, it decided to create a language of its own, called "Caterpillar Fundamental English." The language is limited to about eight hundred words. Words can be used as either nouns or verbs, not both. Every word has only one meaning, and it has to used exactly the same way every time. There are only four sentence structures. Caterpillar saved over $23 million in translation costs the first year. Later the company's training department adopted Caterpillar Fundamental English for its materials. The process of coming up with a universal language that applies only to the use and service of Caterpillar's products forced considerable discipline on those who developed it.

- The manufacturer of HVAC systems developed a standard format for all of its learning materials. Offices in different countries follow this format when they translate their materials. Video is recorded on dual tracks. One track is in English; offices in each country can use the second track for the language of its choice.

- Amway, too, uses a standard format for all of its product and training manuals. Definitions, product features, customer benefits, product specifications, instructions on how to use the product, and examples always appear in the same order and in same place. The use of a standard format has reduced the need to translate, except in countries where learning English is not a viable option. Translations are done in-country, and the standard format better ensures everyone gets the same message in the same way.

Just as you pilot-test training and assessment materials written in English, you should pilot-test translated versions of them as well. The people asked to participate in the pilot test should represent members of the target audience.

## MISSTEPS AND OVERSIGHTS

Here are some mistakes organizations frequently make when they want to deploy a credential internationally:

1. *Overlooking the standards and issues related to equivalency.* The biggest mistake U.S. organizations make when they decide to go global is to focus solely on translating their tests and training materials. They don't think

about confirming the relevance of their standards, the issues of equivalency and reciprocity, or even the cultural bias in their standards. They don't even consider the political benefits of asking foreign nationals for their opinions on what the requirements and standards should be. Instead, they assume foreigners will automatically accept their decisions.

2. *Failing to use professional translators.* Another major mistake is to fail to use a professional translator, preferably someone who works in the country where the translated materials will be used. Bilingual and multilingual Americans can be very useful to international companies—but not for translating test items and training materials for use overseas. For this task, it is better to get someone who is as familiar with the target audience's culture as possible.

## TIPS

Here are some tips to help you in your efforts to go global:

1. *Develop representative standards.* If you want your standards to be accepted in other countries, then select representatives from those countries to help develop them. Consider using the "80-20" rule; that is, make 80 percent of the standards global (appropriate for everyone) and 20 percent customizable by each country to reflect local conditions.

2. *Establish a method for reviewing foreign degrees and coursework.* For international credentials with an education requirement, determine in advance criteria for accepting foreign degrees and coursework. One way to handle this issue is to contract with organizations that specialize in confirming the equivalency of foreign educational programs.

3. *Translate into a foreign language.* If you find it necessary to translate a test, training materials, or any of your marketing and enrollment forms into a foreign language, have the translation done in the country where the materials will be used. Contract with firms that guarantee their translations. If you translate the test, redetermine the passing score based on the translated version. Do not assume that the translated test's passing score will be the same as that of the English test.

 **GUIDELINES**

## Going Global

Here are some guidelines to help you design a credential that will be effective in other countries:

A. If you are going to certify your own employees and the standards apply only to your corporate work rules, then use the same standards for everyone in the target audience, no matter where in the world they work.

B. If you are going to certify your own employees and the standards include compliance with local regulations or local norms, then

- Separate those standards that apply worldwide from those that reflect local conditions.

- Have representatives from the local area develop the standards that apply only in their area.

C. If your certification requires passing a test, then identify any test items that are specific to local regulations or work rules. Then

- Either replace them with items that reflect other localities' rules, as needed for use in different areas of the world, or remove them.

- Pilot the test to confirm that it performs as expected, and redetermine the passing score using the replaced items.

D. If your target audience speaks or reads English as a second language and you do not want to translate the materials,

- Develop a common template or format for all of your materials.

- Decide on a limited number of sentence structures, and adhere to them.

- Look for words that mean different things based on their use, and replace them with single-meaning words.

- Use words in the same way to mean the same thing consistently.

E. If the target audience has little or no opportunity to learn English, then hire someone in-country to translate the standards, training materials, and assessment tools for you.

F. Pilot-test all materials, whether they are in English or in the local language, to confirm that they perform as expected.

G. Put together a team representing all of the nations where you want to implement your certification program.

- Ask them to internationalize your program, using the checklists and guidelines from Chapters Two, Three, Five, Six, and Seven.

- Have them profile the target audience.

- Have them define the role language plays in the standards and assessment.

- Together, decide what, if anything, should be translated.

- If they believe translation is necessary, have them develop a common template.

**SUMMARY**

Taking a certification program global is a very involved process. However, you can avoid the mistakes made by other organizations and build on what others have done well. Begin by confirming why you want an internationally accepted credential. Next, identify the stakeholders in those other countries whose support you will need for your program to be successful. Involve them in designing the program. Build a detailed profile of the target audience, and redo the job or task analysis with a focus on what language ability is required to be successful. Review your standards and identify those that reflect a U.S. cultural bias. Separate the standards that must be met from those that can be modified to better match local working conditions. Decide what local educational and training programs you will accept and what you must provide. Based on your profile of the target audience, the importance of language proficiency, and what you know about access to instruction in English in the target country, decide what materials, if any, you should simplify or translate. Pilot-test all of the materials, whether they were translated or not, with representatives from the target audience.

 **CHECKLIST**

### Going Global

Use this checklist to evaluate existing international certification programs:

|  | | YES | NO |
|---|---|---|---|
| A. | We have documented the driver behind our desire to deploy a credential internationally or develop a global one. | ☐ | ☐ |
| B. | We have evaluated the target audience's language proficiency. | ☐ | ☐ |
| C. | We have compiled a list of local academic and training programs or a description of what standards local programs must meet to be accepted. | ☐ | ☐ |
| D. | We have performed an analysis of the language proficiency required for candidates to perform the task competently. | ☐ | ☐ |
| E. | We have identified standards that are common to all locations and those that must be locally customized. | ☐ | ☐ |
| F. | Representatives from the different countries participated in defining the requirements and standards. | ☐ | ☐ |
| G. | Where appropriate, we developed common formats. | ☐ | ☐ |
| H. | Where appropriate, language was used consistently. | ☐ | ☐ |
| I. | Translations were done in the local country by a professional translator. | ☐ | ☐ |
| J. | Materials were pilot-tested with representatives from the target audience. | ☐ | ☐ |

**WHERE TO LEARN MORE**

The National Organization for Competency Assurance (NOCA) offers conferences and workshops related to translating tests into other languages and deploying certifications internationally. NOCA also lists members who validate educational credentials.

The Center for Quality Assurance in International Education offers conferences and workshops on issues related to trade regulations and how they affect the recognition of education and professional services. The center is concerned with issues of quality and fairness in international academic and professional mobility, credentialing, and recognition. It focuses on three areas: the globalization of the professions, the development or enhancement of quality assurance infrastructures in higher education overseas, and monitoring quality in international higher education.

# Chapter 9

# Implementation

*T*his chapter deals with what is perhaps the most overlooked and under-appreciated aspect of making a certification program successful—giving it staying power. Professional societies, in particular, believe that once they have published the standards, scheduled the test, and announced the requirements, members and practitioners will "line up and sign up." Unfortunately, they are frequently disappointed. They fail to develop a long-term marketing budget and plan to support the program over time. Likewise, organizations that offer internal certifications often fail to understand what it takes for a certification program to become ingrained, institutionalized to the point that it becomes an integral part of the organizational culture. Implementing a certification program should receive the same amount of forethought and resource commitment as a major product launch or culture change. Successful implementation also requires astute project planning and management skills.

The head of finance of a major telecommunications firm shared his dismay over the fact that department heads regularly asked for funds to support the development or purchase of new technologies yet overlooked the costs to implement them and to train people to use them. He finally decided to require all requests over $300,000 to include either funding for training and implementation or a description of how the department would reap the benefits of the new technology without such funding.

A senior manager from another firm had his group go back and identify all of the programs within a five-year period that the company had funded and developed but never fully implemented. Both the number of programs and the amount of funds involved were staggering. He now insists that every new funding request come with an implementation plan, including a cost estimate.

Implementing a certification program is like trying to lose weight. Periodic dieting won't do it; what is required is a lifestyle change. It is helpful to think of implementation as a staged process. Each stage further integrates aspects of the certification program with other programs or functions. Eventually, the credential becomes so ingrained that it is simply the way professionals in a given discipline demonstrate their commitment or the criterion by which an organization selects, evaluates, and promotes employees.

Implementation depends on a well-developed marketing strategy consisting of seven clear steps:

1. Define the market.
2. Brand the credential.
3. Develop and execute a launch strategy.
4. Develop and execute a market penetration (rollout) plan.
5. Develop and execute the communication strategy.
6. Develop the materials.
7. Celebrate successes.

How will you know when you are successful? You will know when you no longer own the certification program; instead, the professional practitioner or the management of the core functions of the business own it. They make it part of their plans and their budgets. They measure how well it is serving their needs, and they commit resources to keeping the program resilient and robust.

## THE MARKETING STRATEGY

*Marketing* is the process of getting a product (in this case, a credential) into the hands of a consumer (the practitioner or employee). Part of that process is acknowledging that the consumer has a choice. The practitioner or employee can choose not to pursue the credential or to pursue a different credential. For a new and unique credential, you have to create a need for it in the eyes of consumers, so that they will desire the certification. When you are competing with other credentials in the same area, you have to demonstrate the superiority of your certification—specifically, how it provides better or greater benefits to the target audience. A *marketing strategy* is a plan for completing the transfer from producer to consumer. In the case of a certification program, it includes reaching the target audience, creating a need for the credential or positioning it as superior to others, and getting people to commit to pursuing it.

Sometimes the consumer is not the buyer. This is the case for internal certifications. The employee is the consumer, but the boss is the buyer—the organizational representative who pays the bill, either in terms of dollars or time. Therefore, your marketing plan should stress the benefits of the credential to both the consumer and the buyer. Similarly, professional associations have to market their credentials both to practitioners and to their potential employers. There is little incentive for practitioners to seek a credential unless they believe it will enhance their employability or earning power.

The marketing process includes packaging, advertising, and selling. Selling is that part of the marketing process when the producer asks the consumer to engage in an exchange. In the case of selling a certification, you have to get the practitioner or employee to agree to meet the requirements in exchange for your awarding them the designation. Therefore, to market your certification you have to

- Package it in ways that reflect its value and communicates its benefits

- Advertise it in ways that build consumer awareness and create a need

- Sell it through distribution channels that enable people to participate in the exchange

## Defining the Market

The market is the target audience—the group of people who might want to be or should be certified. You need to know how many of these individuals there are (or how many there could be if you are successful at generating a need). You also need to know where they are in terms of geography or department affiliation, and you need to know enough about them to be able to effectively design your packaging, advertising, and distribution channels to reach them. This might seem like a simple task, but it is not, because the market has to define itself in the same way that you define it. For example, if you want to certify third-grade teachers, this task is relatively easy—people know whether or not they are or wish to become a third-grade teacher. For newly forming professions, however, people may or may not identify themselves as members or potential members. In corporations, employees may not always associate themselves with the role or task being certified. All of the people who perform the task may not even have the same job title. Some will define themselves by their job title, others by their degrees or professional title, and still others by the tasks they do or the roles they fulfill within the organization. When you target your market, then, you have to decide how to communicate an association between it and the credential—that is, you have to get the members of your target market to say, "this credential is meant for me."

I'm thought of as a practitioner of "human performance technology."
Why? What is it that I do, that makes me one? What do others do to become one? The University of Southern California is the first school to offer
a doctoral degree in this new discipline. People who do the type of work
I do in corporations have numerous job titles. The International Society for
Performance Improvement has devoted over fifteen years to building consumer awareness of the discipline, yet although some members do classify themselves as practitioners of the new discipline, most do not. The
American Society for Training and Development supports the new discipline through its publications and conferences, yet the majority of the
people who attend the conferences are newcomers and work in training.
So, if I were to certify others who do the type of work I do, how would
I find them? By their job title, their education, the scope of their work, or
their membership in a professional society? And how would I package the
certification so that when they saw it, they would recognize it as something for them?

## Branding the Credential

Branding is key to packaging a credential. Branding includes developing a
"mark," a label or logo that identifies it as a certification, sets it apart from other
certifications, and associates it with a standard or a profession. Branding also
involves determining what the designation will be. The designation is the specific language—the term or phrase—that denotes the credential's scope. Professional associations frequently use two- to four-letter abbreviations of the
designation, such as *PE* for Professional Engineer or *CFM* for Certified Facility Manager. The computer industry uses phrases for their designations, such
as *Novell Certified in Version 4.0* or *Certified in Windows 95.* Corporations
brand their certifications through the use of logos, color schemes, and a type-
face that they consistently apply in their marketing and training materials. Corporations may or may not award a designation to employees who become
certified. Other corporations allow their employees to state they are certified
on their business cards.

The main role of branding is to build awareness and eventually widespread
recognition of the credential. This is done by repeatedly using the logo or mark
in all of your marketing materials, training programs, tests, and communications. Also, people who earn the designation will need a way to communicate
to their customers, potential employers, and coworkers that they are certified.
Therefore, part of branding is recommending what people should say about

themselves once they become certified—that is, how they should communicate the designation—and determining how they can "wear" the credential's logo (on their business cards and stationery or on a lapel pin, for example). Just as you pilot-test training materials and tests, you should pilot-test the credential's logo or mark. Some organizations even stage a contest in which potential candidates can submit suggested names and logos. For example:

- ABB established a logo and unifying look for all of its materials, its Web page, and its certificates. Whenever an announcement goes out about a new credential or new requirements for an old one, the logo and look immediately convey what it is about.

- The automotive manufacturer (discussed in previous chapters) had over five different certifications. Every certification had its own logo, color scheme, and marketing materials. The lack of consistency in the look was confusing. Owners of the major dealerships commented that the materials looked like they were from different manufacturers. The company created a single look, a unifying logo, and standardized the design of its materials. It created one Web page for all of the certifications. It established protocols for what people could put on the business cards. It even created banners to hang above each mechanic's work area to display his or her certifications.

### Launching the Credential

The launch is the beginning, but for many organizations it is also the end, as nothing else is planned beyond it. A launch strategy is a plan for introducing the certification program to the organization or to society. The launch is similar to a grand opening or official announcement. Many organizations use the launch as an opportunity to formally certify people who earned the credential through grandfathering or by participating in the pilot program. The launch may also be the first phase of the rollout or implementation strategy. Associations frequently schedule launches to coincide with their national conferences. Other organizations might have a launch coincide with an annual sales conference, an all-employee meeting, or a special anniversary, or they might make it an event all by itself. A well-orchestrated launch introduces the logo or brand image, the communications plan, and the marketing materials, including

- Brochures describing the program, why it was established, who endorses it, and the requirements

- A Web page that includes much of what is in the brochures, along with answers to frequently asked questions

The launch should also include an orientation for the people who will serve as local liaisons, coordinators, and spokespersons. These people should be able to speak knowledgeably about the program and convey enthusiasm for it. For professional associations, a special orientation should be held for the elected officers, key committee chairs, chapter presidents, and senior members of the society. For internal certifications, there should be a letter or announcement from the CEO or top-ranking person in the organization, publicly stating his or her commitment to the program. A special orientation should be done for top managers (especially in marketing and sales) and union officials. The strategy should also include an article in the organization's newsletter or journal, press releases, and perhaps a media event to which the trade or professional press is invited.

## Rolling Out the Credential and Penetrating a Market

A market penetration plan describes how you intend to roll out the certification to the rest of the target audience. Amway did it by country, for example. An association might start with its larger chapters. A company might do it by office, by plant, by region, or by product. However you do it, create an implementation team to share in the responsibility for the continued deployment of the certification program. Ideally, the team should be made up of people who are close to the target audience. For example, the team might consist of chapter leaders, local HR generalists, or local line managers. Whomever you choose to put on the team, publicize their involvement and celebrate their successes.

The team should be trained to introduce the certification program. They should be very familiar with how the program was developed, who participated in it, the requirements for the credential and the rationale behind them, and how candidates can apply for exemptions and assess their readiness. An important role for the implementation team is to solicit candidates' and local stakeholders' feelings about the program and feed that information back to the program administrator and governance board.

For example, one automotive manufacturer displays photographs of every group manager, associate, and team leader in the training and development team's planning room. The position of the photographs reflect the organizational chart. Under each photograph is the person's name. The training and development group that administers the certifications uses this montage of faces to target whom they will approach, and in what order, to communicate how the program works, solicit feedback, and gain support.

## Developing and Executing a Communications Plan

A communications plan is a strategy for reaching the target audience, building their awareness, getting them involved, helping them fulfill the requirements, and recognizing their successes. The strategy includes choosing a distribution channel. Retailers distribute their goods through stores, catalogs, buyer's clubs, and the Internet. Associations distribute their certification enrollment forms, training, and tests through their chapters, local colleges, Web pages, direct mail, and independent testing agencies. Corporations distribute their certification enrollment forms, training, and tests through independent third parties, field trainers, local HR representatives, Web pages, and local colleges.

It is not enough to say you'll build a Web page or distribute brochures. Whatever channel you use, the information has to be continuously available and current. A plan helps you

- Identify events you can use to build awareness and recognize people who have earned the certification

- Coordinate your efforts with others who are also trying to get a message out

- Specify what messages you want to send, when you want to send them, how you want to send them, and to whom you want to send them

Most important, a plan lets you get others to share in the responsibility for getting the message out, because they will know what has to be done and by when. For example:

- Amway uses an eighteen-month calendar. Across the top are the months; down the side are the geographical zones. Every zone has its own color. On the calendar are marked all rallies and major sales events scheduled everywhere in the world. The Merchandising and Global Product Training Group, which administers the certification program, gets on the agenda for every meeting, creates a message for each session, and plans celebrations of success. It uses the calendar to plan its travel and materials budget.

- Some professional associations have regular columns in their membership newsletters and journals just for their certification programs. They also prepare articles for chapter newsletters and earmark part of their annual conferences to celebrate those who have achieved the credential. One association arranges for an elected official to do a dinner speech at a chapter meeting, timed with a mailing to local members that describes the program. At the dinner, those members and local practitioners who have achieved the certification are announced and awarded the designation. Prior to the dinner meeting, local chapter leaders and committee chairs attend an orientation session in which they learn about the certification and are given an opportunity to ask detailed questions about eligibility, exemptions, and so on. The chapters commit to getting local people in the profession to begin the process of earning the credential. The chapters also agree to provide coaches or mentors so candidates will be successful.

### Developing Effective Program Materials

A lot of materials have to be developed and distributed to support the launch and ongoing implementation of the program. In addition to materials for the target audience, you will want materials for the implementation team, organization leaders, the governance board, and any vendors or third parties you might use. All of the materials should wear the mark or logo, including all

- Sales support materials for the implementation team
- Presentation materials used for orientations and executive briefings
- Enrollment forms for the target audience
- Training materials and tests, whether they are distributed via a Web page or intranet, in a classroom, or by direct mail
- The certificates, for when people fulfill the requirements
- Press releases and public or employee relations announcements

Many organizations also produce items such as lapel pins, caps, decals, certificates of completion, and plaques for their certification programs. Before deciding what types of items to make available, consider how the target audience might use them. If the target audience is a professional group, then a statement for their business cards, a certificate or plaque, a prototype press release for their community paper, or a lapel pin might be appropriate. Field technicians might prefer an attachment that can be stapled to work orders and left with the customer, a shirt or jacket patch, or a pin. People who work in a plant might prefer a plaque they can display in a customer receiving area or a decal they can attach to their supply cabinet. Some recognition items are meant to be worn; others are meant to be displayed. What type you choose should be based on the target audience's preference. For example:

- One manufacturer certifies plant workers in discrete tasks associated with specific product groups. Once certified, the worker gets a plastic card (similar in size to a credit card), which he or she wears on a chain around the neck. As new certifications are earned, new cards are added. Some workers have so many cards it looks like they're wearing miniature Venetian blinds down their chest. The cards enable supervisors and production leaders to rapidly assign qualified workers to a task.

- Amway created four attractive lapel pins, one for each level of certification. The pins all contain the logo created for the program. Amway also set up kiosks at its major distribution centers, where affiliates come to pick up merchandise. The kiosks have a touch screen that provides people with the latest information on products, certifications, training, and so on while they wait in line for their orders to be filled.

## Celebrating Success

People who have earned a credential should be held out as special to their coworkers, professional peers, customers, and employers. How best to celebrate their achievement depends on the organization. Some organizations display the photographs and biographies of those who have earned a credential. Some people are formally awarded a certificate during special events like annual banquets and conferences. Although bonus checks and other monetary rewards do provide a form of recognition for people who have earned a credential, they are not the same as celebrating. There is a role for rewards, recognitions, and celebrations. Most organizations remember to recognize, some include rewards, but few think about celebrations. One can argue that the feeling of accomplishment people get from completing a certification program is reward enough or that earning a credential makes people more competitive in the job market and opens the door to greater earning power. Both of these arguments are probably true; however, there can also be joy in having people you respect thank you for your hard work and accomplishment.

Since the goal is to institutionalize the credential—that is, make it part of the fabric of doing business—then you should also celebrate the efforts of those in the background. Supervisors, field trainers, chapter officers, and designated mentors are the people who make a certification program happen. They are the key to getting people involved in the process and actively pursuing the credential. Yet they are almost always overlooked. Certification administrators should go out of their way to recognize and celebrate the people who are key to implementing their programs. For example:

- The pharmaceutical firm (discussed in previous chapters) appointed "mentors" in every local office to be responsible for communicating and explaining the program. The assignment was made part of their regular job duties, and they were evaluated on how effective they were at serving as the local "certification representative." The firm credited the mentors for successfully implementing the program.

- The manufacturer of HVAC systems tracks the number of employees that are in the process of working toward a certification, by their supervisors. Two times a year, the certification administrator publishes the names of the supervisors and the status of their employees' efforts. Supervisors are publicly recognized for supporting the program.

## MISSTEPS AND OVERSIGHTS

Here are some of the more common mistakes organizations make in regard to implementation:

1. *Assuming the target audience will relate to the credential.* One mistake organizations make is that they assume the target audience will identify with the credential—that is, immediately recognize it as something that will benefit them. They also fail to establish a "look," or brand image, and use it consistently in all of their marketing materials. Failure to use the same image makes it harder for the target audience to associate materials (applications, announcements, and so on) with the credential.

2. *Failing to test the brand.* Another mistake organizations make is that they fail to test the name or look of the designation with the potential market. Many years ago one organization invested a lot of money designing a lapel pin and logo, only to have it rejected by the target audience as "too academic looking." The committee had created a design based on the Greek torch symbolizing knowledge. The target audience did not relate to the logo because many had never attended college. They felt that what distinguished them was their practical work experience.

3. *Failing to reward program supporters.* Organizations often fail to reward the team commissioned to help implement the program. One group that is frequently left out are supervisors who support the program.

## TIPS

Here are some tips to help make your implementation successful:

1. *Brand the credential.* A brand image helps you maintain your credential's exclusivity. Involve influential representatives of the target audience and main stakeholders in the process of coming up with a designation and logo. Design a logo that is clear, distinctive, and easily replicated on all of your training, assessment, and marketing materials.

2. *Identify the frequently asked questions (FAQs).* When you pilot-test your marketing, assessment, and training materials, track the most frequently asked questions. Include those in your final print materials. A Web page lends itself well to handling information like this. However, if your candidates do not or cannot access information on-line, then consider using posters, table toppers, reminder cards, and so on to get the message out.

3. *Reward supporters and champions.* Don't overlook your "behind the scenes" helpers. These are the people who go out of their way to give candidates time to study, complete their training, do self-assessments, and the like. Include these individuals at the same time that you recognize those who have fulfilled the requirements and earned the credential.

4. *Draw on your internal expertise.* Most organizations have an individual or department responsible for public relations and marketing. Ask for their help both in designing your materials and in leveraging other events to promote awareness of what you are doing.

5. *Team up with other departments.* Most organizations have several departments that handle training and special events. Join with them to find ways to get your message out and to help them do the same.

6. *Use more than one distribution channel.* Web pages and intranets are effective distribution channels. But even if you make use of these tools, you will still have to put some materials into print. Take advantage of other techniques to get your message out, such as direct mail, table toppers in the employee cafeteria, articles and ads in industry publications, contests, and so on.

7. *Consider getting a registered trademark.* It is difficult to trademark initials or abbreviations, but you might be able to legally protect your designation and logo. At a minimum, you should protect the designation. Consult with an attorney who does this type of work.

8. *Consider outsourcing some implementation tasks.* Companies will now do your material handling for you. Some will administer and score tests. Some will distribute training and information materials. Others will track candidate status and disburse certificates, plaques, pins, and so on.

 **GUIDELINES**

### Implementation

Here are some guidelines to help you plan and execute your implementation strategy:

A. Establish an implementation team.

- Select people from throughout the organization who can be responsible for encouraging participation and answering questions.
- Provide an orientation session in which you explain to them
  How the program is designed and why it was designed that way
  How and why the job or task analysis was done
  What the requirements are and the rationales for them
  What the organizational driver behind the program is
- Train the team in how to conduct the same orientation session for others.
- As a team, describe the target audience as well as you can.
- Ask some selected representatives from the target audience to review your description. (They can be the same people who participated in the job analysis or the pilot test of any of the materials.)

B.  Decide how you will brand the credential.

- Decide what the designation will be (for example, "Certified XYZ Technician" or "XYZ Company–Certified").

- Ask someone from marketing to help you design a logo and a standard look for all of your materials.

- Pilot-test your ideas with representatives from the target audience.

C.  Decide where, how, and when you want to launch the program.

- If possible, coordinate the launch with a high-visibility event that does not conflict with the certification in intent, or pick a time when the launch will not compete with other events.

- Put together a team to support the launch. This group can test the materials you will later use to train others to support the ongoing implementation.

D.  Create a project plan for the full rollout or larger implementation plan.

- Decide which information distribution channels you want to use.

- Commission people skilled in instructional design and technical communications to develop your Web page and other support materials.

- Decide what distribution channels you will use to distribute information about the certification, enrollment forms, answers to frequently asked questions, self-assessments, training materials, and tests.

- Include in your plan opportunities to recognize and celebrate people's successes and contributions.

## SUMMARY

Implementation requires excellent project planning and marketing ability. The marketing strategy lays the groundwork for getting a long-term commitment to supporting the program beyond the first year. It is also the vehicle for getting others committed to the program's success. Certifications, no matter how altruistic their purpose, will not sell themselves. Your message has to effectively compete for people's attention. The benefits to achieving the credential have to be relevant to the target audience. The image the credential conveys has to match what the target audience feels is appropriate. You have to use distribution channels that reach the target audience. If you are clear about the driver behind the certification, have a well-developed business case, and have the support of the target audience and other stakeholders, the marketing plan will be a success. Just don't take it for granted that people will see the relevance of the credential to their role or situation and automatically want to obtain it.

**CHECKLIST**

**Implementation**

Here is a checklist you can use to evaluate how you implemented your program:

|  | YES | NO |
|---|---|---|
| A. The organization developed an implementation strategy for the certification program. | ☐ | ☐ |
| B. Others were involved in its development. | ☐ | ☐ |
| C. The strategy included a description of the target audience. | ☐ | ☐ |
| D. The implementation team was trained in | | |
| • The background of the certification program | ☐ | ☐ |
| • How to communicate that information to others | ☐ | ☐ |
| E. A designation was developed for the credential. | ☐ | ☐ |
| F. A logo was developed. | ☐ | ☐ |
| G. The designation and logo were pilot-tested with the target audience. | ☐ | ☐ |
| H. The logo or other graphic treatment used to brand the credential has been applied to all marketing, training, and assessment materials for the program. | ☐ | ☐ |
| I. There is a plan for distributing information about the certification program. | ☐ | ☐ |
| J. More than one channel is used to distribute information about the program. | ☐ | ☐ |
| K. There is a plan for how the credential will be announced (launched). | ☐ | ☐ |
| L. There is a plan for how the credential will be marketed to the target audience over time. | ☐ | ☐ |

**WHERE TO LEARN MORE**

Fuller, J. *Managing Performance Improvement Projects: Preparing, Planning, Implementing* (San Francisco: Jossey-Bass/Pfeiffer, 1997). This book is a valuable resource for anyone charged with planning and managing a project.

Gelinas, M. V., and James, R. G. *Collaborative Change: Improving Organizational Performance* (San Francisco: Jossey-Bass, 1998). Gelinas and James have created one of the most researched and well-documented processes for successfully deploying and institutionalizing change in an organization. Their book is a must if you are charged with introducing a change in your organization.

Kotler, P. *Marketing Management: Analysis, Planning, Implementation, and Control*, 6th ed. (Englewood Cliffs, NJ: Prentice Hall, 1988). This is the definitive text on marketing. Kotler defines all of the marketing concepts; however, you still have to figure out how to apply them to marketing your credential. It is a big book and weighs a lot, but it is worth it. He also wrote *Strategic Marketing for Organizations,* 4th ed. (Englewood Cliffs, NJ: Prentice Hall, 1991), *Social Marketing: Strategies for Changing Public Behavior* (New York: Free Press, 1989), and *Strategic Marketing for Educational Institutions,* 2nd ed. (Englewood Cliffs, NJ: Prentice Hall, 1995).

# Chapter 10

# Evaluation

**S**ome time ago two business colleagues and I gave a presentation to representatives from about twenty-five associations and credentialing boards on how to measure the impact of international certification programs. My colleagues were from the corporate world, where people are expected to prove the worth of their programs. When we asked the audience to share how they evaluate their programs, the response was silence. Finally one person spoke up and said, "We don't."

It would be unfair to conclude that organizations in the nonprofit world never evaluate their programs. I believe a more accurate conclusion is that what gets evaluated in those organizations depends on the information the organizations want. Some organizations must assess the impact of their programs; others have to prove the efficiency and effectiveness of their administrative processes; still others only track participation demographics. But no matter what gets measured, stakeholders draw conclusions and make judgments about the worth and utility of the certification effort from those measurements. What may be lacking is a candid discussion about what information should be used to judge a certification program's worth and utility.

## DEVELOPING AN EVALUATION STRATEGY

An *evaluation strategy* is an agenda that describes when and how you are going to measure different aspects of your program at particular points in time. For example, initially stakeholders will want to know how people feel about the program and what was produced during the first year (training, tests, logo, Web pages, and so on). Later they will want to know how awarding the credential correlated with key success indicators (retention, costs, compliance, improved performance, customer confidence, and so on). At some point they will want to know about the activities that consume staff time (developing training and tests, maintaining candidate records, answering candidates' questions, and so on)—that is, how efficient the program administrator is at managing the program. The problem is how to get ahead of the curve—that is, to be able to anticipate requests for information about what people think about the program, how well the certification is working, and what you have been doing. You don't want to be caught off guard by requests for information. Putting together an evaluation strategy allows you to anticipate requests, reinforce your business case, and avoid feeling like a victim.

There is some irony to this issue of what and when to evaluate. Most people involved in developing, managing, and deploying certifications are continually gathering data about what people feel, how much is being produced, and so on that can be used to evaluate the program. Unfortunately, they either do not recognize the value of the information they have at hand or they do not frame it as evaluative. They don't label the information they have as legitimate measures of specific aspects of the program, and they don't present the information in such a way that it looks like evaluative data. An evaluation strategy gets you to think about how best to present your findings so that you will be seen as purposely evaluating different aspects of the program.

## DEFINING EVALUATION PROCESSES

When people talk about evaluating their certification program, they aren't always clear about what they mean. Here are some terms associated with evaluating certification programs, with definitions:

1. *Evaluation* is the act of judging something or determining its value. The fact that you got support for your program says that someone thought a certification program was a good idea; but you may not understand how they came to that conclusion, particularly if you inherited a program that has been in place for some time. However, knowing why a program was originally supported will help you identify the information you need to evaluate its success.

2. *Measuring* is the process of gathering data and comparing what you find to some criteria or standard to determine if a gap exists or a change has occurred. This raises all kinds of questions, like "What data?" "How much data?" How do we get it?" and "What do we compare it to?"

3. *Measures* are the factors you are going to gather data about. There are *internal measures,* which deal mostly with a program's efficiency, operating costs, and compliance with professional standards; and there are *external measures,* which deal mostly with how well a program meets stakeholders'

expectations and achieves organizational objectives. A goal of this chapter is to expand the universe of measures you can choose from.

## DETERMINING WHAT TO MEASURE

So what should you measure? It depends on what people want to know. However, just about anything you measure will have to do with what you did (activities), what you produced (outputs), what happened as a result of what you did and produced (outcomes), or how people felt about what you did, how you did it, and the results that occurred (perceptions). Your evaluation strategy should include getting information about all four of these measures over the course of a year and communicating what you learned. Here are some examples of each:

- *Activities* are what you and others did—met with stakeholders, held training classes, administered tests, reviewed applications, heard appeals, and so on.

- *Outputs* are the products of those activities—training programs, tests, certified candidates, the program launch, and so on.

- *Outcomes* are the consequences of what you did—such as fewer losses, fewer accidents, improved employee morale, less turnover in key positions, lower costs, or increased revenues. The variables the program is expected to affect (morale, turnover, accidents, performance, status, consumer confidence, and so on) are the drivers (discussed in Chapter One) and *key success indicators* (discussed in Chapter Four).

- *Perceptions* are how each stakeholder perceives the value of what was done, how it was done, and the results that followed—for example, the public believes the product is safer, the sales department believes customers are more inclined to buy the company's products or services, employees feel the organization is genuinely interested in their professional development, or HR reports that more desirable job candidates are applying for jobs.

## DETERMINING WHERE TO START

Which activities, outputs, outcomes, and perceptions you measure depends on the drivers, or motives, behind the program. Unfortunately, real motives are sometimes disguised by lofty language and unrealistic goals. When this happens, what stakeholders really want to know and what they ask for are frequently not the same. Looking at what other functions or disciplines evaluate can give you ideas about what information would be of real value to you and your stakeholders. As examples, the following paragraphs describe what these functions and disciplines evaluate:

- Marketing and sales
- Political science
- Psychology
- Loss control
- Legal
- Quality assurance
- Finance
- Public relations
- Human resources
- Training and performance improvement

Marketing and sales people measure how well a program identifies consumer trends and buying habits, how well it identifies the size of a market and who has what percentage of it, how well it penetrates a market or expands market share, and how successful it is at getting customers to commit. When you put on your marketing and sales hat, imagine measuring the certification program in terms of

- How much market share you were able to get the first year, the second year, and so on
- How fast you were able to get the program into the marketplace
- In how many locations (offices, sites, and so on) you were able to launch the program the first year, the second year, and so on
- How the credential was perceived by the target market
- Who and how many applied for and achieved the credential

For example, Amway began the rollout of its trainer certification in countries where corporate training had already scheduled visits in conjunction with major sales rallies. After three years, it was certifying trainers in forty-nine countries. Amway tracked how many countries it launched the program in each year, how many trainers participated by country, and how many trainers were in the process of earning their second- and third-level certifications. It then correlated attainment of the certification with retention of trainers and distributors and compared this to data from before the program was launched. This information became its measures of success. If your organization is interested in having its certification become *the* recognized credential in its area—the one most sought after or considered most worthy—then measuring the things that marketing focuses on could be useful.

Political scientists study power and influence, in terms of who has it, how much they have, and how to leverage or minimize it. If you put on the political scientist's hat, you'll think about whether or not your certification program enhanced the power or status of candidates or the organization. For example, IFMA tracks the number of educational programs that apply for approval, the number of major employers seeking certification for their managers, and the number of countries that base their program on its standards. These are indicators that IFMA and its credential are becoming more influential. NCIDQ tracks the number of states that recognize its credential in their licensing process and the number of state licensing boards that have NCIDQ-certified interior designers as members, as both are measures of NCIDQ's influence. If one of your key success indicators is how much your certification enhances the status and influence of the people you certify, then measure those indicators of power and influence.

The discipline of psychology studies people's behavior and its effects on others, and it develops theories about how to shape behavior. Putting on this hat gets you to think about how you might measure your program's effect on consumers' buying behavior or on the target population's behavior. Did certifying sales support personnel positively influence customers' buying decisions? Did it change the way sales support personnel interact with customers? Do employers mention a preference for certified job candidates in their help wanted ads? Do customers ask for certified technicians? If one of your program goals is to change people's behavior, then measure what people do and how they do it.

An organization's loss control function is interested in programs that promote safe practices and reduce the potential for losses. Many certifications are put in place to reduce accidents, promote safe practices, and reduce loss. From this perspective, there are benefits to tracking just who and how many were and were not certified, and why; to what degree awarding the credential correlated with reduced accidents and decreased severity of accidents; and how many people earned an external safety credential because of the internal program. The point is, you can measure those variables that demonstrate due diligence. Over time, you can monitor trends in actual losses and what caused them.

The legal function in an organization is interested in programs that comply with regulations and are legally defensible. Therefore, you might want to track the number of fines the organization incurred in the past year and compare that figure to its precertification days. You might want to show how, as a result of the program, only qualified workers did certain tasks. Again, you would track who did and did not get certified and what distinguished the two groups (capability versus irrelevant factors such as race, gender, and so on), how candidates felt about the fidelity of the experience and the rigor of the process they were put through, and how often performance criteria were reviewed and updated. The point is, you can measure those variables that demonstrate your due diligence in ensuring the validity of the requirements and standards.

Quality assurance people look at processes in terms of their stability and consistency. Certification programs incorporate a number of support processes, such as

- Enrollment and registration
- Test administration
- Test development
- Analyzation of test scores and other assessment results
- Generation of status reports
- Periodic recertification

These processes consume time and resources. The quality assurance perspective gets you to question just how efficient your processes are and how to improve them. It also gets you to question how easy they are to execute, for the candidate and for you. Therefore, if you are interested in improving your processes, you can measure the degree to which they are documented, to what extent people know how to use them, and how people feel about them. Then you can use that information to focus on those processes that are more problematic. For example, ABB has very sophisticated on-line services that candidates can use to register for training and to find out what they have to demonstrate to become certified. That same system allows supervisors and managers to quickly find out who is certified and where each certification candidate is in the process. The quality of the on-line system allows the certification manager to spend time with product managers to ensure that standards are kept current and to correlate the number of certifications attained with important business measures.

The finance function looks at the economic worth of programs. For some programs this is the most important measure, if not the only one considered. Unfortunately some people prefer to focus on one side of the ledger, costs or revenues, but not always both. Associations look to their certification programs not only to support various other organizational goals but also to help generate revenues from training, publications, conference registrations, and chapter memberships, in addition to the fees from seeking the credential itself. Businesses hope their certification programs will support sales and marketing efforts, but they don't always have the ability to correlate the two. However, by looking at your certification program from this perspective, you can begin to question your assumptions about which of your activities add value, which results produce the greatest payback, and what it costs to attend to the feelings of the different stakeholders. You can't be all things to all people; however, finance can help you set priorities, particularly as to what to focus on in the short and long term. Thus if your goal is to increase revenues, then you should measure the revenues from publications the organization sells, training it offers, conferences it sponsors, and so on and compare those figures with the revenues those products and activities generated before the certification program was launched.

Public relations personnel develop programs and messages to inform, attract, and appease groups inside and outside of organizations. Adopting their perspective on your certification program will get you to think about who you want to keep informed and what messages you want to get out. Then you can go about measuring how many people know about the credential and what it represents, the number of press releases that were prepared and disseminated and the number of press conferences held, the number of orientation sessions that were held to explain the program, and the number of articles placed in the company or industry press about candidates and the outcomes of the program. If your program is meant to influence people's perceptions, then measure how people's feelings about the organization (its products or practices) have been affected by the program.

The human resources function in an organization is interested in staffing and recruitment. You could examine data from job candidate interviews to see if the opportunity to become certified influenced people's decision to accept an offer. With HR's help you can measure the impact of the program on hiring and promoting internally versus externally and on employee relations.

The training and performance improvement functions want to know if people are capable and did their job in a way that met standards. With this hat on you would measure whether or not people know more, their performance improved, and management's feelings about employees' readiness to take on new assignments changed.

Every one of these perspectives gives you an opportunity to identify variables to measure that would be of value to one or more of your stakeholders. Much of the information is probably already being collected, if not by you then by some other function. If the information was not collected in the past, then obviously you cannot compare current results to past performance, but you can set a baseline at any point in time and measure trends from then on. Depending on the questions you want to answer and what you want to prove, you can begin to collect information that gives you a more comprehensive picture of what you are doing well, where you need to improve, and what you should celebrate.

## BEING CLEAR ABOUT YOUR PURPOSE

Your evaluation strategy should help you get the information you want when you want it. For example, the sponsors will want to know whether the program lived up to its promise of reducing costs, increasing revenues, and so on. The human resources and legal departments will want information about the procedures you put in place and how they have affected employee relations and staffing. The target audience will want evidence that the program helped them become more secure or competitive in the job market or gave them greater opportunity. Leaders and visionaries will want to know if the program enhanced the stature of the field or ensured greater public well-being. Loss prevention personnel will want to know if the cost of doing business went down because losses were decreased. The finance people will want to know if the assumptions on which you built your business case are holding true. Everyone will want a voice in what gets measured and reported. A strategy will help you negotiate these expectations and stage your evaluation efforts so they won't exhaust your resources.

The process begins by identifying those variables you and the stakeholders want to measure. For example:

- What do I want to focus on this year—program materials, system support, deployment, impact?

- What questions do I want to answer? Did the program support sales? Did it reduce costs? Did candidates like that they could register on-line? Were the training materials adequate? Does the number of candidates who attained the credential correlate with a larger objective (key success indicator)? Did the launch strategy work as planned?

- What will I or someone else do with the answers to those questions? Will we fund revisions to the training program or redesign the training materials? Will we make buying decisions related to system support? Will we more aggressively promote the program based on preliminary results?

- What do I want to "prove"? That the program was a good investment? That behaviors are changing? That the launch strategy worked?

Once you know what to focus on, you can put together a plan for getting the answers. As you would do for any plan, develop a timeline, assign responsibility, get the resources it will take, and set some milestones so you can judge your progress. Whatever you focus on, your strategy should encompass both internal and external measures; one without the other can give you a very misleading picture. Only looking at your activities and what you produced won't tell you if the program is fulfilling its goals. Similarly, only looking at the results and at stakeholder's feelings won't help you identify ways to be more cost- or time-efficient.

For example, the credit card company's measures for the first year of its program (discussed in previous chapters) were (1) the company's readiness (determined using preset milestones) to certify service and sales support for two specific product lines and (2) the number of employees who achieved certification in that period, compared with the number who were eligible. Approximately six months after implementing the certification program, the company planned to track

1. *Perceptions related to employee relations:* the impact on employee morale, as measured by the regular annual survey
2. *Perceptions of the program:* employees' and supervisors' satisfaction with the program, as measured by a special survey
3. *Financial outcomes:* the impact on business growth targets, as measured by analyzing year-end results and seeing if there is any correlation between growth and when employees were certified
4. *Performance outcomes:* if the time to get new hires up to proficiency went down, as measured by conducting interviews with supervisors

Make sure your strategy includes getting data that will help you make improvements and celebrate success.

## DEVELOPING AN AGENDA

Start by replicating the organization's annual calendar. For example, every organization—profit or nonprofit—puts together its budget at the same time every year. All organizations have recurring annual, semiannual, and quarterly events, ranging from conferences to industry trade shows, new-hire orientations, Christmas parties, award banquets, career days, and internal and external audits. There are schedules for getting articles in newsletters and industry trade publications and plans for launching new products and sales campaigns. Organizations also have regularly scheduled routine events such as monthly meetings. You may not know the exact dates, but you can estimate what will happen each quarter or even each month. Do this, and then identify those events for which you might be asked to provide information about the certification program. You can be better prepared for these events if you negotiate up front with stakeholders about what information they can reasonably expect from you, based on their willingness to help you get it.

Next, superimpose on that calendar your own agenda for what you want to communicate. Include certification program events that you will want to evaluate and report on, such as each time you launch the certification to a new audience or location, every exam offering, or whenever a class finishes the required curriculum. Now that you have an idea of what you should be prepared to report and approximately when you will have to report it, you can plan for how you will get and present the necessary data.

## PRESENTING YOUR DATA

The data used to evaluate certification programs consist of facts and perceptions. Most data are expressed as numbers—specifically, means, standard deviations, percentages, and ratios. You can apply statistical formulas to the numbers, such as an analysis of variance or a correlation formula, to determine how much alike or different the numbers are from those derived from other sources or other times. When you present your data, label it "Evaluation Data" and express the results in figures. Figure 10.1 provides an example.

| | |
|---|---|
| Staff's time dedicated to the job or task analysis | 35 percent |
| Number of courses developed | 6 |
| Mean rating of the training | 3.7 |
| Candidates rating the materials at 4 or above | 67 percent |
| Mean rating of the materials | 4.1 |

**Figure 10.1. Evaluation Data**

Some data you will want to collect throughout the year but report only periodically, such as

- The number of training sessions held, the number of tests completed, and the number of people who achieved the certification

- Measures of learners' reactions to the training, test, preparation materials, and so on

- Changes in the key success indicators chosen as measures of the programs' effectiveness

Other data you will collect only once, such as measures of stakeholders' perceptions about the fairness of the criteria and the quality of the materials. Still other data can be gathered every time an event happens, such as measures of learners' reactions to a training course or test scores. For example, the automobile manufacturer developed a three-year evaluation strategy. During the first year it focused on the following activities, outputs, and perceptions:

- *Imposing the same logo and design on all of its existing certification programs.* Measures included the dealerships' perceptions of the new look to the certification materials.

- *Developing a field communications plan.* Measures included the number of printed brochures and Web pages produced and the number and types of calls from candidates about the program.

- *Consolidating its course catalogs for all of its certification programs.* Measures included the cost to redesign and reprint a single catalog versus the cost to print six different catalogs, the number of catalogs disseminated, program managers' perceptions about the catalog's ease of use and representation of the programs' courses.

- *Training field support staff involved in certification.* Measures included the number of training sessions held, the number of staff trained, staff's perceptions of the training (relevant, clear, helps trainees confidently apply the ideas covered), and the dealerships' perceptions of how capable field staff were to support the certification programs. Class evaluation forms were distributed at the end of each session to evaluate staff perceptions of the programs. Questions were added to the annual survey sent to the dealerships about field staff members' ability to support the programs.

• *Replacing the training registration and certification tracking system.* Measures included how well the certification team met its deadline and stayed within budget, and a pilot group's perceptions of the system (ease of use, speed, report-generation capability, report utility, and so on).

To measure the first three activities, all of the dealerships were sent a survey, and twelve, selected at random, were interviewed by phone. The survey and interviews asked dealership managers to rate the materials (for ease of use, clarity of understanding, sense of unity) on a five-point scale. The survey was sent after the newly designed materials had been in the dealerships for approximately three weeks.

Starting with the second year and continuing into the third year, the company focused on measuring

• The number of dealership technicians certified at the first, second, and third levels

• The number of sales staff who attained the required basic certification

• Turnover rates among technicians and sales associates

• Consumer satisfaction (determined using survey scores)

• The number of new courses developed based on the results of needs analyses

• The time required to support the new registration and certification tracking system

This information was tallied and reported quarterly.

## MISSTEPS AND OVERSIGHTS

Here are two common mistakes organizations make when it comes to evaluating their programs:

1. *Failing to develop a strategy.* Perhaps the greatest mistake organizations make is that they fail to agree on an approach or strategy for evaluating their program. That is, they do not define, either in the beginning or at predetermined points along the way, how the program will be evaluated, what will be used as evidence that the program is successful, what data will be tracked, and how that data will be captured and reported.

2. *Having too narrow a focus.* Another mistake organizations make is that they box themselves into one of two narrow models of evaluation. One model is the "save the world" model: "Did we cure cancer or triple profits?" Everyone wants their certification program to save society or the company. But however noble the goal is, it is rarely achieved as a result of a single program. The other narrow model is the "How many did we get?" model: how many took the test, signed up for training, or got a certificate. The information is useful and can support further inquiry into how to improve either the program or the way the program is deployed. However, this information may not tell you how inclined people are to continue to support the program.

**TIPS**

Here are some tips to help you make your evaluation effort successful:

1. *Validate your data by collecting multiple types of data.* Base your evaluations on more than one source or perspective. One source or type of data can give you only a part of the picture. For example, if you measure only how many people applied for candidacy, it will not tell you how many did or did not attain the credential, why they were attracted to the credential, what benefit they foresaw gaining from it, or even what it cost to process the applications.

2. *Make your evaluation agenda public.* Publicize your evaluation agenda. Let candidates and stakeholders know when you plan to collect data and to report on certification activities and results. This will put you in a leadership position but still allow people to suggest modifications.

3. *Don't confuse internal measures with external measures.* Evaluate the design, development, deployment, and maintenance of your certification program separately from its results. (That is, use separate measures to evaluate these things.) Your efficiency and effectiveness at putting the program together are important in the beginning stages of the program. After the program is up and running, you can be more selective about what you measure in terms of marketing the program and its administration. Only measure when you are in a position to do something with the data. Remember that feelings about the certification program and how well it is achieving its goals are important for as long as the program is in use.

4. *Follow good survey design principles.* Many program evaluations depend on the use of surveys, such as customer satisfaction questionnaires and training evaluation forms. The quality of the survey you use will affect the validity of the data you get back. So follow the principles of good survey design, or use the services of a qualified vendor.

5. *Learn some basic statistics.* Many program evaluations use statistical tools, such as correlation formulas, *t* tests, and chi-square goodness-of-fit tests to analyze data. These tools are used to determine how alike or different results are from what was expected or previously found. Work with someone who is proficient in the use of statistics, or take a basic course yourself.

6. *Experiment with how you present the numbers.* Depending on what you want to accomplish, express your results in different ways, and compare how well each way communicates the message you want your audience to get. Always position your data as part of your evaluation agenda. Figure 10.2 provides an example of contrasting ways to present data.

**Figure 10.2. Two Different Ways to Present Data**

| Version 1 | Version 2 |
| --- | --- |
| Twenty-four candidates from the Northwest regional office have started working toward their certification. | *Participation in the Northwest Region*<br>This quarter          30 percent<br>Next quarter          20 percent |
| Most of our customers say they are in favor of the program. | *Customer response*<br>Favorable          18 percent<br>Very favorable          72 percent |
| We plan to reduce the time to process applications by half. | *Processing applications*<br>Current cycle time          6 hours<br>Desired cycle time          3 hours |

 **GUIDELINES**     **Evaluation**

Here are some guidelines you can use to develop an evaluation strategy for your program:

A.  During the planning stages of a new program, meet with stakeholders and together decide what internal and external measures you want to collect as baselines and at key milestones. Consider measuring

- Your ability to meet your deadlines and launch targets as planned

- The number of people you actually involve in the planning, design, development, and launch phases, compared with what you are projecting

- Candidates' perceptions about the process—did they find it easy to understand the process and to get information about what was expected, were they able to do self-assessments easily, and so on

- The number of orientation sessions and presentations given to explain the program
- Reactions to your promotional, enrollment, and assessment materials
- The number of people who enroll within the first six months of the launch
- Your ability to keep stakeholders informed and committed to the project
- Your ability to document the various stakeholders' expectations

B.  After your meeting with the stakeholders, also record

- Stakeholders' initial feelings about the program, its look, how it works, and so on
- Whether or not your were able to get agreement on the external measures for the first year of the program, the second year, and so on
- What the external measures will be for the first year, the second year, and so on

C.  Decide when you will present your measures, to whom you will present them, and how you will present them.

D.  Whether your program is new or established, decide

- What questions you want to be able to answer during the next six months and at the end of the upcoming year
- What data you will need to track or gather to answer those questions
- Who will be responsible for getting the data
- How you will get the data
- When you will track it
- When you will summarize it
- When and to whom you will report your findings
- What future decisions or actions will be based on the data

E.  Whether your program is new or established, consider evaluating

- Your ability to leverage the data-gathering efforts of other programs or initiatives
- The number of materials you developed to carry out the evaluation effort, such as questionnaires, interview questions, observation forms, feedback forms, and so on and how you might leverage these
- How effectively you incorporated information on program participation and results into promotional materials

F.  Build a calendar and indicate what you want to report, to whom you want to report it, and when you want to report it.

- Develop a common template or format for reporting your data.

- Always attach the certification's logo or brand image to your reports and presentations.

## SUMMARY

You can evaluate a certification program by measuring a variety of program aspects: program activities, program products, program outcomes, people's perceptions of the program, how well the program is linked to the business case, and so on. All of these measures are useful, but they serve different purposes. Some will help you improve what you do and how you do it. Others will show how successful the program is, either in terms of what it accomplished or how people feel about it. Some factors can be measured on an ongoing basis, others are measured periodically, and some are measured only once, in response to a specific need. What you evaluate depends on the public promises that were made to get support for your program initially and what your stakeholders want as evidence that their needs are being met over time. Going back to why the organization funded the certification program in the first place begins to get to some of the questions you will want to answer. For example, "Can we, as a result of our certification . . .

- "Deploy people faster or more cost-effectively to where they are needed? How do we know?"

- "Be more confident in the competence of our workers, contractors, and suppliers?"

- "Correlate attainment of the credential with improved performance, fewer fines, higher retention rates, higher customer satisfaction scores, and so on?"

- "Show a reduction in the cost of development, sales, service, and so on?"

- "Show that educational institutions changed their curricula to better match our standards?"

- "Show an increase in revenues from national and chapter memberships, sale of publications, seminars, and regional and national conferences?"

- "Show an improvement in employee or member satisfaction?"

Because evaluations take time and tie up resources, put together a strategy for getting answers to questions when you will need them. Tell others what your agenda is, what you will measure, and when you will report the results. Tie your agenda to your stakeholders' calendar, so you will be prepared to share the results of your evaluation efforts at the appropriate times. Link your strategy to your business case. Express your results in ways that best communicate your findings and that make it clear you are actively evaluating the program.

**CHECKLIST**

### Evaluation

Use this checklist to evaluate your evaluation strategy:

|  | | YES | NO |
|---|---|:---:|:---:|
| A. | An evaluation strategy was developed. | ☐ | ☐ |
| B. | The strategy lists what will be measured. | ☐ | ☐ |
| C. | The strategy indicates when results will be communicated. | ☐ | ☐ |
| D. | The strategy includes an agenda for | | |
| | • How to capture data | ☐ | ☐ |
| | • When to capture data | ☐ | ☐ |
| | • How to report the data | ☐ | ☐ |
| E. | The strategy includes measures related to | | |
| | • The efficiency of the process | ☐ | ☐ |
| | • The effectiveness of materials and systems | ☐ | ☐ |
| | • The effectiveness of deployment | ☐ | ☐ |
| | • Candidates' feelings about the process, standards, and so on | ☐ | ☐ |
| | • Stakeholders' feelings about the process, results, and so on | ☐ | ☐ |
| | • The program's impact on the key success indicators | ☐ | ☐ |
| | • The effectiveness and efficiency of the evaluation effort | ☐ | ☐ |
| F. | The strategy is documented. | ☐ | ☐ |

**WHERE TO LEARN MORE**

There has been a great deal of information written about evaluation; however, there are few good references on how to communicate your data. Here are some books I strongly recommend.

Hayes, B. E. *Measuring Customer Satisfaction: Development and Use of Questionnaires* (Milwaukee, WI: ASQC Quality Press, 1992).

Henry, G. T. *Graphing Data: Techniques for Display and Analysis* (Thousand Oaks, CA: Sage, 1995).

Tufte, E. R. *The Visual Display of Quantitative Information* (Chesire, CT: Graphics Press, 1983), *Envisioning Information* (Chesire, CT: Graphics Press, 1990), and *Visual Explanations* (Chesire, CT: Graphics Press, 1997).

# About the Author

*J*udith Hale has dedicated her career to helping management professionals develop effective, practical ways to improve individual and organizational performance. She has used the techniques, processes, and job aids described in this fieldbook in her own consulting work, which has spanned twenty-five years. Judith's clients speak of the practicality of her approach and the proven results it yields. She is able to explain complex ideas so that people understand their relevance and can apply them to their own situation. She is able to help others come to a shared understanding about what to do and how to commit to action.

Her consulting firm, Hale Associates, was founded in 1974 and enjoys long-term relationships with a variety of major corporations. The services her firm provides include consultation on alignment, assessment, certification, evaluation, integration of performance improvement systems, performance management, and strategic planning.

She is the author of *The Performance Consultant's Fieldbook.* Her book *Achieving a Leadership Role for Training* describes how training can apply the standards espoused by the International Standards Organization and Baldrige to its own operation. She was the topic editor for *Designing Work Groups, Jobs, and Work Flow* and *Designing Cross-Functional Business Processes* and the author of the chapter "The Hierarchy of Interventions" in the *Sourcebook for Performance Improvement.* Judith also wrote *The Training Manager Competencies: The Standards,* as well as *The Training Function Standards* and *Standards for Qualifying Trainers,* and she put together the *Workbook and Job Aids for Good Fair Tests.*

Judith is an appointed member of the Illinois Occupational Skills Standard and Credentialing Council. She was president of the Chicago chapter of the

National Society of Performance and Instruction (NSPI) and served on NSPI's President's Advisory Council. NSPI named her Outstanding Member of the Year in 1987. She has also served as president of the International Board of Standards for Performance and Instruction and president of the Chicago chapter of the Industrial Relations Research Association (IRRA). She was a commercial arbitrator with the American Arbitration Association and has been a member of the American Society for Training and Development (ASTD) for many years. She was nominated for ASTD's Gordon Bliss Award in 1995. She taught graduate courses in management for fourteen years for the Insurance School of Chicago and received the school's Outstanding Educator award in 1986.

Judith speaks regularly at ASTD International, ASTD Technical Skills, Computer Training & Support, the International Society for Performance Improvement, and Lakewood's annual training conferences.

Judith holds a B.A. from Ohio State University (communication), an M.A. from Miami University (theater management), and a Ph.D. from Purdue University (instructional design, with minors in organizational communication and adult education).

# Index

## A

ABB (Asea, Brown, Bovari), a multinational conglomerate, 28, 169, 183; certification roles and levels, 22; employee deployment driver, 3, 140; hypotheses and metrics, 84; on-line services, 11, 140, 198; stakeholders, 11

Abbreviations, professional designation, 182

Ability: domains of, 104–105, 108, 120; levels of, 105–106; testing extraneous, 103; and types of test items, 107–109

Academic credentials, verification of, 120; foreign institution, 171, 174, 177; and fraud, 171

Academic standards: accredited, 170; of foreign institutions, 170

Acceptance of a certification program, ingrained, 93, 179–180, 187

Acceptance of a code of conduct, requirement of, 25, 32, 33

Acceptance test, conducting a certification process, 139

Accomplishment levels: certification recognizing, 22, 23–24

Accreditation: definition of, xxi; and education abroad, 170; voluntary or necessary, xxii, 99

Action maze tests, 108, 110

Activities, program, 195

Activity-based costing, 89–90

Administration procedures. *See* Governance and administration, certification program

Administrative error: assessment and testing, 107; job or task analysis, 50–51, 67–69

Administrator, certification program: five responsibility areas of, 12, 138–141; realistic activity options for, 144–145, 168;

recognition for support people, 187; relationship with governance board, 142–143, 145–146

Advance notice of new credentials or maintenance requirements, 161

Affective domain, 104–105; levels of complexity, 106

Alternatives to certification: business case inclusion of, 86, 89; doing nothing, 85, 86, 94

American Architectural Manufacturers Association: hypothesis and metrics, 84

American Board of Oral and Maxillofacial Surgery (ABOMS): certification, 23, 112, 158

American National Standards Institute (ANSI), xx

American Society for Quality Control (ASQC), xx

Amway, 2–3, 67; certification levels, 24; evaluation measures, 196; hypotheses and metrics, 84; program and training materials, 173, 186–187; training on new products, 159; universal standards, 168; worldwide events calendar, 185

Angoff-Nedelsky (conjectural) method, 114–115

Announcing the credential. *See* Marketing strategy

Answer categories, structured interview, 61–62

Appeals and exemptions policies, governance board, 135–136, 142, 149, 152

Approvals and endorsements, definition of, xxi–xxii

ARAMARK: certification driver, 4

Assessment, 97–130; administrative error, 107; checklists, 124–129; computer-based

testing, 110–111; definition of, 98–104; design error, 104–107; guidelines, 120–123; initial and qualification, 20; measures and tests, 27–28; missteps and oversights, 117–118; non-test types of, 98–100; passing score determination methods, 111–115; recertification, 163, 165; requirements, 98–101; resources and publications, 130; rights and responsibilities, 133, 134; rigor and validity of, 101–107, 116; sampling error, 101–104; summary, 124; test item types, 107–109; testing issues, 101, 115–117; tips, 118–119

Association of Polysomnographic Technologists, 158

Association for Worksite Health Promotion, 6, 158; hypothesis and metric, 83

Associations. *See* Professional associations

Atrophy or evolution, knowledge, 157–159

Audience, the target, 8; assumptions about, 188; communications plan for reaching, 184–185; customer dependency on, 9; designing the process for, 143–144; identifying and defining, 14–15, 181–182; involvement in requirements definition, 35; language proficiency of, 172; market penetration plan for, 184; in other countries, 168, 172, 175, 176; presentation delivery to, 91; recognition items for, 183, 186–187; sample selection methods, 52–54; surveys of, 50. *See also* Candidates, certification

Auditing certification candidates, 98

Auditors, internal, 10

Automobile manufacturer certification program, 5, 6, 11; based on training programs,

# A new edition of a key work in the field of performance improvement!

Harold D. Stolovitch & Erica J. Keeps, Editors

## Handbook of Human Performance Technology

Improving Individual and Organizational Performance Worldwide, Second Edition

Forewords by Thomas F. Gilbert and Robert F. Mager

When you've undertaken a performance initiative at an organization, you need concrete evidence that improvement has occurred. You need to establish a blueprint for change, select efficient tools, and identify whether your work was successful. That's why human performance technology is essential: it provides you with a systematic approach to improving individual and organizational performance.

The first edition of the *Handbook of Human Performance Technology* has been the bible of this rapidly evolving field. This new edition, co-published with the International Society for Performance Improvement, adopts a more international approach and introduces you to many emerging technologies.

### You'll learn how to:

- *Plan* performance improvement projects
- *Analyze* a corporate culture
- *Implement* effective interventions
- *Use* job aids and multimedia-based training
- *Conduct* on-the-job training
- *Evaluate* intervention effectiveness
- *Improve* your own professional life... and much more!

"The difference between ordinary and truly great organizations rests in the quality of leadership and the ability to attract, nurture, and retain brain power. The *Handbook of Human Performance Technology* is an invaluable tool for modern business leaders."
—**François Beaudoin, president and chief executive officer, Business Development Bank of Canada**

"The *Handbook* is the most comprehensive, up-to-date work on human performance technology in print today. It is a must-read for the serious student and an essential reference for the experienced professional."
—**Judith Blumenthal, associate dean, Marshall School of Business, University of Southern California**

"I can now replace several feet of books on my reference shelves with the *Handbook*. It is simply the most comprehensive writing in the field."
—**Joe Harless, inductee, Human Resources Hall of Fame; author, *The Eden Conspiracy***

The contributors to the volume comprise a veritable "who's who" in the field of performance improvement:
- Roger M. Addison • Dale M. Brethower • Ruth Colvin Clark
- William C. Coscarelli • Peter J. Dean • Wellesley R. Foshay
- James Fuller • Diane M. Gayeski • Thomas F. Gilbert
- Roger Kaufman • Danny G. Langdon • Robert F. Mager
- Dana G. Robinson • Allison Rossett • Geary Rummler
- Sharon A. Shrock • Darryl L. Sink • Richard A. Swanson
- Sivasailam "Thiagi" Thiagarajan • Donald Tosti • and many more!

This voluminous work has been exhaustively updated: many new chapters have been added, and all those chapters retained from the first edition have been extensively revised. If you own the trailblazing first edition, you'll want to add this volume to your bookshelf. If you are a trainer, consultant, or a manager engaged in improving performance, this groundbreaking work is indispensable. The answers to your performance improvement questions are here!

Co-published with the International Society for Performance Improvement.

> **The comprehensive sourcebook that defined a whole new approach to the practice of training and consulting.**

hardcover / 928 pages

Handbook of Human Performance Technology
ISBN 0-7879-1108-9

## Achieve measurable gains!

Jim Fuller & Jeanne Farrington

# From Training to Performance Improvement

Navigating the Transition

Training is a quick fix; many managers don't believe that it really works. But even if it isn't the appropriate solution to a problem, many organizations automatically implement training for lack of a more reasoned, thoughtful alternative.

Here's the approach you've waited for: performance improvement. Fuller

and Farrington show you how to achieve measurable gains by implementing this cutting-edge technique at your organization.

*"Clear, concise, and compelling."*
—James J. Hill, manager of executive education, Sun Microsystems

You'll learn how to:

- *Explain* and sell the notion of performance improvement to organizations
- *Surmount* obstacles that can prevent organizations from achieving their full potential
- *Demonstrate* the results of your efforts

As director of performance and learning at a Fortune 20 company, Fuller helped to lead his corporation to a performance breakthrough. With this resource, you'll learn how to start a performance revolution at your organization.

hardcover / 224 pages
. . . . . . . . . . . . . . . . . . .
From Training to Performance Improvement
ISBN 0-7879-1120-8

## So you need some performance magic NOW?

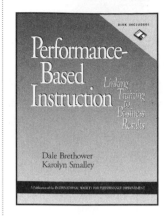

Dale Brethower & Karolyn Smalley

# Performance-Based Instruction

Linking Training to Business Results

With this book as your guide, you'll pinpoint the goal, find the gap between that goal and where you are now, and then close the gap. Using these brilliant designs, you will clarify job expectations and foster pride and confidence in employees' work performance.

*"When performance improvement is vitally needed, the concerned practitioner would do well to heed Smalley and Brethower's thoughtful advice."*
—Robert O. Brinkerhoff, professor of educational leadership, Western Michigan University

This book helps you:

- *Conduct* on-the-job training
- *Design* job aids
- *Perform* needs assessments

Grab this book of spells, add a dash of attentive work, and create some performance magic today!

hardcover / 224 pages includes
Microsoft Word diskette
. . . . . . . . . . . . . . . . . . .
Performance-Based Instruction
ISBN 0-7879-1119-4

## Lead work projects from beginning to end!

Jim Fuller

# Managing Performance Improvement Projects

Preparing, Planning, Implementing

Project teams are growing rapidly as performance improvement solutions become more complex. Develop the skills to effectively manage your budget, time, and the quality of work on performance improvement projects. Learn how to: • obtain sponsorship • manage resources and analyze risks • estimate schedules • and more!

Implement Fuller's process for superior project results. Co-published with the International Society for Performance Improvement (ISPI).

hardcover / 240 pages
. . . . . . . . . . . . . . . . . . .
Managing Performance Improvement Projects
ISBN 0-7879-0959-9

# Roll up your sleeves and make change happen!

> "*Collaborative Change* is a must-read for anyone working within organizations to make them more viable and effective. This book is practical and inspiring. It will give you everything you need to 'roll up your sleeves' and make successful change happen."
> —Ken Blanchard, coauthor, *The One Minute Manager*

FREE diskette includes customizable job aids!

Mary V. Gelinas and Roger G. James

## Collaborative Change

### Improving Organizational Performance

*Collaborative Change* shows you what you need to do in order to launch effective, successful performance improvement initiatives. The authors draw on their forty years of combined experience in the field.

**You'll learn how to:**

- *Build* a strong foundation for change with leaders
- *Apply* best practices for changing organizations
- *Decide* what areas of an organization are ripe for change
- *Involve* key stakeholders in the change process
- *Contract* with internal and external clients
- *Implement* change... and much more!

Integrating models, theories, and practices in a way that is uniquely useful to leaders and practitioners, Gelinas and James have created a modern classic!

"*Collaborative Change* is destined to become a classic, and Gelinas and James have set extraordinarily high standards of practice for all those who accept the challenge of leading change. I heartily recommend it."
—Jim Kouzes, co-author, *The Leadership Challenge* and *The Leadership Practices Inventory (LPI)*; chairman, Tom Peters Group/Learning Systems

"Nowhere else will you find a more comprehensive book that tangibly outlines how organizations can foster and implement collaborative and cooperative changes quickly and effectively."
—Angeles Arrien, cultural anthropologist; author, *The Four-Fold Way* and *Signs of Life*

"The authors' vast experience is shown in the clear organization of their framework, and in the practical and comprehensive way they present each element of their model. Their work leads the change leaders in the effort to lead organizations in change."
—Dennis Jaffe and Cynthia Scott, authors, *Rekindling Commitment*

"*Collaborative Change* is comprehensive, integrated, user-friendly, and pragmatically effective in bringing about lasting and successful hard business results."
—William M. Shine, senior partner, Kurt Salmon Associates

You get a wealth of forms, figures, agendas, and job aids that foster fast implementation. The binder format facilitates photocopying and easy fieldwork, and the enclosed diskette contains all the forms in readily customizable Word format. Grab this guide and make change happen!

Visit the authors at www.gelinasjames.com

looseleaf / 368 pages / includes a Microsoft Word diskette

Collaborative Change
ISBN 0-7879-4204-9

**SATISFACTION GUARANTEED**

# How do you ensure that employees are doing the right things?

Anntoinette D. Lucia &
Richard Lepsinger

## The Art and Science of Competency Models

### Pinpointing Critical Success Factors in Organizations

You'll use this cutting-edge guide to:

- *Clarify* job and work expectations
- *Hire* the best available people
- *Maximize* productivity
- *Enhance* a 360° feedback process
- *Align* behavior with organizational strategies and values
- *Adapt* to change

A competency model is . . . a descriptive tool that identifies the skills, knowledge, personal characteristics, and behaviors needed to effectively perform a role in the organization and help the business meet its strategic objectives.

What skills and knowledge are necessary for effectiveness in a certain job? Does the employee have the appropriate skills and knowledge, or is some kind of training necessary? Are these job expectations aligned with the culture and strategy of the organization as a whole?

These questions are essential to performance improvement efforts. And competency modeling is designed to help you find answers to questions such as these. Cutting through the technical jargon, expert consultants Anntoinette D. Lucia and Richard Lepsinger provide you with a much-needed manual to developing and using effective competency models. Get the results you expect with this practical guide!

From the authors of the best-selling book *The Art and Science of 360° Feedback* comes this guide to the design and implementation of competency models.

"Lucia and Lepsinger have demystified competency models and put in the hands of the reader a blueprint for developing meaningful recruiting, performance measurement, and succession planning systems. They succeed with a straightforward, pragmatic style, using actual examples that make the book an easy read."
—Frank Ashen, senior vice president, New York Stock Exchange

hardcover / 224 pages
. . . . . . . . . . . . . . . . . . . .
The Art and Science of Competency Models
ISBN 0-7879-4602-8

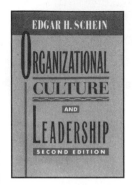

Edgar H. Schein

## Organizational Culture and Leadership

### Second Edition

Focusing on the complex business realities of the '90s, organizational development pioneer Edgar H. Schein lucidly demonstrates the crucial role your leaders play in successfully applying the principles of culture to achieve your organization's goals. With Schein's assistance, you'll drive increased organizational productivity.

You will:

- *Understand* team and organization dynamics
- *See* how new technologies influence organizations
- *Learn* about managing across cultural boundaries
- *Identify* points of resistance at an organization
- *Gain* insight into overcoming cultural resistance to change . . . and much more!

Learn to shape the dynamics of organization and change!

hardcover / 440 pages
. . . . . . . . . . . . . . . . . . . .
Organizational Culture and Leadership
ISBN 1-5554-2487-2

Call Free **1 800 274 4434**   Fax Free **1 800 569 0443**   Online **www.pfeiffer.com**   Or visit your local **bookseller**

# Your performance improvement toolbox!

Danny G. Langdon, Kathleen S. Whiteside,
& Monica M. McKenna, Editors

## Intervention Resource Guide

50 Performance Improvement Tools

### You want to be able to:

- *Increase* your awareness of various performance improvement options
- *Propose* an intervention or a series of interventions to eliminate a performance gap
- *Select* interventions systematically
- *Learn* how to implement interventions more effectively... and more!

Here's your toolbox. Interventions are the tools that you can use to effect changes in performance. While many other resources have identified the importance of interventions as performance tools, and some resources have even singled out select interventions that might be used to drive improvement at an organization, no other resource has offered you so many interventions.

**How would a 360° feedback program improve your organization?**

**How could you design communication, leadership, and mentoring programs?**

**When should you improve your compensation systems and employee orientations?**

**How could you maximize the effectiveness of job aids and on-the-job training?**

This resource not only answers those questions—and many others—but also gives you the field-tested tools you need to produce measurable modifications in performance. You'll be able to solve a host of operational dilemmas!

**Don't worry about how to face performance problems. Just grab your toolbox and go! The *Intervention Resource Guide* has the tools you've waited for.**

First, these experienced editors tell you how to select and implement interventions. Then you get a huge array of 50 interventions designed by the top practitioners in the field. In keeping with the central tenets of human performance technology, all of these interventions are designed to prompt measurable changes at your organization. You'll have an easier time justifying why you're doing what you're doing than ever before!

**Among the many leading contributors to this one-of-a-kind resource are:**

- Jean Barbazette
- Gloria Gery
- Danny Langdon
- William Rothwell
- Sivasailam "Thiagi" Thiagarajan
- Kathleen Whiteside
- and many others!
- Dale Brethower
- Roger Kaufman
- Bob Nelson
- Edgar Schein
- Donald Tosti
- Ron Zemke

You'll get what you need for: • action learning • competency modeling • conflict management • customer feedback • diversity management • electronic performance support systems (EPSS) • performance appraisal • strategic planning • teaming . . . and much more! All these resources are field-tested and formulated for fast implementation.

You've heard about performance improvement and human performance technology. They have sounded promising. But you weren't fully sure what an intervention was, how to select one, or how to implement one. Now you know! *Intervention Resource Guide* is your performance improvement toolbox.

The abundant figures facilitate easy implementation of interventions!

hardcover / 352 pages
• • • • • • • • • • • •
Intervention Resource Guide
ISBN 0-7879-4401-7

Call Free **1 800 274 4434**   Fax Free **1 800 569 0443**   Online **www.pfeiffer.com**   Or visit your local **bookseller**

# The ultimate resource for improvement and planning!

Roger Kaufman, Sivasailam "Thiagi" Thiagarajan, & Paula MacGillis, Editors

## The Guidebook for Performance Improvement

### Working with Individuals and Organizations

This treasure trove of information gives you expert direction for helping your organization and employees improve performance. Unlike most resources on organizational improvement that consider only the micro- (individual) and macro- (organization) levels, this guide incorporates the mega- (customer/client) level in planning success.

**You'll learn vital performance improvement steps including:**

- *Defining* objectives and ensuring that they are useful
- *Determining* what results to achieve
- *Designing* and implementing interventions, programs, and activities that will achieve results
- *Planning* appropriate evaluation efforts... and much more!

**Among the many leading contributors to this volume are:**

- Dale Brethower
- Diane Dormant
- Judith Hale
- Roger Kaufman
- Danny Langdon
- Bette Madson
- Ann Parkman
- Sivasailam "Thiagi" Thiagarajan
- Odin Westgaard
- Jack Zigon . . . and many more!

*The Guidebook for Performance Improvement* draws on all the current improvement approaches—quality, reengineering, job-task analysis, reward programs, and others—synthesizes those ideas, and offers you a wide range of success strategies to maximize workplace performance. A desk reference like no other, this book gives you cutting-edge tips and techniques for achieving organizational breakthroughs.

---

**SELECTED CONTENTS**

- The Origins and Critical Attributes of Human Performance Technology • Research and Development Origins of Performance Systems • Social Responsibility • A Strategic-Planning Framework: Mega Planning • Preparing Performance Indicators and Objectives • Needs-Assessment Basics • Business-Unit Performance Analysis and Development • Organizational Mapping • Job-Task Analysis • The Hierarchy of Interventions • Applications of Total Quality Concepts to Organizational Effectiveness • Developing Front-line Employees: A New Challenge for Achieving Organizational Effectiveness • Job Aids • Recruitment and Turnover • Accountability for Staff Turnover • Performance Management • Program Management: Its Relationship to the Project • Rewards and Performance Incentives • Developing Test and Assessment Items • Quality Management/Continuous Improvement • Performance Appraisal

---

hardcover / 512 pages
. . . . . . . . . . . . . . . . . . . . .
The Guidebook for Performance Improvement
ISBN 0-7879-0353-1

---

Timothy Nolan, Leonard Goodstein, & J. William Pfeiffer

## Plan or Die!

### 10 Keys to Organizational Success

This book explodes the myth that simply coping with unexpected change is effective for the long-term health of an organization. Through a series of parables that illustrate how things are not always as they appear, *Plan or Die* clearly shows you why today's most successful organizations are those that are actively involved in creating their own future.

**Examine the keys critical to shaping your organization's future:**

- *Basing* decisions on values
- *Having* a shared vision
- *Promoting* risk taking
- *Encouraging* innovation and flexibility
- *Maintaining* a market focus

---

"[*Plan or Die!*] provides a highly flexible but very functional road map for firms which need to develop their own planning process."
**—Thomas W. Morgan, president, Hartson Medical Services**

---

Learn how the proven Applied Strategic Planning model can work for you. Take part in your organization's future success right now!

hardcover / 206 pages
. . . . . .
Plan or Die!
ISBN 0-88390-327-X

---

Call Free **1 800 274 4434**   Fax Free **1 800 569 0443**   Online **www.pfeiffer.com**   Or visit your local **bookseller**

# Use tests without fear!

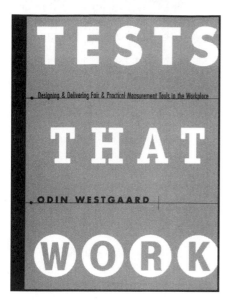

**Odin Westgaard**

## Tests That Work

### Designing and Delivering Fair and Practical Measurement Tools in the Workplace

The only practical business resource available that shows you how to use tests to assess skills and values in the workplace!

Loaded with figures, tips, checklists, and examples, *Tests That Work* gives you everything you need to use assessments responsibly and effectively at your organization.

You know the effects of mediocre workplace performance: reduced profitability, poor productivity, and diminished customer and employee satisfaction. But while you know the effects, finding the causes can seem nearly impossible. Do some of your employees need to improve their execution of basic tasks? Should some of your employees work on expanding their knowledge? How can you answer these questions?

Tests enable you to find answers such as these. But many organizations are afraid to use assessments: test development and execution is complicated. Bad tests can seem punishing or offensive, and yield inconclusive or incorrect results.

That's why noted consultant Odin Westgaard brings you *Tests That Work*, the only practical resource available that shows you how to use tests to assess skills and values in the workplace. Westgaard offers you invaluable advice whether you're developing and administering tests or merely selecting them.

**You'll learn how to:**

- *Test* organizational attitudes
- *Examine* test validity and reliability
- *Manage* ethical issues related to test administration
- *Evaluate* and report test results . . . and more!

You'll use tests to: • discover where training is needed • determine whether training was successful • analyze an organizational culture • assess opinions and preferences . . . and more!

Whether you're a manager who's considering using tests at your organization, a human resource development professional who's designing and implementing tests for your clients, or an educator or student engaged in the study or practice of assessment—this is the resource for you!

hardcover / 400 pages

• • • • • • •

Tests That Work
ISBN 0-7879-4596-X

## The cutting-edge guide for technical and non-technical professionals!

Includes FREE
CD-ROM
with customizable
resources!

Margaret Driscoll

# Web-Based Training

## Using Technology to Design Adult Learning Experiences

The practice of training on the Web and on intranets is growing at an explosive rate. People without technical knowledge need a basic guide that sheds light on best practices for web-based training delivery. People with technical knowledge need a savvy, practical primer on instructional design for web-based training. This is the web-based training book that all of you have waited for. Technical guides come and go. What is cutting-edge today could be obsolete tomorrow. So *Web-Based Training* steps back from the technical whirlwind. This extensively researched handbook shows you how to create web-based training that adheres to the tried-and-true principles of great instructional design.

> **"*Web-Based Training* is important not only because it demystifies web technology, but more importantly because it provides a critical link between the technology and the outcomes of learning."**
>
> John F. O'Connor, educational technology integrator, Motorola University

### Learn how to:

- *Survey* the available training options
- *Prepare* organizations for web-based training delivery
- *Maximize* your training dollars . . . and much more!

This guide offers scores of case studies from both large and small organizations. You'll refer to *Web-Based Training* time and time again to pore over this guide's practical charts, tables, and checklists. Self-study exercises reinforce readers' learning. Plus, the appendix offers a wealth of resources including a list of listservs and relevant organizations, along with a bibliography and glossary. The companion CD-ROM—included FREE with the book—contains even more resources: worksheets, document and presentation templates, job aids, and links to the Web.

"For those of us living and working with technology *Web-Based Training* is a refreshingly concise and easy-to-follow guide to ... successful implementation ... of technology-based training media."
—**Tony Russell, UK education services manager, Informix Software Limited**

"As an anxious technophobe, I found *Web-Based Training* very helpful and reassuring .... Anyone wanting to encourage adult learning through web-based training will find this an invaluable resource."
—**Stephen Brookfield, distinguished professor, University of St. Thomas**

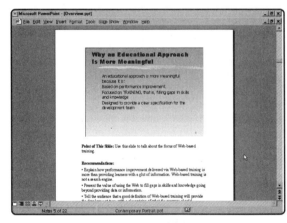

Among the many resources on the CD-ROM are PowerPoint presentations you'll use to explain web-based training to others!

Human resource development professionals have long needed a web-based training book that surveys the available options and makes reasoned recommendations for training delivery. The one-of-a-kind *Web-Based Training* forges the first path through this quickly shifting territory.

hardcover / 256 pages / includes a CD-ROM

. . . . . . . . . .

Web-Based Training
ISBN-0-7879-4203-0

Call Free **1 800 274 4434**    Fax Free **1 800 569 0443**    Online **www.pfeiffer.com**    Or visit your local **bookseller**

# A career guide and a reference tool—in a single source!

Judith Hale

# The Performance Consultant's Fieldbook

## Tools and Techniques for Improving Organizations and People

Internal or external consultant, novice or expert, you've probably heard about performance consulting, a high-impact approach that blends old-fashioned facilitation skills with cutting-edge process and outcome analysis. You want to gain the expertise necessary to identify why an organization is out of alignment, what interventions will correct these problems, and how you can measure your consulting success.

This remarkable book is your skill-builder and resource guide. The step-by-step *Fieldbook* shows you how to make the professional transition to a performance consulting career. You'll use this guide to: • define and describe your consulting skills • determine the costs and measure the effectiveness of your consulting process . . . and much more!

> "Hale has done an outstanding job in this book of contributing to everyone's use of performance technology."
> —Danny Langdon, president, Performance International

The *Fieldbook* details the techniques you need to conduct performance interventions and offers a customizable collection of worksheets, flowcharts, planning guides, and job aids. You'll use these resources to structure your presentations, to ensure clear communication, and to build client confidence.

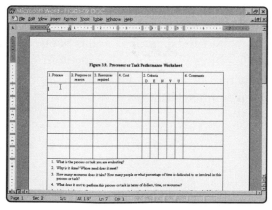

Among the many resources on the diskette are worksheets you'll use to manage your resources!

## The Fieldbook enables you to:

- *Analyze* an organizational environment
- *Diagnose* performance problems
- *Identify* barriers to performance

Includes a FREE diskette with customizable job aids!

- *Select* appropriate interventions
- *Measure* intervention success . . . and much more!

Employees don't need to learn more; they need to perform better. And as a performance consultant armed with Hale's *Fieldbook*, you will have the tools you need to effect measurable enhancements in performance.

## Make the transition to performance consultant today!

## About the Author

Judith Hale is the president of Hale Associates, a consulting firm specializing in performance management, performance improvement systems, and strategic planning. She has contributed to or edited many published works, including *Designing Work Groups, Jobs, and Work Flow* (1995) and *Designing Cross-Functional Business Processes* (1995), both published by Jossey-Bass, as well as *The Guidebook for Performance Improvement* (Jossey-Bass/Pfeiffer, 1997). The recipient of several professional awards and honors, Hale is an active member of both ASTD and ISPI.

## CONTENTS
### Making the Transition
• Performance Consulting • The Transition • Costs • Credibility & Influence
### Performance Consulting
• Environment & Norms • Needs Assessment • Interventions • Measured Results • Evaluating People Performance

paperback / 256 pages / includes a Microsoft Word diskette

The Performance Consultant's Fieldbook
ISBN 0-7879-4019-4

Call Free **1 800 274 4434**    Fax Free **1 800 569 0443**    Online **www.pfeiffer.com**    Or visit your local **bookseller**

## HOW TO USE THIS DISK

The minimum configuration needed to use the files on the disk supplied with this book is a computer system with one 3.5-inch floppy disk drive capable of reading double-sided, high-density, IBM-formatted floppy disks and word processing or desktop publishing software able to read Microsoft Word 6.0/95 files. Document memory needs will vary, but your system should be capable of opening file sizes of 50+K. No monitor requirements other than the ones established by your document software need be met.

Each of the sections in your textbook that are marked with a disk icon have been saved onto the enclosed disk as a Microsoft Word 6.0/95 file. These files can be opened with many Windows- and Macintosh-based word processors or desktop publishers for viewing or editing as you see fit. The files were originally created and saved as Microsoft Word 6.0/95 DOC files by Microsoft Word 97. Not all software will read the files exactly the same, but the DOC format is an honest attempt by Jossey-Bass/Pfeiffer Publishers to preserve the composition of the material such as borders, fonts, character attributes, bullets, and so on as accurately as possible.

Copy all DOC files to a directory/folder in your computer system. To read the files using your Windows-based document software, select File from the main menu, followed by Open to display the Open dialog box. Set the correct drive letter and subdirectory shown in the Open dialog box by using the Look-in control. In the "Files of type" text box, enter *.doc to display the list of DOC files available in the subdirectory.

Each file matches text in the book, and its file name is coded to indicate which text it matches. For example, the checklist in Chapter One has been named CKL01.DOC. You can open the file either by double-clicking your mouse on the file name that you want to open or by clicking once on the file name to select it and then once on the Open command button.